State of Origin

30 YEARS
1980-2009

State of Origin

30 YEARS
1980–2009

The fine line between winning and losing

Liam Hauser

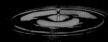

ROCKPOOL
PUBLISHING

A Rockpool book
Published by Rockpool Publishing
24 Constitution Road, Dulwich Hill
NSW 2203, Australia
www.rockpoolpublishing.com.au

First published in 2010

National Library of Australia
Cataloguing-in-Publication entry

Author: Hauser, Liam.
Title: State of origin 30 years : i980-2010
    / Liam Hauser.

1st ed.

9781921295386 (hbk.)

State of Origin (Australia)–History.
Rugby League football–Australia–History
Rugby League football–New South
    Wales–History
Rugby League football–Queensland–History

796.33380994

Cover and internal design by Stan Lamond

Typeset by Diacritec
Printed and bound by Everbest Printing Co Ltd
10 9 8 7 6 5 4 3 2 1

Photographs on previous pages
Page 1: Brent Tate is crunched by two
    NSW defenders in game three of 2006.
Pages 2–3: Up close and personal:
    Terry Hill and Gorden Tallis face off
    in game two of 1999.
Right: The Queensland Maroons are in
    high spirits after winning game three of
    1991, Wally Lewis's final Origin series.

See page 280 for details of the photographs
reproduced on the cover.

cont

1980s 14

1990s 88

ents

2000s 170

Statistics 252

Above, from left:

1980s (also pages 14–15): Two of Queensland's all-time great stars:
Wally Lewis and Allan Langer in 1987.

1990s (also pages 88–89): The Phil Gould-coached Blues celebrate their
1993 series triumph.

2000s (also pages 170–171): Queensland became the first state to win
four consecutive Origin series, at the finish of the third decade of State
of Origin football. Johnathan Thurston, Greg Inglis, Sam Thaiday, Willie
Tonga, Karmichael Hunt, Neville Costigan and Justin Hodges celebrate.

Statistics (also pages 252–253): Queensland's Greg Inglis steps out of a
tackle in game one of the 2009 series.

Foreword

STATE OF ORIGIN football is more than a game, or even a series. It is a glorious and gladiatorial spectacle that captures imaginations around Australia, as well as drawing a capacity crowd, with millions more watching every tension-filled moment on TV.

State of Origin is a panorama of heroics, athleticism, determination and toughness condensed into 80 minutes of compelling drama and electrifying flamboyance.

Its place in rugby league is legendary.

The annual series of three games are as keenly awaited as any event on the Australian sporting program and rival the Melbourne Cup for anticipation.

And remarkably Origin was born of desperation.

Decades of lop-sided series wins by NSW against a Queensland side that was missing key local players who had signed with Sydney clubs lost credibility with the public. A life-reviving change was desperately needed.

In came in 1980 when the first Origin match was played as a one-off after NSW had again beaten Queensland in the opening two games of the traditional series. Massive crowd support and a dramatic win by a Queensland side skippered by Arthur Beetson in that historic game was the pebble that started an avalanche and assured Origin's future. Now, 30 years later, the excitement still grows. The expectations climb higher.

Every year State of Origin taps into the souls of rugby league supporters on both sides of the border. It is a topic of endless argument and passion. Players regard Origin selection as a much-valued highlight of their careers. It's a time when every other sporting loyalty is cast aside and the only thing that matters is winning.

Memories of fabulous Origin moments are seared into the minds of lovers of the game. Some were heartbreaking. Some were triumphant.

What about Mark Coyne's last-minute try to win the first game of the 1994 series after nearly all the Queensland backline handled in a raid that started almost on their own tryline?

And Allan 'Alfie' Langer's secret return from playing with Warrington in England to drive Queensland to a series-winning performance in the final game of the 2001 series at 35 years of age?

NSW have had their moments too. Such as the last-minute tries centre Mark McGaw scored in 1987 and 1991 to win games.

The traditions and folklore of Origin demanded that an illustrated history be made of the most gripping moments and I'm delighted to see that it has not only been done—but done superbly. The descriptions and pictures in this book capture the desperation and toughness of every Origin series year by year.

My congratulations to the author, who has taken time and care with the detailed and illuminating game reports, and to the photographers, who took some memorable pictures. They have ensured this is a valuable addition to rugby league's library.

Colin Love AM
Australian Rugby League chairman

← Steve Mortimer is chaired from the Sydney Cricket Ground in 1985 after leading NSW to its first series win in State of Origin football, following five years of Queensland supremacy.

→ The fierce State of Origin battles were sometimes played in wet weather. Noel Cleal pursues Gene Miles in muddy conditions at the Sydney Cricket Ground in 1984.

↓ Michael O'Connor was one of the most talented footballers of his time, and was always a dangerman for NSW in his Origin days from 1985 to 1991. He had previously represented Queensland in rugby union.

Rugby league's State of Origin competition has emerged from an uncertain start to become an iconic part of the Australian sporting calendar. With New South Wales donning sky blue and Queensland in maroon, the best players from each of the two states vie for interstate supremacy. Over 30 years, the speed, skill, intensity, and physical and mental nature of the Origin games have taken rugby league to greater and greater heights. The accepted ferocity of the games has often allowed players to get away with antics that could incur hefty punishment in club football. The fierce nature of Origin football has also caused tempers to flare, making it not unusual for fist-fights to break out during the games.

Here we take a close look at the first 30 years of the competition, exploring each game in close detail. Those who have witnessed many a State of Origin game can relive their favourite moments and reflect on the triumphs, disappointments, controversies and unexpectedness that have shaped the great spectacle—and, in particular, how thin the line is between success and failure. One or two vital incidents may determine the complexion and outcome of each game. As Australia's best players go hammer and tongs at each other, the margin for error is almost non-existent. If both teams are at peak performance, the score is often very close. But if one side is even five per cent below its best, the opposition can easily inflict a thrashing. One team may win a game convincingly but the result could just as easily be reversed next time round, such is the small margin for error.

Numerous rugby league fans and journalists have referred to certain Origin results as upsets. However, when the key moments in each game are examined, it becomes clear there really is no such thing as an

upset result in State of Origin. In a nutshell, the degree to which each side makes mistakes, and capitalises on the opposition's mistakes, goes a long way to deciding match results. The unpredictability of how it eventually pans out in each game makes for compelling viewing.

State of Origin's match officials often attract the ire of losing teams, as is the case in most sports. Controversial rulings and referees' errors of judgement may change the complexion of a game as much as a mistake by a player. But when scrutinising the

teams have only a week or so to prepare for each game. The players come from an array of clubs and have to put aside club allegiances to focus on beating the opposite state. That also means forgetting about their club colleagues playing for the other team. For three games each year, they are enemies.

The same issues apply to the coaches, many of whom coach against their club players in State of Origin. The coaching role in Origin football is a challenge. In the early years, there was little time for developing game plans or building up a team. But as Origin went into its third decade, more extensive coaching panels and advance planning become the established approach.

Although there can be only one premiership-winning team each year in club competitions, other sides may be judged to have been somewhat successful. In State of Origin, however, winners and losers are much more clearly defined. As the legendary Queensland coach Wayne Bennett noted in *Big League, State of Origin Special*: 'If you lose, you feel as though you have let every bugger in the state down, whereas in club football you rally for a game next week and just get on with the job. It's the most stressful coaching job I've had, yet the most wonderful.'

Indeed, fans have felt unhappy for days afterwards when their state has lost an Origin game. Because of the aura surrounding State of Origin, it becomes too easy to forget that, as with any sport, it is just a game—a game where players are merely playing with a football. Many sports are like that: simply playing with a ball. Yet State of Origin fans and players feel that their state is at stake.

The fervour that Origin football has created is not confined to NSW and Queensland. Although rugby league has always had a comparatively small following outside the two states, Origin is something different. A lot of people who are normally uninterested in the sport have eagerly followed Origin football. Apart from NSW and Queensland, the competition has generated huge interest not just

↑ The gifted Darren Lockyer, a rugby league star at club, state and international level in the 1990s and 2000s.

key moments in a game, it becomes evident that if a team does well enough to achieve victory, it will usually win regardless of match officials.

The Challenges of Origin

Apart from the first two years of Origin football, the NSW Blues and Queensland Maroons have battled out a series of three games each year. The demands on the players are far different from club football, in more ways than one. Whereas club teams play on a weekly basis throughout the season, State of Origin

in the other Australian states but in Papua New Guinea, New Zealand and even in some parts of Europe and Asia.

In the Beginning ...

Historically, interstate series involving NSW and Queensland have been a part of rugby league since the code began in Australia in 1908. Yet it took 72 years for the State of Origin competition to materialise. Before 1980, the accepted rule was that players represented the state in which they lived and worked and played. As Sydney had developed into the premier club competition in the world, NSW always boasted the best teams. It was not unusual for Queensland-based players to head south for greater opportunities. This proved commonplace until the 1980s and 1990s, when Queensland and other non-NSW based clubs were introduced to a geographically expanded Sydney premiership competition. Nevertheless, NSW still had more players to choose from than Queensland. Thus, as Origin history shows, Queensland and NSW have very different selection policies. With so many players available, NSW selectors often pick players based on their form at the time of Origin selection. Consequently, it has not been unusual for NSW teams to change considerably within the space of a year or two.

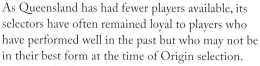

↑ NSW's Timana Tahu in action during the 2002 State of Origin series.

As Queensland has had fewer players available, its selectors have often remained loyal to players who have performed well in the past but who may not be in their best form at the time of Origin selection.

From the first interstate game in 1908, NSW won all 22 matches until the end of the 1921 series. The Queenslanders enjoyed an eight-game winning streak from 1922 to 1925, but NSW won far more often than not in the ensuing decades. In both 1960 and 1961, the series was tied at two games all, but there was little joy for Queensland for the rest of that decade. Indeed, in the 1960s, NSW won 31 games to Queensland's seven, with one drawn. In 1964, rugby league writer Jack Reardon raised an idea in the *Courier-Mail* that Queensland should be allowed to call on their players from Sydney clubs. The idea went nowhere.

The 1970s produced even worse results for Queensland—it won just three games and drew one compared with NSW's 26 victories. When tallying the history of the interstate competition results at the end of 1979, the readings were: NSW 156 wins, Queensland 54 wins, seven draws. Even worse for the Maroons was that more and more Queensland players were heading south and playing for NSW. Barry Muir, a Queensland halfback in the 1970s, used the term 'cockroaches' to describe his contempt towards NSW. This nickname stuck, and to this day NSW Origin teams are sometimes called the 'cockroaches'. On the other side of the fence, Queensland acquired the nickname of the 'cane toads'.

Politics was as big a factor when it came to the number of players moving south. The financially secure Sydney clubs could offer much larger sums of money, thanks to revenue from poker machines, which were outlawed in Queensland until 1992.

Establishing Origin

In 1977, Western Australia and Victoria contested a state-of-origin game in Australian Football League. Of the two states, Victoria always had the strongest club competition and, like NSW in rugby league, attracted players from other AFL states to play in Melbourne, win selection for the Big V and then play against their home states. But WA won the game because it was able to call on its players who had moved to Victoria.

Queensland Rugby League president Ron McAuliffe liked the WA-Victoria concept and began talking to a number of key sports administrators, including Victorian Football League president and fellow Rothmans Sports Foundation board member Dr Allen Aylett. They formed the idea that Queensland and NSW play on a 'state of origin' basis. McAuliffe pushed the idea to the New South Wales Rugby League president and Australian Rugby League chairman Kevin Humphreys. Although Humphreys saw merit in the idea, there were concerns that Sydney clubs would be reluctant to accept the concept, for two major reasons. Firstly, Sydney clubs would have to supply players for Queensland as well as NSW. Secondly, club team-mates were going to oppose each other, so it was unclear if the players would take it seriously.

Many informal discussions took place before the state-of-origin concept was discussed at a NSWRL meeting in 1980. Delegates from each of the 12 NSWRL clubs were present. Nine were in favour (Balmain, Canterbury, Cronulla, Manly, Newtown, North Sydney, Parramatta, Penrith and Western Suburbs) and three opposed (Eastern Suburbs, South Sydney and St George). The 9–3 vote in favour was a hugely successful result, considering the reservations about the concept. Nonetheless, the idea had not won wide favour among rugby league followers and the media. Hence, McAuliffe and Humphreys agreed that the first two games of the 1980 series would be played on the traditional state-of-residence basis. But if one side won both of those games, the third would be played on a state-of-origin basis.

State of Origin was set to begin. And the rest, as they say, is history.

← NSW defenders often found Queenslander Matt Bowen elusive when he played in the 2000s.

↓ Mercurial Queenslander Billy Slater beats David Williams to the ball to score a try in the 30th year of Origin football.

1980s

1980

The Evolution of League's Interstate Rivalries

Under the traditional state of residence format, NSW won the first game of the 1980 interstate series 35–3 at Lang Park in Brisbane. The Blues were somewhat weakened in the second game at Leichhardt Oval in Sydney, but still won 17–7. NSW's two wins ensured the third interstate encounter would be a State of Origin game, which was played at Lang Park.

The Origin concept had many critics and so was a calculated risk. There was a lot of scepticism as to whether or not players would play seriously against their regular club team-mates. But with Queensland's selectors able to choose both resident and expatriate players, there was every chance that the intensity and competitiveness of interstate rugby league might reach levels not seen for decades. There was the very real risk, though, that if NSW won the one-off State of Origin game, interstate football was potentially doomed.

Queensland was coached by former test centre John McDonald. NSW was coached by Ted Glossop, who was also coaching Canterbury in club football.

← English referee Billy Thompson looks on as tempers flare in the inaugural State of Origin game. It put paid to the notion that club team-mates would go easy on each other when playing for opposing states.

↑ Opposing halfbacks Tom Raudonikis and Greg Oliphant in a friendlier frame of mind off the field.

The Teams

Queensland's selectors named eight Sydney-based players before one of them, the injured Graham Quinn, was replaced in the squad by the Queensland-based Brad Backer. The captain, 35-year-old Arthur Beetson, was playing his first game in Queensland colours after he had represented NSW for 12 years.

Captained by Tom Raudonikis, NSW selected a strong team despite Ray Price, Garry Dowling, George Peponis and Les Boyd having to pull out with injuries. The states took different approaches in the lead-up to the game. NSW players represented their clubs on the weekend before the Origin game, and four of the selected players subsequently failed the medical examination. The Blues held one training session. In contrast, the Maroons withdrew from club football and held several training sessions.

Englishman Billy Thompson officiated.

The Game

↓ The front page of the Brisbane *Telegraph* salutes Queensland's win in the first State of Origin game.

A parochial crowd roared as their home-grown heroes entered the arena, with Beetson receiving a particularly loud ovation. Beetson was fortunate not to be penalised for a high tackle on Hambly in the first minute. After Eadie kicked early, Wynn was

punished for holding Lang down after he darted through from acting-half. Meninga opened the scoring, kicking a 25-metre penalty goal.

The forwards from both sides tackled vigorously. Close looked dangerous in attack but twice threw a poor pass with the tryline beckoning. Scrums proved farcical as a swarm of legs and bodies moved around clumsily, and the referee's interpretations of the rules puzzled players, commentators and spectators alike. When Raudonikis was oddly penalised for taking too long to feed a messy scrum, Meninga kicked another penalty goal.

After the Maroons lost possession near halfway, Alan Thompson got away with a knock-on in a play-the-ball, even though players momentarily stopped and waited for the referee to intervene. Moments later, Edge switched play to the left where Raudonikis, Cronin and Eadie combined. Eadie veered right into a wall of defence but flicked a one-handed pass to Cronin, who shrugged off Boustead and evaded Scott's diving tackle. Cronin turned the ball left to Leis, who drew Lang and linked up with Edge, who drifted left and fired the ball to the unmarked Brentnall. He raced to the left corner and rolled over to score in Boustead's tackle. Cronin's conversion attempt just failed, leaving NSW one point behind.

An all-in brawl broke out when Wynn retaliated after Oliphant held him down too long. Club-mates displayed the passion involved in state representation as they tore into each other. Once the violence had calmed down somewhat, referee Thompson mysteriously awarded Queensland a scrum feed.

Telegraph   FINAL

52-6011 (Classified 52-0461)   15 CENTS*

BRISBANE, WEDNESDAY, JULY 9, 1980   Treasure 1293: P65

MAROONS VICTORY SPECIAL

Artie says 'let's do it again' after...

By DAVID FALKENMIRE

Arthur Beetson was nursing a sore head this morning — but he reckons it was worth it.

Beetson, Queensland's favorite son, celebrated after leading the Maroons to their memorable 20-10 win over New South Wales at Lang Park last night.

And just for good measure . . . at the age of 35 . . . he

was one of the best players on the field.

"I had never played for Queensland and I doubt if I have ever been so determined to win," Beetson said today.

"It is one of the highlights of my career."

Beetson said he had no doubts a state-of-origin match should be played annually.

"I am more convinced than ever after last night," he said.

It was Beetson's first representative match since 1971 and it may well be his last.

After 15 years of Sydney football with Balmain, Easts, and now Parramatta, he admits his career is nearly finished.

● More pictures, stories, Pages 3, 72, 73 and Back Page.

THE NIGHT WE BEAT THE BLUES

Queensland last night produced the magic to beat New South Wales 20-10 in an historic state-of-origin rugby league match at Lang Park.

Queensland league followers have been saying it for years: Give us our players back, Sydney, and we will beat the Blues.

So they gave us back a Magnificent Seven — seven players from Queensland playing with Sydney clubs — who combined with the best north of the border to defeat "the Unbeatables."

Evergreen Artie Beetson, Johnny Lang, Kerry Boustead, Greg Oliphant, Rod Morris, Allan Smith and Rod Reddy provided experience to galvanise the locals.
And the lo...

...ay's KEITH MORRIS picture of Artie Beetson the morning after.

Triplets in

Queensland attacked in NSW's quarter after Anderson fumbled a wild pass from Young. Beetson took the ball up and unloaded back to Lewis. The ball moved right to Oliphant, Smith and Meninga, who drew Cronin and fed Close. Stepping around the fast-approaching Rogers, Close drew Brentnall, stepped right and fed Boustead, who sprinted unopposed to the line. Meninga's acutely angled conversion made the score 9–3, before Scott fumbled from the kick-off. The Maroons were penalised from the ensuing scrum, and Cronin closed the margin to four points with a penalty goal. Both teams showed some ill-discipline within the last ten minutes of the half, but there was no further change to the score.

After a handling error each way after the break, NSW was penalised from two scrums in quick succession. From the latter, Meninga kicked another penalty goal. After Brentnall fumbled an awkward pass from Thompson, Young was penalised for tripping, and Meninga's fifth goal made the score 13–5. Brentnall conceded a silly penalty in the ensuing tackle count, kneeing a tackled Boustead while a linesman was nearby. A few tackles later, inside NSW's half, the ball went left before Meninga turned an inside ball to Close. Close stumbled but stepped around Thompson and out of Leis's tackle. Accelerating ahead, Close veered right and evaded Eadie's attempted ankle-tap before crossing near the right post. Queensland held a commanding 13-point lead after Meninga's sixth goal.

Scott stepped over the dead-ball line as he fielded the kick-off, but the match officials missed it. NSW received two quick penalties, the latter when Beetson struck Hambly. Moments later, Cronin was held when Beetson arrived and hit him on the jaw with a swinging left hand. Near the tryline, Edge sent a well-timed pass to Raudonikis, who surged over to score inside the left upright. Cronin's conversion narrowed the score to 18–10 midway through the second half.

Lewis stole the ball in a tackle soon after the restart, and an ensuing offside penalty led to Meninga landing his seventh goal from seven attempts. The

Maroons conceded four successive penalties but their defence hung on. The crowd chanted 'Artie, Artie, Artie' as the historic game neared its conclusion.

The Verdict

Two tries each and a penalty count of 11–9 Queensland's way suggested an even game. The penalties conceded by NSW within kicking range, coupled with Meninga's faultless accuracy, proved crucial. Regardless, Origin football was on its way. Naturally, Queenslanders savoured their 20–10 victory. Meanwhile, the Sydney reporter Alan Clarkson commented that the game was a winner as a promotion and for the code itself, and that an annual Origin fixture would be a welcome part of the rugby league season.

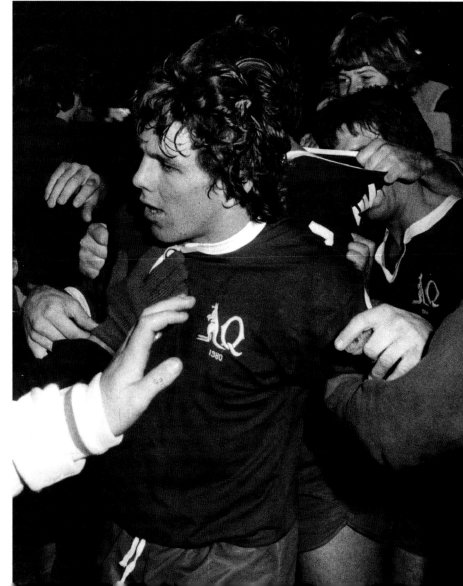

↓ The Maroons winger Kerry Boustead scored Queensland's first try in Origin football.

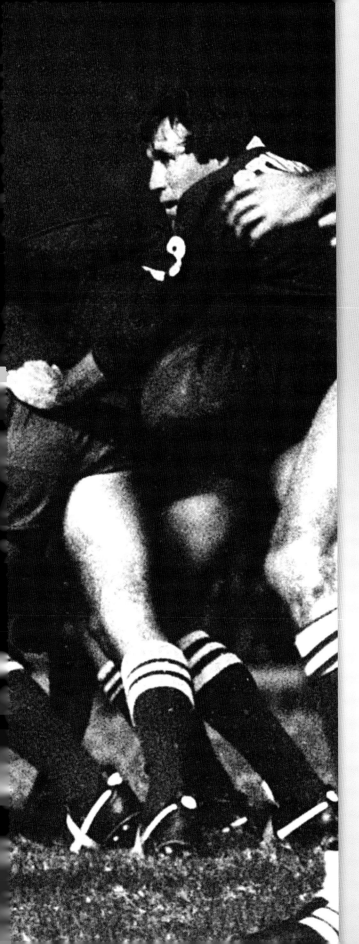

1981

Flying Fists and Fighting Back

In spite of the success of the inaugural State of Origin match in 1980, the format for interstate football remained the same in 1981. Two games were to be played on the traditional state-of-residence basis with an Origin game to follow only if one state won both games. The Blues won the first interstate game 10–2 at Lang Park and the second 22–9 at Leichhardt Oval. Some six weeks later, the second State of Origin game was played at Lang Park.

Currently playing for Redcliffe in Queensland, Arthur Beetson captained and coached the Maroons. Ted Glossop remained the coach of the NSW side.

← Queensland halfback Ross Henrick darts away from a scrum. A late inclusion in the team, Henrick made several mistakes as NSW shot to a 15–0 lead before the Maroons fought back.

The Teams

Both teams differed significantly from those chosen for the 1980 game. Queensland's newcomers were Greg Conescu, Mark Murray, Terry Saunders, Mitch Brennan, Chris Phelan, John Ribot and Paul McCabe. But Beetson, Saunders and Ribot failed fitness tests. Backer returned and Ross Henrick and Paul Khan joined the list of debutants. With Beetson as coach, Lewis was named captain.

NSW's only survivors were centres Cronin and Rogers, who was the new captain. Michael Pattison (illness) and Royce Ayliffe (injured) were replaced by Terry Lamb and Graham O'Grady.

New Zealander Kevin Steele was appointed referee.

Players & Statistics

QLD Colin Scott, Brad Backer, Mal Meninga, Chris Close, Mitch Brennan, Wally Lewis (c), Ross Henrick, Chris Phelan, Rohan Hancock, Paul McCabe, Paul Khan, Greg Conescu, Rod Morris. **RESERVES** Norm Carr, Mark Murray.
COACH Arthur Beetson

NSW Phil Sigsworth, Terry Fahey, Michael Cronin, Steve Rogers (c), Eric Grothe, Terry Lamb, Peter Sterling, Ray Price, Les Boyd, Peter Tunks, Ron Hilditch, Barry Jensen, Steve Bowden. **RESERVES** Garry Dowling, Graham O'Grady (not used).
COACH Ted Glossop

Result Queensland 22 (Backer, Lewis, Close, Meninga [penalty] tries; Meninga 5 goals) beat NSW 15 (Grothe 2, Cronin tries; Cronin 3 goals)

Referee Kevin Steele (New Zealand)

Crowd 25 613

Man of the Match Chris Close (Queensland)

The Game

McCabe made a long break from dummy-half in the first minute, then an offside penalty in front of the posts offered Meninga a 23-metre goal-kick but he pulled it. Fighting erupted after Bowden and Morris collided, and further brawls soon broke out, after Hancock was gang-tackled and when the ensuing scrum collapsed. Referee Steele penalised NSW from the scrum but changed his mind and penalised Queensland for fighting. Morris and Bowden were sin-binned for ten minutes, and NSW had its first possession after six minutes.

↑ Queensland's Rohan Hancock in a close encounter with the NSW duo Ron Hilditch and Peter Sterling.

Penalties and goal-line drop-outs were traded. After forcing a drop-out, the Maroons were attacking dangerously in the 10-metre zone. But Brennan fumbled Conescu's short pass, and Grothe counterattacked down the left touchline. Backer chased from the opposite wing but failed to stop Grothe, who stumbled over to score in Scott's last-gasp tackle. Cronin converted from the sideline.

After an error by Henrick, the Blues opted to run on the last tackle, about 30 metres from Queensland's tryline. Rogers passed left to Price, who turned his back to the defence as Rogers ran around to his left. Khan moved up as Price turned the ball to the short side where Sterling scurried through. Drawing Scott, Sterling sent Cronin scampering to score a try, which he converted. NSW led 10–0 just before Bowden and Morris returned.

Scrums were as farcical as those in the 1980 Origin game. Queensland lost a scrum that was fed by Henrick, who was then penalised for not retiring behind another scrum. In Queensland's quarter, Sterling took the penalty tap and fed Price, who again turned his back in a set play. Sterling ran a decoy as Price fed Grothe. He sprinted through Phelan's tackle to score behind the posts.

NSW comically lost possession when Jensen's pass hit the hip of Boyd, who wasn't looking. A few moments later, Conescu passed left where Henrick, Khan and McCabe handled. As Fahey moved in, McCabe fired the ball to the unmarked Backer, who beat Sigsworth to the left corner. Meninga's impressive conversion narrowed NSW's lead to 15–5 eight minutes before half-time. After receiving an offside penalty, the Maroons might have scored twice in quick succession had passes to Backer found their mark. After errors by Sterling and Boyd, Meninga sliced a goal-kick from near the left wing.

Following the break, Queensland's defence held on after Henrick faltered with three consecutive scrum feeds. Brennan threatened in attack but Grothe made a try-saving tackle from behind. NSW conceded three quick penalties, one of which led to the hookers fighting. Soon after Rogers knocked-on, Henrick passed to Lewis, who baulked, looked right, wrong-footed Sterling, stepped between two defenders and out of Price's tackle to stumble over the line. Meninga's crucial conversion closed NSW's lead to a converted try with 20 minutes remaining.

The Blues failed to kick at the end of their next set, giving Queensland a scrum feed near halfway. Scott broke through and was brought down from behind by another great tackle from Grothe. Close raced to dummy-half, desperate for a quick play-the-ball. He pulled Grothe's hair, back-handed him in the face and pushed him over. Scott played the ball to Close, who stepped left and crashed over the line in Rogers's tackle. A penalty against Close was warranted but Steele awarded the try, to the disbelief of the Blues. Meninga's conversion levelled the scores.

Penalties each way led to wasted opportunities. In the 73rd minute, Sigsworth was too slow to recover a grubber and was forced in-goal. Then Phelan was held in front of the posts when a frustrated Price foolishly head-butted him. It provided Meninga with a 20-metre goal to break the deadlock.

Rogers kicked short but a jumping Bowden knocked it forward to an offside Price. Five tackles later, Lewis chip-kicked to the left where Price dived for the ball but fumbled it. Meninga toed the ball ahead and was just short of the tryline when he kicked it again and was tackled from behind by Rogers. The ball went dead and Steele awarded a penalty try. Replays suggested a penalty may have been fairer as there appeared doubt that Meninga would have scored. Meninga's conversion from in front of the posts sealed the game for Queensland.

← Kerry Boustead (left) turned out for NSW in the state-of-residence series, but injury robbed him of representing Queensland in the State of Origin game.

The Verdict

Recovering from a sizeable deficit was something that Queensland had not been able to do in traditional interstate football. But NSW could just as easily have won the game, bearing in mind the controversy in the lead-up to Close's try, Price's moment of madness and the questionable nature of the final penalty try.

One thing was clear, however: State of Origin football was a winner because Queensland was becoming competitive.

↓ Arthur Beetson played for Queensland in the state-of-residence series, but he pulled out of the Origin game with injury. Regardless, he coached the Maroons to a memorable come-from-behind win.

1982

Best of Three: Queensland Triumph Again

The clear acceptance of State of Origin football over a residence format ensured that the Blues would have to put past successes behind them and concentrate on achieving similar results in a new era. In 1982, the format expanded to a two-game series with provision for a third if the series were level after two games.

NSW made two notable changes in its approach. The Australian coach Frank Stanton was appointed to guide the Blues, and the NSW team was chosen a week before the opening clash, thus allowing the side a longer preparation time than previously.

← Steve Mortimer scores a try for NSW in game one of the 1982 series, the first year that three games were played in the State of Origin format.

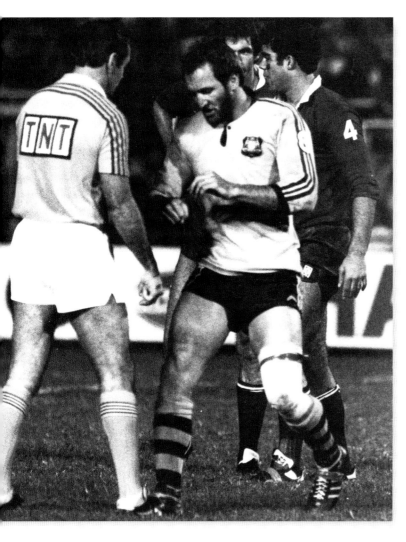

↑ Ray Price stresses his
point to referee Kevin
Roberts, the first Australian
to officiate an Origin game.

Players & Statistics

NSW Greg Brentnall, Chris Anderson, Michael Cronin, Steve Rogers, Ziggy Niszczot, Alan Thompson, Steve Mortimer, Ray Price, John Muggleton, Tony Rampling, Craig Young, Max Krilich (c), John Coveney. **RESERVES** Brad Izzard, Royce Ayliffe. **COACH** Frank Stanton

QLD Colin Scott, John Ribot, Mitch Brennan, Mal Meninga, Kerry Boustead, Wally Lewis, Mark Murray, Paul Vautin, Paul McCabe, Bruce Walker, Paul Khan, John Dowling, Rohan Hancock. **RESERVES** Bob Kellaway, Gene Miles. **COACH** Arthur Beetson

Result NSW 20 (Niszczot 2, Mortimer, Izzard tries; Cronin 4 goals) beat Queensland 16 (Ribot, Brennan tries; Meninga 5 goals)

Referee Kevin Roberts (NSW)

Crowd 27 326

Man of the Match Mal Meninga (Queensland)

The Teams

NSW made wholesale changes to its 1981 Origin side. Eight players were discarded, and Brentnall, Anderson and Thompson were recalled. Ziggy Niszczot, Steve Mortimer, John Muggleton, John Coveney, Brad Izzard and Royce Ayliffe made their first appearances, along with Max Krilich, a representative from pre-Origin days. The injured Hilditch and Boyd were late withdrawals, replaced by Young and another debutant, Tony Rampling.

Queensland fielded four debutants in its starting team—John Ribot, John Dowling, Paul Vautin and Bruce Walker—and reserves Bob Kellaway and Gene Miles were also newcomers. Kellaway was chosen after Morris was ruled unfit. The other players had played in at least one Origin game.

Sydney's Kevin Roberts became the first Australian State of Origin referee.

The Game

The Blues conceded three penalties before gaining possession. From the third, Meninga landed a great goal from the left sideline. Mortimer employed an unusual ploy from a penalty tap, hoisting a kick over his head, only for Brentnall to fumble beyond the tryline. The Blues conceded six penalties to two in an ill-disciplined opening 18 minutes, and the Maroons led 4–0 after an indiscretion by Price.

Krilich made up for earlier mistakes with an intercept. Mortimer put up a bomb, and Scott missed the ball as Brennan accidentally impeded him. Brentnall collected it and passed to Mortimer, who drifted left and fed Muggleton. He veered towards the corner and was held by Boustead, but he freed his left arm and flung an inside pass to Niszczot, who reached for the line. NSW led 5–4 as Cronin landed the difficult conversion.

NSW enjoyed territory after some errors from Queensland. Rampling lofted a pass to an unmarked Anderson just 10 metres out, but Anderson fumbled on the half-volley. The Blues, however, won the scrum against the feed. Two tackles later, Price passed left to Muggleton. He drifted and delayed a long pass to Niszczot, who got outside Boustead to score another try. NSW led 10–4 as Cronin again converted superbly. NSW won another scrum against the feed and forced a repeat set of tackles. An ensuing offside penalty enabled Cronin to extend the Blues' lead to eight points.

Successive penalties against Mortimer and Krilich led to Meninga landing another goal. The Blues forced goal-line drop-outs leading up to half-time but were unable to extend their 12–6 lead. However, they looked the goods after converting more chances.

The first three penalties after the break went to Queensland but they made little impact, and Meninga fumbled an intercept with a try on offer. Murray conceded a costly penalty for not retiring from a scrum. Near the tryline, Krilich shovelled the ball to Mortimer, who looked left but stepped right to change the point of attack. Burrowing between Hancock and Khan, Mortimer exploited some soft goal-line defence to cross the line. Cronin converted, and NSW held a strong 17–6 lead.

After Price was penalised for stealing the ball, the Maroons decided to pocket another penalty goal rather than press for a try. They failed to profit from further penalties, before Young fumbled. Dowling then off-loaded back to Meninga, who veered both ways and evaded Thompson and Price. Drifting right, Meninga busted Young's tackle and fended off Mortimer before off-loading to Boustead. He ran down the sideline and was blocked by cover defence, but spun around and passed to Ribot, who sprinted through to score near the right post. Meninga skewed the easy conversion attempt, crucially leaving Queensland more than a converted try behind.

One tackle after the restart, Brennan delayed a short ball to Meninga, who burst through Rogers's tackle and fended off Mortimer. Meninga drew Brentnall and sent Brennan running to score near the left post. Meninga converted to narrow NSW's lead to one point and set up a thrilling final ten minutes.

Brennan made a dangerous break soon after the restart, but Ribot was penalised for a shepherd. NSW held the ball for six tackles, then received a penalty from a scrum. Five tackles later, Mortimer received the first pass on the left but stopped and sent a long pass to the right to Ayliffe. Drawing Ribot, Ayliffe slipped a short ball to Izzard, who reached to score in a tackle. Cronin's goal-kick veered right. Queensland could win with a converted try in the last four minutes.

A fumble by Ayliffe and a ball-stripping penalty against Mortimer increased the Maroons' prospects. Their attack was lack-lustre before Lewis put up a testing bomb on the last tackle. But Brentnall leapt high to catch the ball safely as Khan and Niszczot flanked him. In the final minute, Mortimer was penalised for incorrectly feeding a scrum, then was marched 10 metres for dissent. Queensland had one last chance but Mortimer smothered Dowling's kick. The siren sounded as Walker's last-gasp kick sliced out.

The Verdict

The Blues deserved their victory after being the better side for most of the game. Meninga's late impact could have led Queensland to another incredible come-from-behind win, but his failure to convert Ribot's try proved costly. NSW, however, had to defend desperately until the end as Queensland remained in the hunt. Like the previous year, the old saying 'it isn't over till the fat lady sings' was a good description of the nature of the game.

↓ John Dowling was beaten to the ball by counterpart Max Krilich in several scrums, but Dowling produced a vital pass as Queensland fought back from a 17–8 deficit.

The Teams

Queensland lost Meninga and Brennan to injury, and Boustead, Walker and Kellaway were dropped. Quinn was named after injury denied him in 1980, and newcomer Greg Holben was on the bench. Backer, Carr and Morris were recalled, and some positional changes occurred.

NSW was also forced into changes as Anderson and Cronin were unfit. Tony Melrose was named to debut as Grothe and Fahey were overlooked. Izzard was promoted to centre and Brett Kenny was a new reserve. Rampling was dropped but returned when the recalled Boyd again succumbed to injury.

Mackay referee Barry Gomersall was plucked out of Queensland country football to control the game.

↓ NSW forward John Muggleton holds on tight as Wally Lewis tries to break free. The first two games of the 1982 series were Muggleton's only Origin appearances.

The Game

Greasy conditions caused some players to slip early on. Referee Gomersall penalised NSW from the first scrum and then for offside in front of the posts, but Scott's 24-metre goal-kick pushed to the right. In a mistake-riddled period, Gomersall once restarted Queensland's tackle count when no NSW player touched the ball, and a couple of Queensland knock-ons were overlooked. The Blues threatened when they moved the ball right but Ribot had Melrose's measure. Melrose later evaded Ribot but threw a hugely forward pass that incurred a penalty. After Ribot made good ground in a well-coordinated move, Mortimer was penalised for offside at marker. Scott's goal-kick from wide to the left was a horror —the ball dribbled about 10 metres along the ground. Soon after, Brentnall fumbled a Lewis bomb before an offside Young dived on the ball. Ten metres from the right post, Scott finally kicked Queensland to a 2–0 lead.

After Krilich conceded a scrum penalty, the Maroons attacked in NSW's 30-metre zone. The ball moved left from Quinn to Murray and Khan, who surged into Izzard and turned it inside to Dowling. He drifted left and passed back to Miles, who ran powerfully through a gap and charged into Brentnall before bulldozing over him to score. Lewis took over the goal-kicking but his conversion attempt swung wide. Queensland led 5–0.

Murray was penalised soon afterwards, then a brawl erupted when McCabe pulled off a heavy tackle. The referee ignored the fighting and allowed play to continue. Near halfway, Thompson and Rogers moved the ball left where Izzard used his fend to surge through Quinn's tackle before accelerating to crash over in the corner. Melrose's hooked goal-kick left Queensland with a two-point lead. There was no further change to the score before half-time.

The Blues made a couple of mistakes in their half soon after

play resumed, and then Mortimer was penalised for another incorrect scrum feed. Near the tryline five tackles later, Dowling passed left to Khan, who fired a cut-out pass to Ribot. He stepped inside Melrose, straightened and then stepped inside Rampling to score. Lewis's hooked goal-kick kept the margin to one converted try. McCabe and Price exchanged knock-ons before NSW received a penalty from a scrum. Morris was penalised five tackles later when he held Krilich down too long, and Melrose landed a goal to narrow Queensland's lead to three points.

After a fumble from Price, the Maroons forced a goal-line drop-out, then the Blues were penalised from successive scrums. NSW's defence held firm before Mortimer chip-kicked from his quarter and received a penalty when obstructed. NSW moved downfield and dominated field position for several minutes. Miles escaped being penalised for almost spear tackling Brentnall, before penalties occurred each way. Referee Gomersall continued to miss some Maroons indiscretions, including a sideways play-the-ball

from Scott. But Mortimer was penalised yet again for feeding a scrum in the second-row. The Maroons attacked briefly and then Rogers and Mortimer made half-breaks. After a penalty against Murray, the Blues opted not to push for a try, Melrose instead potting a 22-metre goal. Queensland led 8–7 with a tense ten minutes remaining.

Price made a break to the halfway line after the restart, but Izzard fumbled from dummy-half a couple of tackles later. Mortimer was in disbelief after Queensland was awarded another penalty from a scrum. Lewis hoisted a bomb which Brentnall caught, and Brentnall just entered the field of play as he was tackled. Miles pushed him back behind the tryline and it seemed an obvious penalty to NSW, but Gomersall ordered a goal-line drop-out. The Blues defused further Lewis bombs before Young was penalised for using his feet in a tackle. NSW's defence held for another tackle count until Brentnall caught another bomb and was legitimately pinned in-goal. Four tackles later, Queensland pressed and, after a series of fumbled passes backwards, Hancock scooped up the ball then slipped it to Vautin, who dived to score in Rampling's tackle. Lewis messed up the conversion from almost in front but the siren was imminent. The Maroons had squared the series.

The Verdict

Queensland's win ensured a third Origin game was required to decide the series. Although both sides seemed to have enough opportunities to win game two, Queensland scrambled just that little bit better to finish ahead. In NSW, Gomersall's refereeing was loudly criticised, with reporter Alan Clarkson saying it would have tested the patience of a saint. It would be the first of several controversial performances by Gomersall in Origin football.

← Ray Price locked the scrum for NSW in all three games of the 1982 series.

Players & Statistics

QLD Colin Scott, John Ribot, Graham Quinn, Gene Miles, Brad Backer, Wally Lewis (c), Mark Murray, Norm Carr, Paul McCabe, Rod Morris, Paul Khan, John Dowling, Rohan Hancock. **RESERVES** Paul Vautin, Greg Holben. **COACH** Arthur Beetson

NSW Greg Brentnall, Tony Melrose, Brad Izzard, Steve Rogers, Ziggy Niszczot, Alan Thompson, Steve Mortimer, Ray Price, John Muggleton, Tony Rampling, Craig Young, Max Krilich (c), John Coveney. **RESERVES** Brett Kenny, Royce Ayliffe. **COACH** Frank Stanton

Result Queensland 11 (Miles, Ribot, Vautin tries; Scott goal) beat NSW 7 (Izzard try; Melrose 2 goals)

Referee Barry Gomersall (Queensland)

Crowd 19 435

Man of the Match Rod Morris (Queensland)

The Teams

The Blues made multiple changes. Young, Rampling, Melrose and Thompson were dropped, Boyd and Cronin recalled, and Phil Duke and Don McKinnon named to debut. NSW players still played club football on the weekend before Origin games, and injuries caused further disruptions, sidelining Muggleton, Brentnall, Niszczot, Rogers and Coveney. Young and Thompson returned to the squad, Fahey and Sigsworth were recalled, and debutant Paul Merlo was added.

For Queensland, Scott and Quinn were injured, and Backer and Holben were omitted. Brennan, Meninga and Boustead returned, and Tony Currie was a new reserve.

The refereee was New Zealander Don Wilson.

The Game

Just over 20 000 spectators attended the first Origin game played on NSW turf. Each team received an early penalty, and a swinging arm from Ayliffe on Hancock triggered a brawl. Poor co-ordination and sloppy handling from both teams saw possession turn over early in tackle counts. After an offside penalty to Queensland in the tenth minute, Dowling took the tap nearly 30 metres out. He passed left to Lewis, who spun the ball to Murray. Noticing Boyd coming up too quickly, Murray stepped right and scurried between two Blues before drawing Sigsworth and sending Hancock in to score. Queensland led 5–0 as Meninga converted.

During a scrappy period, Cronin was penalised for punching Hancock, referee Wilson incredibly gave NSW a scrum feed after McKinnon clearly raked the ball, and a one-on-one brawl between Dowling and Boyd saw the offenders dismissed for five minutes. The Blues forced a goal-line drop-out but NSW's ball control was dreadful and Mortimer conceded penalties for improper scrum feeds. The Maroons were also wayward. After a penalty against Duke, Meninga pulled a goal-kick from the left of the posts.

After Murray inadvertently passed straight to Kenny, the Blues finally completed a tackle count and were 30 metres from Queensland's line.

Mortimer and Ayliffe played a run-around movement on the left before Mortimer veered right and fed Merlo. He drew two defenders and linked with Kenny and Cronin, who attracted Meninga and Miles before feeding Duke. The Moree winger juggled the ball but beat Brennan to score in the corner. Two minutes before the break, Queensland led 5–3 as Cronin's conversion attempt failed.

Errors continued. Boyd made a break before passing to Miles; Fahey dropped an easy pass; Boyd conceded a penalty for striking Meninga. Queensland applied pressure without penetrating and the Blues were pinned in their own half before receiving a penalty. NSW entered Queensland's 10-metre zone but Duke was taken over the sideline. Queensland thus had a scrum feed but the ball bounced NSW's way. Astonishingly, referee Wilson penalised Mortimer for feeding the scrum in the

second-row. When Mortimer protested, he was marched 10 metres. Moments later, Lewis put in a long kick, which rolled past the tryline. Sigsworth was first to the ball but was held by McCabe. Sigsworth unloaded to Duke, but he fumbled the ball over his shoulder and was beaten by Lewis in the dive for it. Meninga easily converted. A refereeing howler followed by a NSW blunder enabled Queensland to gain a 10–3 lead with 25 minutes left.

A series of blunders from the Maroons opened the door for NSW, but Cronin and Ayliffe took it in turns to pass straight to an opponent. After Morris was penalised for reefing the ball in a three-man tackle, Dowling was marched 10 metres for dissent. From 25 metres out, Cronin hooked a goal-kick. The Maroons opted not to kick six tackles later, then Lewis was penalised and sin-binned for five minutes for flinging the ball into Ayliffe after Ayliffe accidentally stepped on his hand. Cronin made no mistake this time, narrowing Queensland's lead to one converted try with 17 minutes remaining.

The Blues failed to capitalise while Lewis was off the field, although they briefly looked dangerous when Duke made a break. Brennan broke through for Queensland but threw a bad pass in the red zone. Errors each way made the game go backwards and forwards. NSW neared Queensland's tryline with six minutes left, and the Maroons were farcically offside as they sped out of the defensive line before a play-the-ball. Price charged from dummy-half but was held up over the line.

The Maroons worked their way out of trouble and received a repeat set, but Lewis hooked a field goal that would have sealed the game. The Blues returned to the attack after Murray was penalised for an incorrect scrum feed. Mortimer hoisted a

bomb which came down near the tryline but a teammate fumbled it in a bunch of players. Murray was penalised again for a feed into the second-row. Mortimer took a quick tap to get within 10 metres before Price's desperate kick was safely caught by Boustead.

The Verdict
The Blues could have won but their error rate hurt them badly. However, Queensland benefited from a major controversy—referee Wilson's clanger—followed by the blunder by Sigsworth and Duke, which cost NSW five crucial points. Regardless, the Maroons showed they could beat the Blues more than once within a month. The ongoing popularity of Origin football suggested some great years lay ahead.

← The Queensland team. *Back row*: unknown trainer or strapper, John Dowling, Colin Scott, Mal Meninga, Paul McCabe, Gene Miles, Paul Khan, Rohan Hancock, Paul Vautin, Arthur Beetson (coach). *Front row*: Dick Turner (co-manager), Rod Morris, Norm Carr, Mark Murray, Wally Lewis, Kerry Boustead, Graham Quinn, John Ribot, Kevin Brasch (co-manager).

↓ Mark Murray cemented his position as the Maroons' premier halfback in the 1982 Origin series.

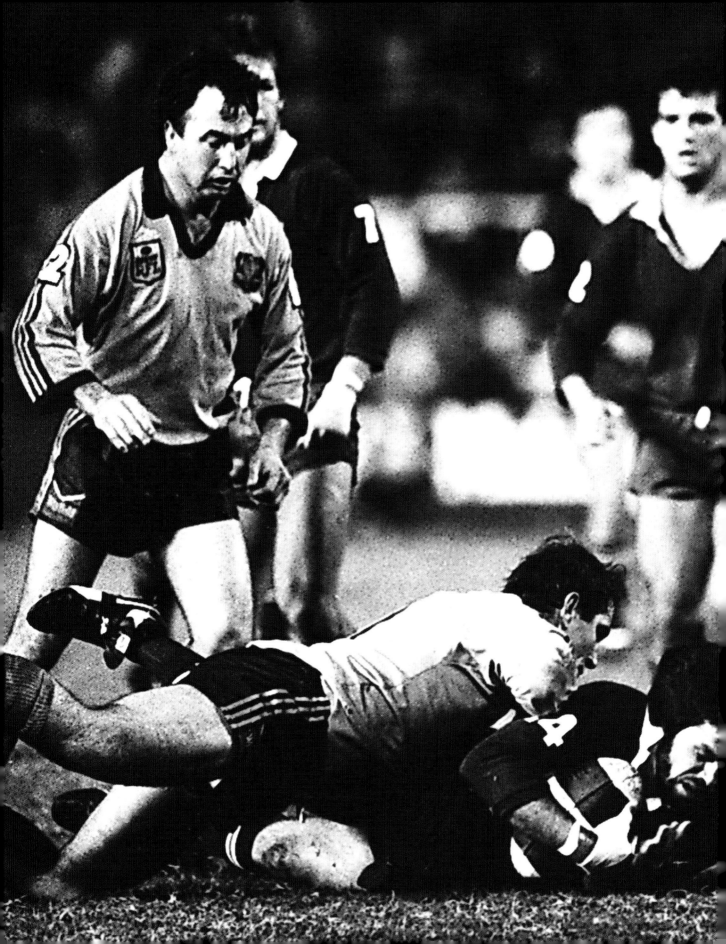

1983

Elbow Ends Forward's Dream, but Wally Has Last Laugh

The burgeoning popularity of State of Origin football was clear, and the all-conquering Kangaroo tour of England and France late in 1982 established Australia as the indisputable force in international rugby league. Origin football thus pitted the best against the best. The series also provided the setting to reinforce the strength of the game in Australia and the opportunity for players to prove themselves in front of the national selectors.

Glossop returned as NSW coach after Stanton stood down from representative coaching. The Blues had one major setback before the series, as Rogers was injured.

← Queensland reserve Bruce Astill is tackled during the last game of the 1983 series. A third game was again needed to decide the series winner, and again it was the Maroons who emerged triumphant.

The Teams

NSW fielded a new-look team, 11 of whom were Kangaroo tourists. Wayne Pearce, Geoff Bugden, Geoff Gerard, Steve Ella and Ray Brown were State of Origin debutants, and Grothe and Sterling were recalled.

Wally Fullerton Smith, Bryan Niebling, Darryl Brohman and Brad Tessmann debuted for Queensland, and Scott and Conescu were recalled. In late changes, more newcomers were added, with Steve Stacey and Brett French replacing injured duo Boustead and Close, and Brett French taking the place of an ill McCabe.

NSW's preparation was unsettled several hours before kick-off when Glossop announced that Ella was relegated to the bench and Thompson would start at five-eighth.

↑ Colin Scott returned to fullback for Queensland after missing the 1982 series decider.

The Game

Immediately after Queensland kicked off, Brentnall kicked downfield, where Miles surprisingly returned the favour from near halfway. An offside infringement by Sigsworth was followed by Conescu playing a run-around movement with Murray and turning a reverse ball to Vautin. Flashing past Gerard, Vautin drew Brentnall before sending Lewis in to score beneath the crossbar.

The Blues held on, conceding a couple of penalties, and then attacked after receiving a penalty. Sterling was tackled a metre out before the Blues sent the ball left. Receiving an undetected forward pass, Sigsworth headed for the tryline but Fullerton Smith and Scott thwarted him. Scott was penalised for pinning Sigsworth down, and Sigsworth sliced a relatively straightforward goal-kick from the left of the posts.

When Queensland next had the ball, Brohman made a hit-up towards the halfway line. Bugden and Ella tackled low, but Boyd came in high and led with his elbow, smashing the ball-carrier's jaw. Referee Gomersall penalised

→ Greg Conescu was an automatic selection at hooker for Queensland for several years.

Boyd but amazingly did not dismiss him. NSW was subsequently caught offside in front of its posts, and Meninga's 25-metre goal made the score 8–0. After a knock-on from Bugden, Niebling fell as he was tackled when Boyd came in and swung wildly with his right arm, narrowly missing Niebling's head. This time Boyd was sin-binned for ten minutes, and the penalty provided another two points for Meninga.

Queensland enjoyed better field position amid a high mistake rate each way. After an offside infringement from NSW, the penalty count favoured the Maroons 9–3, and Meninga landed a 40-metre goal to take the score to 12–0.

Brohman succumbed to his injury and was replaced. After more errors from each team, Conescu played the ball near the right post on tackle five. From dummy-half, Lewis leaned left and dived low between Price and Pearce to score. A penalty to NSW in the 35th minute enabled the Blues to attack. In the ensuing set, Sterling stepped right and looked to pass but instead surged into Fullerton Smith and Tessmann. Sterling's pass to Boyd was relayed on to an unmarked Grothe, who fielded it after one bounce and scored wide out. NSW trailed 18–6 as Sigsworth converted brilliantly.

Gerard set up a break by Pearce soon after the restart, only for Pearce to knock-on as he was tackled. The Maroons soon raided, but the final pass to Tessmann went astray. Vautin was penalised for infringing Boyd in a tackle just before the break, and Dave Brown subsequently slapped Boyd and was sin-binned for five minutes. With the siren about to sound, Sterling put up a bomb but Scott caught it safely.

Early in the second half, Sterling put up another bomb, which Stacey fumbled over his shoulder. Thompson picked up the loose ball and burrowed for the line but was ruled to have been held up. In an exciting play, Meninga chipped and chased, then Brentnall fielded the ball and copped a Meninga shoulder-charge. An unhurt Brentnall quickly played the ball before Grothe made a break. NSW received another tackle count after a penalty against Dave Brown, but Anderson was penalised for shepherding.

After another mistake from Dave Brown, Kenny threw a dummy and split Queensland's defence. He stepped down the blindside but an airborne Scott tackled him over the sideline as the tryline beckoned. An indiscretion by Ray Brown sparked a brief brawl, and Boyd interestingly tried to break it up.

NSW received four successive penalties and pressed the Queensland line. Ella and Sterling exchanged passes on the left before Ella sliced between two Maroons, veered right and evaded a couple of defenders before diving over the line. Sigsworth converted to narrow NSW's deficit to a converted try with 14 minutes left.

Scrappy play continued, and Sigsworth twice wasted possession by kicking short in NSW's half. After further errors each way, NSW entered Queensland's half but lost possession. Five minutes from full-time, the Blues were penalised when they fed another scrum. Five tackles later, Queensland seemed well-placed for a field-goal attempt. Conescu fired the ball right to

Murray, who stepped each way then straightened as he passed two defenders before reaching to score in Sterling's tackle. Meninga's sixth goal from as many attempts made the score 24–12, in Queensland's favour, as it remained until full-time.

The Verdict

The Blues had fought back but, as in 1982, they let themselves down with too many errors. Referee Gomersall attracted criticism in NSW, and Glossop came under fire for opting to start with Thompson rather than Ella.

Although more borderline decisions went Queensland's way, Boyd was fortunate not to be sent off for his elbow-charge on Brohman. But he had to pay a heavy price afterwards because he was suspended for one year.

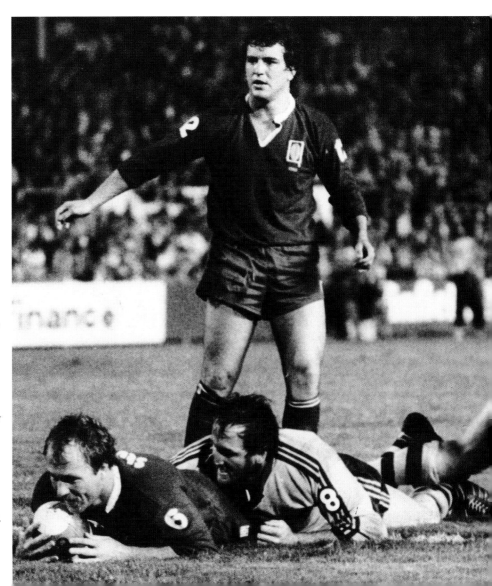

↓ Wally Lewis dives over to score his and Queensland's second try of the game.

The Teams

The Blues had another major shake-up. Sigsworth, Thompson, Bugden and Brown were dropped, Boyd was suspended, and Brentnall, Anderson and Pearce were injured. Cronin, Young and (reserve) Mortimer were recalled, and debutants were Marty Gurr, Brian Johnston, Gavin Miller, Pat Jarvis and Paul Field. NSW was rocked when Krilich, Young, Johnston and Jarvis were ruled out at the medical examination. Peter Tunks and Lindsay Johnston were named as replacements, but Tunks was ruled unfit. Brown was reprieved, and Neil Hunt and Stan Jurd joined the squad. There were eight Parramatta players in the squad, including six backs (Gurr was the exception).

Parramatta forward, Price, took over the captaincy. A journalist in the *Sydney Morning Herald* commented that it was Parramatta versus Queensland.

Queensland also had injury concerns, with Ribot, Brohman, McCabe and Stacey unavailable. Close, Henrick and Boustead were reinstated, but Boustead was later ruled out with injury and replaced by the newcomer Terry Butler.

The Game

Following rain, several areas of the field resembled a swamp. After NSW kicked off in the muddy conditions, Lewis kicked downfield after just two tackles. Following an offside penalty to NSW, Butler did well to defuse Sterling's bomb. The Blues raided numerous times in the early stages, but were unable to find a way through.

After a mistake by each team, Conescu played the ball 35 metres from NSW's tryline. Long passes were thrown right to Lewis, Murray and Scott before Scott slipped a well-timed pass to Meninga after Kenny moved up too quickly. Meninga charged through and veered right to evade Ella, before running in to score with Gurr clinging to his legs. Meninga converted his own try, and the visitors led 6–0 after absorbing the early pressure.

Soon after the restart, referee John Gocher awarded the Blues a questionable penalty for an offside pass against Niebling. Cronin kicked for goal but his 40-metre attempt pushed to the right. Miles created a raid, only for Scott to spill Miles's pass. Scott defused Sterling's bombs, before a stray offload from Tessmann was followed by a penalty against Vautin. One tackle after the penalty, Johnston played the ball 8 metres from the tryline and near the right wing. Long passes were thrown left from Ray Brown to Sterling and Kenny, who unloaded to Cronin. He barged into Scott, who fell over, and then Cronin

The NSW forwards pack into a scrum. After the Blues appeared in disarray following injuries and player unavailability, the different-looking Blues forward pack performed admirably in difficult conditions.

lobbed a high pass over Butler to an unmarked Hunt, who dived over the line. Cronin's impressive wide-angled conversion tied the scores after 31 minutes. The Maroons trailed 7–1 in the penalty count at half-time yet the score was 6-all.

Just after the break, the Blues were caught offside, but Scott fumbled. After winning a scrum against the feed, the Blues ventured into attack but they too were foiled by a handling error. After a play-the-ball in NSW's territory, Gerard changed the point of play and linked with Johnston, Miller and Price, who drew an opponent and fed Gurr. He broke away from Close and kicked ahead. In the chase for the ball, Cronin beat Close and miscued a kick, and the ball went between Grothe's legs. But Ella scooped it up and dived over to score with Lewis snapping at his feet. NSW led 10–6.

After the Blues were penalised for collapsing a scrum in which they had the feed, Meninga made a half-break inside his quarter before Niebling charged for the line. Sterling made a crucial tackle but damaged the AC joint in his shoulder before Gurr ensured Niebling was thwarted agonisingly short of the line. Acting-half Tessmann torpedoed the ball left to Murray. He drifted behind Miles, who surged into Ray Brown. Murray fed Lewis, who crossed near the left upright, but the referee correctly penalised Queensland for an obstruction.

The game ebbed and flowed as penalties were exchanged, and NSW won two scrums against the feed. After a relieving penalty to Queensland, Gurr fumbled Lewis's bomb backwards in NSW's quarter. Miles raced through and kicked the loose ball but

just failed to reach it before it went dead. Three minutes remained. As soon as Queensland retrieved the ball, Close made a strong run on a kick return. The Maroons sent the ball right on the next tackle, with Murray feeding Vautin, who swung a long ball out to Lewis. He passed long to Miles, who charged ahead before rifling a pass to Butler, but Butler fumbled into touch just 10 metres from the tryline as Hunt struggled to keep up. Queensland's last chance to snatch a win or draw was gone, ensuring game three would decide the series.

The Verdict

After their horror lead-up, the Blues deserved credit for their two-tries-to-one victory. This time around there was criticism of the referee from north of the border. However, it was worth noting that the Maroons bombed three potentially winning tries after NSW's final try. Sterling became the first NSW player to win an Origin man-of-the-match award.

↑ Mal Meninga scored all Queensland's points in game two, including a try from a trademark run.

↓ Wally Fullerton Smith on the burst. Queensland's forwards were well and truly outplayed.

Players & Statistics

NSW Marty Gurr, Neil Hunt, Michael Cronin, Steve Ella, Eric Grothe, Brett Kenny, Peter Sterling, Ray Price (c), Paul Field, Gavin Miller, Lindsay Johnston, Ray Brown, Geoff Gerard. **RESERVES** Steve Mortimer, Stan Jurd. **COACH** Ted Glossop

QLD Colin Scott, Terry Butler, Mal Meninga, Gene Miles, Chris Close, Wally Lewis (c), Mark Murray, Paul Vautin, Wally Fullerton Smith, Bryan Niebling, Dave Brown, Greg Conescu, Brad Tessmann. **RESERVES** Brett French (not used), Ross Henrick. **COACH** Arthur Beetson

Result NSW 10 (Hunt, Ella tries; Cronin goal) beat Queensland 6 (Meninga try; Meninga goal)

Referee John Gocher (NSW)

Crowd 21 620

Man of the Match Peter Sterling (NSW)

The Teams

Queensland made three changes with Butler, French and Henrick omitted and replaced by the recalled Stacey and Astill and debutant Gavin Jones. Closer to the game, Close was forced out with injury, leading to a recall for Brennan.

NSW lost Gerard, Price, Sterling and Grothe to injury, and Rogers and Pearce were unavailable. Jurd was initially omitted but later reprieved. Krilich, Mortimer, Bugden and Anderson won recalls. So did Sigsworth but he too was forced out, allowing Kevin Hastings to make his debut.

Englishman Robin Whitfield was appointed to officiate in game three.

The Game

Queensland received an offside penalty in its first tackle count, but Meninga hooked a 26-metre goal-kick. Following NSW's quarter-line drop-out, Miller and Johnston were penalised for a high tackle. The Maroons neared the posts, and then Murray stepped both ways and passed right towards Lewis.

But Lewis tripped over and the ball ended with Conescu, who caught it behind him and turned to dive over the line. Meninga made no mistake with the goal-kick this time. Queensland fumbled soon after, but Bugden and Cronin made unforced errors in quick succession. NSW conceded a scrum penalty and Queensland soon returned the favour.

Brennan was fortunate not to be pulled up for a knock-on before Lewis broke through some feeble defence. He linked with Murray, who sped away and was brought down just short of the tryline. Kenny deliberately slowed the play-the-ball, and Queensland led 8–0 from Meninga's penalty goal.

↑ NSW's defence appears dominant in this tackle, but the defence cracked many times as Queensland racked up the biggest score in State of Origin, before the record was broken 17 years later.

Brennan fumbled from the kick-off, then Jurd and Miller knocked-on in the ensuing minutes. Five tackles later, Lewis's chip-kick bounced unpredictably and was fielded by Meninga, who veered left and charged 30 metres. He reached over his head to ground the ball as Gurr snapped at his legs, but the ball came loose and a try went begging. Gurr saved NSW again when he forced a knock-on from Lewis after Lewis regathered his own kick over

the line. Further mistakes by Queensland gave the Blues chances, but poor handling let them down. Lewis was in fine form with his kicking; however, the same could not be said for NSW. Cronin sliced a bomb out on the full before failing to find the sideline from a penalty kick.

When Mortimer dropped a regulation pass 35 metres from NSW's tryline, Meninga scooped it up, then darted to the right and drew Jurd before feeding Miles. He forged ahead before linking with Niebling, who sent Stacey diving over in the right corner. Meninga's conversion gave Queensland a 14–0 lead. The game was slipping away from NSW.

The Maroons again fumbled after the restart. Murray safely defused Krilich's bomb. Immediately Tessmann drifted left and stepped out of two tackles before unloading to Brennan, who sprinted 70 metres to score beneath the crossbar. The teams exchanged more fumbles after the kick-off, then Queensland received a repeat set of tackles. Lewis accepted a pass 10 metres from the posts and chose to kick a field goal. Queensland held a 21–0 lead at the break.

Mortimer made a costly mistake soon after the break when he knocked-on at the scrum base. Three tackles later, Meninga sliced through NSW's defence to set up a try for Brennan. Within minutes, Murray darted through after a run-around movement with Lewis. Niebling scooped up Murray's pass on the half-volley and broke free of Jurd's tackle to score. Queensland led 33–0 with 30 minutes left.

Following some scrappy play by Queensland, Mortimer veered right from halfway and combined

← Queensland reserve Bruce Astill is thwarted in the 1983 decider. It was the second of Astill's two Origin appearances, although he didn't have any game time in his first, the inaugural 1980 game.

↓ NSW centre Michael Cronin and lock Gavin Miller in the thick of the action. The veteran Cronin had a game he would rather forget as the Blues lost heavily. It was not a happy introduction to Origin football for Miller and he had a while to wait before earning another Origin cap.

with Hastings and Cronin, who linked with Gurr and Kenny. He drew three Maroons and then sent Anderson across in the right corner. Cronin converted, but soon erred again when he dropped a straightforward pass. After errors from Kenny and Mortimer, Brown powered over to score from dummy-half despite the attention of three defenders.

Queensland led 37–6 until the 65th minute, when Scott spilled Hastings's bomb for Mortimer to catch the rebound and score. NSW earned a penalty from a scrum a few minutes later, and then Anderson scored in the right corner. Cronin converted again, but continued to have a poor game when he dropped a simple pass. From NSW's quarter soon afterwards, Hunt, Mortimer and Kenny combined before Kenny drew the defence and sent Gurr scurrying away. Gurr kicked but Stacey made a mess of it, and Ella scooped up the ball and sent Anderson over again.

NSW had scored three tries in eight minutes to reduce Queensland's lead to 37–22 with seven minutes left. In the final three minutes, Murray sent Jones through a gap before Gurr was penalised for a second tackle on Jones. Lewis took a tap 5 metres from the tryline and threw a long pass left. It bounced to Miles, who evaded Kenny before scampering over beside the left upright. Scott added the extras for a final score of 43–22.

The Verdict

Considering Queensland romped to a 33–0 lead soon after half-time, it was hard to imagine that the series was on the line before the game. Although the Blues clawed back from 33–0, it was all too little and it came far too late. Lewis won the man-of-the-match award for the third time in four games, having made a decisive impact on the Origin competition.

1984

Maroons Register Hat-trick of Series Wins

With State of Origin entering its fifth year, the Blues took a new approach to Origin football, requiring that selected players be released from club commitments on the weekend before each game. Some NSW players commented that it had been hard to give their best in Origin when they had played in club games as little as 48 hours beforehand. By comparison, Queensland's home-based players had had week-long breaks to prepare before each game. Thus, the Maroons arguably always had a pre-game advantage. With both teams now having equal preparation opportunities, a NSW loss could no longer be attributed to a short lead-up.

Arthur Beetson remained coach of the Maroons for the fourth straight year. The Blues reinstated Frank Stanton as their coach, after he made himself eligible for the position.

← Passion spilled over into violence in game two of the 1984 series. Queensland went on to win its third consecutive three-game State of Origin series.

The Teams

NSW again fielded a new-look side. Garry Jack, Ross Conlon, Andrew Farrar, Rex Wright, Noel Cleal, Steve Roach and Pat Jarvis were first-timers. Sterling was recalled as a reserve and Mortimer at halfback. However, Mortimer (injured) and Farrar (suspended) withdrew, and Sterling returned to halfback. Ella was recalled and Brian Hetherington was the new reserve.

Queensland had a familiar team, with Boustead returning, and Stacey and Brennan omitted. Newcomers were Greg Dowling and Bob Lindner.

The ARL announced on game day that Stanton was now the Australian coach instead of Beetson. Whether this would impact on the Origin game was arguable, but the Maroons felt that Beetson was harshly treated.

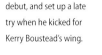

↓ Bob Lindner came off the bench in his Origin debut, and set up a late try when he kicked for Kerry Boustead's wing.

The Game

Vautin fumbled as he was tackled in the first minute, then Brown was penalised for punching. Conlon's ensuing goal gave NSW a quick two-point lead. Queensland failed to capitalise on two penalties before Conlon landed a 43-metre goal from NSW's second penalty. In Queensland's next set in possession, Murray fed Miles, who drifted left and broke past the tackles of Sterling and Pearce. Miles drew Jack and sent Vautin running in for a try near the left upright, but the scores remained level as Meninga's easy goal-kick struck the right post.

After Scott fumbled in a tackle, Miles was penalised for holding an opponent down too long. Miles was marched 10 metres for dissent, allowing Conlon to restore NSW's lead. After Pearce dropped a pass in his quarter, NSW's defence held for five tackles. Kenny knocked down Murray's pass to a trybound Miles, but Wright was penalised from the scrum. NSW again held for five tackles before a leaping Jack fumbled Lewis's high ball, which went straight to Boustead, who fell to score at the posts. Meninga converted, and Queensland led 10–6.

NSW lost possession after looking threatening, before being penalised from the ensuing scrum. Dowling took the ball up from the tap and unloaded to Boustead, who dashed ahead. A few tackles later, Boustead played the ball 4 metres from the tryline near the right wing. Dummy-half Lewis cleverly darted to the blindside, evaded Jack and dived under Cleal's tackle to score. It was 14–6 after 31 minutes.

Price sold Boustead a dummy and linked with Sterling and Pearce before Price broke away, only for Close to come across and knock him down with a heavy shoulder charge just short of the line. Two minutes from half-time, Jack ran onto Conlon's pass and fumbled as he collided with Conlon. Kenny conceded a penalty before the Maroons forced a goal-line drop-out. The siren sounded one tackle later as Lewis received a pass, and he booted a 35-metre field-goal, for Queensland to lead 15–6.

Sterling surrendered possession with a risky chip-kick from his quarter soon after the break. A penalty against Price for tripping saw Meninga hook a straightforward 15-metre goal-kick. After successive errors by Wright, Meninga sliced another easy kick. Lewis sent a clearing kick out on the full but Queensland won the scrum against the feed.

Following some mistakes each way, field position began to favour NSW. Queensland was penalised from a couple of scrums that Murray fed. After the latter, NSW ran on the last tackle from inside the quarter. On the left, Ella combined in a run-around movement with Sterling before Young's stray pass was fielded by Thompson. He fed Kenny and Price, whose round-the-corner pass was parried by Wright. He caught it on the second attempt. The ball moved to Roach and Cleal, who threw Meninga a dummy and veered towards the posts to score. Each team's goal-kicking was telling as Queensland led by just three points with 19 minutes left.

Players & Statistics

QLD Colin Scott, Kerry Boustead, Mal Meninga, Gene Miles, Chris Close, Wally Lewis (c), Mark Murray, Paul Vautin, Wally Fullerton-Smith, Bryan Niebling, Dave Brown, Greg Conescu, Greg Dowling. **RESERVES** Brett French, Bob Lindner. **COACH** Arthur Beetson.

NSW Garry Jack, Eric Grothe, Brett Kenny, Steve Ella, Ross Conlon, Alan Thompson, Peter Sterling, Ray Price (c), Wayne Pearce, Noel Cleal, Craig Young, Rex Wright, Steve Roach. **RESERVES** Pat Jarvis, Brian Hetherington. **COACH** Frank Stanton.

Result Queensland 29 (Boustead 3, Vautin, Lewis, Miles tries; Meninga 2 goals; Lewis field goal) beat NSW 12 (Cleal try; Conlon 4 goals)

Referee Kevin Roberts (NSW)

Crowd 33 662

Man of the Match Wally Lewis (Queensland)

Young soon turned over possession with a poor pass. From 30 metres out, Conescu spread the ball right to Murray and Lewis before a cut-out pass found Meninga. Drawing Conlon, Meninga fed Boustead, who flashed ahead before stepping inside Jack. His ankle-tap sent Boustead into the air before Boustead spun over the line. Queensland looked much safer, leading 19–12.

Kenny made a break without result, before Jack dropped Miles's kick, which went straight to him. Both teams turned over possession wastefully. NSW raided from its half, but Boustead drove Hetherington over the sideline. Murray was penalised for another improper scrum feed, but Jarvis dropped Sterling's easy pass from the penalty tap in Queensland's quarter. In NSW's quarter, Jarvis dropped another easy pass. Moments later, Scott drifted right

and drew two Blues before sending Miles past Price's tackle to score. Queensland looked safe at 23–12 with four-and-a-half minutes left.

The Blues crumbled further as they lost two scrums that Sterling fed. Queensland attacked, and Lindner's chip-kick to the right was perfectly placed as Boustead caught the ball outside Conlon and scored. Queensland won 29–12 after Meninga finally kicked another goal, ironically from wide out.

The Verdict

NSW was within sight until the late stages. However, Queensland scored six tries to one, and would have won more convincingly had Meninga's goal-kicking been better. No excuses were offered for NSW's demise. Some Queensland players said they wanted to win for Beetson more than anything else.

↓ Colin Scott represented the Maroons at fullback in 17 of the first 18 State of Origin games.

↑ Peter Tunks showed some roughhouse tactics early on after being recalled for the Blues.

The Teams

NSW's selectors dropped Thompson, Sterling, Wright, Young and Hethering-ton, and Ella was relegated to the bench. Tunks, Lamb and Mortimer were recalled, and debutants were Andrew Farrar and Royce Simmons.

For the Maroons, Currie was recalled as a reserve in place of French. Meninga and Close swapped positions.

The Game

Heavy rain before kick-off turned the field into a quagmire, and a very strong wind blew as rain continued to fall. Lewis riskily elected to run into the wind in the first half. An all-in fight broke out after Roach struck Miles in the first tackle. Roach was penalised, but it was some time before play resumed. Miles and Farrar exchanged kicks for field position before Tunks and Roach gave away penalties for ill-disciplined play. From the latter, Meninga kicked for goal but his 35-metre attempt fell short in the wind. After Miles was punished for raking the ball, Conlon's 28-metre penalty attempt pushed to the right.

The slippery ball was hard to control. Miles spilled a bomb in his quarter, then Mortimer was penalised from the ensuing scrum. After Close dropped a pass on his quarter-line, Fullerton Smith was penalised for obstructing Lamb, who had chipped into the in-goal area. From 14 metres out and almost in front, Conlon's kick bounced off the post.

The Maroons had a higher mistake rate, although Lewis sometimes kicked effectively early in tackle counts. Miles made a rare break after Roach fumbled, and Queensland entered NSW's 10-metre zone before Conescu spilled a pass just a few metres from the uprights. The rain became heavier and the

water became ankle-deep in many places. Lamb and Mortimer surrendered possession with risky short kicks in their own half. There was no score at half-time—neither side could break through strong defence in the atrocious conditions.

Tunks knocked on in a tackle soon after the resumption, enabling the Maroons to camp in NSW's red zone. Jack defused Lewis's bomb behind the tryline but was pinned in-goal. The Blues had to drop-kick from their posts (it was not until 1986 that catching the ball behind one's tryline would produce a quarter-line tap). Cleal's attempted goal-line drop-out stuck in the mud and rolled only a metre after Cleal's boot barely touched it. Meninga's penalty kick from in front wobbled over the crossbar to give the Maroons a key 2–0 lead.

Lewis repeatedly kicked early in Queensland's tackle counts. Handling errors were frequent and Cleal did better with his next goal-line drop-out, which rolled 20 metres. Farrar's sub-standard kicking game helped the Maroons gain good field position. Six metres from the tryline, Miles swung the ball to Lewis, whose chip-kick hit the middle of the crossbar. A reacting Dowling reached down and juggled the ball below his knees, but hung on to plunge over for a spectacular try in a pool of mud. Meninga converted to put Queensland well on top with an 8–0 lead after 57 minutes.

The kick-off rolled dead in-goal to force a goal-line drop-out, before NSW forced another drop-out. The difference in the teams' kicking games was highlighted as Lewis sent the latter drop-out past halfway. After Lewis put in another long clearing

← Wally Fullerton Smith looks to offload the ball as his momentum is brought to a stop.

kick, the Blues forced another repeat set of tackles. They threatened again when Lewis illegally stole the ball from Pearce in a tackle just 2 metres from the posts. Conlon finally kicked a goal, and NSW was hanging in there at 8–2 down with 18 minutes left.

Grothe made a break before Scott fumbled Farrar's downfield kick. On Queensland's quarter-line, NSW's forwards conceded a costly scrum penalty for moving off the mark, before both sides traded errors. From a scrum on NSW's 40-metre line, Lamb kicked hopefully but wastefully as Miles was first to the ball. NSW chose not to push for a try after an infringement by Conescu with 12 minutes left, but Conlon's 20-metre goal-kick pushed to the right. Ella made a half-break from inside his half but the ball came loose as Lewis hit him. The Maroons forced a repeat set of tackles and were 7 metres from NSW's uprights on the last tackle. From acting-half, Miles evaded a diving Cleal and bustled over the line in a tackle. Meninga's conversion with barely four minutes left sealed a 14–2 win to Queensland.

The Verdict

The game was more even than the score suggested. Conlon's poor goal-kicking, Cleal's muffed drop-out and Dowling's freakish try all proved decisive. In the conditions, Lewis's excellent kicking and passing gave the Maroons an edge over their opponents.

Players & Statistics

QLD Colin Scott, Kerry Boustead, Chris Close, Gene Miles, Mal Meninga, Wally Lewis (c), Mark Murray, Paul Vautin, Wally Fullerton Smith, Bryan Niebling, Dave Brown, Greg Conescu, Greg Dowling. **RESERVES** Tony Currie (not used), Bob Lindner. **COACH** Arthur Beetson

NSW Garry Jack, Eric Grothe, Andrew Farrar, Brett Kenny, Ross Conlon, Terry Lamb, Steve Mortimer, Ray Price (c), Wayne Pearce, Noel Cleal, Peter Tunks, Royce Simmons, Steve Roach. **RESERVES** Steve Ella, Pat Jarvis. **COACH** Frank Stanton

Result Queensland 14 (Dowling, Miles tries; Meninga 3 goals) beat NSW 2 (Conlon goal)

Referee Barry Gomersall (Queensland)

Crowd 29 088

Man of the Match Wally Lewis (Queensland)

← Kerry Boustead tries to break away in the sloppy conditions that marred the Sydney game.

The Teams

The NSW selectors again chopped and changed. Tunks was dropped and Price was overlooked after saying he would retire from representative football after the third test between Australia and Great Britain. NSW's newcomers were Chris Walsh and Peter Wynn. The NSWRL released players for club football because the Origin series was decided, and the Blues lost Grothe, Farrar, Pearce and Lamb to injury and Ella to illness. Tunks returned as a reserve and Brian Johnston was recalled. Chris Mortimer, Steve Morris and Michael Potter won their first Origin jerseys. Steve Mortimer became captain after Price and Pearce were omitted.

Queensland was also depleted, with injuries ruling out Close, Miles, Murray, Niebling and Vautin. They were replaced by Ribot, French, Henrick, Phelan and Kellaway.

The Game

Rain before the game made for sloppy conditions, although the field was not nearly as saturated as in Sydney. The teams exchanged early kicks before Scott fumbled, and then knocked Steve Mortimer's bomb over the dead-ball line when the ball looked likely to go out. Referee Roberts penalised Queensland for being inside the five, and Conlon subsequently kicked NSW to a 2–0 lead. Henrick charged down Chris Mortimer's clearing kick soon after the restart, before the Maroons lost possession twice within two minutes, then were caught offside. Conlon doubled NSW's lead with a 22-metre goal.

Scott combined with Ribot to send Meninga charging down the left side, but Steve Mortimer brilliantly tackled his much larger opponent over the sideline. However, the halfback undid his good work as he was penalised for incorrectly feeding the ensuing scrum, and Meninga threatened again. He unloaded to Henrick, who touched down, but the pass was well forward. After a break by Scott and a penalty against Conlon, Queensland entered NSW's quarter. Dowling, Henrick, Lewis and Meninga handled as the ball moved right before an unmarked Boustead stepped inside Chris Mortimer and Conlon. Boustead passed to the shortside and Lindner ran past Jack's tackle to score. Queensland led 6–4 as Meninga's conversion attempt bounced through off the left upright.

The contest became scrappy in the wet conditions, and neither side was able to gain good field position. Queensland was set back when an injured Conescu exited the game. With half-time looming, the Blues co-ordinated well and headed into an attacking position. Near the quarter-line, Morris passed left to Steve Mortimer, and a run-around movement looked likely as Morris looped to Mortimer's left. However, the halfback veered right instead and offloaded to Kenny. Drawing Scott, Kenny sent Johnston running for the corner to score. Conlon's kick just missed, but NSW had struck a crucial blow within two minutes of half-time to grab a two-point lead.

Jarvis was penalised in the first minute after the resumption, but Meninga hooked his 25-metre goal-kick. A couple of minutes later, Brown's offload went astray in Queensland's half. Five tackles later, Cleal's high bomb was spilled by Scott behind the posts. Cleal was on the spot to ground the ball, and

Players & Statistics

NSW Garry Jack, Steve Morris, Chris Mortimer, Brian Johnston, Ross Conlon, Brett Kenny, Steve Mortimer (c), Peter Wynn, Noel Cleal, Chris Walsh, Pat Jarvis, Royce Simmons, Steve Roach. **RESERVES** Michael Potter, Peter Tunks. **COACH** Frank Stanton

QLD Colin Scott, John Ribot, Mal Meninga, Brett French, Kerry Boustead, Wally Lewis (c), Ross Henrick, Bob Lindner, Wally Fullerton Smith, Chris Phelan, Dave Brown, Greg Conescu, Greg Dowling. **RESERVES** Tony Currie, Bob Kellaway. **COACH** Arthur Beetson

Result NSW 22 (Johnston 2, Cleal tries; Conlon 5 goals) beat Queensland 12 (Lindner, Boustead tries; Meninga 2 goals)

Referee Kevin Roberts (NSW)

Crowd 16 559

Man of the Match Steve Mortimer (NSW)

Conlon's conversion gave NSW an eight-point lead soon after Queensland could have levelled the scores.

The Blues attacked following the restart and forced a goal-line drop-out. Henrick was penalised for holding Jack down too long, and Conlon extended NSW's lead with another penalty goal. A fumble by Simmons soon after allowed Queensland a chance to fight back, but a poor attacking set ended with Henrick slicing a bomb over the sideline. After Meninga was caught running a shepherd, NSW led by two converted tries as Conlon landed another goal.

Brown made Queensland's cause even harder when he raised his right forearm and struck Steve Mortimer in the face in an attempt to fend him off. Brown earned a ten-minute stint in the sin-bin, but Queensland managed to hold out. However, when Lewis fumbled while tackled in his quarter, Kenny quickly fielded the ball before drawing Scott and passing right to Johnston. He ran past the diving Scott and threw Currie a dummy before diving to score. Conlon's goal-kick hit the left upright, and NSW's 22–6 lead looked match-winning.

The Maroons finally worked their way into good field position but Jack caught a bomb under great pressure behind his tryline. Following the goal-line drop-out, Lewis stepped right and swung a long pass to Boustead, who got outside Conlon and ran in for a try. Meninga's conversion bridged NSW's lead to 10 points with eight minutes left, but Queensland's comeback ended quickly as the Maroons reverted to their error-prone form.

NSW launched one more attacking raid with Potter reaching the tryline after good lead-up work from Morris, Johnston and Kenny, but referee Roberts ruled Kenny's pass to Potter forward.

The Verdict

The Blues earned their 22–12 win as the Maroons were uncharacteristically incoherent throughout the duration of the game. The Blues stuck to their game plan and capitalised on Queensland's errors at crucial times. Steve Mortimer was a worthy man of the match.

Lewis had an unusually ordinary game, although he had shown before that he was the most influential rugby league player in Australia. He was revered in Queensland, where he was known as 'The King' or 'The Emperor'. But in NSW he was reviled, even when he was representing Australia.

↓ Down but not out. Noel Cleal played a key role in NSW's face-saving win, and scored a vital try after half-time.

1985

Turvey Conjures Blues Breakthrough

Queensland entered the 1985 series having won eight of the 11 Origin games played and all of the three-game series to date. However, almost every game had been highly competitive with little between the winners and losers. The new series promised more of the same intensity and fierce rivalry.

Arthur Beetson stepped down from the Queensland coaching job to concentrate on club football. So, for the first time in Origin football, he was not involved with the Queensland team in any capacity. The new coach was Des Morris, who had built up a strong record in the Brisbane Rugby League. He was coaching Wynnum-Manly, which included Lewis, Dowling and Miles.

Frank Stanton also stepped down from representative coaching. The NSWRL appointed Terry Fearnley, who had extensive experience at club, state and international levels. He had coached the current NSW captain Steve Mortimer in the 1977 interstate series. Mortimer was unhappy at being replaced by Tom Raudonikis in one game. Eight years later, Mortimer and Fearnley had the task of working together to end Queensland's dominance in the updated interstate rugby league competition.

Queensland's chances of winning another Origin series were set back as the injured Miles and Boustead were unavailable for all three games.

← Steve Mortimer looks to the heavens and clenches his fists as he is chaired from the Sydney Cricket Ground. The Blues had finally won a State of Origin series, and Mortimer had the honour of captaining NSW to this milestone.

The Teams

Queensland teenager Dale Shearer was named to
debut. Ian French became another newcomer when
an injured Ian French withdrew.

Grothe, Pearce and Ella were recalled for NSW,
which fielded eight players from game three of 1984.
John Ferguson, Michael O'Connor and Ben Elias
were newcomers. O'Connor transferred from rugby
union, in which he had represented Queensland.

The Game

Rainy weather ensured the game was played in mud.
Lewis kicked after just two tackles, then scuffling
broke out. NSW raided down the left wing where
Lewis tackled Grothe into touch. But NSW was
awarded a penalty from the altercation, and
O'Connor landed a goal to open the scoring.

Rough play and the difficult conditions somewhat
limited the standard of play. When Queensland
risked moving the ball wide, Meninga fumbled to
give NSW possession and field position. However,
O'Connor was tackled into touch after veering right
from dummy-half. Soon after, Kenny kicked downfield from a scrum but O'Connor was caught offside.

The teams exchanged fumbles before Steve
Mortimer was penalised for a late hit on Lewis.
Eight metres in from the left wing, Meninga's
penalty attempt drifted to the left. Meninga made a
break from his own half when the Maroons tried to
move the ball again, but Vautin fumbled in a tackle
in NSW's quarter. Meninga retrieved a lofted pass

by Kenny and the Blues were caught
offside. Meninga levelled the scores.

A few minutes later, Murray
fumbled a chip-kick over the sideline.
Dowling was caught offside as NSW
attacked, and O'Connor kicked the
goal on offer for NSW to regain a
two-point lead. Scott vitally fumbled
as he was tackled on a kick return.
Then Kenny made a darting run after
retrieving a loose pass, but he was
thwarted centimetres the tryline.
Steve Mortimer's bomb bounced
crazily in-goal, causing problems for
Vautin, who just managed to ground
the ball ahead of the fast-approaching
Ferguson. Jarvis fumbled as he was
tackled in NSW's next sets in possession. NSW led 4–2 at the break.

Chris Mortimer immediately
returned a kick downfield after the resumption.
Pearce was penalised for a late hit on Lewis, whose
retaliation sparked a fight. Queensland's attacking
chances were lost when Murray fumbled, before
Shearer threw a stray pass. Cleal stole the ball in a
tackle to put NSW on the attack before Close
fumbled a bomb on the last tackle. NSW looked
certain to score when Pearce swung the ball left, but
it crossed the sideline as Grothe was out of position.

Cleal gave away a penalty but Brown lost the
ball in a hit-up. The Blues enjoyed field position and
forced successive goal-line drop-outs, the latter
after Kenny kicked from a scrum. Pearce was driven

Players & Statistics

NSW Garry Jack, Eric Grothe, Michael O'Connor, Chris Mortimer,
John Ferguson, Brett Kenny, Steve Mortimer (c), Wayne Pearce,
Peter Wynn, Noel Cleal, Steve Roach, Ben Elias, Pat Jarvis.
RESERVES Steve Ella (not used), Peter Tunks. **COACH** Terry Fearnley

QLD Colin Scott, John Ribot, Mal Meninga, Chris Close, Dale Shearer,
Wally Lewis (c), Mark Murray, Bob Lindner, Paul McCabe,
Paul Vautin, Dave Brown, Greg Conescu, Greg Dowling.
RESERVES Brett French (not used), Ian French (not used).
COACH Des Morris.

Result NSW 18 (O'Connor 2 tries; O'Connor 5 goals) beat
Queensland 2 (Meninga goal)

Referee Kevin Roberts (NSW)

Crowd 33 011

Man of the Match Peter Wynn (NSW)

backwards by Murray but managed to shovel the ball right to Kenny, who offloaded to Chris Mortimer. He lofted the ball to O'Connor, who stepped left and shrugged off Scott before diving over with Lewis and Vautin hanging on. O'Connor converted.

From just inside Queensland's half, the Maroons moved the ball quickly to the right where Lindner broke away. Confronted by Jack, Lindner kicked ahead to no avail. Ribot made a break, then Meninga threatened moments later before Lindner's unload was intercepted by Ferguson. When Murray's chip-kick was regained by Kenny near halfway, Close was penalised for dislodging the ball and marched 10 metres for dissent. O'Connor subsequently landed a 40-metre goal to make the score 12–2.

The Maroons kept trying. Their prospects became increasingly tough with eight minutes left when McCabe fumbled in a tackle near his quarter-line.

Kenny picked up the ball, evaded Murray and broke away from Lindner. Kenny lofted the ball left to O'Connor, who had an open run to score out wide. NSW held a 14-point lead as O'Connor pushed the conversion attempt to the right. Poor handling cost Queensland any chance of coming back. Steve Mortimer forced a goal-line drop-out with a bomb, before he chip-kicked in the ensuing tackle count and received a penalty when Conescu impeded him. O'Connor kicked a subsequent goal to bring up the final score to 18–2.

The Verdict

The game was closer than the score suggested, but the Blues capitalised on their limited opportunities whereas the Maroons created some chances but could not finish them off. Despite O'Connor's sensational debut, Wynn was man of the match.

↓ Debutant Michael O'Connor scored all of NSW's 18 points as the Blues triumphed in muddy conditions to draw first blood in the 1985 series.

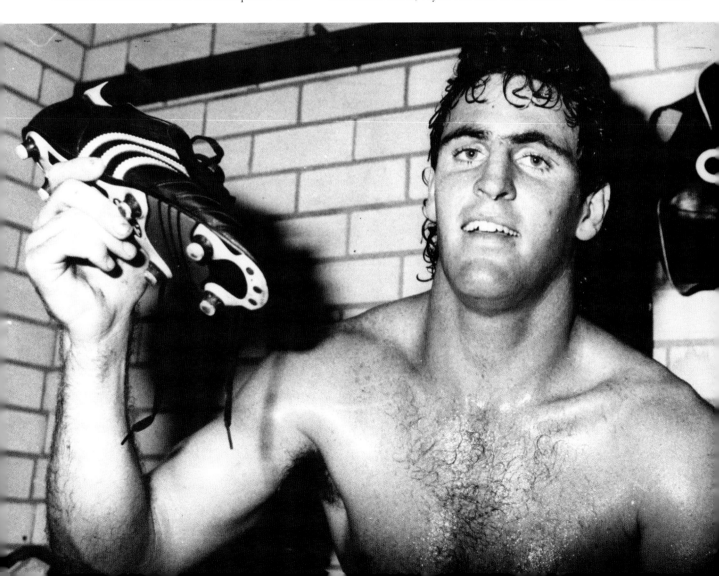

The Teams

For the first time, a NSW Origin team was unchanged. Having played a lot without a break, Kenny asked to be rested but eventually agreed to play at the insistence of Fearnley.

Queensland selectors made only one unforced change, with Fullerton Smith replacing McCabe. Currie was recalled when an injured Brett French withdrew.

The Game

In the opening minutes, both teams kicked early in tackle counts. When Queensland attacked in the eighth minute, Lindner broke away and fed Meninga on the inside. Meninga charged for the right corner but fumbled when tackled by Cleal and Jack.

Jack ran strongly on a kick return, and NSW attacked vigorously before Steve Mortimer's bomb

was caught by an acrobatic Kenny in the 10-metre zone. At acting-half, Mortimer put up another bomb and his brother Chris jumped and scored. NSW led 6–0 as O'Connor converted.

The Blues raided again before a fumble occurred with the tryline beckoning. From dummy-half near the quarter-line in NSW's next set, Elias stepped right, then veered left through sloppy marker defence. Elias threw a dummy to fool Scott and ran to score behind the posts. Ten minutes after Queensland could have scored first, NSW led 12–0.

From inside NSW's half, Conescu passed right where Murray, Meninga and Close combined. Close unloaded to Shearer, who immediately passed inside to Murray. He drew the fullback and sent Lindner scurrying to score behind the crossbar. Meninga goaled and NSW's lead was back to a converted try. Queensland was in trouble as Scott and Lindner fell badly as they were tackled, and both exited the game. After Jack dropped an easy pass, Dowling passed straight to Ferguson, but Chris Mortimer was punished for a high and slinging tackle on Dowling. Meninga landed the goal on offer to lower the Maroons' deficit.

Meninga sliced a simple goal-kick after another penalty, and Queensland had one more attacking chance before half-time. Lewis drifted left near halfway and broke through, but held the ball when an unmarked Ribot was trybound. Lewis was tackled 2 metres short before Murray charged and was also thwarted. NSW still led 12–8.

Soon after the resumption, Dowling and Roach spent five minutes in the sin-bin for squaring off. The teams exchanged a series of errors, before Queensland won a scrum against the feed for the second time since half-time. In NSW's quarter, Dowling drifted right before changing direction. Held in a tackle, Dowling freed one arm and passed inside. French reached to catch the awkward pass before crashing over the

Players & Statistics

NSW Garry Jack, Eric Grothe, Michael O'Connor, Chris Mortimer, John Ferguson, Brett Kenny, Steve Mortimer (c), Wayne Pearce, Peter Wynn, Noel Cleal, Steve Roach, Ben Elias, Pat Jarvis. **RESERVES** Steve Ella, Peter Tunks (not used). **COACH** Terry Fearnley

QLD Colin Scott, John Ribot, Mal Meninga, Chris Close, Dale Shearer, Wally Lewis (c), Mark Murray, Bob Lindner, Wally Fullerton Smith, Paul Vautin, Dave Brown, Greg Conescu, Greg Dowling. **RESERVES** Tony Currie, Ian French. **COACH** Des Morris

Result NSW 21 (C Mortimer, Elias, Kenny tries; O'Connor 4 goals; O'Connor field-goal) beat Queensland 14 (Lindner, French tries; Meninga 3 goals)

Referee Barry Gomersall (Queensland)

Crowd 39 068

Man of the Match Wally Lewis (Queensland)

tryline in a tackle. The Maroons hit the lead with 23 minutes left as Meninga converted.

The Blues soon returned downfield after Ferguson produced some exhilarating footwork and beat a few defenders, then Pearce and Grothe continued the raid. Ribot held Grothe down to allow team-mates to return onside and was penalised. O'Connor's goal-kick from the right wing drifted to the left. Moments later, Conescu erred from his quarter-line as his long pass found a gap and crossed the tryline. Fullerton Smith subsequently knocked-on as Elias tackled him near the tryline, before Shearer fumbled while pouncing on Jack's stray pass. Close and Murray were penalised for blatantly obstructing Steve Mortimer after he chip-kicked. O'Connor landed the gift two points to level the scores with 15 minutes remaining.

A few minutes later, Steve Mortimer sent Pearce charging away before Grothe continued the movement down the right wing, flattening Currie along the way. Vautin attempted to drive Grothe over the sideline but Grothe freed his right arm and fed a trybound Jarvis. The linesman ruled Grothe had stepped into touch, but replays showed the Blues were wronged as Grothe's foot was inside the sideline. The faltering Maroons failed to kick in their half on the last tackle, putting NSW on the attack. On tackle five, Jarvis passed back where O'Connor landed a field goal.

Trailing 15–14 with nine minutes left, the Maroons returned to the attack and were reprieved when a knock-on was overlooked. Queensland set up for a field goal but Elias smothered Lewis's attempt

before Steve Mortimer beat Dowling to the loose ball. When Conescu smothered Elias's clearing kick near halfway, Elias regained the ball. The Maroons were on the back foot and held on, before losing a scrum that Murray fed. Ribot took an intercept but then Shearer's desperate kick landed out on the full. After NSW returned to the 10-metre zone, Jarvis passed right to Steve Mortimer and Kenny, who threw Lewis a dummy, then burrowed into Currie and Brown. Kenny freed his left arm to reach out and score the series-clinching try. As the Blues celebrated a famous victory, Steve Mortimer fell to his knees, kissed the ground and pounded his clenched fists into the turf. O'Connor converted, and there was no time left to restart.

↑ Chris Close did not have the impact he did in 1980 and 1981, but he still helped Queensland fight back from 12–0 down.

The Verdict

The Blues not only won their first Origin series, but they also won under Gomersall's refereeing for the first time. The game could have gone either way, but the Blues survived better under pressure. They would have been unlucky to lose after Jarvis was disallowed a fair try. A triumphant Steve Mortimer immediately retired from representative football.

← Despite being on a State of Origin series-losing team for the first time, Wally Lewis won the man-of-the-match award. He was loudly jeered by the SCG crowd when the announcement was made.

The Teams

Although NSW had won the series, plenty was still at stake. Before Origin III, the Kangaroos played three tests against New Zealand. After Australia won the first at Lang Park, there were rumours that the Kangaroos did not gel off the field during the New Zealand tour. Fearnley and captain Lewis seemingly did not get along. After Australia narrowly won the second test, Fearnley axed Queenslanders Close, Murray, Dowling and Conescu. Four NSW players replaced the out-of-favour Queenslanders, and New Zealand won the third test 18–0. The Maroons became fired up to beat Fearnley's Blues in Origin III to prove a point.

With the Origin series decided, the NSWRL released its players for club football the weekend before game three, and Cleal and Tunks suffered injuries that forced them out. Rampling was recalled, and David Brooks and Kangaroo Des Hasler were named to debut. Pearce took over the NSW captaincy. The Maroons lost Lindner to injury, and debutant Cavill Heugh came into the squad.

The Game

Referee Gomersall penalised NSW twice in the opening minutes, before Meninga hooked a straight-forward goal-kick. Scott fumbled after taking the ball up. The ensuing scrum erupted but Gomersall

Players & Statistics

QLD Colin Scott, John Ribot, Mal Meninga, Chris Close, Dale Shearer, Wally Lewis (c), Mark Murray, Paul Vautin, Wally Fullerton Smith, Ian French, Dave Brown, Greg Conescu, Greg Dowling. **RESERVES** Tony Currie, Cavill Heugh. **COACH** Des Morris

NSW Garry Jack, John Ferguson, Chris Mortimer, Michael O'Connor, Eric Grothe, Brett Kenny, Des Hasler, Wayne Pearce (c), David Brooks, Peter Wynn, Steve Roach, Ben Elias, Pat Jarvis. **RESERVES** Steve Ella, Tony Rampling. **COACH** Terry Fearnley.

Result Queensland 20 (Shearer 2, French, Ribot tries; Meninga 2 goals) beat NSW 6 (Ella try; O'Connor goal)

Referee Barry Gomersall (Queensland)

Crowd 18 825

Man of the Match Wally Fullerton Smith (Queensland)

ignored the scuffle. The Maroons repeatedly attacked NSW's tryline without breaking through.

Another scuffle broke out after Ribot was penalised for niggling an opponent. With NSW finally in Queensland's quarter, Roach charged into the defence and slipped a forward pass to a try-bound Hasler, who was questionably ruled offside. After a different offside penalty against NSW, Meninga landed a 30-metre goal.

Conescu fumbled taking a penalty tap and Grothe ran from dummy-half and was held, seemingly unaware that it was the last tackle. A scuffle involving the hookers was ignored as Shearer made a threatening break, but a try was bombed when Close knocked-on in support. Murray passed right to Scott from a scrum near halfway. With Jack in the defensive line, Scott kicked downfield where Shearer led the chase and received a fortuitous bounce before claiming the ball and scoring. Queensland led 6–0 in the 24th minute after Meninga's kick shaved the post.

Kenny employed a kick from a scrum near halfway, but Shearer was quick to save the Maroons. Queensland surrendered possession after a penalty against Wynn, then Rampling dropped the ball soon after entering the game. Lewis pushed Rampling, who responded by throwing the ball into Lewis to start another scuffle. Kenny's kicking ploy from a scrum worked well just before half-time, but then Kenny was tackled across the sideline. The Maroons held on until the break, and led by just six points despite a favourable penalty count of 7–1.

At the start of the second half, Jack put in a massive clearing kick. But the Blues seemed to lack

← Paul Vautin prepares to tackle tough NSW prop Steve Roach, who was always a formidable presence for the Blues.

organisation in attack. Kenny's kicking tactic from a scrum failed when the ball rolled dead. In NSW's next set, Chris Mortimer's stray pass crossed the sideline. Queensland attacked immediately to 10 metres from the posts. Conescu passed left to Murray and Lewis, who delayed a pass to Ian French. He busted Brooks's tackle and charged over to score. Meninga's kick hit the post but rebounded through to make the score 12–0.

Elias was penalised for a scrum breach, before Conescu surged from acting-half and was held up. Fullerton Smith conceded a penalty, and the Blues forced a goal-line drop-out but never looked like penetrating. French counter-attacked after an O'Connor fumble, but a wayward pass spoiled the move. The Blues spread the ball left in their quarter when Grothe fumbled a poor pass from Chris Mortimer. Another brawl soon erupted and, as a linesman tried to stop the fighting, Gomersall again concentrated only on the football.

The Blues received a scrum penalty before Ella, Kenny and Mortimer moved the ball left on the attack. Kenny slipped a short pass to O'Connor, but O'Connor momentarily looked ahead and dropped the ball. French again counter-attacked and unloaded inside to Shearer, who sprinted 55 metres down the right wing and scored. Queensland led 16–0 with nine minutes left.

Five metres inside Queensland's half, Meninga passed left to Lewis, who rifled a long pass to Murray. Drawing two defenders, Murray lofted a blatant but undetected forward pass to Currie, who dashed ahead and drew defenders before sending Ribot in for a try in his Origin farewell.

A chip-kick from Murray soon after gave NSW a chance. On the last tackle, Ella combined with Kenny, then Ella fended off Murray and dived to score. O'Connor converted. The score remained 20–6 as scrappy play dominated the last five minutes.

The Verdict

The Maroons had proven their point to Fearnley, and Dowling could not help himself as he called out at Fearnley late in the game. Referee Gomersall was controversial but there was little doubt the Maroons had played the better football. The game could have panned out differently had NSW not bombed a chance to score the first try. By contrast, the Maroons took their opportunities as their first 16 points came off the back of NSW errors.

Regardless, NSW's series win ensured that 1985 marked a significant point in Origin history.

↑ John Ribot had a triumphant farewell to Origin football as Queensland prevented NSW from clean-sweeping the series.

1986

Blues Inflict First Whitewash

The 1986 State of Origin series was set to sizzle, with Queensland determined to win back supremacy and NSW keen to emulate its 1985 series win. With an Australian tour of Britain and France scheduled for later in the year, Origin players had an extra incentive to play well.

Citing lack of enthusiasm, Terry Fearnley stood aside as NSW coach and was replaced by Ron Willey, who had coached Manly to the club's first two premierships (in 1972 and 1973). Queensland also changed coach, after Des Morris had had problems at Wynnum-Manly after the club lost the 1985 Brisbane league grand final to Souths. The triumphant Souths coach, Wayne Bennett, was appointed to the coaching position.

← NSW's Wayne Pearce had the honour of being the first captain to lead a state to a series clean-sweep in State of Origin football. But the series was close, as all three games could have gone either way.

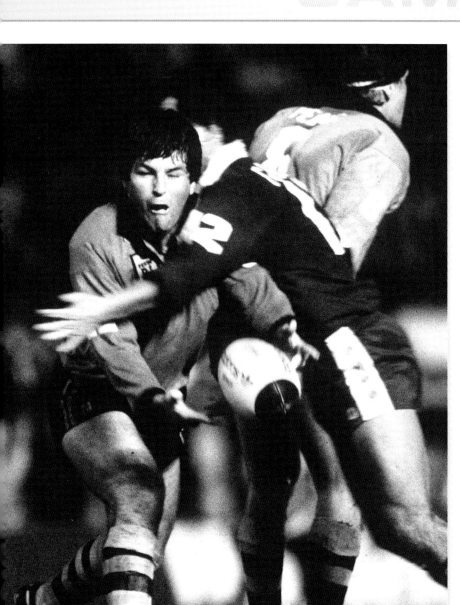

↑ Greg Conescu's tackle fails to stop his counterpart Royce Simmons firing a pass away.

The Game

The Blues were offside when Chris Mortimer kicked downfield in the first minute. An offside penalty against O'Connor enabled Meninga to kick Queensland to a 2–0 lead. Simmons, who crashed to the ground when his head hit Dowling's hip as Dowling made a hit-up, took several moments to return to action.

After Farrar spilled Lewis's kick, the Maroons attacked from a scrum but Morris intercepted to quickly change the momentum. Ten metres from Queensland's tryline, Pearce unloaded to Roach, who fed Sterling and Folkes. With Murray advancing, Folkes delayed a pass to Jack, who juggled the ball and scurried through to tumble over near the right post. NSW led 6–2 after ten minutes.

Jack fumbled from the restart but NSW's defence held as Conescu was foiled just short of the tryline on the last tackle. Jack knocked-on again when he dived to catch Lewis's downfield kick, then Murray was penalised for improperly feeding the scrum. NSW forced a repeat set of tackles before O'Connor miscued a field-goal attempt. After Brown knocked-on in a tackle, the Blues approached the tryline again. Sterling, Cleal, Pearce and Morris handled before Sterling lofted the ball left to Mortimer. He veered right, wrong-footing three defenders, before burrowing over the line. NSW's tries were superbly executed, and the Blues led 12–2 after O'Connor's second conversion.

The Maroons returned to the attack after a penalty but Close spilled a pass. Queensland won the scrum against the feed before Roach was caught offside. Meninga surprisingly kicked for goal from near the right wing, and narrowed Queensland's deficit to eight points. Roach was penalised for collapsing a scrum, then the Maroons were 5 metres from NSW's line. Conescu spun the ball left to Murray and Lewis, whose skillfully delayed short pass enabled Miles to beat two defenders and crash over beside the right upright. Meninga converted, and Queensland trailed by just two points in the 30th minute. Roach conceded another penalty when he hit Jones with a swinging

The Teams

NSW's team was similar to those from the first two games of 1985. Morris, Farrar, Sterling, Simmons and Lamb were recalled, and debutants Steve Folkes and David Gillespie were named. Queensland's side also looked familiar, with Peter Jackson the only newcomer. Miles returned, and Vautin and Fullerton Smith were injured. Jones was recalled for his second Origin match, almost three years after his debut.

arm. The teams exchanged mistakes, and Lewis made a couple of handling errors. With half-time looming, NSW conceded a fifth offside penalty, before Meninga made a menacing run. The Maroons moved the ball right but Jones dropped a pass, and NSW maintained its lead.

Soon after play resumed, Farrar ran to the shortside from a kick return and was driven over the sideline. Lewis put up a bomb five tackles later, and a leaping Jack spilled it near the quarter-line. Miles re-gathered the ball and unloaded to Dowling, who powered over to score between the posts. Meninga landed his fourth goal, and Queensland had scored 14 unanswered points to lead 16–12.

Farrar was taken over the sideline again but Queensland faltered, with knock-ons by Miles and Lindner in quick succession. Lewis attempted a long-range field goal but it fell beside the left post. Referee Roberts overlooked an improper play-the-ball from Folkes, and Pearce chip-kicked and forced a goal-line drop-out on the following tackle. Cleal charged and got close to the tryline before playing the ball on tackle five. Dummy-half Simmons scooped up the ball, spun clockwise and dived for a soft try. O'Connor converted. NSW led by two points with 22 minutes left.

Scott exited the game with a head knock. After Mortimer kicked downfield, makeshift fullback

Shearer crucially fumbled the rolling ball. The scrum twisted and swivelled towards the sideline as Sterling scooped the ball to Pearce, who drew Close and sent Farrar to the left corner. NSW led by a converted try with 15 minutes left.

The Maroons were becoming desperate. Lewis mishandled twice before NSW ventured downfield from a penalty. O'Connor evaded two defenders, but hooked a field-goal attempt. Farrar dropped a high kick inside the final four minutes. Queensland moved the ball right but Lewis's pass was fumbled by Close over his shoulder with the tryline less than 10 metres away. Queensland's forwards were punished for collapsing the ensuing scrum, allowing the Blues to exit their danger zone and win 22–16.

↑ After suffering a head knock early in the game, Royce Simmons became the first hooker to receive man-of-the-match honours in State of Origin.

↓ Gene Miles made a welcome return for the Maroons after missing the 1985 series with injury.

The Verdict

NSW's win was well-earned after scoring four tries to two and overcoming a penalty count favouring Queensland 9–4 (after it was 8–2 at half-time). Although the Blues were sometimes ill-disciplined, the Maroons wavered at crucial times, particularly with ball handling in the second half. Simmons recovered from a setback to be named man of the match.

Players & Statistics

NSW Garry Jack, Steve Morris, Michael O'Connor, Chris Mortimer, Andrew Farrar, Brett Kenny, Peter Sterling, Wayne Pearce (c), Noel Cleal, Steve Folkes, Peter Tunks, Royce Simmons, Steve Roach. **RESERVES** Terry Lamb, David Gillespie. **COACH** Ron Willey

QLD Colin Scott, Dale Shearer, Mal Meninga, Gene Miles, Chris Close, Wally Lewis (c), Mark Murray, Bob Lindner, Gavin Jones, Bryan Niebling, Dave Brown, Greg Conescu, Greg Dowling. **RESERVES** Peter Jackson, Ian French. **COACH** Wayne Bennett

Result NSW 22 (Jack, Mortimer, Simmons, Farrar tries; O'Connor 3 goals) beat Queensland 16 (Miles, Dowling tries; Meninga 4 goals)

Referee Kevin Roberts (NSW)

Crowd 33 066

Man of the Match Royce Simmons (NSW)

The Teams

NSW made one forced change, with Hetherington replacing an injured Morris. Queensland dropped Scott, Close and Brown, and Dowling was forced out by injury. Brohman and Heugh were recalled, and Gary Belcher and Les Kiss were named to debut. The Maroons were set back further when Niebling withdrew. Tessmann was subsequently recalled.

The Game

The Maroons attacked from a scrum in the third minute. Belcher cut through and fed Miles but Shearer fumbled with a try in sight. When Queensland had another scrum feed in enemy territory, Kenny was caught offside. Roach was penalised and sin-binned for five minutes for kneeing Brohman in a tackle. Meninga landed the two points on offer.

Queensland was unable to score while Roach was off the field. After he returned, Kenny made a break but threw a pass over the sideline. The Maroons approached NSW's quarter-line, where Conescu passed left to Lewis. Attracting two Blues, Lewis released a one-handed pass to Meninga, who broke through and sent French running to score under the crossbar. Queensland led 8–0 after 17 minutes.

↓ Peter Sterling formed a formidable halves combination with Brett Kenny for NSW and Parramatta. Their running and passing games were crucial as the Blues wrapped up the series.

↓ Brett Kenny scored a crucial breakthrough try in the second half.

Miles crucially knocked the ball down when NSW had it near halfway, and the Blues forced a goal-line drop-out before Folkes wriggled free from a three-man tackle. Just short of the tryline on the next tackle, Cleal spread the ball left to Sterling and Kenny. He fired a cut-out pass to O'Connor, who drew Shearer and hurled the ball to Farrar. He scored in the corner. NSW soon received a scrum penalty, before nearing the 22-metre line on tackle five. Simmons turned the ball left to Sterling, who drew Murray and delayed a pass to Kenny. He flashed between Shearer and Jones before sending O'Connor over the line. The score was 8-all.

Eight minutes from the break, near the halfway line, Pearce stepped right to evade Murray, and then turned a reverse pass to Hetherington. He fed Roach, who ran ahead and passed right to Mortimer. Confronted by defenders, Mortimer fed a charging Pearce, who scored with Lindner hanging around his legs. As O'Connor was offline with another difficult kick, NSW led by just four points, despite scoring three tries to one.

Three minutes from half-time, Folkes dropped an offload from Tunks near NSW's quarter-line. The Blues were penalised for collapsing the ensuing scrum, and Queensland pushed for a try. On tackle five, Brohman put up a kick to the left. Hetherington won the jump but he fumbled as several players converged. The ricochet was caught by Lindner, who fell on his back as he was tackled in-goal. Referee Gomersall awarded a try despite claims from NSW that Lindner was held up. Replays were inconclusive, and the score was 12-all at the break after Meninga hooked the conversion attempt.

In the 52nd minute, Queensland sent the ball left from 40 metres out as Sterling was slow to return to the defensive line. Miles unloaded to Belcher, who broke away before drawing Jack and passing to Kiss. Hetherington reached for an intercept, knocked the ball towards the tryline and juggled his attempt to regain it as he fell backwards. Kiss freakishly flew over Hetherington to grab the ball and score. Queensland led 16–12 when Meninga hooked another difficult goal-kick.

Queensland's defence was forced to dig deep after NSW had several sets of tackles in attack. From an offside penalty, O'Connor landed a goal to close the deficit to two points with 19 minutes remaining. NSW received another offside penalty but Farrar dropped a pass. The Maroons conceded a differential penalty from the ensuing scrum, and the Blues ventured downfield. O'Connor made a weaving run to get within 12 metres of the uprights. Simmons passed right to Sterling, who ran the ball on the last tackle. Sterling drew Lewis and slipped a short ball to Kenny, who evaded Brohman and scored as French collared him. O'Connor surprisingly hooked the easy goal-kick. NSW had momentum and an 18–16 lead with 14 minutes left.

With the series slipping away, the Maroons seemed to tire. They were pinned in their half before Farrar caught Lewis's kick and broke three tackles on an electrifying run. On the ensuing tackle, Roach veered left and brushed off Heugh in a storming run before sending the unmarked Cleal running behind the posts. The series was there for NSW's taking as O'Connor's conversion took the team to an eight-point lead with ten minutes remaining.

Queensland won a scrum against the feed in NSW's half, but the Maroons were running out of puff and couldn't seem to threaten. The Blues played

safely before Murray scurried from a scrum in his quarter and fed Belcher, who wrong-footed Farrar and then broke away. Belcher sent Shearer sprinting down the right sideline for a 55-metre try despite briefly stumbling as Jack ankle-tapped him. The Maroons declined the conversion attempt because they needed another try. Ninety seconds remained when NSW kicked off. But Queensland's hopes of a last-minute miracle died after the first tackle when NSW retrieved Shearer's risky offload.

The Verdict

In a tit-for-tat game, the Blues again capitalised more often and finished stronger. It was telling that they scored two tries from running on the last tackle, whereas the Maroons seemed to lose direction after the speculative try to Kiss could have turned the game their way.

↑ Peter Sterling harasses Wally Lewis, who manages to get his kick away. Sterling and Kenny were quick to move up to the dangerous Lewis in an attempt to nullify him.

→ Greg Conescu scored Queensland's third try as the Maroons shot to a 12–0 lead, before NSW came back.

The Teams

NSW dropped Hetherington and recalled Grothe. Hetherington was called up to replace an injured Farrar, then Hetherington became injured and was replaced by Brian Johnston.

Queensland's selectors dropped Heugh in favour of Niebling, before Brohman and Jackson withdrew injured, allowing Heugh to return and Grant Rix to debut.

↓ Chris Mortimer sometimes took on the kicking duties for NSW, taking the pressure off Sterling and Kenny.

The Game

The Maroons raided early as Meninga and Lindner set up a break by Kiss, who entered NSW's quarter. On the right, Lewis spun a huge pass which cut out four attackers. Miles linked with Meninga and Shearer, who stepped inside Grothe and dived over in the corner. NSW had the next attacking chance but it didn't materialise. Queensland returned downfield after Roach was penalised for raking the ball. Lewis fired the ball right to Miles, whose short pass sent Belcher slicing between Sterling and Grothe for another try in the corner. Queensland led 8–0 as Meninga hooked another kick.

Both sides made a succession of errors before Heugh broke through. Kenny and Lamb conceded a penalty, but Meninga badly miscued a 33-metre goal-kick. Soon after, Miles released an around-the-corner pass, which was knocked down by Simmons. Shearer fielded the loose ball and sent Conescu running to score near the right post. Kiss took over the goal-kicking but hooked the straightforward attempt.

Jones erred from the restart but the Maroons won the ensuing scrum against the feed. Kiss made another break before Murray chip-kicked on tackle five, regained the ball and fed Lindner, who fumbled as he was tackled. Jack instantly counter-attacked from his quarter and fed Kenny, who passed to O'Connor. He bolted down the left wing and ran to the posts for a 60-metre try before adding the extras. Queensland's poor goal-kicking was costly as NSW had halved the lead in the blink of an eye.

Cleal fumbled twice in quick succession. Straight after the second error, Shearer took the ball up then lost it in a tackle. Five metres into NSW's half, Jack retrieved the ball and combined with Folkes, Pearce and Kenny, who stepped right and sped between Kiss and French. Kenny passed inside to Pearce, who scored. It was 12-all as O'Connor converted.

Queensland returned to the attack after Mortimer dropped a pass as he was about to kick from his quarter. A tackle later, Lewis spun the ball left to Meninga, whose cut-out pass found Kiss outside the defensive cordon. Kiss had a free run to the corner to put Queensland back in front, but his goal-kick sliced badly.

With half-time looming, Cleal blatantly raked the ball off Jones, but referee Roberts did not penalise Cleal. On tackle five, NSW was within a metre of the line. Acting-half Tunks surged into three defenders and fumbled the ball with his right hand, then placed his left hand on the ball and claimed a try. A knock-on seemed obvious but

Players & Statistics

NSW Garry Jack, Brian Johnston, Michael O'Connor, Chris Mortimer, Eric Grothe, Brett Kenny, Peter Sterling, Wayne Pearce (c), Noel Cleal, Steve Folkes, Peter Tunks, Royce Simmons, Steve Roach. **RESERVES** Terry Lamb, David Gillespie. **COACH** Ron Willey

QLD Gary Belcher, Dale Shearer, Mal Meninga, Gene Miles, Les Kiss, Wally Lewis (c), Mark Murray, Bob Lindner, Gavin Jones, Bryan Niebling, Cavill Heugh, Greg Conescu, Brad Tessmann. **RESERVES** Grant Rix (not used), Ian French. **COACH** Wayne Bennett

Result NSW 18 (O'Connor, Pearce, Tunks tries; O'Connor 3 goals) beat Queensland 16 (Shearer, Belcher, Conescu, Kiss tries)

Referee Kevin Roberts (NSW)

Crowd 21 097

Man of the Match Brett Kenny (NSW)

Roberts awarded a try, to the disgust of the Maroons. The scores were tied at the break after O'Connor hooked his goal-kick.

Both teams made a myriad of mistakes throughout the second half, making it hard to predict what would happen next. Scoring opportunities were rare. Lamb was held up over the tryline after regaining a bomb, and Heugh was thwarted near NSW's tryline. Lamb and Lewis each pushed a long-range field-goal attempt to the right.

Queensland launched a raid but Kiss slipped and fumbled 10 metres out. Meninga conceded a critical penalty on the last tackle before Roberts's refereeing came under scrutiny again. Simmons fumbled from dummy-half while Lewis lingered in the ruck, and Lewis was penalised despite his claim that he had a twisted leg and could not get out of the way. In an ironic twist, Roberts then called for a trainer for Lewis. O'Connor landed the gift penalty goal, putting NSW in front with eight minutes left.

In a hectic finale, Lamb soared to pursue Sterling's bomb, but fumbled a match-winning try. With two minutes left, Belcher sent Meninga breaking away from Queensland's half. Meninga kicked towards the right wing, where O'Connor fumbled the ball over his head, but the crowd showed that it was incensed as once again the referee waved the play on.

Belcher caught Lamb's clearing kick on the last tackle, drifted right and kicked where Sterling spilled it. Roberts detected a knock-on this time, giving Queensland one last chance. The siren was sounding as Murray fed Lewis from the scrum 43 metres from the tryline. Lewis skied a bomb where Jack leapt but fumbled over his shoulder. The ball rolled towards the tryline where Kenny fielded it. Meninga tackled Kenny over the tryline and Kenny grounded the ball before it rolled away. Shearer pounced and claimed a try as the crowd roared, but Roberts correctly ruled Kenny had forced the ball. Thus, NSW became the first state to clean-sweep an Origin series.

The Verdict

Queensland scored four tries to three against, but it was another case of so near and yet so far. The Maroons were not helped by Roberts's enigmatic refereeing, but they had let themselves down with five missed goal-kicks and conceding two tries against the run of play.

The series was much more even than the 3–0 result suggested, considering the margins in each game ranged from only two to six points.

↓ NSW enforcer Steve Roach does some boxing drills at training. The 1986 series, however, was one of the cleanest Origin series, as there was little spite on show compared with previous years.

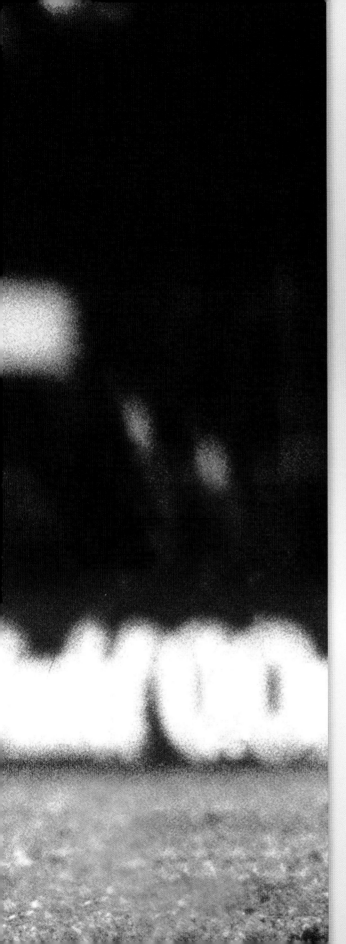

1987

The Emergence of
a Superstar

Coaches are often the first scapegoats when a team is on a losing streak. Wayne Bennett's time as Queensland's Origin coach in 1986 resulted in three defeats. Bennett had since become a co-coach of Canberra, and the QRL had ruled that the Queensland coach could not be based south of the border. But when Wally Lewis said he wanted Bennett to continue coaching Queensland, the QRL reversed its residency rule and retained Bennett.

Having lost two series in a row, the Maroons were set back with Murray (retired after suffering an off-field eye injury) and Meninga (broken arm) unavailable. The selectors used a one-off game of Sydney Residents against Queensland Residents to help choose the team.

The release of Adrian McGregor's biography *King Wally* a few weeks before the series caused a stir when extracts from the book were published in newspapers. Some sections appeared to reflect negatively on certain Sydney league players and officials. The drama was little more than a media beat-up, but ARL chief Ken Arthurson deemed it necessary to warn Origin players against committing foul play in retaliation to any grievances about the book.

An addition to the State of Origin program was an exhibition match featuring the Origin teams, scheduled for California after the series was completed. The ARL staged the exhibition match in an effort to promote rugby league in the United States of America. (See the Statistics at the end of the book for details of the game.)

← Allan Langer came of age after being a surprise selection for Queensland. Many observers had grave doubts about him, as he stood only 165 centimetres and was not yet 21 years old. But he silenced the critics in the best way possible, by letting his football do the talking.

The Teams

Sydney Residents beat Queensland Residents 20–10, making Queensland-based Allan Langer a contentious selection ahead of Laurie Spina. Martin Bella, Alan McIndoe and Trevor Gillmeister were other newcomers. When McIndoe and Lindner were injured, Currie and debutant Gary Smith were brought in.

The Blues retained nine players from their 1986 triumph. Mark McGaw, Andrew Ettingshausen, Les Davidson and David Boyle were debutants, and Jarvis was recalled. Roach and Tunks were injured and thus unavailable.

The Game

The opening stages were characterised by strong defence and handling errors. First-time Origin referee Mick Stone awarded two scrum penalties, one each way, within the space of five minutes. The Maroons forced repeat sets of tackles but could not break through.

After O'Connor conceded a silly penalty in possession midway through the first half, stopgap goal-kicker Jackson landed the two points on offer. After a NSW error, a Queensland try beckoned, but Belcher's pass to the unmarked Currie found the sideline. Langer's confidence grew as he nailed Ettingshausen in-goal. After another NSW mistake, Miles, Dowling and Jackson combined to send Langer to the left. He passed inside to Currie who crashed over in the corner, but Langer's pass was ruled forward.

Queensland controlled the run of play but led only 2–0, before Cleal stepped left down the short side from inside NSW's half. He surged past Jackson and lobbed a pass to O'Connor, who sprinted away and kicked past the advancing Belcher, then beat Langer to swoop on the ball. O'Connor converted for NSW to lead 6–2.

Jackson charged down Sterling's kick but it went over the sideline. Jack sliced through from the subsequent scrum, reaching the danger zone before Langer knocked down Sterling's pass to foil a raid. But NSW remained on the attack. Inside the 10-metre zone, Simmons stepped left but passed the other way where a rampaging Davidson charged through to score in a tackle.

Players & Statistics

NSW Garry Jack, Andrew Ettingshausen, Mark McGaw, Brian Johnston, Michael O'Connor, Brett Kenny, Peter Sterling, Wayne Pearce (c), Noel Cleal, Steve Folkes, Les Davidson, Royce Simmons, Pat Jarvis. **RESERVES** David Boyle, Des Hasler (not used). **COACH** Ron Willey

QLD Gary Belcher, Tony Currie, Peter Jackson, Gene Miles, Dale Shearer, Wally Lewis (c), Allan Langer, Ian French, Paul Vautin, Trevor Gillmeister, Martin Bella, Greg Conescu, Greg Dowling. **RESERVES** Colin Scott (not used), Gary Smith. **COACH** Wayne Bennett

Result NSW 20 (O'Connor 2, Davidson, McGaw tries; O'Connor 2 goals) beat Queensland 16 (Dowling, Shearer, Currie tries; Jackson, Belcher goals)

Referee Mick Stone (NSW)

Crowd 33 411

Man of the Match Les Davidson (NSW)

Martin Bella shovels the ball away in a tackle during his Origin debut. It was to be another year before Bella cemented his place in the Queensland forward pack.

NSW led 10–2 as O'Connor hooked the straight-forward goal-kick.

With Queensland back in possession, Shearer ducked through two tacklers and kicked ahead but Ettingshausen saved NSW in the in-goal area. Davidson conceded a penalty, and Queensland entered the danger zone. On the last tackle, Conescu passed right to Lewis who held the ball, drew Jack and, with Johnston a bit wide in defence, sent a short pass to Dowling, who rolled over to score in a tackle. The Blues led by four points after Jackson's wide-angled goal-kick barely rose above ground level.

NSW had a scoring chance soon after half-time, but Cleal was held up over the line. After successive penalties against the Blues, Jackson put in another horror goal-kick. In the 63rd minute, the Blues moved the ball left. Sterling's cut-out pass found Kenny, who drew Vautin and Shearer, creating a gap on the wing. Kenny sent O'Connor over in the corner, and O'Connor's splendid kick stretched NSW's lead to ten points.

The game changed within two minutes. From his own quarter-line, Jackson passed to Lewis, regained the ball in a run-around movement and flashed through, sending an unmarked Shearer on a sprint to crash over between the posts. Taking over goal-kicking, Belcher narrowed the gap to four points.

Referee Stone controversially penalised McGaw for interference in the 74th minute after Shearer fumbled the ball. Boyle conceded another penalty a few tackles later when he stole the ball. Conescu took the tap on NSW's quarter-line and fed Lewis, who darted down the blindside where the defence was short. Lewis popped an overhead pass to Currie, who raced to dive in the left corner. Belcher hooked a pressure conversion attempt, leaving the scores deadlocked at 16-all in the final four minutes.

Boyle stripped the ball off Miles soon after the restart. NSW set up for a field goal after four tackles but Sterling's attempt wobbled to the right. Currie's kick dribbled feebly before the Maroons reached tackle five, and the Blues regained possession near the halfway line. Just outside the 40-metre zone on

tackle four, Pearce passed right where Sterling and Kenny handled before Ettingshausen drew Currie and sent McGaw dashing down the wing. McGaw's inside pass to Ettingshausen was knocked towards the tryline by a desperate Currie. Ettingshausen crashed into Jackson, who kicked the loose ball as he ran at it. He held McGaw's jersey as they chased the ball, which rolled towards the dead-ball line. McGaw reached out with O'Connor and Jackson in pursuit and momentum took the three and the ball past the line. Stone consulted the nearby linesman and awarded a try. Replays showed Stone's courageous decision was correct: McGaw grounded the ball centimetres inside the dead-ball line. NSW had snatched a thrilling 20–16 victory with 48 seconds to spare. O'Connor's goal-kick hit the right post.

The Verdict

With NSW having won four consecutive close games, Bennett was waiting for something to go Queensland's way. Like in game three of 1986, the Maroons were let down by poor handling and poor goal-kicking. The pint-sized Langer justified selection. Davidson, who'd seen the team doctor before the start to overcome nerves, was man of the match.

↑ Mark McGaw's debut was one to remember, as he scored a thrilling try in the final minute to clinch victory for NSW in one of the remarkable finishes to an Origin game.

↓ Les Davidson forces his way over to score NSW's second try despite Wally Lewis's and Ian French's tackles.

↑ Greg Dowling showed his ability to play wet-weather football, and he was a shade unlucky not to receive man-of-the-match honours.

→ Garry Jack did some kicking in general play for NSW, and he threw a forward pass that incurred a decisive penalty in the second half.

The Teams

The Maroons regained Lindner from injury, promoted Scott to the run-on team and relegated Currie and French to the bench. Smith was omitted.

Farrar returned for the Blues in place of the injured Ettingshausen. Cleal broke down with injury at training and Boyle came into the starting line-up. Paul Langmack was the new reserve.

The Game

The SCG was wet and muddy following heavy rain. Referee Gomersall penalised Queensland after the first tackle as a couple of Maroons were offside when Belcher kicked downfield. O'Connor kicked the Blues to a 2–0 lead before they had possession. Queensland was penalised for a scrum infringement soon after, and the Blues forced a goal-line drop-out following Sterling's chip-kick. Sterling's next chip-kick stopped in a splash of mud as Belcher retrieved it near the tryline. Shearer veered left from acting-half and fumbled as he was tackled by Pearce and Kenny. Kenny picked up the ball and passed to Johnston. He fed Farrar, who beat Scott's tackle to score, and NSW led 6–0 as O'Connor's goal-kick pushed to the right.

The Blues were caught offside as Jack kicked downfield soon after the restart. Scott's 27-metre goal-kick landed beside the left post. Knock-ons both ways were followed by two scrum penalties against NSW when the Blues had the feed. Farrar and Belcher kicked for field position and Gomersall ignored a scuffle involving six players. McGaw, Pearce and Kenny combined before O'Connor made a breathtaking burst, stepping around defenders as if they were markers at a training drill. With Folkes continuing the move-ment, Gillmeister came from behind and hammered him with a savage tackle. The injured Folkes had to exit the game.

A contentious penalty against Jarvis for an improper play-the-ball gave the Maroons an opportunity. Vautin subsequently made a good run and bumped off a couple of defenders before Queensland forced a goal-line drop-out. The teams traded knock-ons, and then Langer had the ball a metre from the tryline. From dummy-half, Shearer stepped right and burrowed into three defenders to graze the ball on the line. Scott's conversion attempt thudded into the crossbar to leave NSW leading 6–4. Downfield kicks were exchanged by Sterling, Belcher, O'Connor and Belcher again. Farrar knocked-on as he looked up while bending down to field Belcher's kick, but the Maroons didn't capitalise. As half-time loomed, Davidson took an intercept and flashed beyond halfway before his low pass was kicked by Kenny. Johnston and Shearer contested before Kenny kicked again and threatened to score, but the ball crossed the dead-ball line.

Another kicking duel opened the second half. Belcher exchanged kicks with Farrar and Jack, and NSW gradually gained territory before Kenny charged down Belcher's kick on Queensland's 10-metre line. O'Connor made another dangerous run, but Johnston fumbled in support as Lewis hammered him front-on. Another knock-on from Johnston prevented another scoring chance. More NSW handling errors and kicks by Belcher, Lewis and Jackson improved field position for Queensland.

The game see-sawed. Langmack was penalised for stripping, Sterling fumbled an intercept, Queensland was penalised in the ensuing scrum, then Jarvis and Bella knocked-on. The Blues won a scrum against the feed but were penalised for offside when Sterling kicked. Davidson hit Dowling with a bone-crunching tackle , then Jack fielded a Lewis kick and broke clear. He passed to Farrar, a metre in front of him, and Gomersall gave the Maroons an offside penalty, not a scrum feed. Five tackles later, Miles drifted right from dummy-half in the 10-metre zone and pushed a chest pass to Dowling, who threw a dummy, bumped off Kenny and crashed over the line. Queensland grabbed an 8–6 lead with 19 minutes left.

Belcher kicked the ball back from the restart before Jack's instant return almost reached the corner flag. Dowling was penalised from

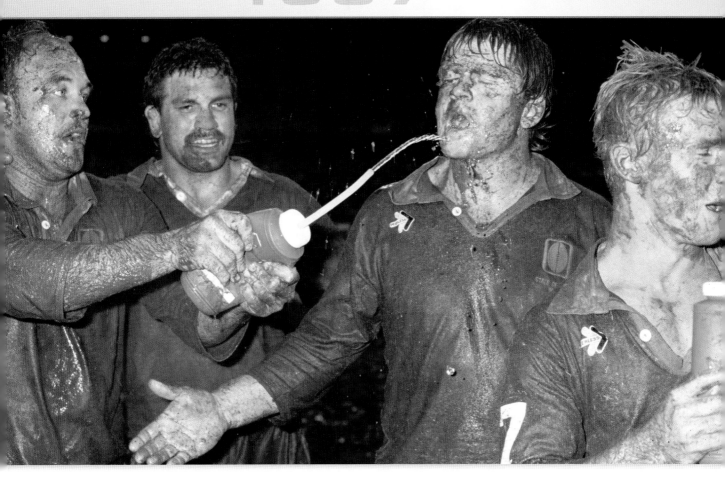

the scrum but NSW failed to break through. Possession changed regularly. McGaw was forced from the field injured. After a penalty against Farrar, Conescu and Langer went close to scoring before Gillmeister passed left to Lewis and Miles, who drew O'Connor. Miles released a trademark right-handed pass to the unmarked Scott, who dived across to score. Taking over the goal-kicking, Lewis failed to make the distance. Queensland led 12–6 with ten minutes left.

The Maroons were content to kick early in the tackle count, and Hasler knocked-on in his half with five minutes left. Miles attempted a field goal but was unable to lift the heavy ball high enough. NSW threw the ball around and entered Queensland's half before Belcher chased Sterling's kick and forced the ball in-goal. In the final minute, the Blues again threw the ball around but went too close to the left sideline where O'Connor was forced into touch. Bennett finally tasted victory in Origin football.

The Verdict

Queensland did well to fight back from 6–0 down in the slushy conditions. The Sydney media targeted Gomersall's refereeing, as the penalty count finished 10-4 Queensland's way. Willey pointed to Queensland's better kicking game and his players' handling, not Gomersall, as the reason for NSW's loss. It was notable that NSW fumbled 22 times to ten.

↑ Muddy but happy: Wally Lewis, Colin Scott, Paul Vautin and Allan Langer after the Maroons snapped a four-game losing sequence.

Players & Statistics

QLD Gary Belcher, Colin Scott, Peter Jackson, Gene Miles, Dale Shearer, Wally Lewis (c), Allan Langer, Bob Lindner, Paul Vautin, Trevor Gillmeister, Martin Bella, Greg Conescu, Greg Dowling. **RESERVES** Tony Currie (not used), Ian French. **COACH** Wayne Bennett

NSW Garry Jack, Michael O'Connor, Mark McGaw, Brian Johnston, Andrew Farrar, Brett Kenny, Peter Sterling, Wayne Pearce (c), Les Davidson, Steve Folkes, Pat Jarvis, Royce Simmons, David Boyle. **RESERVES** Des Hasler, Paul Langmack. **COACH** Ron Willey

Result Queensland 12 (Shearer, Dowling, Scott tries) beat NSW 6 (Farrar try; O'Connor goal)

Referee Barry Gomersall (Queensland)

Crowd 42 048

Man of the Match Peter Sterling (NSW)

↑ Wally Lewis leads the Maroons on a lap of honour after they won a tense decider at Lang Park.

↓ In his final Origin series, Greg Dowling again played a key role for Queensland.

The Teams

NSW's selectors surprisingly made mass changes. Numerous positional changes occurred, including Kenny from five-eighth to centre. Farrar, Hasler and Langmack were dropped, Ettingshausen returned, and Cliff Lyons and Phil Daley were debutants. Tunks returned to replace the injured Jarvis.

Queensland made just one change, with Niebling back from injury to replace Bella.

The Game

Lyons accepted Kenny's offload and split Queensland's defence, before the duo pinned Belcher behind his tryline. After a relieving penalty to Queensland from a scrum, Langer grubber-kicked but just failed to ground the ball before it rolled dead. A scrum breach from Simmons enabled Conescu to take a penalty tap 15 metres from NSW's tryline. Langer and Dowling exchanged passes before Langer looked right but turned the ball to the shortside. Lewis stepped around Tunks and drew Boyle before feeding Belcher. He wrong-footed Simmons and was held by Jack but slipped a low pass inside to Lindner, who spun over the line.

After errors by each team, Miles offloaded to Jackson, who sliced through from halfway. Seconds later, Langer scampered for the right corner but Johnston tackled him just short. Then Pearce smothered Lewis's clearing kick near halfway and regained possession. Pearce fed Johnston, who drew Belcher and quickly passed to Boyle. He galloped away and crashed over beneath the posts. NSW led 6–4 as O'Connor converted. Soon after the restart, Davidson dropped a regulation pass and Niebling instantly counterattacked. In NSW's quarter on tackle four, Conescu passed right to Dowling, who grubbered to the right. The ball bounced awkwardly but Shearer pounced for a try. Queensland led 8–6 but Scott sliced a goal-kick from an achievable angle.

The Maroons failed to capitalise after Boyle and Sterling sliced kicks out on the full. Lyons threw a bad pass but then took an intercept. He dashed ahead and was stopped on the quarter-line by Lewis, who pinned him down as the defenders struggled to get onside. The obvious penalty provided O'Connor

Players & Statistics

QLD Gary Belcher, Colin Scott, Peter Jackson, Gene Miles, Dale Shearer, Wally Lewis (c), Allan Langer, Bob Lindner, Paul Vautin, Trevor Gillmeister, Bryan Niebling, Greg Conescu, Greg Dowling. **RESERVES** Tony Currie, Ian French. **COACH** Wayne Bennett

NSW Garry Jack, Brian Johnston, Brett Kenny, Michael O'Connor, Andrew Ettingshausen, Cliff Lyons, Peter Sterling, Wayne Pearce (c), Les Davidson, David Boyle, Phil Daley, Royce Simmons, Peter Tunks. **RESERVES** Mark McGaw, Steve Folkes. **COACH** Ron Willey

Result Queensland 10 (Lindner, Shearer tries; Shearer goal) beat NSW 8 (Boyle try; O'Connor 2 goals)

Referee Barry Gomersall (Queensland)

Crowd 32 602

Man of the Match Allan Langer (Queensland)

with a simple goal to equalise. Lyons riskily chip-kicked after a scrum win as half-time loomed, and O'Connor was a step offside as he pursued the ball. From 27 metres out and to the right of the posts, Shearer kicked a goal to give Queensland the lead.

The Maroons threatened soon after play resumed, but Shearer ran too close to the left wing and passed straight to Boyle. Jack broke away on a kick return before Johnston was driven over the sideline. A Langer chip-kick put the Maroons back in dangerous territory, but Jackson passed straight to Jack. In Queensland's next set, Langer regained his chip-kick. On the following tackle, Dowling drew the defence and fed Miles. He hurled the ball right to the unmarked Scott, but the winger spilled the awkward shin-height pass almost on the try-line. After Tunks was penalised in the scrum, Miles charged for the line but was held up by a flock of defenders. Scott fumbled Sterling's clearing kick and Lyons lost possession.

With 20 minutes remaining, the game moved from one end to the other as pressure mounted. From NSW's half, Kenny sent O'Connor flashing through with only Lewis in front. O'Connor stepped inside, but Lewis anticipated the movement and the two crashed fiercely. Then Shearer sent a massive kick into NSW's quarter but Jack beat Shearer to it. After Sterling and Kenny handled, O'Connor delivered a spectacular blind overhead pass to send Johnston running down the left wing. Johnston drew Belcher and sent Lyons away, but Belcher chased and caught him from behind. A try was still on but Lyons's pass was poor and Johnston stepped out as he retrieved the ball. The see-sawing game

continued. Simmons was again penalised before Jackson turned over possession. Lyons was injured and replaced by McGaw. Miles conceded a penalty and Kenny chipped beyond the tryline, where McGaw dived for the ball but just missed it as Jackson kicked it dead.

The Blues were offside after Sterling hoisted a kick in the 71st minute, and the Maroons attacked and then gained a repeat set. For several minutes they rucked the ball up, then kicked into the in-goal area to force repeat sets. Queensland looked safe when Lewis and two teammates drove Johnston over the sideline in NSW's quarter with one minute left. But O'Connor raced out of the defensive line and plucked an intercept with 39 seconds remaining. With 90 metres to travel, the Blues threw the ball around as the clock wound down but were still in their half when Dowling knocked down Kenny's pass in the last five seconds.

The Verdict

The game was played at a frantic pace and it was incredible that no points were scored after half-time. Either team could have won, as scoring chances were squandered both ways. As in 1986, all the games were won by small margins, but this time the balance favoured Queensland.

The series was particularly memorable for Langer, who overcame criticism of his selection to show that he belonged in State of Origin football.

↓ Colin Scott (far right) has the ball to kick for goal while his team-mates move back into position after Dale Shearer scored Queensland's second try.

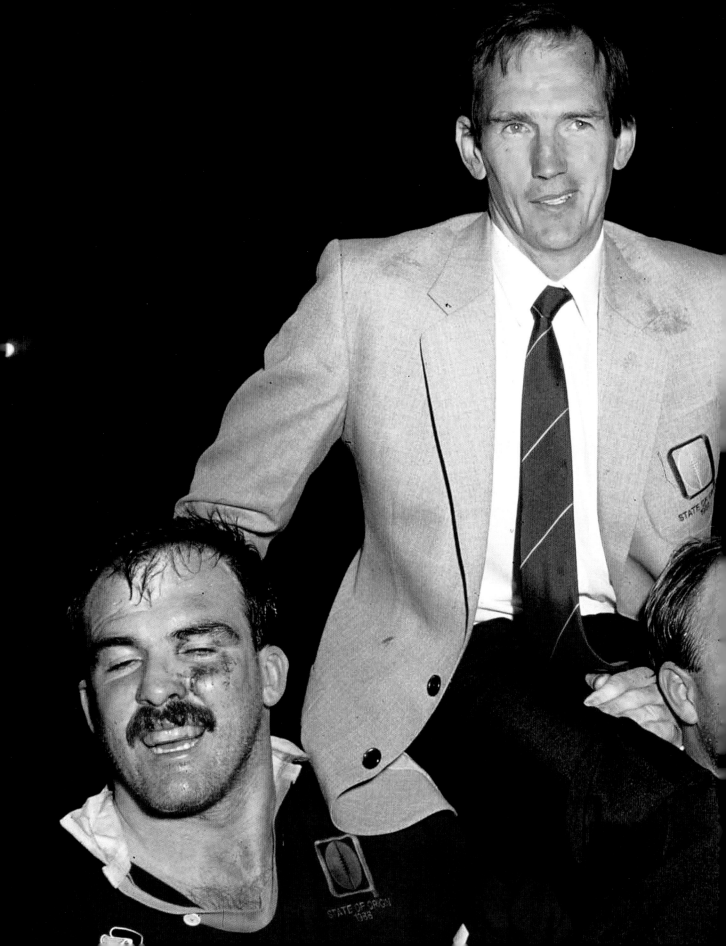

1988

Jacko, Backo, Beer Cans and Revenge

Expansion of the NSWRL competition to include teams from Newcastle, Gold Coast and Brisbane brought opportunities to more players. The introduction of the Brisbane Broncos in particular exposed more Queensland players to the week-to-week grind of the NSWRL, and the fitness and skill levels required in the competition. By contrast, the Brisbane Rugby League was undermined, making it increasingly difficult for players from that competition to make it into Origin ranks.

Wayne Bennett continued as Queensland coach despite also coaching the Broncos. By comparison, the NSWRL retained its rule that the NSW coach could not be coaching a club as well. This ruled Ron Willey out of contention after he took on the coaching job at Penrith. NSW's new coach was John Peard, who had previously achieved modest results as a club coach.

For the first time in Origin football, two games were scheduled in Sydney. The newly built Sydney Football Stadium replaced the SCG as the main rugby league arena.

← Martin Bella and Wally Lewis chair their coach Wayne Bennett after Queensland wrapped up the series in game two at Lang Park. Bennett enjoyed the triumphant clean-sweep two years after being on the other side of a whitewash.

The Teams

For NSW, Jack (suspended) and Kenny (injured) were unavailable, and Tunks was a late withdrawal (injured). Roach was recalled, and debutants were David Trewhella and Jonathan Docking (although Docking had played in the 1987 exhibition game).

With Dowling retired from representative football and injured duo Shearer and Meninga already missing, Queensland lost Lewis (injured) for the first time in Origin football. Jackson moved to five-eighth, and Vautin was named the new captain. Debutants were Sam Backo, Joe Kilroy, Alan McIndoe and Scott Tronc.

The Game

Belcher kicked Queensland to an early 2–0 lead after referee Gomersall dubiously penalised Lyons for reefing the ball in a three-man tackle. Soon after, Langer soccered the ball through but fumbled it a metre from the tryline. Queensland maintained the momentum as Lindner split the NSW defence, but Jackson's unload to a trybound Miles went forward.

Several minutes later, Cleal ran onto Lyons's reverse pass and was tackled 26 metres from the tryline. McGaw flung the ball left to Sterling, whose long pass found O'Connor. He threw a dummy, rushed past Vautin and Belcher and dived for the line. NSW led 4–2.

McIndoe made a long break after Belcher offloaded to him on a kick return, but Miles knocked-on a few rucks later. Sterling fed the ensuing scrum in NSW's quarter and the ball unexpectedly bounced out Queensland's way. Langer picked it up, scurried past Sterling's tackle and touched down in the right corner. Queensland regained a two-point lead.

McGaw, O'Connor and Ettingshausen were all guilty of kicking when there was no need, before the Blues threw the ball around and made inroads. A pass was touched by a Queenslander, then Currie was caught offside. NSW levelled the scores with O'Connor's penalty goal.

NSW looked dangerous after the restart but Ettingshausen fumbled in a tackle. A few tackles later, Langer grubber-kicked through. He bent to pick up the ball but, with Sterling approaching, kicked it to the right where Johnston was about to swoop. Langer kicked again, slightly infield towards the tryline, then chased it down to score. Belcher converted, and Queensland led 12–6 at the break.

Belcher fumbled Sterling's clearing kick on Queensland's quarter-line just after the resumption,

↓ Prop Sam Backo played a leading role in his Origin debut as the Maroons won the series opener. Coach Wayne Bennett criticised Backo before the game, focusing on his form, attitude and ball control.

Players & Statistics

QLD   Gary Belcher, Alan McIndoe, Tony Currie, Gene Miles, Joe Kilroy, Peter Jackson, Allan Langer, Paul Vautin (c), Bob Lindner, Wally Fullerton Smith, Sam Backo, Greg Conescu, Martin Bella. **RESERVES** Brett French, Scott Tronc. **COACH** Wayne Bennett

NSW   Jonathan Docking, Brian Johnston, Mark McGaw, Michael O'Connor, Andrew Ettingshausen, Cliff Lyons, Peter Sterling, Wayne Pearce (c), Noel Cleal, Steve Folkes, Steve Roach, Royce Simmons, Les Davidson. **RESERVES** Terry Lamb, David Trewhella. **COACH** John Peard

Result   Queensland 26 (Langer 2, Jackson, McIndoe, Belcher tries; Belcher 3 goals) beat NSW 18 (O'Connor, Ettingshausen, McGaw tries; O'Connor 3 goals)

Referee   Barry Gomersall (Queensland)

Crowd   26 441

Man of the Match   Allan Langer (Queensland)

but Cleal soon knocked-on. Langer threatened after a chip-and-chase but fumbled as he looked for support. Within the next minutes, Roach unloaded to Davidson, who broke away and neared halfway. He fed Lyons, who fumbled in Belcher's tackle. Three rucks later, Currie offloaded to Vautin, who shrugged off Simmons and veered right before powering ahead. Ten metres out, Vautin played the ball to Conescu, who passed right to Bella and Jackson. He stepped past McGaw as the defender came up too quickly, then Jackson stepped out of Folkes's tackle and reached to score while held. Queensland was lucky the try was awarded: Vautin played the ball without getting to his feet and Bella's pass was slightly forward. Belcher missed the kick but Queensland had a fortunate 16–6 lead.

NSW became less cohesive in attack. Backo and Bella led as the Maroons dominated in the ruck. After Sterling's kick reached the in-goal area, poor defence enabled Kilroy to make a long break. Queensland's tackle count restarted, before Lindner sent a cut-out pass to Belcher, who kicked to the left. McIndoe chased from the outside and beat Pearce in the dive for the ball. The try was awarded, although replays showed McIndoe had knocked-on. The Maroons held a 14-point lead with 17 minutes left.

The Blues gained good field position but their attack was sub-par. NSW forced a goal-line drop-out before Pearce spilled Lamb's inside pass. On a kick return soon afterwards, Docking linked with Ettingshausen and O'Connor, who broke away but was dragged over the sideline by McIndoe. One tackle later, 5 metres inside NSW's half, Miles stepped right, drew three defenders and unloaded to Langer. He also drew defenders before sending Belcher scurrying through to score under the cross-bar. Belcher's conversion made the score 26–6 with nine minutes left.

After scrappy play by both sides, Lamb drew the defence and fed Ettingshausen, who got outside McIndoe and flashed down the right wing. ET linked with McGaw and Lamb. He veered towards the posts but tripped, then got up and flung a high pass to Ettingshausen, who scored in Belcher's tackle. In the final 30 seconds, Johnston passed left to Sterling and Lamb, who drew four Maroons. Lamb slipped the ball to Roach, who threw a dummy and veered left before sending McGaw over in the corner. Replays showed Pearce knocked-on in the play-the-ball. O'Connor's conversion made the final score somewhat respectable at 26–18.

← Allan Langer won another man-of-the-match award after taking a leading role in Queensland's win in the first Origin game to be played at the Sydney Football Stadium.

The Verdict

The growing stature of Langer and the excellent performances by Jackson, Bella and Backo highlighted Queensland's win without Lewis. The Blues were heavily criticised amid calls for mass sackings. However, the fine line between winning and losing was overlooked. Queensland's first try came from a scrum win against the feed, NSW missed chances to score when behind 12–6, and Queensland's ensuing two tries should not have been awarded. Taken altogether, the result could have been very different. Yet Gomersall's refereeing did not attract much attention, as the penalty count finished 5–1 to NSW.

↓ Peter Jackson was adept at five-eighth, filling the giant shoes of the injured Wally Lewis.

GAME two

The Teams

NSW selectors were ruthless, dropping Docking, Johnston, Lyons, Simmons, Davidson and Cleal. Recalled were Jack, Ferguson, Elias, Hasler and Phil Daley. Paul Dunn was named to debut. Later Trewhella (injured) was replaced by Langmack.

Predictably, Queensland recalled Lewis along with Shearer and Gillmeister. Kilroy, Tronc and French were unluckily omitted. French returned after Shearer was injured in a club game.

The Game

NSW failed to capitalise on an early unforced knock-on by Jackson, before McGaw conceded a penalty. Daley and Roach got away with high tackles, then Folkes committed an offside infringement. Daley escaped penalty for another swinging arm. Lindner fumbled with the tryline under threat, then niggled Roach in a tackle and, when Elias kicked from dummy-half, Roach inexplicably flattened Lindner. A groggy Lindner was replaced, and Roach was penalised but not dismissed. Both teams surrendered possession before Folkes conceded another penalty, from which Belcher kicked Queensland to a 2–0 lead.

↓ All hell is about to break loose. Wally Lewis (obscured), Greg Conescu, Wayne Pearce (obscured) and Phil Daley listen to the match officials after a scuffle involving Conescu and Daley sparked an all-in brawl. Conescu and Daley each received a ten-minute stint in the sin-bin, but the sin-binning of Lewis led to the infamous beer-can throwing from the crowd.

Players & Statistics

QLD Gary Belcher, Alan McIndoe, Peter Jackson, Gene Miles, Tony Currie, Wally Lewis (c), Allan Langer, Paul Vautin, Bob Lindner, Wally Fullerton Smith, Sam Backo, Greg Conescu, Martin Bella. **RESERVES** Brett French, Trevor Gillmeister. **COACH** Wayne Bennett

NSW Garry Jack, John Ferguson, Mark McGaw, Michael O'Connor, Andrew Ettingshausen, Terry Lamb, Peter Sterling, Paul Langmack, Steve Folkes, Wayne Pearce (c), Steve Roach, Ben Elias, Phil Daley. **RESERVES** Paul Dunn, Des Hasler. **COACH** John Peard

Result Queensland 16 (Backo, Langer tries; Belcher 4 goals) beat NSW 6 (O'Connor try; O'Connor goal)

Referee Mick Stone (NSW)

Crowd 31 817

Man of the Match Sam Backo (Queensland)

From NSW's first penalty, O'Connor's 32-metre goal-kick pushed to the right. Both teams showed sub-par ball control before Elias gave away a silly penalty on the last tackle with the Maroons pinned in their quarter. Bella fumbled and then O'Connor made a break. Inside Queensland's quarter, Lamb veered left and turned a reverse pass to Sterling. He fed Pearce, Elias and O'Connor, who drifted into

open space after Lewis tried to intercept. O'Connor dived across the line. NSW led 4–2.

Lewis grubbered for Jackson, who beat Ettingshausen to the ball but fumbled it over the line to bomb a certain try. Referee Stone sin-binned Roach for ten minutes after he swung a punch which missed Lindner, who had returned. After a period of scrappy play, NSW conceded a penalty for an offside infringement, allowing Belcher to level the scores after 33 minutes. Lewis sent McIndoe away down the left wing before Jack's cover tackle forced McIndoe to throw a stray pass. The Blues raided and forced a goal-line drop-out, then Bella, who had a bloodied face, foolishly threw punches at Daley. O'Connor's penalty goal gave NSW a 6–4 lead.

The game's see-sawing nature continued as light rain began to fall after the resumption. Belcher put in a long kick before Jack fielded it and made a long break. McIndoe kicked ahead soon after, and followed through to tackle Ferguson over the dead-ball line. NSW's defence held as the Maroons applied repeated pressure. O'Connor made another break, only for McGaw to spill a pass. Lindner counterattacked but Miles threw a dreadful pass.

The Blues forced two goal-line drop-outs and briefly threatened, but the mistakes continued. In the 58th minute, Conescu fielded a loose ball and became involved in a scrap with Daley. Lewis raced in and shoved Daley in an effort to protect Conescu as an all-in fight erupted. Stone sin-binned Conescu and Daley for ten minutes and Lewis for five. Stone awarded NSW a penalty, and Sterling kicked for the sideline as irate spectators threw beer cans onto the field. There was a brief halt as the field was cleared.

The Blues immediately attacked, and Lamb drew Queensland's defence before Jackson intercepted his pass and flashed away. Ferguson dragged Jackson down 10 metres from NSW's line before Folkes deliberately slowed the play as NSW players scurried to return onside. Folkes was sin-binned for five minutes, reducing both sides to 11 players. NSW's defence held before Vautin played the ball 2 metres out on tackle five. From dummy-half, Backo powered over the tryline amid three tacklers. Belcher converted, and Queensland led 10–6 after 63 minutes.

Elias was fortunate not to be penalised for ball-stripping, and then McGaw made a bustling run. He was nearly driven out but his desperate kick was spilled by Belcher. From the scrum, Lamb kicked to the right corner where O'Connor dived for the ball but missed a certain try. NSW won the scrum

against the feed and again moved the ball right. Conescu made a crucial tackle but the linesman intervened, reporting Conescu had returned prematurely. NSW received a penalty but faltered when Langmack turned over possession. Ettingshausen made a break but NSW failed to penetrate.

French busted a couple of tackles and broke away. Elias unsuccessfully tried to regain the ball and the tackle count restarted. Then Jack spilled Langer's bomb to concede a goal-line drop-out. Five tackles later, Queensland was in the 10-metre zone. Conescu stepped left but turned the ball right to Langer, who stepped through to score near the posts. Belcher converted, and the score remained 16–6 to the Maroons for the final few minutes.

The Verdict

There were claims the can-throwing incident turned the game in Queensland's favour. However, NSW subsequently had 12 players to 11 on the field and attacked from a penalty. Rather, Jackson's ensuing intercept proved decisive. Queensland's series win was largely overlooked amidst unsavoury scenes, particularly the beer-can storm. Lewis was considered a scapegoat in NSW, and Bennett was furious about Roach's violent antics.

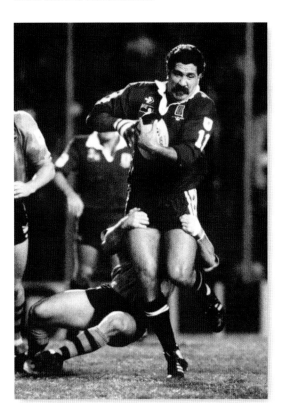

↑ Michael O'Connor was still a danger, and he scored another clever try. But as in game one, it wasn't enough to prevent a Queensland win.

← Sam Backo scored a crucial try when both teams were down to 11 players soon after the beer-can storm.

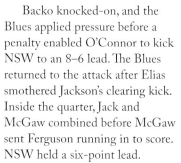

↑ Gary Belcher, Peter Jackson and Sam Backo are happy after another Queensland win.

↑ NSW's series loss was a disappointing end to coach Wayne Pearce's Origin career.

The Teams

For NSW, reserves Dunn and Hasler were replaced by Lyons and Cleal, before Lyons and Hasler became the halves pairing when Lamb and Sterling withdrew injured. Greg Florimo was the new reserve. Daley was expelled for leaving the camp to visit his pregnant wife. Steve Hanson replaced Daley.

Queensland named an unchanged team but Miles succumbed to injury, and Kilroy was recalled.

The Game

The Blues withstood an early raid by the Maroons. After a penalty against Backo, Lyons set up a break for Jack, who scurried to within 12 metres of the tryline. On the right, Lyons changed the point of attack and fed Langmack. He rucked the ball up and unloaded to Pearce, who crashed over to score. Ettingshausen then fumbled in his 10-metre zone from the kick-off. From the ensuing scrum, Langer fed Lewis, who threw a dummy, then drifted right and scampered through to score a soft try near the posts. The score was 6–all after seven minutes.

Backo knocked-on, and the Blues applied pressure before a penalty enabled O'Connor to kick NSW to an 8–6 lead. The Blues returned to the attack after Elias smothered Jackson's clearing kick. Inside the quarter, Jack and McGaw combined before McGaw sent Ferguson running in to score. NSW held a six-point lead.

Belcher scooped up a loose ball and kicked during a counterattack, but Jack beat him to the ball. A stray offload from Fullerton Smith was followed by a Blues raid. Near the right corner, Elias turned the ball left to Lyons. The five-eighth drew the defence and cleverly delayed a pass that sent Hanson galloping through to score beneath the crossbar. NSW had a handy 18–6 lead after 24 minutes.

McIndoe knocked-on before Jackson's heavy tackle on Jack forced a mistake. Backo made a hit-up and fed Lindner, who veered right, broke away from Hasler, drew Jack and sent Langer scurrying to score. Belcher's conversion closed the margin to six points with 11 minutes left before half-time. The Maroons made a few quick errors but NSW couldn't capitalise. Three minutes from the break, Currie fumbled in his quarter but NSW lost the scrum, which Hasler fed before Ferguson dropped a pass in his 30-metre zone. Elias fumbled as he stripped the ball off Vautin, giving Queensland another scrum feed. After four tackles, Lewis veered right and swivelled left in a tackle to pop the ball to Backo, who dived through to score just 17 seconds before the break. Belcher's conversion levelled the scores.

The Blues attacked early in the second half but executed poorly. They turned over possession straight after receiving a penalty, before Hanson threw an intercept during a promising raid. Five tackles later, Langer grubbered through, regained the ball in NSW's quarter and unloaded to Jackson. He veered towards the posts and reached over his head to score despite O'Connor rolling him on his back. Queensland held a 24–18 lead.

Currie's knock-on after the restart enabled NSW to attack, but Cleal threw a forward pass. After some mistake-riddled play from each team, NSW had the ball from a scrum near the 22-metre line. It moved left to Lyons, Hasler and Roach, who threw a dummy and cleverly drew Lewis and Vautin. Roach slipped the ball to Hasler, who veered, drew three defenders and flung a pass to O'Connor. He stepped outside Kilroy to score then hooked his conversion attempt, but the Blues were back, trailing 24–22 in the 62nd minute.

NSW turned over possession and the Maroons progressed very close to the tryline. Backo barged forward but first-time Origin referee Greg McCallum ruled he was held up. Replays revealed Backo had scored a fair try. On the last tackle of their next set, the Maroons moved right for Kilroy to touch down in the corner, but he had stepped over the sideline and the try was denied. Ferguson fumbled again one tackle later. Conescu stepped right from dummy-half and turned the ball inside to Backo, who scored. Queensland led by eight points with 12 minutes left.

Gillmeister stole the ball from Pearce and Queensland forced a goal-line drop-out. A forward pass from Gill-meister went unnoticed before Backo made another charge. Langer drifted left and drew the defence before passing right to Kilroy, who ran through to score. Queensland led 34–22. NSW faltered when the

kick-off failed to travel the required 10 metres. Langer grubber-kicked early in the next tackle count, and French scored as he beat Ettingshausen to the ball. Leading 38–22, the Maroons forced two goal-line drop-outs in the final three minutes.

The Verdict

The Blues appeared well in the game until the 74th minute. But, having led 18–6 after 24 minutes, they were subsequently outscored 32–4. Queensland converted more opportunities, and overcame a penalty count of 7–3 to NSW, after it was 6–1 at one stage.

The Maroons were a settled unit as they won their first series whitewash. By contrast, the Blues seemed unsettled by some mystifying team selections, including a high number of changes after game one, and the sacking of Daley before game three.

In a sad postscript to the series, Ron McAuliffe, the 'father of State of Origin', passed away in August from a brain haemorrhage.

↑ Paul Vautin was captain in game one when Wally Lewis was absent.

↓ Experienced forward Wally Fullerton Smith was crucial to the series win.

Players & Statistics

QLD Gary Belcher, Alan McIndoe, Peter Jackson, Tony Currie, Joe Kilroy, Wally Lewis (c), Allan Langer, Paul Vautin, Bob Lindner, Wally Fullerton Smith, Sam Backo, Greg Conescu, Martin Bella. **RESERVES** Brett French, Trevor Gillmeister. **COACH** Wayne Bennett

NSW Garry Jack, John Ferguson, Mark McGaw, Michael O'Connor, Andrew Ettingshausen, Cliff Lyons, Des Hasler, Paul Langmack, Steve Folkes, Wayne Pearce (c), Steve Roach, Ben Elias, Steve Hanson. **RESERVES** Noel Cleal, Greg Florimo. **COACH** John Peard

Result Queensland 38 (Backo 2, Lewis, Langer, Jackson, Kilroy French tries; Belcher 5 goals) beat NSW 22 (Pearce, Ferguson, Hanson, O'Connor tries; O'Connor 3 goals)

Referee Greg McCallum (NSW)

Crowd 16 910

Man of the Match Sam Backo (Queensland)

1989

Maroons Maul Mastercoach's Mutants

After losing five consecutive games, NSW set about regaining Origin supremacy with the appointment of the vastly experienced Jack Gibson as coach. Gibson had won five Sydney premierships with Easts and Parramatta and was widely regarded as the best coach in rugby league. Arthur Beetson returned as Queensland coach after Wayne Bennett opted to concentrate on his commitments with the Brisbane Broncos. Gibson and Beetson were close friends and had a lot of history together. Gibson was the coach of the 1974 and 1975 Easts premiership-winning teams, which were captained by Beetson. John Peard, who Gibson was replacing, had been in those Easts teams too.

NSW was forced to make changes to its team as well, because Kenny, Sterling and Pearce had retired from representative rugby league.

← Gene Miles takes on Paul Dunn as Bob Lindner prepares to back up in support. Having moved from centre to the second row, Miles was still at his destructive best as the Maroons won a series 3–0 for the second year running.

The Teams

Already without Kenny, Sterling and Pearce, the Blues were further weakened because O'Connor, Roach and McGaw were unfit. Several players from the 1988 series were omitted, and Farrar, Miller and Chris Mortimer were recalled. Miller was named captain even though he was not captaining a club and had not played Origin since 1983. A string of debutants comprised Chris Johns, Laurie Daley, Bradley Clyde, Paul Sironen, Ian Roberts, Mario Fenech, Greg Alexander and John Cartwright. Roberts succumbed to injury and was replaced by another debutant, Glenn Lazarus.

For the Maroons, Jackson and Backo were omitted because of injury problems. Meninga returned from injury, and debutants were Michael Hancock, Kerrod Walters, Dan Stains, Gary Coyne and Michael Hagan. Meanwhile, Miles was a second-rower after years as a centre.

The Game

McIndoe fumbled the kick-off on the half-volley behind his tryline, before Lewis's goal-line drop-out went more than 70 metres and was followed by a NSW mistake. After an offside penalty, the Maroons forced repeat sets of tackles, but Langer's third grubber-kick was too deep. After receiving an offside penalty, the Blues also forced repeat sets without

> ↓ The dejected NSW players gather after one of seven Queensland tries in game one, which the Maroons won by an Origin record margin of 30 points.

breaking through. Lamb fumbled, and the Maroons threw the ball around and attacked from their 10-metre zone. NSW was offside after one tackle, and Langer took a quick tap 30 metres from NSW's tryline. With the defence off guard, Langer scampered right and swung a long pass to McIndoe, who flashed past Farrar and veered towards the posts to score. Meninga converted and Queensland led 6–0.

Lindner fumbled from the restart before Miles was penalised for obstruction in front of the posts. But Daley hooked a simple 14-metre goal-kick. On the last tackle in Queensland's next set, Walters looked right but turned the ball the other way to Lewis. He dummied before pushing a pass to Stains, who fed Currie. Drawing Jack and Farrar, Currie turned a reverse pass to Hancock, who plunged over for a try. Meninga converted for a 12–0 lead.

Soon after the restart, Walters exploited poor marker defence and sent Meninga powering ahead. On tackle five, Langer grubbered past the upright and beat Jack to the ball. Meninga landed another two points.

Daley hooked the restart out on the full, but Langer's next grubber-kick was too long. After NSW forced a goal-line drop-out, Lewis commit-

Players & Statistics

QLD Gary Belcher, Michael Hancock, Tony Currie, Mal Meninga, Alan McIndoe, Wally Lewis (c), Allan Langer, Bob Lindner, Gene Miles, Paul Vautin, Dan Stains, Kerrod Walters, Martin Bella. **RESERVES** Trevor Gillmeister, Dale Shearer, Gary Coyne, Michael Hagan. **COACH** Arthur Beetson

NSW Garry Jack, Chris Johns, Andrew Farrar, Laurie Daley, John Ferguson, Terry Lamb, Des Hasler, Bradley Clyde, Gavin Miller (c), Paul Sironen, Paul Dunn, Mario Fenech, John Cartwright. **RESERVES** Glenn Lazarus, Greg Alexander, Andrew Ettingshausen, Chris Mortimer. **COACH** Jack Gibson

Result Queensland 36 (Hancock 2, Meninga 2, McIndoe, Langer, Lindner tries; Meninga 4 goals) beat NSW 6 (Ettingshausen try; Daley goal)

Referee Mick Stone (NSW)

Crowd 33 088

Man of the Match Martin Bella (Queensland)

ted a professional foul to slow a play-the-ball near the tryline. Referee Stone sin-binned Lewis for five minutes, and no cans were thrown this time. Fenech incredibly fumbled as soon as he took the penalty tap before Lewis exited the field. As half-time loomed, the normally speedy Ferguson was slow to get to Langer's clearing kick into the in-goal area. Ferguson reached down and touched the ball when McIndoe dived on it and claimed a try. After consulting the linesman, Stone ordered a goal-line drop-out. Replays suggested a try could have been given considering Ferguson did not apply downward pressure.

Half-breaks by Fenech, Ferguson and Miller gave the Blues an early chance in the second half, but Clyde dropped a pass. He produced a thumping tackle on Miles, before Miller conceded a silly penalty in a play-the-ball soon afterwards. Walters, Lewis and Belcher combined, Lewis handled again, and then Miles veered right. Drawing Ferguson, Miles sent an overhead pass to Meninga, who scored.

Ettingshausen, Alexander and Lazarus came on in place of Farrar, Clyde and Cartwright. After a fumble from Dunn, Queensland attacked again. Langer fired the ball right to Lindner, who busted Sironen's and Hasler's tackles before slicing through. Lindner unloaded inside to Meninga, who scored again. Replays showed Lindner's pass was forward but Queensland was too far ahead, at 26–0.

After a penalty against Dunn, the Maroons raided again. Miles's knee touched the sideline as he was tackled but noone noticed. Queensland soon sent the ball right, where Miles drifted, before sending Lindner over to score. Meninga converted and Queensland led 32–0 with nearly 20 minutes left.

Soon after the restart, Lewis's clearing kick was charged down by Mortimer. Five tackles later, Miller grubber-kicked past the left upright. Ettingshausen sped through and forced the ball down. Lazarus's fumble in the play-the-ball went unnoticed. Daley's conversion made the score 32–6.

From near the halfway line inside the last five minutes, the Maroons moved the ball left and Meninga linked with Currie in a run-around move-ment. Meninga charged between Johns and Lamb, fended off Lamb and drew Jack before hurling an inside pass to Belcher. He sent a short pass to Hagan, who turned and swung the ball left. Jack dropped it. Hancock was on the spot and powered out of Johns's tackle to score in the corner. The margin remained 30 points. On the last play of the game, Langer's high downfield kick was dropped by Ferguson.

↑ The Maroons celebrate as they produced their biggest win in State of Origin history.

← Mal Meninga shows his elation after scoring his second try in his comeback to Origin, after he suffered a series of broken arms.

The Verdict

The Blues looked like a second-rate team as the Maroons took their chances to register the biggest win in the competition. After failing to capitalise on a mistake at the beginning, and then missing a simple goal-kick when only six points down, NSW was outplayed in every department.

Queensland coach Arthur Beetson (right) with Mal Meninga, who was forced to exit the game in the first half with a fractured eye socket after being struck by NSW firebrand Peter Kelly.

The Teams

NSW's selectors dropped Ferguson, Farrar, Sironen and Lazarus. The injured Lamb was unavailable. Debutants were Peter Kelly, Bruce McGuire, Brad Mackay and Alan Wilson, and some positional changes occurred. Brian Johnston was recalled but then withdrew because of injury, and Ferguson was reinstated. Meanwhile, Backo returned for Queensland after the injured Stains withdrew.

With Gomersall retired, Queensland whistle-blower David Manson was chosen to officiate.

Kerrod Walters grabbed his opportunity with both hands after being selected at hooker to replace Greg Conescu. Walters had been playing reserve grade for the Brisbane Broncos not that long beforehand.

The Game

The Blues applied early pressure after McIndoe had the ball dislodged in the first 30 seconds. Miller's bomb appeared to bounce on the dead-ball line and Belcher was trapped in-goal. Referee Manson ignored Belcher's and Lewis's protests and ordered a goal-line drop-out. The Maroons held before Hancock fielded Alexander's grubber behind the tryline and made a burst. As Queensland moved the ball left three tackles later, the defence advanced on Lewis. He fed Lindner, who broke through, then Langer veered left and fired the

ball to Belcher, whose quick pass sent Hancock across. Meninga converted and Queensland led 6–0 after NSW made the early running.

After Backo and Dunn exchanged fumbles, Belcher made a break and kicked where Alexander was nailed in-goal. The Maroons attacked a few minutes later, but Miles's basketball pass to Currie was forward. Then Lindner and Belcher were penalised, but Daley's 41-metre goal-kick barely left the ground. The Maroons turned over possession quickly, then had to withstand repeated attacks. Daley stepped out of Meninga's tackle and headed for the left corner but Currie forced him out.

Queensland was set back when Langer slipped and broke his ankle. Lewis's 30-metre attempt at a field goal fell short. After Bella was penalised for striking McGuire in an off-the-ball incident, NSW ventured downfield but McGuire dropped a head-high pass. In NSW's next set, Belcher dropped Alexander's towering bomb and Daley grabbed the ball and powered over between the posts. Alexander's conversion levelled the scores.

Kelly escaped scrutiny for punching Meninga, who exited the game with a fractured eye socket. McGuire fumbled again after NSW gained momentum, before the Blues attacked further. After a try wouldn't come, Alexander hooked a 25-metre drop-goal attempt. As the siren sounded, Fenech broke through and found McGuire, only for McGuire to surrender possession with a wild pass as he was caught by desperate cover defence. Coyne became Queensland's sole reserve as Vautin departed at half-time with an elbow injury.

The Blues raided from their half just after the break, but Clyde's pass to McGuire was forward. Johns soon made a break, and NSW threatened but Ettingshausen's bomb was regained by Queensland. Moments later, Lewis moved left and swung a high pass to Hagan. Evading tacklers, Hagan linked with Belcher and McIndoe, who immediately passed inside where Shearer fed Hagan. Drawing two defenders, Hagan sent Walters running away to dive beneath the posts. Again the Maroons had scored against the run of play to take a six-point lead.

Players & Statistics

QLD Gary Belcher, Alan McIndoe, Tony Currie, Mal Meninga, Michael Hancock, Wally Lewis (c), Allan Langer, Bob Lindner, Gene Miles, Paul Vautin, Sam Backo, Kerrod Walters, Martin Bella. **RESERVES** Michael Hagan, Dale Shearer, Trevor Gillmeister, Gary Coyne. **COACH** Arthur Beetson

NSW Garry Jack, Chris Johns, Andrew Ettingshausen, Laurie Daley, John Ferguson, Chris Mortimer, Greg Alexander, Bradley Clyde, Gavin Miller (c), Bruce McGuire, Paul Dunn, Mario Fenech, Peter Kelly. **RESERVES** Des Hasler, John Cartwright, Brad Mackay, Alan Wilson. **COACH** Jack Gibson

Result Queensland 16 (Hancock, Walters, Lewis tries; Meninga, Belcher goals) beat NSW 12 (Daley, Johns tries; Alexander 2 goals)

Referee David Manson (Queensland)

Crowd 40 000

Man of the Match Wally Lewis (Queensland)

NSW forced an error but Queensland won the scrum against the feed. After Gillmeister and Miles were stopped near the tryline on successive tackles, the Maroons had no replacements left as Hancock finally succumbed to a shoulder injury. Clyde fumbled in a typical Gillmeister bone-rattler, and Hagan flicked the loose ball to Lewis 33 metres from the tryline. Lewis veered right, changing pace as he shaped to pass but instead accelerated between Mortimer and Daley. Jack grabbed Lewis's jersey but Lewis dragged Jack along with him and crashed over for a brilliant try. Queensland led 16–6 with 20 minutes left as Belcher hooked the kick.

NSW brought on three fresh players. Cartwright set up a break by McGuire, but the Maroons halted the raid with an intercept, only for Shearer to deflect the ball to an offside Hagan. Four tackles later, Fenech spun the ball right to Alexander and Cartwright, who stood in a tackle and passed inside to Johns. Seeing a hole, Johns headed through to score. Alexander's conversion narrowed NSW's deficit to four points with 12 minutes remaining.

The game fluctuated as both sides showed poor ball control. When the Blues eventually entered Queensland's half, play was halted when Lindner, who had broken a bone in his leg earlier, was carried off. Down to 12 men, the Maroons tried to cling to their lead. In the final three minutes, Queensland conceded a penalty for an offside mistake. Near the halfway line, Cartwright was about to rise and play the ball when Miles knocked it from his grasp. Referee Manson incorrectly ruled a knock-on against

Cartwright. Instead of NSW having the chance to push for the converted try it needed, the clock wound down after the Maroons ventured downfield.

The Verdict

The Maroons' win to clinch their third series in a row was something special as they had to overcome a dreadful injury toll. The Blues may have beaten the tiring Queenslanders had play continued for another five or ten minutes. And NSW was unlucky not to receive what could have been a decisive penalty in the final minutes, but there were several close calls throughout the game. The fact was that the Blues faltered at a few crucial times, and Queensland's three tries came against the run of play.

↑ Greg Alexander has an interesting time trying to tackle Sam Backo. The injury-ravaged Maroons were fortunate that four reserves rather than two were now the norm in rugby league, as they were left one player short in the closing stages of the game.

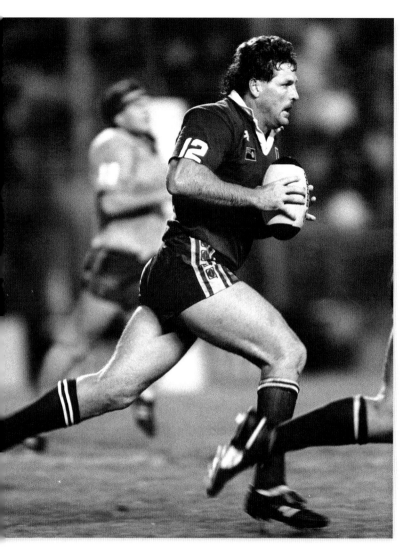

↑ Gene Miles makes another break in what was his final year of representative football.

The Teams

Ferguson, Ettingshausen and Dunn were dropped for NSW, and injuries to Mortimer, Daley, Clyde and Fenech forced further changes. Johnston, O'Connor and Trewhella were recalled, and Phil Blake, Mark Geyer and Terry Matterson were the debutants. Ferguson again earned a reprieve, and several positional changes occurred.

The Maroons lost Meninga, Langer and Lindner to injury. Jackson and Stains returned and newcomer Kevin Walters was a reserve.

The Game

At dummy-half from his 30-metre line in Queensland's first set of tackles, Kerrod Walters broke through before drawing Jack and passing right to McIndoe. The winger reached to impressively catch the ball left-handed as he sped down the sideline before running in to score after 85 seconds of play.

The teams traded errors until the Blues dominated field position. Belcher knocked-on in a tackle before a Miles pass was ruled forward. From a scrum 9 metres from the tryline, Alexander accelerated to the right and stepped between Vautin and Lewis before releasing an inside ball to Hasler, who dived over beside the right post. O'Connor's easy goal-kick pushed NSW to a 6–4 lead.

McGuire fumbled a few minutes later, and Hagan kicked downfield to the left on the next tackle as Jack was out of position. Ferguson appeared to have the ball covered but it suddenly bounced left. Shearer put his hands into Ferguson's back as he tried to get around him before retrieving the ball and scoring. Referee McCallum awarded the try, which was unconverted. Queensland was ahead by two points.

McGuire conceded a penalty for a high tackle. At the end of the next set, Shearer caught Lewis's bomb ahead of the two fullbacks to touch down, but McCallum gave a penalty to NSW. It was unclear why, but McCallum marched Lewis 10 metres for dissent. Then he penalised Miles for stripping when Ferguson appeared to drop the ball as he was about to play it. Just one tackle later, Hasler passed left to Mackay, who threw a dummy to Hasler, fooling the defence. Mackay ducked under Bella's tackle, ran ahead and unloaded to Trewhella, who stepped out of a tackle to score behind the posts. O'Connor's conversion gave NSW a 12–8 lead.

Successive knock-ons by Kerrod Walters and Lewis gave NSW another tryscoring chance. Miller grubbered for the left corner, where O'Connor touched down but he was penalised for offside. The Blues were back on the attack when Alexander threw a dummy and broke through before feeding Geyer. Geyer linked with Kelly, who sent Hasler to the posts, but Geyer's pass was ruled forward. After a penalty against Backo, O'Connor pushed a long range goal-kick to the right.

Almost on half-time, Alexander ran left and threw a dummy before sending Hasler a blatantly forward pass. It went undetected and Hasler scampered away towards the quarter-line with the defence in disarray. Hasler lofted another forward pass, which O'Connor fumbled. The Blues could have led by more than four points, but the Maroons also had a try controversially disallowed.

Both teams made errors early in the second half before Kerrod Walters darted from dummy-half and linked with Miles and Currie, who drew Johns and fed Hancock. He dived over in the left corner and Shearer converted superbly to put Queensland in front 14–12. The game continued to turn the Maroons' way on the last tackle of NSW's next set. A scrappy pass by Trewhella forced Jack into a left-footed kick as the defence pressured him. Five tackles later, Lewis stepped around Alexander and grubber-kicked into the right corner. Jack had ample time to field the ball but fumbled, allowing Kerrod Walters to pounce for an easy try. Shearer landed another conversion to give Queensland a 20–12 lead.

NSW went on the attack through Johnston, who weaved his way through Queensland's defence and linked up with Johns, Matterson and Mackay to send Ferguson heading for the right corner. But Ferguson was dragged into touch 5 metres short by Hancock. After Hasler knocked-on a few minutes later, Queensland used the ball well as Vautin, Shearer, Bella, Vautin again and Hagan handled before Belcher broke away to score. Shearer converted and the Maroons held a convincing 26–12 lead.

Another splendid exhibition of ball handling a couple of minutes later led to Currie scoring in the left corner to make it 30–12. Jackson made a long break, and the Maroons exploited some more fragile

defence after forcing a goal-line drop-out. On the quarter-line, Shearer looped around Lewis's left in a run-around movement before Shearer raced through a yawning gap to score near the uprights. Lewis finally left the field with arm and shoulder injuries. Queensland conceded two quick penalties in the last five minutes before McGuire scored a late try. The final margin was a resounding 20 points.

The Verdict

The result was misleading, considering NSW came close to scoring on three occasions before the break. It was anyone's guess whether the Maroons' second-half dominance would have occurred had they been more than six points behind at half-time. As they had racked up an eight-game winning streak, the fine line between winning and losing was easily overlooked.

← Alan McIndoe scored the opening try in the first and third games of the series.

↓ Gary Belcher puts a kick through. Belcher had become an automatic choice for the Maroons at fullback since his Origin debut in 1986.

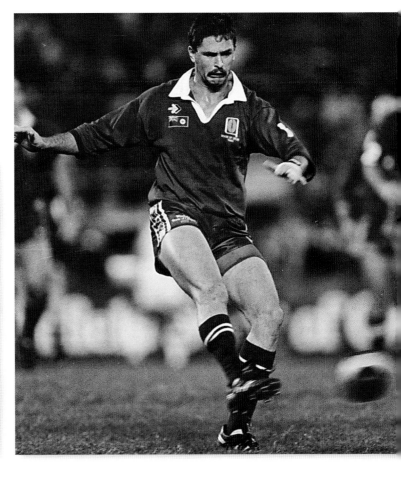

1990s

1990

A Melbourne Excursion

The start of the second decade of State of Origin football took a different turn, with one of the three games scheduled for Melbourne. Origin football had emerged from an uncertain beginning in 1980 to being a proven winner in Queensland and NSW. The next step was to take a game interstate to Melbourne, the heart of the AFL. The first game of the series was scheduled for the Sydney Football Stadium, the second in Melbourne and the third at Lang Park. Despite NSW's comprehensive series loss in 1989, the Blues retained Jack Gibson as coach, and once again his counterpart was Arthur Beetson.

Queensland's quest for continuing supremacy was hampered by injuries. Currie and Hancock were unavailable for the series, and Backo, Kerrod Walters and Peter Jackson were absent for at least game one. Furthermore, Miles had retired from representative football.

← NSW defenders end a charge from Mal Meninga in game two. It was the first time that any part of a three-game State of Origin series was played outside Brisbane and Sydney.

→ Mark McGaw (left) had the better of the battle against the man he struggles to halt in this photo, Mal Meninga.

↓ Mark McGaw wraps up Dale Shearer with a ball-and-all tackle.

The Teams

The Blues team was quite different from the previous year's teams. Ricky Walford, Ricky Stuart, Ian Roberts and Rod Wishart gained their first Origin jerseys, with the rest of the side containing a balance of players from the City versus Country trial. Geoff Toovey and Graham Lyons were late additions after injuries to Alexander and Hasler.

Despite injury problems, the Maroons fielded many seasoned players in a recast side. The only debutant was Steve Walters, who replaced brother Kerrod. The Maroons were set back further when Lewis pulled out with injury. Mark Coyne was the new reserve, while Vautin took over the captaincy.

The Game

The first scoring opportunity came in the eighth minute when O'Connor sent Clyde through a gap. Clyde fed Gillespie. He drew Kiss but threw a forward pass left to Walford, who was heading for the uprights. After mistakes by both sides, Roberts broke through and sent O'Connor down the wing. O'Connor lobbed a pass to Wishart, who fumbled as he was caught by frantic defence near the tryline. Queensland gave away two silly penalties in quick succession. From the latter, O'Connor pushed a goal-kick offline from the left sideline.

NSW appeared fortunate to receive a repeat set of tackles after Daley's kick ricocheted off Fullerton Smith, who did not play at the ball. Near Queensland's posts on the next tackle, Stuart swung the ball right where the defence was thin. But Clyde's pass went to ground before Ettingshausen was shoved over the sideline as another try bombed. NSW

dominated field position, but silly errors squandered any advantage. Roach conceded a penalty when he was tackled because he foolishly struck Vautin. Daley and O'Connor broke through, then O'Connor drew Belcher but threw a wild forward pass to the try-bound McGaw. The Blues had blown four try-scoring opportunities and missed a penalty goal.

The breakthrough came two minutes later. From 8 metres inside NSW's half, Elias fired the ball left to Stuart and Daley, who drifted before attracting Vautin and Meninga. Daley fed McGaw, whose pass inside to Ettingshausen looked forward. Evading Langer's tackle, ET shovelled a long pass inside to Elias. As Kiss was about to swoop, Elias flung the ball left to Walford, who wrong-footed Langer. Confronted by Belcher, Walford unloaded to McGaw, who scooped the ball up low down and crashed over the line in McIndoe's tackle.

Elias and Steve Walters exchanged mistakes soon after, and then some ill-disciplined play resulted in a couple of penalties each way. Bella surrendered a rare attacking chance when he replicated Roach's earlier mistake, by striking Gillespie. The Maroons were fortunate to trail by only six points at half-time.

Queensland had a chance to strike very soon after play resumed. Steve Walters's heavy tackle on Ettingshausen forced a knock-on, but the northerners were caught offside five tackles later as Langer put up a high ball. A few Blues mistakes enabled Queensland to have three sets of possession in NSW's half in three minutes. But the Maroons just couldn't get their act together. Langer kicked needlessly early in a tackle count, Stains coughed up the ball in the quarter, and then Hagan kicked wastefully after the first tackle.

In Queensland's next tackle count, Fullerton Smith spilled possession when tackled on his 30-metre line. The ball propelled forwards off Daley, who picked it up and ran away to score in the corner, but referee Manson ruled a knock-on both ways. Replays showed the ball touched Daley's shoulder and not his hands, costing NSW a fair try. NSW nonetheless had the scrum feed, and then Stains conceded a blatant penalty when he came down on Roberts with a forceful right arm strike. O'Connor landed the goal on offer from in front of the posts.

NSW's lead was more than handy as the Maroons did not look like scoring. Both teams completed most of their sets of possession in the last 20 minutes, and NSW looked in control in defence. In the dying minutes, a Daley chip-kick was touched by Belcher and retrieved by Ettingshausen, who was tackled near the tryline. Lazarus charged at the line but was held up by three defenders. The Maroons threw the ball around but a knock-on by Kevin Walters concluded Queensland's disappointing night.

The Verdict

NSW's win was its first for three years. It was its first win at the SFS after three losses. And Queensland became the first Origin team to be kept scoreless. The game tally of eight points was easily the lowest in an Origin game. The Blues were strong in defence and deserved praise for keeping their tryline intact. According to O'Connor, Gibson and the players from the previous year were much more relaxed and team spirit more evident. Queensland was not disgraced, and Lewis said the Maroons showed tenacity to keep NSW to a single try.

↓ Michael Hagan (top) and Allan Langer (bottom) bring down Laurie Daley, who tasted success in Origin for the first time after two losses in 1989.

The Teams

Vautin lost the Maroons captaincy and his place in the team, marking the end of his Origin playing career. Fullerton Smith, Steve Walters and Hagan were also axed. Lewis and Backo returned, and Kerrod Walters replaced brother Steve. Coyne was called up from the bench and Andrew Gee was a new reserve.

NSW made just one change, with Hasler replacing Toovey on the bench. However, Daley and O'Connor were later ruled out with injuries, and Brad Mackay returned as a centre, Hasler was promoted to five-eighth, and the new reserve was Brad 'Freddie' Fittler, who became the youngest player in Origin history at 18 years and 114 days. Walford (injured) was a late withdrawal, and Lyons moved to wing while Farrar was recalled as a reserve.

The Game

On a slippery surface, both teams exchanged handling errors early on. NSW suffered a blow when Hasler exited the game injured. The Maroons moved the ball left inside the quarter but Stains threw a poor pass to Meninga, who fumbled with a try beckoning.

Lyons made a few dashing runs but repeatedly lost his footing. Lewis made a break after Kerrod Walters won a scrum against the feed in NSW's territory, but this scoring chance was squandered when Langer dropped an easy pass. After being hit across the face by McGaw in a tackle, Shearer was controversially penalised for shouting at referee McCallum. Elias fumbled the penalty tap, and then Lewis knocked on before conceding a penalty for roughing up Roach. Wishart subsequently landed a 32-metre penalty goal.

After a fumble from Roberts, McGaw was penalised, but Meninga's easy 15-metre goal-kick crashed into the right upright. Queensland forced a goal-line drop-out, and Meninga made a menacing burst. On the next play, the ball moved left to Lewis and Stains, whose inside pass to Belcher was intercepted by Stuart. From inside his quarter, Stuart scurried away and crashed over to score. Wishart's

↓ Wally Lewis (right) acknowledges NSW captain Ben Elias as the victor after the Blues secured the series.

goal-kick pushed to the right, but NSW led 6–0 against the run of play. Soon after, an offside penalty enabled Queensland to venture downfield. Kerrod Walters turned the ball right to Lewis and Meninga, who drew the defence and sent Lindner through to the tryline. But McCallum ruled Meninga's pass forward, although replays showed it was marginal but fair. Despite missing a few scoring chances, the Maroons were unlucky to trail 6–0 at half-time.

A mixture of sloppy and entertaining football took place when play resumed. Following an exchange of fumbles, Elias put in a long kick and Belcher only just escaped his in-goal area. Belcher badly spilled a towering bomb from Stuart, and McGaw fielded the loose ball but bombed a certain try with a massively forward pass to Stuart. Backo turned the ball over almost straight away but then Elias pushed a field-goal attempt just outside the right post. Errors continued, and match officials overlooked indiscretions, including swinging arms, an obvious forward pass from Belcher and a blatant knock-on by Gillespie.

After Belcher and Lindner combined to send McIndoe scurrying down the left wing, McIndoe was tackled 25 metres from NSW's line. Long passes were thrown right to Kerrod Walters, Lewis and Gillmeister, whose pass was touched by Mackay before Belcher sent Kiss over in the corner. Meninga landed a great conversion to tie the scores with ten minutes left.

Kiss had the ball stolen by Elias on the first tackle after the restart. The Blues threw the ball to the right

and Wishart was in sight of scoring before McIndoe and Shearer bundled him over the sideline. Kiss fumbled again in his half, before McCallum ensured the game would be remembered for his refereeing. Lazarus was tackled by Lewis but rose and stepped forward. Langer stole the ball, a legitimate-looking action considering Lazarus's actions. McCallum claimed he had called 'held' and thus penalised Langer. Lewis argued with McCallum in vain, and Wishart's straightforward penalty kick took the Blues to an 8–6 lead.

The Maroons searched for a way to score in the last minutes. Lindner briefly found open space with about three minutes left, but his pass was intercepted by Roberts 10 metres in NSW's half. In the final minute, the Maroons went sideways and backwards as they threw the ball right inside their half. McIndoe,

Lewis, Langer and Walters handled before Walters's pass hit the ground. Coyne fielded passed inside to Meninga but Mackay intercepted and scurried 30 metres to score and seal the game and series.

The Verdict

NSW's 12–6 triumph and its first series win in four years were tainted by intense debate over the penalty against Langer for stealing the ball. Lewis insisted the Queenslanders heard the referee call 'play on' but McCallum said he had called 'held' four times before penalising Langer. The next day he said he'd called 'held' once and 'let him go' three times.

Although McCallum did Queensland no favours, it was telling that the Maroons made 21 handling errors to NSW's 13. Furthermore, both of NSW's tries resulted from wayward passes by Queensland.

↑ Rod Wishart, Graham Lyons, Andrew Farrar and Brad Mackay savour NSW's first Origin series win for four years.

↑ Although Queensland had lost the series, Gary Coyne, Martin Bella, Sam Backo and an injured Peter Jackson found reason to cheer after their success in game three.

The Teams

Kiss and Coyne were the only Maroons players dropped. It was the end of Kiss's Origin career and he had not been in a winning team. Willie Carne was the new winger and Hagan returned as a reserve. Gillmeister was promoted from the bench and Steve Jackson was the new reserve forward.

The NSW selectors surprisingly chose Mackay at five-eighth, despite him being a regular lock for St George. Alexander was back in place of Fittler and O'Connor returned as a centre.

Closer to the game, hamstring injuries caused Roach (NSW) and Meninga (Queensland) to withdraw. Lazarus moved to the front-row for NSW and Mark Sargent was the new reserve. Peter Jackson returned at centre for the Maroons.

The Game

Concerns for spectator safety saw 400 ticketholders locked out of Lang Park. But many of the banished kicked at the gates, and they were granted entry after persuasion from members of the Lang Park Trust.

Dropped balls and silly penalties marred the start of the game. After a penalty for offside, the Maroons attacked with Kerrod Walters exploiting poor marker defence. Elias raked the ball from his opponent's grasp and Belcher kicked the home side to a 2–0 lead from the ensuing penalty. An offside penalty against the Maroons just a couple of minutes later put the Blues in the attacking zone. Gillespie played the ball 3 metres from the tryline. From dummy-half, Lazarus looked right and, as the defence looked that way, he straightened, ducked and crashed over for a soft try. Wishart landed the wide-angled conversion, and the Blues jumped to a 6–2 lead.

Neither side looked like gaining the upper hand and repeatedly failed to complete sets of tackles. After a fumble from Clyde, O'Connor was penalised for tackling Peter Jackson before he received the ball. Belcher landed a 30-metre penalty goal to bridge the margin to two points. A few tackles after a knock-on by Shearer, Clyde played the ball on the quarter-line to the right of the posts. Elias stepped around some feeble marker defence and cleverly wrong-footed

Players & Statistics

QLD Gary Belcher, Alan McIndoe, Dale Shearer, Peter Jackson, Willie Carne, Wally Lewis (c), Allan Langer, Bob Lindner, Trevor Gillmeister, Gary Coyne, Martin Bella, Steve Walters, Sam Backo. **RESERVES** Andrew Gee, Kevin Walters, Steve Jackson, Michael Hagan. **COACH** Arthur Beetson

NSW Andrew Ettingshausen, Graham Lyons, Michael O'Connor, Mark McGaw, Rod Wishart, Brad Mackay, Ricky Stuart, Bradley Clyde, David Gillespie, Bruce McGuire, Glenn Lazarus, Ben Elias (c), Ian Roberts. **RESERVES** Mark Sargent, Paul Sironen, Greg Alexander, Andrew Farrar. **COACH** Jack Gibson

Result Queensland 14 (Belcher, S Jackson tries; Belcher 2, Lewis goals) beat NSW 10 (Lazarus, McGaw tries; Wishart goal)

Referee David Manson (Queensland)

Crowd 31 416

Man of the Match Bob Lindner (Queensland)

straightening and, as he committed three defenders, slipped the ball right to replacement Steve Jackson, who surged over. Belcher pushed the goal-kick off to the right, and the Maroons led by four points with ten minutes left. After a Queensland error, McGaw was tackled over the sideline. NSW was unlucky not to receive a penalty as McGaw appeared to be halted before the defenders dragged him out.

The final five minutes were frantic. Lewis sliced a straightforward 20-metre penalty goal-kick, before Clyde scurried through before being bundled into touch 4 metres short of the tryline. Lewis knocked on to give NSW one last chance, but the Maroons held on.

↓ Mark McGaw scored a try to carry NSW to a 10-4 lead in the first half.

Gillmeister, then sliced between Kerrod Walters and McIndoe to send McGaw crashing over in the corner. Wishart pulled the conversion attempt, and NSW led by only six points despite two tries to nil.

Handling errors stifled NSW's progress. The Maroons threatened to score six minutes from half-time but Lindner's long pass to the right went forward. But an immediate knock-on by NSW put Queensland back in attacking mode. Langer evaded numerous tackles from the scrum win before being held 10 metres out. In the next play, the ball passed right through Lindner, Gillmeister, Walters and Peter Jackson before Belcher whirled over to score with O'Connor clinging to him. Lewis surprisingly took the conversion attempt from near the right wing, and landed his first goal in Origin football to level the scores at 10-all. Lewis failed with a 45-metre field-goal attempt just before the break. Players became involved in some pushing and shoving as the siren was about to sound.

Roberts was unable to resume because of a neck injury. Both sides fumbled the ball early in the second half as play swung from end to end. Gillmeister came close for Queensland but he was held up by numerous defenders. Coyne looked to have a try on offer in the 57th minute after Ettingshausen fumbled Belcher's kick inside the NSW quarter, but Coyne lost the ball in the tackle. Queensland forced a repeat set, then the Blues touched the ball to restart the tackle count. On the last tackle, Belcher played the ball to Kerrod Walters in the 10-metre zone. On the left, first receiver Langer drifted before

The Verdict

For the third successive game, scoring points proved difficult as chances were restricted by strong defence and handling errors. Goal-kicking proved decisive, with the Blues conceding a couple of penalties within range of their posts. Beetson and Lewis were satisfied after the disappointment of Melbourne but said it was no moral victory because Queensland had lost the Origin series.

← Trevor Gillmeister was promoted to Queensland's starting team after being selected for the bench in the first two games.

1991

The Emperor Strikes Back and Says Good-bye

The 1991 State of Origin games were played in Brisbane and Sydney only, as an Australia–New Zealand test was scheduled for Olympic Park after the Origin series.

In a shock decision, Arthur Beetson was sacked as Queensland coach and replaced by New Zealander Graham Lowe. Beetson, who heard the news from a Brisbane radio journalist, was hurt by the decision. Controversy over the sacking and the appointment of a New Zealander dominated pre-series discussions. Lowe suffered a brain haemmorhage early in 1991, but he recovered to take up his Origin coaching appointment.

Jack Gibson decided not to continue as NSW coach after having disagreements with the NSWRL management. He was unhappy with his lack of influence in team selections. Canberra coach Tim Sheens was appointed after taking the Raiders to successive premierships in 1989 and 1990. The NSWRL took the unusual step of choosing a coach who also had club commitments.

For Queensland, Backo, Shearer and Lindner had injury problems, although it was possible Lindner and Shearer could return during the Origin series. For NSW, an injured Clyde was in a similar situation.

← Wally Lewis, the mainstay of Queensland's dominance during the 1980s, in the thick of the action in his last State of Origin series.

The Teams

Queensland fielded a familiar backline but an inexperienced forward pack. Debutants were lock Gary Larson, second-rower Mike McLean and reserves Gavin Allen and Steve Renouf. Gillmeister was omitted and Steve Jackson and Gee were in the starting line-up for the first time.

An argument over sponsorship threatened to derail the Maroons. XXXX sponsored the Origin team and Power's Brewing the Brisbane Broncos. The Broncos management objected to Brisbane's seven Origin players wearing the XXXX logo. Threats and counter-threats were hurled around before the Broncos management relented. The dispute highlighted the growing influence of commercial interests in the game. Fullback Paul Hauff became another Broncos player and Origin debutant when an injured Belcher withdrew. Gary Coyne was recalled to replace an injured Stains.

Every member of NSW's starting line-up had Origin experience, although the Blues made some positional changes. Geyer was recalled and the only debutant was replacement Col Van der Voort. Lazarus and Fenech were notable omissions, but Lazarus was called up when an injured Van der Voort had to withdraw.

↓ Queensland fullback Paul Hauff made a good start to the game and held off early NSW attacks, but left the field injured midway through the second half.

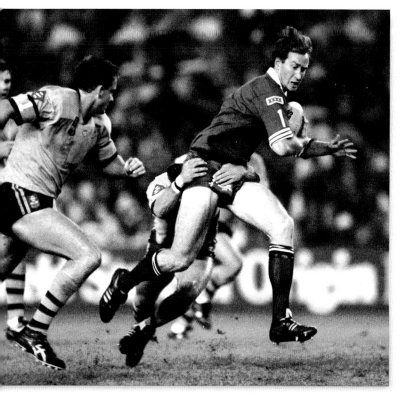

Players & Statistics

QLD Paul Hauff, Michael Hancock, Peter Jackson, Mal Meninga, Willie Carne, Wally Lewis (c), Allan Langer, Gary Larson, Mike McLean, Andrew Gee, Steve Jackson, Steve Walters, Martin Bella. **RESERVES** Kevin Walters, Steve Renouf, Gary Coyne, Gavin Allen. **COACH** Graham Lowe

NSW Greg Alexander, Chris Johns, Andrew Ettingshausen, Laurie Daley, Michael O'Connor, Cliff Lyons, Ricky Stuart, Des Hasler, Paul Sironen, Mark Geyer, Ian Roberts, Ben Elias (c), Steve Roach. **RESERVES** Glenn Lazarus, David Gillespie, Mark McGaw, Brad Fittler. **COACH** Tim Sheens

Result Queensland 6 (Meninga try; Meninga goal) beat NSW 4 (Daley try)

Referee Bill Harrigan (NSW)

Crowd 32 400

Man of the Match Wally Lewis (Queensland)

The Game

An old-style kicking duel between Stuart and Hauff started the game. A few minutes in, Lyons came up with the ball after he and Ettingshausen tackled Hauff. Lyons scurried to the tryline, only to be penalised for stealing the ball. Lyons kicked ahead from a scrum shortly afterwards, but Hauff easily beat Ettingshausen to the ball. The Queensland fullback had no trouble when Stuart tested him with a high punt soon afterwards. Hauff had a lot of work to do as the NSW backs attacked. Lyons then cleverly drew the defence and sent Alexander through, but Hauff tackled him over the left sideline with the tryline beckoning. Ettingshausen broke through two minutes later but the trybound ET grubber-kicked where Hauff recovered the ball. Alexander made another break several minutes later and combined with Ettingshausen, who flashed away but couldn't get past Hauff inside Queensland's half.

The Maroons had little possession before half-breaks by Carne and Hancock created a rare attacking opportunity. A late tackle on Steve Jackson by Gillespie and Stuart led to Meninga opening the scoring with a penalty goal. Queensland's 2–0 lead was no reflection of the flow of the game, as the Blues failed to finish off their attacking plays.

Having withstood NSW raids in the first half, Queensland gained momentum after the break. The Maroons attacked dangerously in the 55th minute when an offside Hasler took an intercept. Ten metres in from the left sideline, Meninga pushed the penalty goal attempt to the right. Hauff's Origin debut took an unfortunate twist when he fell awkwardly and left the field injured. Carne moved to fullback after Hauff had done a sterling job there, and Renouf came onto the wing. The Blues threatened to break through when Daley scooped up a stray Maroons pass, only to be tackled within 10 metres of the tryline. The Blues turned the ball over twice in quick succession, with the second one inside their own half proving crucial.

In the following set, Bella played the ball 26 metres from NSW's posts, and it went left to Langer and Lewis, who threw a dummy and darted between two defenders. Lewis turned a reverse pass inside to Meninga, who powered ahead and crashed into Alexander before barging over the line. Queensland led 6–0 with 15 minutes left after Meninga sliced his conversion attempt. Following a break by Steve Walters, Meninga sliced a goal-kick from the right of the posts after Roberts was penalised for holding down in the tackle. The Maroons tried to set up for a field goal with 11 minutes left, but the NSW defence came up too quickly.

NSW was error-prone with the ball and the Maroons looked capable of holding the Blues out. But with three minutes left, Kevin Walters ran down the blindside in his territory and was tackled into touch. Fourteen metres from Queensland's uprights, Sironen played the ball to Elias, who passed it right to Alexander. He threw a cut-out pass to Daley, who kicked around Hancock and beat him to the ball for a try. O'Connor had a sideline conversion attempt to level the scores but he skewed the crucial kick well to the right.

Meninga incredibly sent the kick-off over the dead-ball line on the full in the final 10 seconds, giving NSW one last throw of the dice from the resultant penalty. Alexander opted to kick for goal from halfway to draw the game, but the distance proved beyond his reach. Lewis caught the ball and took a tackle. Queensland won 6–4.

The Verdict

The Blues could have avoided a loss in the dying stages. But, as coach Sheens said, they were outplayed and guilty of too many mistakes, poor kicking and sloppy defence. Lewis, whose leadership was crucial to Queensland's success, won his eighth Origin man-of-the-match award. Lewis said that his players were always confident they would win.

↑ Balmain Tigers' second-rower Paul Sironen —in the middle of his Origin career—powers into a Maroons tackle.

The Teams

A fit Clyde returned for NSW. Fittler and McGaw were dropped; Sironen, Lazarus and Alexander sidelined by injuries and there were some positional changes. Brad Mackay, Wishart and Cartwright were recalled, as was McGaw after Alexander withdrew.

Queensland named the same starting line-up. Shearer returned to the bench in place of Renouf.

The Game

The field was damp following rain. After Hancock fumbled from dummy-half in the first minute, a contentious penalty for ball-stripping gave O'Connor a goal-kick from the right of the posts but he pulled it. He made no mistake from a wider angle two minutes later after a Larson indiscretion. A kick from Langer bounced favourably for Carne to pin Wishart in-goal, but Carne was controversially ruled offside. The NSW pack produced some thundering tackles before Geyer flattened Hancock with a brutal shoulder charge on a kick return. Hancock lost the ball and was left in a groggy state.

After the heavens opened midway through the first half, both sides turned over possession early in tackle counts. Near the middle of the field in the 28th minute, Elias passed left to Stuart, who threw a dummy and sped between Steve Walters and Gee on a 35-metre dash, before passing inside to Johns. He ran to score 10 metres left of the posts and O'Connor's conversion gave NSW an 8–0 lead. But that advantage was in jeopardy as Clyde dropped the ball in a tackle from the restart. A few tackles later, Steve Walters played the ball to Gee 10 metres from the tryline and near the posts. Gee turned the ball left to Langer, who spread it to Peter Jackson. As O'Connor came up quickly, Jackson handballed the ball to Hauff. He stepped around Geyer and burst through Roberts and Ettingshausen before feeding Carne, who busted a tackle to dive over the line. From a wide angle, Meninga landed an impressive conversion.

The game turned nasty on half-time. Geyer roughed up Steve Walters in a tackle and was pushed away by Gee. The two exchanged punches as an all-in scuffle developed, before Lewis stood toe-to-toe remonstrating with Geyer. Referee Manson

↑ Laurie Daley celebrates the Blues' last-minute victory, but he was out of the decider with injuries sustained in game two.

lectured the players sternly, but when he turned away Lewis and Geyer resumed their heated exchange. Manson was forced to stand between the players to separate them.

Needing a win to keep the series alive, NSW had to continue without injured trio Daley, Wishart and Roberts. The NSW players returned to the field after the break in fresh jerseys and, although the rain had eased, there were still numerous pools of water. The Blues enjoyed field position early but Gillespie knocked on contesting a high kick with Hauff near the tryline. At the other end, Ettingshausen fumbled Shearer's downfield kick from a penalty tap. Rough play ensued with Geyer again in the thick of it. As Stuart tackled Hauff low down, Geyer raised his left elbow and struck the ball-carrier on the jaw. Peter Jackson retaliated, throwing a flurry of punches as another fight broke out. Strangely, Manson did not banish anyone, merely giving Queensland a penalty, which levelled the scores through Meninga's goal.

As heavy rain returned, knock-ons became regular. The momentum swung dramatically when Queensland won a scrum against the feed. In the 10-metre zone a couple of tackles later, Steve Walters turned the ball left to Langer, who fired it to Lewis as an overlap developed. About to cop a high tackle from Geyer, Lewis threw a superbly timed pass to Shearer, who stepped between Johns and Stuart to slide in the left corner. Meninga hooked the goal-kick, and Queensland was tantalisingly within sight of a series win, leading by four points with 12 minutes left.

Both teams strove to play in their opponent's half. After NSW had its tackle count restarted with about five minutes left, Clyde surged to within 5 metres of the tryline. From the play-the-ball, Elias passed right to Stuart, who swung a decisively long pass to McGaw. He stepped inside Hancock and showed amazing determination as he surged across the tryline with two defenders clinging to him. His try tied the scores with barely four minutes left. From a similar angle to his kick in the dying stages of game one, O'Connor faced an enormous challenge due to the boggy field, heavy ball and teeming rain. The kick curved beautifully from outside the right post and sailed between the uprights. The crowd roared as the Blues snatched a 14–12 lead, before they fumbled from a short kick-off. Langer kicked dangerously a few tackles later and Hasler scurried to beat Carne to the ball in-goal. Queensland mounted a last-minute raid from the goal-line drop-out, but a stray pass from Shearer ensured a NSW victory.

The Verdict

For the second successive game, the margin was just two points. In post-match discussions, O'Connor's majestic goal-kick paled into insignificance compared with the focus on Geyer's tactics. Threats of boycotts, character attacks and calls for send-offs dominated commentary, taking the focus away from another Origin spectacle that set up a thrilling finale to the series.

↓ Mark Geyer, here with Ben Elias, was widely criticised for his roughhouse tactics. It was later revealed Geyer had been instructed by NSWRL management to get stuck into the Maroons.

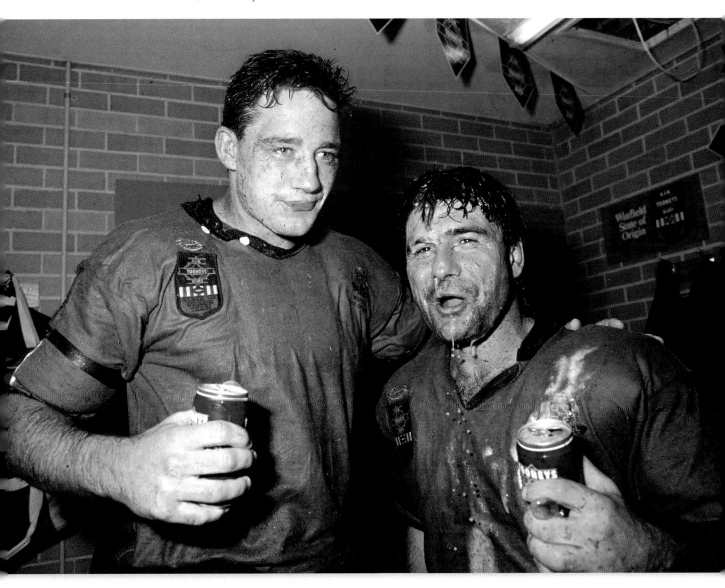

The Teams

NSW was without Geyer, who was suspended, and the injured Daley, Ettingshausen and Roberts. Lyons was dropped, and McGaw, Fittler and Alexander were recalled. Craig Salvatori and David Fairleigh were debutants. The 19-year-old Fittler opposed Lewis as NSW made some positional changes.

Queensland made just one change on the bench, with Lindner replacing Allen. When coach Lowe was hospitalised, Lewis took on the coaching role until Lowe returned two days before the game.

↓ Wally Lewis retired from State of Origin on a high. The crowd chanted 'Wally, Wally, Wally' and sang 'For he's a jolly good fellow' as he made a victory lap.

ARL chief Ken Arthurson warned that players found guilty of rough play risked lengthy suspension and missing test selection.

The Game

NSW enjoyed early territorial advantage. Fittler grubber-kicked to the right corner where Johns beat Hancock to pounce for a try. O'Connor sliced the conversion attempt. Queensland ventured downfield after NSW chasers were caught offside following Stuart's clearing kick. The ball moved right where Meninga drew McGaw and Fittler and slipped a clever pass to Hauff, who raced ahead before his deft inside step left Alexander clutching at thin air. Hauff beat Wishart to the tryline but Meninga hooked the conversion attempt from a handy position.

O'Connor was dazed after feeling the brute force of Meninga's front-on tackle, then McGaw was injured by Gee's swinging arm. Gee was penalised, and O'Connor's 47-metre goal-kick fell short. Queensland lost momentum until Bella made a powerful burst in the 17th minute. After exchanges of possession, Langer innocuously chip-kicked over the NSW defence from inside Queensland's half. Stuart tried to nudge the loose ball to Johns but it bounced off his knee. Hancock fielded the loose ball and sprinted 25 metres to score. Another sliced goal-kick left Queensland with a four-point lead. Before half-time, Wishart butchered an intercept with a try beckoning and Fittler fumbled just one metre from the tryline. Carne dived over the line as the Maroons sought to capitalise but he astonishingly had the ball jolted loose by Mackay's tackle.

NSW lost McGaw to a rib injury, after half-time. The Blues had an attacking chance in the 55th minute after Coyne fumbled Alexander's chip-kick. Creating an overlap as they spread the ball right, Alexander, Stuart, Izzard and Salvatori handled before O'Connor scampered across in the corner. Replays showed Salvatori's pass was borderline; the Maroons insisted it was forward and a dissenting Bella was dismissed for ten minutes by Harrigan. O'Connor's badly sliced kick left the scores level.

After the restart, Stuart's kick was touched in flight by Lindner's attempted chargedown. Fairleigh beat Lewis to catch the ball near halfway and sent Hasler racing towards the tryline. Hasler was brought down from behind by Hancock, but momentum took the ball-carrier across the line. NSW had vitally scored with Queensland a player short, but O'Connor sliced another hard goal-kick.

Players & Statistics

QLD Paul Hauff, Michael Hancock, Peter Jackson, Mal Meninga, Willie Carne, Wally Lewis (c), Allan Langer, Gary Larson, Mike McLean, Andrew Gee, Steve Jackson, Steve Walters, Martin Bella. **RESERVES** Dale Shearer, Gary Coyne, Bob Lindner, Kevin Walters (not used). **COACH** Graham Lowe

NSW Greg Alexander, Chris Johns, Mark McGaw, Michael O'Connor, Rod Wishart, Brad Fittler, Ricky Stuart, Brad Mackay, Bradley Clyde, John Cartwright, David Gillespie, Ben Elias (c), Steve Roach. **RESERVES** Des Hasler, Brad Izzard, Craig Salvatori, David Fairleigh. **COACH** Tim Sheens

Result Queensland 14 (Hauff, Hancock, Shearer tries; Meninga goal) beat NSW 12 (Johns, O'Connor, Hasler tries)

Referee Bill Harrigan (NSW)

Crowd 33 226

Man of the Match Martin Bella (Queensland)

↑ New Zealander Graham Lowe (left) guided the Maroons to a series victory in his maiden year as an Origin coach, after controversy over his appointment. Wally Lewis (right) was all smiles after a successful farewell, which was prompted the previous day when he was rocked to learn that his daughter was profoundly deaf.

The game see-sawed. Hancock helped thwart NSW with a pummelling tackle on the hapless O'Connor. Half-breaks by Carne and Meninga led the Maroons back on the attack, before Fittler conceded a costly penalty for collaring Langer after he kicked. In the attacking zone, Steve Walters, Peter Jackson, Langer, Hauff and Meninga kept the ball alive before Langer swung it left to Shearer. From a standing start, Shearer drifted and dummied through to cross the line and level the scores again. From a wide angle, Meninga landed the first goal all night.

With Queensland clinging to a slender 14–12 lead, the ground announcer broke the news that the crowd's favourite son was making his last Origin appearance. A significant chapter in Origin football was just 11 minutes from the end. The parochial crowd cheered Lewis on, before opportunities flowed both ways in a hectic finale.

Queensland was on the front foot after a Blues knock-on. Then an offside call against the Maroons gave NSW a chance, before Stuart kicked out on the full. After another mistake from Stuart, Meninga hooked a penalty kick from a similar position to his successful goal-kick. After NSW got the ball back with three minutes left, Gee crucially fumbled a loose ball to enable the Blues to head downfield. They spread it left but Wishart fumbled. Queensland needed to secure the ball for just one minute but Lindner coughed it up with 30 seconds left. Finally, Elias's pass went astray and was fielded by a Maroon. The Queenslanders had survived and sent the King into retirement a winner.

The Verdict

For the third time in the series, only two points separated the teams. Inaccurate goal kicking was one of many decisive factors. All three games could have gone either way and all the best features of Origin were on display—ferocious defence, some fortuitous bounces, attacking flair, passion for the jersey and many close calls. The Blues appeared unsporting after game three as they exited the field before the trophy presentation began. They were unhappy with referee Harrigan's performance.

But it was a night to remember. Lewis had a triumphant farewell from Origin football and he received a sustained ovation from the crowd.

1992

The New King's Reign Begins

The 1992 series promised a changing of the guard with the end of the Wally Lewis era. Graham Lowe remained as Queensland's coach and the new captain was Mal Meninga, the only surviving member from the competition's beginning.

NSW axed Tim Sheens as coach. He had lost favour with the NSWRL hierarchy because of his team's walkout before the on-field presentations at the end of the 1991 series. Phil Gould took over as coach. His impressive coaching background included premierships with Canterbury (1988) and Penrith (1991). Gould was the youngest coach of a premiership-winning side when he guided Canterbury to the 1988 title, as a 30-year-old in his maiden year of first-grade coaching. Ben Elias was stripped of the NSW captaincy but held his place in the team under new captain Laurie Daley.

For the first time, the two Origin captains came from the same club team. The 22-year-old Daley was NSW's youngest captain. Meninga, his club captain, was 31.

← Blood, guts and glory: Ben Elias, who had lost the NSW captaincy, was a bloodied mess after copping a nasty head gash in game one, but he soldiered on to help NSW to victory.

The Teams

Queensland's selectors retained many players from the 1991 series. Shearer was named at fullback as Hauff and Belcher were injured. Having been a reserve seven times, Kevin Walters stepped into the five-eighth role vacated by Lewis. With Gee injured, Gillmeister returned.

The Blues fielded four newcomers: Paul Harragon, Paul McGregor, Graham Mackay and Robbie McCormack. Some players changed positions, including Fittler (now at centre) and Daley (in the contentious five-eighth spot). Lazarus was named at prop after a strong display in Country's 17–10 win over City. Alexander, Johns, Roach and McGaw were sidelined with injuries, and O'Connor's State of Origin career was over in his final year of football. NSW was set back when Stuart pulled out injured. Illawarra teenager John Simon was named as the new halfback.

The Game

Lazarus was penalised in the first tackle, then Cartwright and Gillmeister were fortunate to escape punishment for high shots. Shearer and Gillmeister were on the receiving end of heavy tackles before Steve Jackson was concussed and exited the game. Referee Manson finally awarded a penalty for rough play when Sironen floored Larson with a high tackle, then used his elbow to niggle the ball-carrier.

Graham Mackay made the first line-break of the game after a clever pass from Fittler. The Blues had the early momentum, and a penalty against Hancock in the seventh minute enabled them to enter Queensland's quarter. On the left, Elias played a run-around movement with Cartwright before feeding Clyde, who drifted and sliced through to dive over in the corner. Wishart converted to give NSW a 6–0 lead, but the Blues soon faltered. They failed to get a last-tackle kick away, then were caught offside.

Meninga hooked a penalty kick from wide to the right of the posts, then Peter Jackson nailed McGregor behind the tryline. In the repeat set, good lead-up work from Meninga sent Lindner crashing over in the right corner, but the try was disallowed as Lindner's foot touched the sideline before he grounded the ball.

In the 17th minute, Clyde suffered match-ending bone and ligament damage while making a tackle. After Queensland attacked in the 21st minute, Shearer's bomb bounced wickedly and Elias was trapped in-goal. In the next set, Meninga fired a long pass left to Allen, who offloaded to Langer. He scurried straight through and touched down beside the right post in a tackle. Meninga's easy conversion levelled the scores.

Larson, who suffered concussion and bleeding from a high hit by Harragon, left the field on a stretcher. Referee Manson was lenient again, ruling a scrum to NSW for Larson's knock-on rather than penalising Harragon. The Blues had a couple of attacking chances but were kept out by Queensland's strong, scrambling defence. As half-time loomed, both sides created chances but did not

↓ Andrew Ettingshausen (with ball) played at fullback for NSW in the 1992 series, and winger Graham Mackay (left) was in his first Origin game.

score. The Maroons had repeat sets after forcing a goal-line drop-out; McGregor made a threatening break but kicked to no avail; Ettingshausen threw a careless pass which Kevin Walters toed towards the tryline but Daley saved the Blues.

The ferocity continued after the break. Daley decked Gillmeister with a savage front-on tackle before Elias was swamped near the tryline. Coyne was penalised for tackling in back-play, and McCormack replaced Elias, who was bleeding from a cut. After Wishart's wide-angled penalty kick hit the right post, Daley collided heavily with Peter Jackson's hip and was taken off with concussion.

A bandaged Elias returned and the Blues threatened the error-prone Maroons. Simon attempted a field goal but Gary Coyne smothered it. A crucial incident occurred soon afterwards. From marker, Elias raced to dummy-half Shearer and forced a knock-on, which was exacerbated when an offside Steve Walters caught the ball. It provided a straightforward goal-kick for Wishart to take NSW to an 8–6 lead.

Meninga threw a bad pass that Lindner fumbled before Cartwright surrendered possession early in the following tackle count. The Maroons spread the ball left in their quarter but Hancock ran too close to

the sideline and was driven out by Wishart. Simon soccer-kicked through five tackles later, and Shearer vitally fumbled again. In the 10-metre zone on the next tackle, Elias threw a well-timed pass to from Salvatori, who surged forward and crashed over beside the left post while being tackled. Wishart's conversion gave NSW the breathing space of an eight-point lead with 15 minutes left.

The Maroons threatened when Peter Jackson sent Meninga through a gap but the pass was forward. The visitors continued to attack after an accidental offside penalty against NSW, but the Blues held on superbly before Gary Coyne knocked on. In a scrappy final few minutes, Queensland was desperate but still mistake-ridden while NSW defended strongly to ensure the Maroons did not break through.

The Verdict

In a famous on-field scene, Elias's mother attended to her son, whose face was a bloodied mess. Man-of-the-match Elias was full of praise for his team-mates after they overcame the losses of Clyde and Daley. The match's brutality was a major talking point in post-match discussions. Referee Manson's skinny 5 metres and leniency with high tackles attracted criticism. Long-term league reporter Alan Clarkson described the match as 'one of the most potentially lethal games' since Origin began.

↑ Bradley Clyde scores the first try of the 1992 Origin series. He had to call the game to a than ten minutes later after suffering bone and ligament damage.

Players & Statistics

NSW Andrew Ettingshausen, Rod Wishart, Paul McGregor, Brad Fittler, Graham Mackay, Laurie Daley (c), John Simon, Bradley Clyde, John Cartwright, Paul Sironen, Paul Harragon, Ben Elias, Glenn Lazarus. **RESERVES** Robbie McCormack, Craig Salvatori, Brad Mackay, David Gillespie. **COACH** Phil Gould

QLD Dale Shearer, Michael Hancock, Peter Jackson, Mal Meninga (c), Willie Carne, Kevin Walters, Allan Langer, Gary Larson, Bob Lindner, Trevor Gillmeister, Steve Jackson, Steve Walters, Martin Bella. **RESERVES** Mark Coyne, Gary Coyne, Steve Renouf, Gavin Allen. **COACH** Graham Lowe

Result NSW 14 (Clyde, Salvatori tries; Wishart 3 goals) beat Queensland 6 (Langer try; Meninga goal)

Referee David Manson (Queensland)

Crowd 40 039

Man of the Match Ben Elias (NSW)

The Teams

With Clyde and Daley recovering from injury, NSW made two changes: a fit Stuart replaced Simon and debutant Steve Carter replaced McCormack on the bench. The Maroons lost Carne to injury, and Steve Jackson, Gary Coyne and Renouf were omitted. McLean was recalled, and first caps were given to Adrian Brunker, Billy Moore and Darren Smith. Kevin Walters was relegated to the bench, with Peter Jackson moving to five-eighth as Mark Coyne was promoted to centre.

Before the game, Queensland premier Wayne Goss unveiled a statue of Wally Lewis outside Lang Park.

The Game

The game was played in light rain. Shearer kicked early in the first tackle count, and Queensland forced the Blues into error and then to drop-kick from the uprights. After Langer's grubber bounced off Clyde in the repeat set, Langer passed right to Shearer, who drew two Blues to create an overlap. Brunker sent the unmarked Meninga across in the corner but referee Harrigan ruled Brunker's pass forward. Video replays did not support the ruling, and Harrigan warned Jackson and Bella for abusing the decision.

Jackson hit Sironen with a high tackle moments later and Bella engaged in some push-and-shove with Clyde as a brawl broke out. NSW received the penalty, then quickly received two more for offside infringements by the Maroons. Jackson and Bella dissented again and were sin-binned. Wishart landed the penalty goal on offer, 10 metres from the uprights.

↑ Steve Carter made his Origin debut off the bench during the game.

NSW led 2–0 and had 13 players against 11 for the following ten minutes. But the Blues did not throw the ball wide where Queensland's defence may have been caught short. After finally receiving a penalty when NSW was offside, the Maroons enjoyed a glut of possession. A restarted tackle count put them deep in attack before Langer's grubber forced a goal-line drop-out. The sin-binned players returned and Ettingshausen fumbled a kick from Shearer. Near the posts a few tackles later, Steve Walters turned the ball left to Langer and Meninga,

Players & Statistics

QLD Dale Shearer, Michael Hancock, Mark Coyne, Mal Meninga (c), Adrian Brunker, Peter Jackson, Allan Langer, Billy Moore, Bob Lindner, Gary Larson, Gavin Allen, Steve Walters, Martin Bella. **RESERVES** Kevin Walters, Trevor Gillmeister, Darren Smith, Mike McLean. **COACH** Graham Lowe

NSW Andrew Ettingshausen, Rod Wishart, Paul McGregor, Brad Fittler, Graham Mackay, Laurie Daley (c), Ricky Stuart, Bradley Clyde, John Cartwright, Paul Sironen, Paul Harragon, Ben Elias, Glenn Lazarus. **RESERVES** Craig Salvatori, Brad Mackay, David Gillespie, Steve Carter. **COACH** Phil Gould

Result Queensland 5 (Moore try; Langer field goal) beat NSW 4 (Wishart 2 goals)

Referee Bill Harrigan (NSW)

Crowd 31 500

Man of the Match Bob Lindner (Queensland)

who veered left as the defence held off him and fed Coyne. He fell as he was tackled but shovelled the ball back to Moore, who plunged over to score. Meninga's conversion sliced wide, but Queensland's 4–2 lead was psychologically significant.

Queensland's plan to play the game in NSW's half was evident when Shearer kicked downfield from the restart, before repeating the tactic after fielding Stuart's clearing kick soon afterwards. After handling errors each way, Daley's well-placed kick to the left corner lingered near the sideline in-goal, forcing Shearer to take it dead. After the drop-out, Harrigan controversially penalised Langer after he tackled Elias, who held onto Langer and forced him to hover in the tackle. Wishart levelled the scores.

The Blues were set back early in the second half when the injured Graham Mackay was unable to continue. Stuart, Daley and Shearer appeared more interested in a prolonged kicking duel, with the NSW duo gaining greater distance before Shearer finally ran with the ball.

When Larson smothered Stuart's clearing kick in the 57th minute, the ball bounced close to NSW's tryline, forcing a goal-line drop-out. Fittler conceded a penalty in the next set when he punched the ball out of Hancock's grasp after the tackle had been completed. From 28 metres out and just to the right of the posts, Meninga badly sliced a penalty kick. Neither side appeared to gain control.

Meninga made a dangerous burst to create a try-scoring opportunity, only for Stuart to swamp him in a great tackle and force a knock-on. Ten minutes from full-time, Jackson threw a poor pass which Coyne fumbled. Four tackles later, the Blues set up for a field goal and Elias spun the ball back to Stuart but the halfback's attempt hooked just wide. The same scenario occurred a few moments later after NSW forced a mistake, but this time Stuart's attempt pushed to the right.

Harragon committed a crucial knock-on in his half in the 76th minute, before Meninga riskily kicked from the ensuing scrum and effectively wasted possession. Coyne knocked-on in Queensland's next set, then Fittler fumbled in his half one tackle later as he crucially didn't secure the ball when pulled to ground. The Maroons forged downfield in the final two minutes, and were 15 metres out and just left of the posts on tackle four. Steve Walters passed right to Langer and, with no defenders moving up quickly, Langer kicked a one-pointer to break the deadlock. NSW tried a short kick-off with less than a minute left but Meninga retrieved the ball and the Maroons were safe.

The Verdict

The result could just as easily been a draw or a win to NSW. The Maroons admirably overcame adversity, having had a fair try disallowed and being down

two players for ten minutes. It was odd NSW did not appear to try to exploit the shortened defensive cordon during that time. Langer earned most attention for his match-winning field goal, and he reckoned his previous field goal occurred when he was a youngster in his backyard.

← North Sydney and Queensland forwards Billy Moore and Gary Larson are in buoyant spirits after game two. Moore scored the only try of the match in his Origin debut.

↓ Queensland coach Graham Lowe is delighted when the Maroons levelled the series with a thrilling 5–4 win.

→ Despite a disappointing performance in game one, Queensland skipper Mal Meninga proved dangerous in games two and three. But it wasn't enough for the Maroons to win the series.

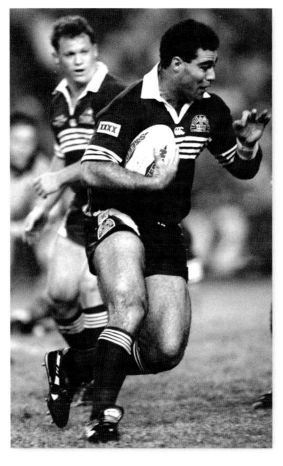

charged but was halted by three defenders. Queensland forced a repeat set but then Steve Walters fumbled. Allen flattened Harragon with a thundering shoulder-charge, and the groggy NSW prop was assisted from the field. Ettingshausen produced a strong tackle when he drove Brunker back several metres.

Queensland won a scrum against the feed but an ensuing knock-on by Langer wasted another scoring opportunity. A few minutes later, an offside penalty against Mark Coyne led NSW downfield. In front of the uprights, Elias looked right but turned the ball to Stuart on the other side. As Stuart drifted left and threw dummies to decoy runners Daley and McGregor, a huge gap opened, allowing Stuart through to score. Wishart's goal-kick swung just outside the right post. Steve Walters escaped penalty for almost spear-tackling Elias shortly after the restart.

Defence continued to dominate, and NSW applied pressure after Brunker spilled a poor pass from Shearer. But Queensland held on despite a poor goal-line drop-out from Shearer. At the other end, Ettingshausen fielded Langer's grubber in NSW's in-goal area and nearly stepped on the dead-ball line, but ET managed to enter the field of play. The Maroons released the pressure further as they were penalised for pushing McGregor behind the tryline. But they raided again after Hancock broke away and linked with Brunker. Elias and Cartwright were penalised for holding Langer down, and Meninga reduced NSW's lead to 4–2 with a 20-metre goal.

↓ After building a strong record as a club coach before his 35th birthday, Phil Gould earned another achievement as he guided NSW to supremacy in his first series as Origin coach.

The Teams

NSW replaced injured duo Graham Mackay and Carter with the recalled Johns and newcomer Tim Brasher.

Queensland made one change on the bench, with Gillmeister omitted in favour of Steve Jackson. But the Maroons endured a major setback on match day when an ill Lindner withdrew. Gary Coyne was subsequently recalled.

The Game

Shearer fielded the ball from the kick-off and kicked from near his tryline before following through and pouncing on Johns. An early penalty to the Blues gave them an attacking chance, but Ettingshausen fumbled Stuart's pass to concede an offside penalty. After Ettingshausen spilled a grubber from Langer, the Blues were caught offside from the ensuing scrum near their posts. Peter Jackson took a quick tap and fed Meninga, who

Harragon returned to the field, and both teams showed wayward ball control. In the shadows of half-time, Langer played the ball forward 10 metres from the tryline and darted to the left where he saw a gap. He sent the ball to the unmarked Mark Coyne, but Johns reached to knock down the pass to save a certain try. NSW still had to defend desperately as Queensland had a scrum feed, but Peter Jackson threw a stray pass late in the tackle count.

An injured Wishart was unable to resume after the break. Two minutes in, a penalty against Elias enabled Meninga to level the scores with a simple goal. With the game and series in the balance, the Maroons dominated territory and gathered momentum, but NSW's defence was up to the task. Smith made a break before Johns was penalised for slowing a play-the-ball, then Queensland was punished for an obstruction and Shearer suffered a leg injury.

The game turned in the 54th minute. Following a play-the-ball near the 40-metre line, Daley kicked through and McGregor regained the ball. As defenders closed in, McGregor passed inside to Daley. He drew Hancock and fed Ettingshausen, who scored in a tackle. Brasher's goal attempt from the right of the posts hooked just wide. The Blues led 8–4.

After the restart, Daley milked a penalty by running into a defender, who was returning onside. NSW received further possession when Hancock dropped Elias's high punt. A couple of tackles later, Cartwright veered left from dummy-half, burrowed low and powered over to score in Bella's and Darren Smith's tackles. Smith claimed Cartwright was held up but the try was awarded. Brasher's goal-kick was on target this time, and NSW suddenly led 14–4.

Brasher landed a 35-metre penalty goal after Langer was penalised for running a shepherd behind Kevin Walters. NSW was offside with 13 minutes to go but the Maroons failed to profit. From Peter Jackson's chip-kick a few minutes later, Mark Coyne recovered the loose ball and broke away down the left wing. He

reached for the corner but was denied when Brasher dragged his legs over the sideline.

With eight minutes left, Larson made a break but Ettingshausen intercepted near the NSW quarter-line. After a penalty against Harragon, another Queensland attacking raid went begging through a poor pass. Brasher showed courage and experience beyond his years when he tackled a surging Meninga within the final two minutes. The Blues reclaimed the Origin shield, and NSW had won a third and deciding match for the first time in Origin football.

The Verdict

The Blues deserved their win after taking chances when it counted. They did remarkably well to keep Queensland tryless, considering the attacking opportunities the Maroons had. The Blues had restricted Queensland to two tries in the series and were well served by Gould's coaching and Daley's captaincy. Daley had matched Wally Lewis's achievements of a decade earlier: a five-eighth captaining a team to an Origin series victory at the age of 22.

↓ Laurie Daley and John Cartwright ensure that a Queensland ball-carrier is thwarted.

1993

Emperor's Coaching Crusade Eclipsed by King Lozza

Graham Lowe pulled the pin as Queensland coach after his health worsened, marking the return of Wally Lewis to Origin football, albeit as a coach. He had become the head coach of Gold Coast after retiring as a player at the end of 1992, and his club was losing constantly. Thus he had the challenge of coaching a failing club and coaching an Origin team virtually full of players he had played with in Origin football. Lewis had utilised excellent skills and vision as a player, but these things couldn't necessarily be coached.

Phil Gould opted to stay on as NSW coach following talks with NSWRL officials, even though he had indicated after the 1992 Origin series that he would step down from the role.

Rugby league underwent a major rule change in 1993: players had to stand back 10 metres in defence rather than 5 metres as previously.

← Laurie Daley became the first skipper to lead the Blues to successive series wins. The Sydney-based coach Warren Ryan had predicted in 1990 that Daley would become the new king of Origin football. There was nothing to discredit the claim in the first two series after Wally Lewis's retirement, including when Lewis returned as a coach in 1993.

↑ Andrew Ettingshausen played on the wing in the first two games of 1993, and then in the centre after Tim Brasher took over the fullback role.

Players & Statistics

NSW Tim Brasher, Rod Wishart, Brad Fittler, Paul McGregor, Andrew Ettingshausen, Laurie Daley (c), Ricky Stuart, Brad Mackay, Paul Harragon, Paul Sironen, Ian Roberts, Ben Elias, Glenn Lazarus. **RESERVES** David Fairleigh, Craig Salvatori, Brett Mullins (not used), Jason Taylor (not used). **COACH** Phil Gould

QLD Gary Belcher, Michael Hancock, Mal Meninga (c), Steve Renouf, Willie Carne, Kevin Walters, Allan Langer, Billy Moore, Gary Larson, Bob Lindner, Martin Bella, Steve Walters, Steve Jackson. **RESERVES** Mark Coyne, Dale Shearer, Mark Hohn, Andrew Gee. **COACH** Wally Lewis

Result NSW 14 (Wishart, Stuart tries; Wishart 3 goals) beat Queensland 10 (Lindner, Carne tries; Meninga goal)

Referee Greg McCallum (NSW)

Crowd 33 000

Man of the Match Ricky Stuart (NSW)

was recalled, and Harragon was chosen in the second-row as an injured Clyde was unavailable. The only newcomers were reserves Jason Taylor and Brett Mullins. Mullins was called up after injured centre Chris Johns withdrew, and McGregor was promoted from the bench to the starting team.

The Game

In an unsavoury start to the series, Channel Nine microphones picked up Meninga barking a string of expletives as he gave his team a pep talk.

There were a couple of poor kicks early on and plenty of heavy hits, with Moore dazed after a high tackle in the seventh minute. NSW gained territorial advantage after handling errors by Queensland. From a play-the-ball 10 metres out, Elias passed left to Stuart and Daley, who drifted, threw a dummy on the inside and drew the defence before sending Brasher through. Brasher drifted left and fed Wishart, who crossed in the corner and then converted.

The Maroons squandered possession in their half again, then Steve Walters was penalised for dislodging the ball from Harragon in the ruck. Wishart landed a 30-metre penalty goal to make the score 8–0. Scrappy play by both sides followed. Langer took a quick tap from a penalty instead of accepting a gift penalty goal, a move that backfired when Steve Walters pushed a risky pass. But after an offside penalty, Meninga landed a 15-metre goal to bridge the gap to 8–2.

The game quickly swung back NSW's way after Larson fumbled. Five tackles later, Stuart's bomb struck a leaping Belcher on the shoulder as

The Teams

Queensland selected a familiar team, with the recall of fullback Belcher the most notable change. The only newcomer was reserve forward Mark Hohn. Gillmeister was again a controversial omission.

NSW also had a familiar team with an obvious change at fullback, where Brasher was picked ahead of Ettingshausen, who moved to the wing. Roberts

Ettingshausen and Brasher contested with him. Stuart caught the rebound and touched down, and NSW held a handy 12–2 lead. Queensland suffered another major blow just before half-time when Renouf broke his ankle after falling in a tackle.

Soon after play resumed, Sironen suffered match-ending injuries. NSW was kept in its own half, and then Stuart fumbled a Meninga grubber-kick. NSW's defence scrambled well before Langer grubber-kicked through to the corner, where Lindner beat Wishart and Brasher to the ball. Queensland was back in the contest, trailing by six points after Meninga hooked the goal-kick.

A decisive passage of play began soon afterwards, as Queensland forced three consecutive goal-line drop-outs with last-tackle grubber-kicks that Brasher had to take out behind his tryline. But NSW's defence held solid under enormous pressure for 19 consecutive tackles as Queensland attacked persistently until Steve Walters had the ball jolted loose by Elias. In Queensland's next set, Langer sent Kevin Walters away, and Langer backed up but fumbled 5 metres from the tryline in desperate cover defence. Steve Walters conceded another penalty,

before Hancock gave away a potentially match-surrendering penalty after Queensland regained the ball. Elias niggled Hancock in a tackle and, as he rose to his feet, Hancock pushed Elias down before playing the ball. Just 15 metres from Queensland's posts, the penalty was a gift two points for Wishart. Twenty minutes remained but NSW had stretched its lead to eight points and halted Queensland's momentum.

After Steve Walters played the ball to brother Kevin 25 metres from NSW's tryline on tackle five, Langer took the first pass on the right but, instead of kicking, stepped right. He spread the ball to Meninga, who drew the defence and lofted a pass that a jumping Wishart touched. Carne caught the ball and stepped inside Fittler before showing impressive strength as he surged to score with two Blues tackling him. NSW led 14–10 as Meninga hooked another wide-angled goal-kick.

Queensland was well in contention with about ten minutes remaining, and Gee made a thundering run from the kick-off. Meninga made a break a few tackles later but kicked to no avail. Lazarus committed a vital knock-on before Kevin Walters fumbled as he was swamped. In Queensland's next set, Elias knocked down Langer's pass to restart the tackle count, and Steve Walters made a half-break before being tackled 5 metres from the uprights. Jackson barged for the tryline but was held up. However, Roberts was penalised for obstructing Langer in backplay during Steve Walters's break. The Maroons pushed for a try instead of an easy penalty goal, and attacked vigorously but were met by strong defence. Jackson neared the tryline again but his grubber-kick dribbled past the dead-ball line. The Blues completed their next two tackle counts and kicked to push the Maroons further downfield, and NSW hung on to win. NSW's triumph was its first at Lang Park since game one of 1987.

↑ Paul Harragon charges into the Queensland defence.

The Verdict

The Blues deserved credit for keeping their tryline intact under heavy pressure during the second half. According to Gould, a major turning point was when Queensland had possession for 19 successive tackles without scoring. Strong defence proved vital, as did goal-kicking. Lewis conceded that his team played nowhere near its ability in the first half.

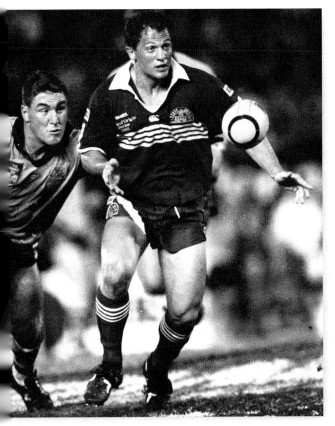

← Steve Walters made a few costly errors for the Maroons as their eight-match winning streak at Lang Park came to an end.

→ Having been man of the match in the previous two Origin games, Ricky Stuart again played a key role for NSW, particularly with his kicking game.

↓ NSW prop Ian Roberts was in a series-winning team for the second time, after he had come back from injury problems.

The Teams

Queensland's sacking of Belcher ended his Origin career and injuries ruled out Renouf, Hancock and Gee. Brunker and Gillmeister were recalled, Coyne, Hohn and Shearer moved to the starting line-up, and Darren Smith and debutant Julian O'Neill were reserves.

McCormack and Gillespie returned for NSW in place of Elias (suspended) and Salvatori (injured). Mullins was omitted, and Jason Croker was the new reserve after injury ruled out Chris Johns and Terry Hill.

The Game

Stuart repeatedly gained 55 to 65 metres with his clearing kicks in the first half. After Queensland

received the first two penalties, Langer kicked to the right where Carne jumped for the ball and crashed over the line but was penalised. Replays showed that referee Ward's decision was a shocker as Carne was a metre onside. Soon after, Larson suffered a match-ending ankle injury as he collided with Brasher.

Brunker sliced a penalty kick from the left of the posts after Harragon was offside in the 24th minute. Early on, Harragon pummelled Gillmeister, who responded with a tackle that made Harragon airborne and fumble. The Maroons forced a goal-line drop-out, before a clearly forward pass from Moore to Hohn was overlooked as Queensland sent the ball left. Meninga was almost on the tryline when he confronted Ettingshausen and fed the unmarked Brunker. But Brunker fumbled the knee-high pass while the empty-handed Meninga crossed the tryline in ET's tackle. Brunker subsequently sliced another penalty goal-kick.

Five tackles later, Meninga moved right and fed Shearer, who only had to dive to score but instead stepped inside two defenders. He whirled over the tryline untouched but unbelievably the ball rolled loose as another certain try was bombed. NSW was lucky there was no score after the Maroons crossed the tryline three times and missed two goal-kicks.

Queensland had another chance two minutes before half-time, with a scrum-feed 25 metres from the tryline. Moving right, Langer, Kevin Walters and Shearer handled before Coyne, flung an overhead pass inside to Meninga. He charged to finally score Queensland's first try. Brunker landed a brilliant conversion. However, Queensland's 6–0 lead did not faze the Blues.

Four minutes after half-time, Langer hooked an unexpected field-goal attempt. It was another costly miss, and then Moore conceded a penalty before Coyne produced a trysaving tackle on Brad Mackay. On the next tackle, Gillespie fired a long pass left to Daley, who stepped both ways and evaded Hohn before crashing through two defenders to score. Wishart hooked the goal-kick. Queensland led 6–4.

The game changed dramatically just four tackles later. Stuart's clearing kick was touched in flight by Moore before landing 5 metres beyond halfway. Fittler got a fortuitous bounce as he beat Carne in the jump for the ball before racing ahead and

Players & Statistics

NSW Tim Brasher, Rod Wishart, Brad Fittler, Paul McGregor, Andrew Ettingshausen, Laurie Daley (c), Ricky Stuart, Brad Mackay, Paul Harragon, Paul Sironen, Ian Roberts, Robbie McCormack, Glenn Lazarus. **RESERVES** David Fairleigh, David Gillespie, Jason Taylor, Jason Croker. **COACH** Phil Gould

QLD Dale Shearer, Willie Carne, Mal Meninga (c), Mark Coyne, Adrian Brunker, Kevin Walters, Allan Langer, Bob Lindner, Trevor Gillmeister, Gary Larson, Mark Hohn, Steve Walters, Martin Bella. **RESERVES** Julian O'Neill, Steve Jackson, Darren Smith, Billy Moore. **COACH** Wally Lewis

Result NSW 16 (Daley, B Mackay, Wishart tries; Wishart 2 goals) beat Queensland 12 (Meninga, K Walters tries; Brunker, Shearer goals)

Referee Eddie Ward (Queensland)

Crowd 41 895

Man of the Match Tim Brasher (NSW)

drawing Shearer to send Mackay running to the posts. NSW suddenly led 10–6.

Queensland made a couple of errors before both teams created half chances without finishing them. Coyne was sin-binned for a professional foul during a raid as Queensland's defence struggled to regroup. But the Maroons launched the next attack, with Smith breaking through before fumbling in Wishart's desperate tackle.

Daley sent McGregor breaking away a few moments later before Ettingshausen sprinted to the left and was caught by Shearer in the quarter. With the defence well behind, Ettingshausen quickly played the ball to Croker, who fed Wishart. He easily evaded Queensland's only defender to score near the posts and then convert. With about ten minutes left, NSW led 16–6 and looked secure.

Shearer regained possession from his short kick-off, then Queensland forced a goal-line drop-out before NSW was caught offside. In the 10-metre zone, the ball went left to Kevin Walters, who threw a dummy, stepped right and evaded Fairleigh before diving over the line in a tackle. Shearer converted, and NSW's lead was back to four points with five minutes remaining.

With an injured Carne leaving the field and time ticking away, the Maroons fumbled. Moore was held 11 metres from their posts with barely a minute remaining. When Queensland sent the ball right, NSW's defence closed in as Gillmeister sent a cut-out ball to Meninga, who quickly fed Lindner. He evaded Fittler and fed Meninga, who broke away

down the right side and entered NSW's 40-metre zone with Daley pursuing. Meninga slowed down and passed to Hohn, who was sandwiched just inside NSW's quarter. He attempted to unload to Meninga but lost the ball forward. Queensland's last chance was gone. Meninga later admitted he should have taken Daley on rather than pass the ball.

The Verdict

The Maroons came agonisingly close to snatching victory, but their failure to regularly capitalise cost them the series. They were understandably upset over Ward disallowing a fair try to Carne but they had ample chances to compensate.

↑ Bob Lindner gave his all for Queensland in his final Origin year, but the Maroons had lost the series before he had a successful finish in game three.

Players & Statistics

QLD Dale Shearer, Brett Dallas, Mal Meninga (c), Mark Coyne, Willie Carne, Julian O'Neill, Allan Langer, Bob Lindner, Trevor Gillmeister, Gary Larson, Mark Hohn, Steve Walters, Martin Bella. **RESERVES** Kevin Walters, Darren Smith, Steve Jackson, Billy Moore. **COACH** Wally Lewis

NSW Tim Brasher, Rod Wishart, Brad Fittler, Andrew Ettingshausen, Graham Mackay, Laurie Daley (c), Ricky Stuart, Brad Mackay, Paul Harragon, Paul Sironen, David Fairleigh, Ben Elias, Glenn Lazarus. **RESERVES** David Gillespie, Terry Hill, Scott Gourley, Jason Taylor. **COACH** Phil Gould

Result Queensland 24 (Carne 2, S Walters, Lindner tries; Meninga 2, O'Neill 2 goals) beat NSW 12 (Ettingshausen, Harragon tries; Wishart 2 goals)

Referee Greg McCallum (NSW)

Crowd 31 500

Man of the Match Dale Shearer (Queensland)

↑ Paul Sironen tries to fight his way through a swarm of Maroons. After being in and out of NSW sides from 1989 to 1991, Sironen established himself as a first-choice second-rower for the Blues.

→ For the second straight year, Laurie Daley enjoyed the spoils of an Origin series win as captain.

The Teams

Queensland's selectors demoted Kevin Walters to the bench and regular fullback O'Neill was promoted to pivot. Brunker was axed and replaced by Brett Dallas, who became Queensland's youngest Origin player at 18 years and 225 days.

The Blues were set back when McGregor and Roberts were forced out with injury, resulting in some positional changes as well as the recall of Graham Mackay. Croker was omitted from the bench, and Terry Hill and Scott Gourley were the new reserves.

The Game

In his Origin farewell, Lindner led the Maroons onto Lang Park. NSW conceded two penalties within the first five tackles, but Queensland again failed to capitalise on ample possession. There were some typically stinging tackles early on. When the Blues finally had possession after more than three minutes of play, they received a relieving penalty. After NSW forced a goal-line drop-out, Stuart's high punt bounced off a Queenslander. As the ball rolled towards the posts with Elias in pursuit, Dallas came from the right and unwisely kicked the ball across-field in-goal. Evading Coyne's outstretched hand, the ball ended up with Ettingshausen for an easy try. Wishart's conversion put NSW in front 6–0.

Queensland had a lucky break in its next set of tackles, as Lindner burst onto a clearly forward pass that referee McCallum didn't detect. On the last tackle, Langer's bomb was spilled by Brasher under pressure just inside the right post. Carne and Coyne were quick to pounce, and Carne was awarded the try. O'Neill's conversion levelled the scores.

Both teams made handling errors before rough play crept into the game. Meninga was penalised for a swinging arm that just missed Brasher, then Brad Mackay fumbled in Steve Walters's heavy tackle. Stuart was punished for a swinging arm on Bella, before a brawl erupted from a scrum on Queensland's quarter-line. Hookers Steve Walters and Elias engaged in a one-on-one punch-up, as did Harragon and Bella. McCallum sin-binned the four for ten minutes. The Maroons were awarded a penalty from the scuffle, and O'Neill's goal took Queensland to an 8–6 lead. Soon afterwards, Brad Mackay was penalised for throwing a punch at Carne.

Queensland received two more lucky calls in quick succession but nothing came of them. Ettingshausen made a break after a good pass from Stuart, then Ettingshausen's pass to Wishart found the sideline. With both sides back to full strength, play remained in Queensland's half after handling mistakes from O'Neill and Bella. A few tackles later, Stuart fired a cut-out pass right to Fittler, who threw a dummy to Meninga before stepping left to wrong-foot Gillmeister. Fittler slipped the ball to Harragon, who veered right and sliced through before reaching to score in a tackle. Ten seconds from half-time, an offside infringement by Queensland gave Wishart a penalty kick, but he hooked the straightforward attempt, leaving the score 12–8.

Kevin Walters came on at five-eighth for the Maroons after the break. NSW conceded two early penalties but again repelled Queensland's attack. After a high tackle from Gillmeister forced Brad Mackay from the field, the Maroons raced downfield, but Fittler was in place to intercept Carne's inside pass. NSW earned six more tackles when Shearer spilled Stuart's towering kick. In the repeat set, the Blues moved the ball right and Ettingshausen darted between Meninga and Dallas and headed for the corner. Ettingshausen reached for the tryline but Meninga grabbed him and dragged him into touch just short of the corner post. A few minutes later, Langer, Coyne and Shearer raided before Shearer was tackled 5 metres from the uprights. On the left, Kevin Walters drifted before passing to brother Steve, who straightened, stepped right and burrowed past two defenders to score. Meninga converted to give Queensland a two-point lead in a decisive turnaround after Ettingshausen's near-miss.

NSW squandered possession when Graham Mackay spilled Fittler's inside pass. Near NSW's quarter-line a few tackles later, Smith stepped both ways from dummy-half before unloading to Lindner. He ran ahead and was held by Stuart before powering into Brasher and reaching out to score in the tackle. Meninga's kick stretched the margin to eight points.

NSW's loss of direction was further evident in its next two sets with knock-ons inside its own half. After the second of these, Kevin Walters grubber-kicked through and Ettingshausen tried to escape the in-goal area. As he reached the tryline, the ball spilled in a tackle and Carne pounced for a try. Meninga sliced the conversion and Queensland led 24–12 with eight minutes left. There was no way back for NSW.

Smith and Sironen came to blows in the final two minutes, then Wishart intercepted a pass and raced more than 70 metres until Dallas brought him down.

The Verdict

Although the margin was 12 points, the game was as close as the previous two. A few controversial refereeing decisions favoured Queensland this time, and the Blues may well have won were it not for Meninga's try-saving tackle on Ettingshausen in the second half. When Steve Walters scored at the other end soon afterwards, the complexion of the game changed. Although NSW won the series, Queensland's win in game three provided a memorable farewell for Lindner, who jogged a lap of honour after full-time.

↑ Losing Queensland skipper Mal Meninga was Laurie Daley's club captain.

1994

Benny Gatecrashes Mal's Farewell Dream

The NSWRL decided to take Origin to Melbourne again, with the second game of the 1994 series scheduled to be played at the Melbourne Cricket Ground. As was the case in 1990, game one would be in Sydney, game two in Melbourne and game three in Brisbane. Lang Park was now officially called Suncorp Stadium. The venue's look was somewhat changed as the sponsor's name was emblazoned on the advertising boards of both grandstands.

A notable aspect of the 1994 Origin series was that Mal Meninga and Ben Elias were in their final series, before retiring from the sport at the end of the year. The final survivor from the inaugural Origin match in 1980, Meninga had a long list of achievements in rugby league. But the one thing he had not achieved was captaining Queensland to an Origin series win.

← Billy Moore is on the receiving end of a lifting tackle from Laurie Daley. Moore was in his third successive Origin series, but was still to taste a series win.

↑ Gary Larson, Chris Close and Andrew Gee enjoy Queensland's remarkable come-from-behind win in the last minute, following arguably the greatest try scored in Origin history. The ball went through ten sets of hands in a 60-metre movement. The Maroons went into a frenzy while the mood of the NSW players and crowd was one of disbelief. Television commentator Ray Warren's cry, 'That's not a try, that's a miracle!', became part of Origin legend.

The Teams

The NSW team remained similar to the Blues teams of the previous two series. Injury forced Clyde out again, Brad Mackay moved from the bench to lock, and David Barnhill was named for his Origin debut.

Queensland's team also looked familiar, although Shearer and Steve Jackson were ignored after injury spells. Meninga was the only non-Brisbane player in the backline, which included O'Neill at fullback. Reserve forward Darren Fritz was the only newcomer.

The Game

In the first set, Stuart spun the ball left to Daley, who sliced through and crossed halfway, but Carne intercepted his pass to Wishart. Meninga paid the price for stepping down the blindside from dummy-half, as he was tackled over the sideline. Bella was driven head first into the ground in a tackle facing

the Queensland tryline. Rising, perhaps disoriented, Bella still faced his tryline as he played the ball. He picked the ball up as he realised his error, but the damage was done and a scrum was awarded to NSW. Fortunately for Bella, NSW did not profit from his clanger. Queensland also failed to make the most of back-to-back penalties.

After an offside penalty to NSW in the 16th minute, Meninga was punished for shouldering Fittler off the ball. From Daley's quick play-the-ball near the posts three tackles later, dummy-half Harragon barged into three defenders and grounded the point of the ball on the line. Referee Harrigan awarded the try, but replays showed Daley should have been penalised for rolling the ball between his legs. Wishart converted to give NSW a 6–0 lead.

Stuart pushed an unexpected field-goal attempt to the right in the 25th minute. NSW had successive sets in possession but McGregor fumbled in Renouf's tackle near the tryline. Carne made a long break before Langer's grubber was trapped by Daley, then retrieved by Roberts, who was offside. Three tackles later, Steve Walters turned the ball right, where Langer, Kevin Walters, Renouf and Meninga combined to send O'Neill diving over in the corner. O'Neill's missed kick left NSW leading 6–4.

An offside penalty against NSW gave Queensland a chance to attack with half-time looming, but Gillmeister's flick pass went astray. The Maroons conceded successive penalties, although the second looked doubtful. NSW had another lucky break in Queensland's quarter when the referee failed to spot a knock-on by Harragon. With the siren imminent, Stuart grubber-kicked to the left where Brasher grounded the ball, only to be ruled offside.

Following the break, both teams showed sub-par cohesion in attack. Queensland forced a repeat set, and then threw several reverse passes, but NSW's defence was strong. A penalty against Stuart for an improper play-the-ball gave Queensland a chance to level the scores, 31 metres from the right upright,

Players & Statistics

QLD Julian O'Neill, Michael Hancock, Mal Meninga (c), Steve Renouf, Willie Carne, Kevin Walters, Allan Langer, Billy Moore, Gary Larson, Trevor Gillmeister, Martin Bella, Steve Walters, Andrew Gee. **RESERVES** Mark Coyne, Darren Smith, Mark Hohn, Darren Fritz. **COACH** Wally Lewis

NSW Tim Brasher, Graham Mackay, Brad Fittler, Paul McGregor, Rod Wishart, Laurie Daley (c), Ricky Stuart, Brad Mackay, Paul Harragon, Paul Sironen, Ian Roberts, Ben Elias, Glenn Lazarus. **RESERVES** Andrew Ettingshausen, Chris Johns, David Gillespie, David Barnhill. **COACH** Phil Gould

Result Queensland 16 (O'Neill, Carne, Coyne tries; Meninga 2 goals) beat NSW 12 (Harragon, B Mackay tries; Wishart, G Mackay goals)

Referee Bill Harrigan (NSW)

Crowd 41 859

Man of the Match Willie Carne (Queensland)

Hancock, who was driven back by Ettingshausen but fed Darren Smith, who drifted right. Drawing two Blues, Smith passed to Langer, who moved past the quarter line and flung the ball right as Brad Mackay brought him down from behind. Meninga accepted Langer's pass and drifted right to feed Coyne, who stepped inside and surged forward with Fittler wrapped around his waist. With the ball under his right arm, Coyne reached for the line and grounded the ball as Stuart and Elias arrived.

With 40 seconds left, Queensland had snatched an incredible victory. Meninga converted to make the score 16–12.

The Verdict

The Blues did not trail until the last minute, losing at the death to one of the truly great tries. NSW was the better team for most of the game but the Maroons deserved credit for producing the unthinkable when they looked gone. If ever there was an example of the unpredictability of Origin games, here was the proof.

↑ Paul McGregor shapes to pass while being tackled low down.

↓ Caught in a tackle with Paul Sironen approaching, Maroons lock Billy Moore looks right for support.

but O'Neill hooked his goal-kick. Queensland had repeat sets when Brasher and Lazarus knocked on consecutively while repelling attacking raids, but the Maroons fumbled their chances.

Steve Walters and O'Neill left the field injured. From the halfway line, Elias passed left to Stuart and Fittler, who put a grubber into the 30-metre zone where Daley raced to the ball. He beat Carne before drawing Coyne to send Brad Mackay in to score behind the posts. The Blues were well-placed as Graham Mackay's conversion gave them a 12–4 lead with 11 minutes left.

Queensland faltered in its next two sets before Carne caught a kick behind his tryline. The Maroons worked their way downfield with Langer making a darting run before being tackled 28 metres out. The ball went right to Kevin Walters, Carne, Walters again, Renouf, Meninga and Coyne, who broke down the wing. He threw an overhead pass inside, and Fritz touched it before Carne caught it and scored in Elias's last-gasp tackle. Meninga's conversion closed NSW's lead to two points with four minutes remaining.

Queensland's last chance came in the final two minutes as the Maroons had a scrum feed near their 30-metre line. After two tackles, Coyne played the ball 10 metres short of halfway. In a sweeping movement to the left, long passes were thrown from Meninga to Langer, Kevin Walters and Carne, who lobbed an overhead pass to Renouf as he was tackled. Renouf scurried past halfway before passing inside to

The Teams

The Maroons made just one change, dropping Bella and naming Gorden Tallis for the first time. When Renouf and Steve Walters withdrew injured, Kerrod Walters returned at hooker and Adrian Vowles was the new reserve as Coyne was promoted to centre.

The Blues omitted Graham Mackay, Barnhill and Gillespie, and Wishart was injured. Clyde was recalled, Brad Mackay reverted to the bench, and Brett Mullins was named on one wing and Ettingshausen moved to the other. Dean Pay and Ken Nagas were the new reserves. Injury forced Roberts out and allowed Barnhill to regain his spot. Pay was moved to second-row and Harragon to prop.

Nagus's eligibility was contentious. Born and bred in Bundaberg in Queensland, he played junior football there before moving to Kyogle in NSW at the age of 16, where he played under-18 football and a first-grade game. Although he admitted being a Queensland supporter, he played for Country against City, and thus became eligible for NSW.

The Game

A record crowd of 87 161, more than double that at any previous Origin game, packed the MCG. Queensland dominated field position early after Ettingshausen and Clyde made silly handling mistakes in NSW's half. The Blues defended well, with Mullins defusing a bomb before Meninga put in a poor grubber. After a further penalty each way, NSW's defence muscled up brilliantly in Queensland's half. Langer was forced to kick from inside his 10-metre zone, and Brasher and Mullins combined to enter the quarter on tackle one. Near the uprights on tackle three, Elias looked left but turned a reverse pass to Lazarus as Pay held marker Gee's jersey. Pay let go but Lazarus veered right and charged over the line in Gee's tackle. Although the Maroons claimed Gee was obstructed, Annesley awarded the try. Brasher converted, and NSW led 6–0 after ten minutes.

Sironen flattened Gillmeister with a thumping tackle before an Elias mistake restarted Queensland's tackle count. The Maroons went downfield and received successive penalties, the latter when Elias infringed in a play-the-ball. Just 12 metres from the left post, O'Neill's goal-kick crashed straight into the upright. The Maroons

↓ Kerrod Walters (centre) is involved in some push and shove in his first Origin appearance for four years.

let themselves down further as they conceded back-to-back offside penalties. NSW headed downfield where Mullins and Daley made breaks, with Meninga producing a try-saving tackle on Daley. NSW forced a repeat set of tackles and Kerrod Walters conceded a foolish penalty for raking the ball, allowing Brasher to kick a penalty goal for an 8–0 lead.

The Maroons continued to falter, but did well to withstand repeated attacks on their tryline as NSW forced consecutive goal-line drop-outs. A high tackle by McGregor gave Queensland a relieving penalty, but Larson put in an ineffective grubber. Meninga lost possession just before half-time, enabling Mullins to instantly counter-attack. He fed Harragon, who charged for the left corner, but Carne produced a superb cover tackle while O'Neill arrived to jolt the ball loose as a try looked certain.

Mackay and Hohn exchanged errors early in the second half. Then Moore charged down Stuart's clearing kick but Gillmeister fumbled the loose ball. Soon after, Gee niggled Harragon in a tackle, leading to a fight. Harragon could have been penalised but referee Annesley penalised Gee. NSW led 10–0 as Brasher landed the resultant penalty attempt.

Queensland had the chance to strike back after consecutive penalties but NSW's defence held firm. Annesley blew several further penalties. With about 20 minutes remaining, Ettingshausen fumbled a bomb from Langer to give the Maroons another six tackles. NSW's scrambling defence thwarted Queensland three times near the tryline in the one set.

Kerrod Walters gave away two penalties within

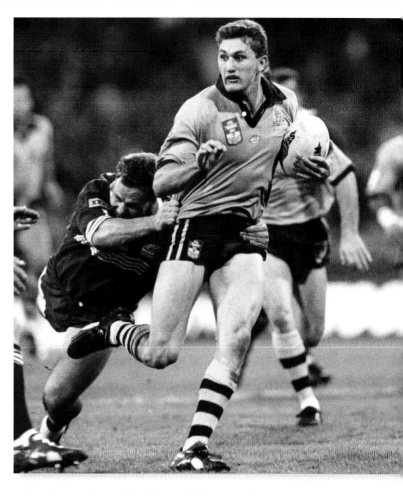

↑ Brett Mullins tries to break away from a tackle. Mullins was picked on the wing after having no game time in his only previous Origin match the year before.

a few minutes. Two tackles later and 14 metres from the posts, Elias looked left but again threw a reverse pass, this time to Stuart, who veered right, drew two defenders and slipped a pass inside to McGregor. He flashed through a yawning gap to score behind the posts. Brasher kicked into the upright from almost in front. The Blues led 14–0 with ten minutes left.

NSW errors enabled the Maroons to press the tryline, but they couldn't crack a wall of defence. The Maroons received a couple of penalties in the final minutes, including after a brawl broke out. Queensland's last scoring chance went begging as Smith dropped Langer's pass just 4 metres out.

The Verdict

The game might have panned out differently had O'Neill not missed a simple goal-kick in the first half. However, NSW's defence was magnificent all night, holding Queensland scoreless for the second time in Origin football. The Blues took their scoring chances while the Maroons squandered theirs.

Players & Statistics

NSW Tim Brasher, Andrew Ettingshausen, Brad Fittler, Paul McGregor, Brett Mullins, Laurie Daley (c), Ricky Stuart, Bradley Clyde, Dean Pay, Paul Sironen, Paul Harragon, Ben Elias, Glenn Lazarus. **RESERVES** Brad Mackay, David Barnhill, Ken Nagas, Chris Johns (not used). **COACH** Phil Gould

QLD Julian O'Neill, Michael Hancock, Mal Meninga (c), Mark Coyne, Willie Carne, Kevin Walters, Allan Langer, Billy Moore, Gary Larson, Trevor Gillmeister, Darren Fritz, Kerrod Walters, Andrew Gee. **RESERVES** Darren Smith, Mark Hohn, Gorden Tallis, Adrian Vowles. **COACH** Wally Lewis

Result NSW 14 (Lazarus, McGregor tries; Brasher 3 goals) beat Queensland 0

Referee Graham Annesley (NSW)

Crowd 87 161

Man of the Match Paul Harragon (NSW)

→ NSW captain Laurie Daley is chaired from the field after the game. For the third year in a row, Daley captained NSW to a series win at the expense of his club captain at Canberra, Queensland skipper Mal Meninga.

Players & Statistics

NSW Tim Brasher, Andrew Ettingshausen, Brad Fittler, Paul McGregor, Brett Mullins, Laurie Daley (c), Ricky Stuart, Bradley Clyde, Dean Pay, Paul Sironen, Paul Harragon, Ben Elias, Ian Roberts. **RESERVES** Ken Nagas, Chris Johns, Brad Mackay, David Barnhill. **COACH** Phil Gould

QLD Julian O'Neill, Michael Hancock, Mal Meninga (c), Steve Renouf, Willie Carne, Kevin Walters, Allan Langer, Jason Smith, Gary Larson, Billy Moore, Darren Fritz, Steve Walters, Mark Hohn. **RESERVES** Mark Coyne, Darren Smith, Andrew Gee, Gorden Tallis. **COACH** Wally Lewis

Result NSW 27 (Clyde, Daley, Mullins, Fittler tries; Brasher 4 goals; Elias 2, Fittler field goals) beat Queensland 12 (Gee, Renouf tries; O'Neill 2 goals)

Referee Bill Harrigan (NSW)

Crowd 40 665

Man of the Match Ben Elias (NSW)

The Teams

Queensland's selectors omitted Kerrod Walters, Gillmeister and Vowles, and recalled Renouf and Steve Walters. Jason Smith was the new lock, and some positional changes occurred. The Blues made one change: the injured Lazarus replaced by Roberts.

Would Meninga exit a winner on home soil or would the last laugh go to Elias, who was strongly disliked by Maroon fans?

↓ Ben Elias (middle) had a successful Origin farewell from a personal and team perspective, at the venue where fans loved to hate him. He is pictured with Balmain team-mates Tim Brasher and Paul Sironen.

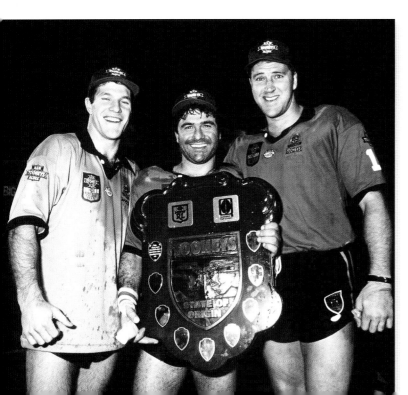

The Game

NSW had an attacking opportunity after a Steve Walters knock-on. Elias darted from dummy-half before Hancock was penalised for a tackle infringement. Brasher hooked a penalty goal-kick from the right of the posts, then fumbled in the following set. A penalty against Roberts allowed the Maroons to enter enemy territory. Their ineffective attack was followed by a major blow: a head clash with Roberts in an off-the-ball incident forced a dazed Jason Smith out of the game.

Queensland's successive last tackle options were poor. Langer sliced a kick out on the full, before throwing a desperate pass to the right when Elias advanced on him. Elias intercepted and sent Clyde rushing away to score near the left post.

The teams exchanged errors, then NSW gained a repeat set of tackles after Renouf botched an intercept. Four metres from the tryline, Elias passed left to Stuart, who spun it to Daley. He stepped left then right to evade Langer and Darren Smith. Straightening, he brushed past Moore and O'Neill and had Steve Walters clinging to him as he completed a brilliant individual try near the posts. NSW led 12–0 after 22 minutes.

Sironen fumbled from the restart but Queensland failed to capitalise. After another Maroons mistake, Stuart just missed a 35-metre field-goal attempt. The Maroons threw the ball around in their half, and Renouf hurled it right for Carne but instead found Mullins, who raced away unopposed to score under the crossbar. Having let themselves down again, the Maroons trailed 18-0 in the 33rd minute.

Queensland finally launched a coordinated raid two minutes before the break. From 20 metres out, Carne passed right to Kevin Walters, who grubbered through and regathered before passing to Gee. He fooled Stuart with a dummy and crashed over the line. O'Neill's goal left NSW leading 18–6.

Gee made costly mistakes soon after half-time, throwing a poor pass and then conceding a penalty for punching. Three tackles later, Mackay passed to Elias, who kicked an unexpected field-goal to stretch NSW's lead beyond two converted tries.

For several minutes, individual plays influenced the tide of the game. Daley feigned to kick and instead split the defence and raced ahead but lacked support. Carne dropped a straightforward downfield kick but Queensland's defence held out, and did so again after Gee conceded another penalty. Daley caught Queensland's defence off guard again, and he sent McGregor striding through but Brasher fumbled a head-high pass. O'Neill counter-attacked immediately and, from the ensuing play, Carne, Langer and Kevin Walters handled before Walters unloaded to Renouf, who flashed through. He was grabbed by Mullins just short of the tryline but the momentum carried him across the line. O'Neill landed his conversion attempt, and the Maroons were back in the game, trailing 19–12 with 24 minutes remaining.

But Queensland's poor handling continued, with mistakes in consecutive sets by Kevin Walters and Langer. The handling error count was 15–7 to Queensland when Meninga fumbled in the 64th minute. Soon after, Carne fielded Stuart's kick and broke through. Nearing halfway, Carne threw a forward pass and was hit high by Clyde's swinging right arm. Play was halted and Carne was carried off on a stretcher. No penalty was awarded because Carne fell into the tackle. Two minutes later, Steve Walters threw a bad pass. NSW attacked for five tackles before Fittler steadied and kicked a field goal. NSW thus led 20–12.

Soon afterwards, the Maroons had a scrum feed on their 20-metre line. Langer passed right to Kevin Walters, who threw a long, high and desperate pass towards Meninga. Meninga jumped to catch it but could only knock the ball in the air, allowing Fittler to catch it and run behind the posts for the easiest of tries. Brasher's conversion gave the Blues an unbeatable 14-point lead with five minutes left.

At the end of the next set, Elias potted another field goal for a final scoreline of 27–12.

The Verdict

The Blues deserved their win as they remained composed while capitalising on Queensland's errors. Three of their four tries came from intercepts and the fourth soon after an opposition error. Elias was named man of the match in a memorable Origin farewell. But it was a disappointing Origin finale for Meninga. Nevertheless, he walked a lap of honour to a rousing and appreciative home crowd.

NSW's win was its first in an Origin decider in Brisbane, and NSW had won three consecutive Origin series for the first time. It was also the first time the Blues had won an Origin series after losing game one.

Under the coaching of Gould and captaincy of Daley, NSW's Origin achievements from 1992 to 1994 were similar to those achieved by Queensland a decade earlier under Arthur Beetson and Wally Lewis.

↑ Mal Meninga leads the Maroons for the last time.

↓ Meninga makes a typical burst. His dream of a successful Origin farewell was dashed as the Maroons crumbled in the decider on their home turf.

1995

Fatty's Nobodies Achieve Mission Impossible

Representative football was severely affected by the developing rugby league 'war' between the traditionalist ARL and the proposed Super League. The rebel competition was mooted by media empire News Limited in order to help meet pay-television requirements. Eight of the 20 clubs in the ARL competition jumped on the Super League bandwagon. The Super League-aligned players remained in club football but were barred from representative teams.

Both state teams suffered from this restriction, although Queensland appeared worse off because Brisbane Bronco players signed with Super League, depriving the Maroons of a substantial portion of their first-choice side. It also cost them their coach when Wayne Bennett resigned because of the ban on Super League players. Paul Vautin was the new man in charge. The ARL seemingly relaxed the player eligibility rule for the Maroons since they had so few players available. Two cases in point were Adrian Lam and Wayne Bartrim. Lam had started his career in Brisbane but had played a test for his home country Papua New Guinea. Bartrim was raised in NSW and had played for two NSW senior teams. His only link to Queensland was living in Brisbane and the Gold Coast briefly. He confessed being a NSW supporter but was happy to play for Queensland. Also eligible for Queensland were Gavin Allen and Brett Dallas, both of whom had not signed with Super League but were with Super League-aligned clubs.

Daley, Ettingshausen, Lazarus, Mullins, Nagas and Stuart were among the players who were unavailable for NSW. Additionally, Sironen had retired from representative football. NSW retained Phil Gould as coach as he was strongly associated with the ARL.

← Adrian Lam, Mark Coyne, Wayne Bartrim and Gavin Allen celebrate Queensland's series win, a remarkable achievement in the light of the turmoil in rugby league at the time.

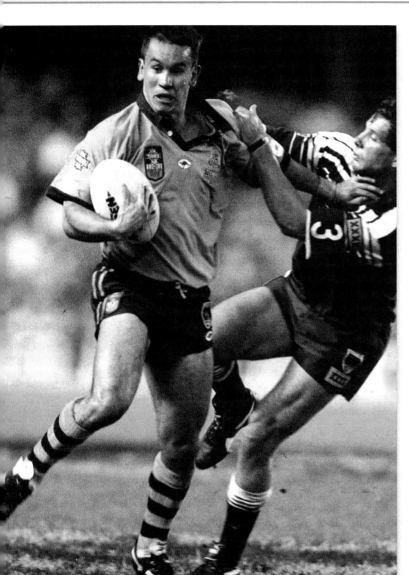

↑ Matthew Johns made his Origin debut at five-eighth in the same game as his brother Andrew, who was playing at halfback. Here, Mark Coyne struggles to thwart Matthew Johns's progress.

Players & Statistics

QLD Robbie O'Davis, Brett Dallas, Mark Coyne, Danny Moore, Matt Sing, Dale Shearer, Adrian Lam, Billy Moore, Gary Larson, Trevor Gillmeister (c), Tony Hearn, Wayne Bartrim, Gavin Allen. **RESERVES** Terry Cook, Ben Ikin, Mark Hohn, Craig Teevan. **COACH** Paul Vautin

NSW Tim Brasher, Rod Wishart, Terry Hill, Paul McGregor, Craig Hancock, Matthew Johns, Andrew Johns, Brad Fittler (c), Brad Mackay, Steve Menzies, Mark Carroll, Jim Serdaris, Paul Harragon. **RESERVES** Greg Florimo, David Fairleigh, Matt Seers, Adam Muir. **COACH** Phil Gould

Result Queensland 2 (Bartrim goal) beat NSW 0

Referee Eddie Ward (Queensland)

Crowd 39 841

Man of the Match Gary Larson (Queensland)

The Teams

NSW was still able to field familiar Origin and international players such as Brasher, Wishart, Fittler, Brad Mackay and Harragon. Debutants were Craig Hancock, Matthew and Andrew Johns, Jim Serdaris, Steve Menzies, Mark Carroll, Matt Seers and Adam Muir. Florimo was recalled as a reserve after seven years in the wilderness, and Fittler was named captain.

Queensland fielded eight players with Origin experience but only Shearer and Hohn had represented Australia. Allen and Dallas were picked out of reserve grade. Newcomers were Robbie O'Davis, Danny Moore, Matt Sing, Adrian Lam, Tony Hearn, Wayne Bartrim, Ben Ikin, Terry Cook and Craig Teevan. Ikin, who had played only three club games for the Gold Coast, became the youngest player in Origin history at 18 years and 83 days. The expectation was that the series would be a David-Goliath encounter with NSW trouncing the Maroons.

As Super League-aligned referees including Harrigan and Annesley were also part of the selection ban, ARL-aligned referee Eddie Ward was appointed to officiate.

The Game

Billy Moore tried to inspire his team-mates as he repeatedly shouted 'Queenslander' as the Maroons headed down the tunnel to the playing arena.

After an early penalty to NSW, Andrew Johns kicked to the right, where Wishart caught the ball but momentum took him into the corner post. A swinging arm from Harragon triggered a brawl, before a penalty against Andrew Johns a few minutes later led the Maroons downfield. Coyne made a darting run in the quarter but eased off as Brasher confronted him, squandering a scoring chance. After a knock-on from Bartrim, Hearn was penalised for a late hit on Serdaris, and Wishart hooked a goal-kick from 10 metres inside the left wing.

After a badly sliced clearing kick from Andrew Johns was caught by Shearer 10 metres in NSW's half, McGregor appeared harshly penalised for a supposed high tackle on Sing. Bartrim's kick for goal was from a similar angle to Wishart's, with a similar result. Queensland forced the pressure with repeat sets of tackles but couldn't penetrate NSW's defence.

However, Harragon was punished for impeding Larson as Larson advanced towards Andrew Johns's kick. Bartrim subsequently kicked Queensland to a 2–0 lead with a 25-metre goal.

Queensland attacked NSW's line again just before half-time but could not find a way through to score. Coyne again went close but was tackled barely a metre short. The maligned Maroons were proving to be very competitive as they led by two points at the break.

Billy Moore resumed shouting 'Queenslander' as the Maroons returned to the field. They conceded two early penalties before NSW's tackle count restarted. Andrew Johns threw a long pass

left to Mackay, who unloaded to Serdaris. He threw a long bouncing ball to Hill, who bumped off Dallas to touch down in the corner. But Serdaris's pass was ruled forward and, although the pass looked marginal, replays suggested Hill had stepped on the sideline before grounding the ball.

The teams took it in turns to apply pressure and then lose possession. Play ebbed and flowed with Larson's strong tackling and hard running a feature. Andrew Johns, Serdaris and McGregor helped push the Blues to Queensland's 10-metre line before the ball moved right in the following play. Hill surged over the line but was held up by Sing, Hohn and Danny Moore. Ikin's moment of truth came in the 66th minute as he replaced Shearer. After Dallas made a half-break, a movement featuring Dallas, Gillmeister, Larson and Danny Moore led to Ikin breaking through before passing to Billy Moore. But Ikin was unable to take the return pass and the movement broke down. Play was halted when Danny Moore was unable to get up after copping Wishart's shoulder to the jaw during the passing rush. The injured Queenslander needed a neck brace and was carried off on a stretcher. Soon after, Bartrim hooked a penalty goal-kick from 12 metres in from the right wing. After the Maroons again failed to break through, NSW received a relieving penalty.

The contest could not have been tenser as the Maroons tried to hang on while the Blues searched for an opening. Harragon was thwarted just short of the tryline on tackle four before Serdaris grubber-

kicked to the left, where Brasher just failed to ground the ball before it rolled into touch in-goal. A knock-on from Billy Moore gave NSW another chance, but Wishart was bundled over the sideline within 10 metres of the line in the last two minutes. After a final fumble from NSW, Vautin's 'nobodies' had pulled off a shock win.

The Verdict

Origin's first tryless game, the lowest scoring game, NSW held scoreless for the first time and a Queensland win against the odds—all were remarkable aspects and showed that the Blues were no certainties for the series. ARL chairman Ken Arthurson said the game maintained the best traditions of Origin football in spite of rugby league's off-field turmoil.

Vautin spoke of his players' courage and determination. Gould acknowledged his team had enough opportunities to score but seemed to get nervous.

← Gary Larson earned the man-of-the-match award after a heavily involved game with the ball and in defence.

↓ Nervous Queensland coach Paul Vautin had plenty of anxious moments during his underdog team's memorable 2–0 win to go one-up in the series.

→ Gavin Allen spilled blood and spent time in the sin-bin in an Origin match as ferocious as ever.

The Teams

Queensland kept an unchanged squad before Shearer withdrew with injury. Jason Smith returned at five-eighth after becoming eligible when he signed with the ARL-aligned Parramatta.

For NSW, an injured Matthew Johns was replaced in the squad by Barnhill, and positional changes were made. When the injured Hancock and Seers and suspended Carroll became unavailable, Pay returned, and John Hopoate and Brett Rodwell were introduced to Origin.

The Game

↓ State against state, mate against mate: John Hopoate comes to grips with Manly team-mate Danny Moore as tempers flare in Origin II.

A crowd of nearly 53 000 was impressive in light of the Super League crisis. The contest began at a frantic pace with hard-hitting tackles, and the first scrum erupted into a brawl. Strangely, referee Ward did not call time-off and more than three minutes of play were lost as the fighting continued. NSW

dominated field position after consecutive penalties against Smith, but the Maroons held out before a relieving penalty allowed them to move downfield.

Inside NSW's 30-metre zone, Smith chip-kicked where Brasher fumbled the bouncing ball before Smith appeared to knock on. Coyne picked the ball up and crossed near the left upright. The try was awarded, although replays showed that both Brasher and Smith had knocked-on and that Queensland should have only been awarded a scrum feed.

Both teams squandered possession before Bartrim kicked Queensland to an 8–0 lead after a penalty against Pay. The Blues had a good chance to hit back in a repeat set but a Hopoate blunder at dummy-half allowed Sing to swoop from marker. Barnhill also blundered before Allen was penalised for starting a scuffle after Harragon's tackle on Allen appeared high. Allen and Harragon were sin-binned, and Allen bled from a head wound for the second time in the game. A few minutes before half-time, Danny Moore was penalised for obstructing Fittler, and Wishart's ensuing goal left the Maroons 8–2 leaders. An injured Billy Moore was unable to return after half-time.

After play resumed, NSW dominated field position through strong defence and thanks to handling errors from Queensland. Near the 10-metre line, Andrew Johns fired a cut-out pass right to Fittler, who stepped, drew O'Davis and sent a well-timed pass to Rodwell. He, in turn, stepped between O'Davis and Sing to score in the corner in a tackle. The consequences were horrific as Rodwell suffered medial and cruciate ligament damage and left the field on a medi-cab. Wishart's hooked goal-kick left Queensland leading 8–6. After a Harragon infringement a few minutes later, Bartrim landed a penalty goal to make the score 10–6.

Poor handling robbed both teams of momentum, with Smith and Serdaris repeat offenders. The Maroons had a good scoring chance but Cook fumbled Gillmeister's pass to foil the move. NSW threatened next and a clearly offside Hearn intercepted but escaped the referee's attention. At the other end, a fumble by McGregor in Bartrim's tackle was followed by Smith's grubber forcing a goal-line drop-out. Five tackles later, Teevan passed left to Lam in the quarter. The halfback stepped past the

Players & Statistics

QLD Robbie O'Davis, Brett Dallas, Mark Coyne, Danny Moore, Matt Sing, Jason Smith, Adrian Lam, Billy Moore, Gary Larson, Trevor Gillmeister (c), Tony Hearn, Wayne Bartrim, Gavin Allen. **RESERVES** Ben Ikin, Terry Cook, Mark Hohn, Craig Teevan. **COACH** Paul Vautin

NSW Tim Brasher, Rod Wishart, Terry Hill, Paul McGregor, John Hopoate, Brad Fittler (c), Andrew Johns, Brad Mackay, David Barnhill, Greg Florimo, Paul Harragon, Jim Serdaris, Dean Pay. **RESERVES** Brett Rodwell, Adam Muir, Steve Menzies, David Fairleigh. **COACH** Phil Gould

Result Queensland 20 (Coyne, Lam, Dallas tries; Bartrim 4 goals) beat NSW 12 (Rodwell, Serdaris tries; Wishart 2 goals)

Referee Eddie Ward (Queensland)

Crowd 52 994

Man of the Match Jason Smith (Queensland)

advancing Serdaris and linked with Gillmeister and Cook, who threw a dummy and drifted left. Cook stood in Brasher's tackle and shovelled the ball inside to Lam, who ran through a yawning gap to score. The ecstatic Queenslanders sensed an historic series victory as they led 14–6, but Bartrim hooked the relatively straightforward goal-kick.

After errors from the Maroons, Hearn was forced off with injury, and then a penalty against Larson gave NSW another chance. Johns passed right to Fittler. He stepped and fed Serdaris, who crashed through tired defence to score between the uprights. After Wishart quickly added the extras, the Maroons led 14–12 with four-and-a-half minutes left.

The Blues looked invigorated as they gained good territory while the Queenslanders looked fatigued. At the end of an attacking raid, Menzies surged for the line and swivelled but was held up over the line by O'Davis, Cook and Bartrim. NSW nevertheless had a scrum feed on Queensland's 10-metre line with 77 seconds remaining. After two tackles, Serdaris swung the ball left to Fittler, who cleverly delayed a short pass to draw the defence. Fittler sent Brasher past Coyne and over the line in Larson's tackle, but NSW's celebrations were stunningly short-lived as Ward ruled Fittler's pass forward. The Maroons played safely as the clock counted down. From dummy-half on Queensland's 10-metre line in the final 10 seconds, Dallas jinked between Johns and Muir and raced away to score under the posts. Bartrim converted, and Queensland's 20–12 win secured the state's first series win in four years.

The Verdict

Replays showed that Ward ruled correctly against the Blues in the final minutes. Vautin said he was an emotional wreck and had never experienced anything like the final two minutes of the game. Gould, who coached a series-losing Origin team for the first time, said the game and the series were wonderful and a great advertisement for the future of league.

The Blues had been regarded as certain series-winners, yet Queensland secured the series with a game to spare. Interestingly, the Maroons secured the series without having played on their home turf.

↑ Brett Rodwell scored a try in his only Origin game, but he was in agony when he injured his knee in the process and was forced from the field.

↑ Jubilant Queenslanders celebrate the clean-sweep. NSW had been regarded as certain to win a landslide.

↓ Adrian Lam was one of his team's best throughout the 1995 series.

The Teams

NSW dropped Hopoate, Andrew Johns, Pay and Mackay. Matthew Johns, Toovey, Seers and Carroll returned. David Hall was the only debutant. Some positional changes occurred again.

Queensland retained the same squad but Gillmeister was in hospital with a serious leg infection. Doctors warned Gillmeister he would be risking his life if he played. Regardless, he checked out of hospital, hell-bent on leading his side to a series clean-sweep.

David Manson was named to referee his first Origin game for three years.

The Game

After the Blues were unable to capitalise on early field position, Bartrim's 35-metre penalty goal-kick hit the right post. Lam made a half-break in the next couple of minutes and played the ball in the 10-metre zone on the last tackle. Coyne passed left to Smith, who dummied before surging through Harragon's and Menzies's tackles to score near the right upright. Bartrim's conversion ensured Queensland led 6–0.

Errors in their quarter a few minutes later had the Maroons under pressure. Eventually the Blues moved the ball left through a few hands before McGregor palmed off Ikin. McGregor drew Dallas and sent an around-the-corner pass for Brasher to run through and score. Wishart's excellent sideline conversion tied the scores.

Soon after the restart, the Blues headed downfield from a penalty before Brasher fumbled Toovey's pass with the tryline beckoning. After Hearn rose to his feet from a tackle, he head-butted Carroll in the face, prompting Carroll to lash out as a brawl erupted. The Maroons controversially received the penalty but didn't profit. After an offside penalty to NSW, Wishart missed an angled 30-metre goal-kick. But O'Davis blundered as he fumbled the ball over the dead-ball line to ensure a goal-line drop-out. From a play-the-ball on the 20-metre line, the ball went right before Fittler veered left, confused the defence

Players & Statistics

QLD Robbie O'Davis, Brett Dallas, Mark Coyne, Danny Moore, Matt Sing, Jason Smith, Adrian Lam, Billy Moore, Gary Larson, Trevor Gillmeister (c), Tony Hearn, Wayne Bartrim, Gavin Allen. **RESERVES** Ben Ikin, Terry Cook, Mark Hohn, Craig Teevan. **COACH** Paul Vautin

NSW Tim Brasher, Rod Wishart, Terry Hill, Paul McGregor, David Hall, Matthew Johns, Geoff Toovey, Brad Fittler (c), Adam Muir, Steve Menzies, Mark Carroll, Jim Serdaris, Paul Harragon. **RESERVES** Matt Seers, Greg Florimo, David Fairleigh, David Barnhill. **COACH** Phil Gould

Result Queensland 24 (Smith, D Moore, Dallas, Ikin tries; Bartrim 4 goals) beat NSW 16 (Brasher, Wishart, Muir tries; Wishart 2 goals)

Referee David Manson (Queensland)

Crowd 40 189

Man of the Match Adrian Lam (Queensland)

and sent Brasher through. Brasher's pass was fumbled backwards by McGregor before Wishart fielded it and stepped past Dallas to score. NSW led in a game for the first time all series, but Wishart hooked the relatively comfortable conversion attempt.

After an error from NSW, Smith forced a goal-line drop-out just before half-time with a well-placed chip-kick. On the 10-metre line after three tackles, a few Maroons sent the ball right. Drawing the defence, Coyne fed Danny Moore, who stepped inside Brasher and ran in to score behind the posts. It was a decisive blow, and Bartrim's conversion took the Maroons to a 12–10 lead. An injured Allen was unable to resume after the break.

In the first set after half-time, a Billy Moore handling error gifted NSW possession. After Johns played the ball in the attacking zone, Serdaris's pass bounced to Fittler, who passed inside to Muir. He raced through a gap and out of O'Davis's tackle to score inside the right post. Wishart's conversion gave his team a 16–12 lead. A penalty against Hohn after the kick-off led NSW downfield again, but Serdaris lost possession as he pushed a needless pass. The Blues maintained the momentum, but another threatening raid in the 50th minute was lost when McGregor's pass went off track.

A few tackles later, Smith found an opening and drew Brasher near halfway before sending Dallas scurrying to score under the crossbar. Bartrim's conversion ensured Queensland led 18–16 in a see-sawing game.

Smith left the field injured, then NSW had the next chance to attack after a break by Brasher and another penalty against Hohn. Queensland showed great scrambling defence and Hall was thwarted within a metre of the line. Gillmeister's exit with 23 minutes remaining left his team with just one fresh reserve. The Blues attacked again and received six more tackles after Cook knocked down a pass. The Maroons held out before an errant Fittler pass went over the touchline.

Midway through the half, Fairleigh was penalised for a strip but Bartrim struck an upright from a penalty kick for the second time in the game. Following through, Teevan raced to the ball but he propelled it forward with a try beckoning. The momentum swung back NSW's way but Dallas, Sing and O'Davis took turns to escape from the in-goal area after Fittler kicked through in successive sets for the Blues.

The Maroons appeared within reach of winning again for a clean-sweep of the series. With four minutes left, Lam hoisted a bomb, which Seers dropped on his 20-metre line as Coyne closed in. Ikin fielded the loose ball and ran in to score 12 metres inside the left wing. Bartrim's conversion gave Queensland an unassailable 24–16 lead. In the closing stages, NSW captain Fittler fumbled as a series he would rather forget came to a close.

The Verdict

Gillmeister returned to his hospital bed, describing his players as incredible after they had been written off before the series had even begun. According to McGregor, Queensland was more committed and played with more passion than the Blues who, Mal Meninga suggested, seemed to lack the urgency and energy of their opponents.

Phil Gould offered no excuses for his team's losses and gave full credit to Queensland for achieving a clean sweep.

The extraordinary 1995 State of Origin series was a highlight in a year of turmoil for rugby league.

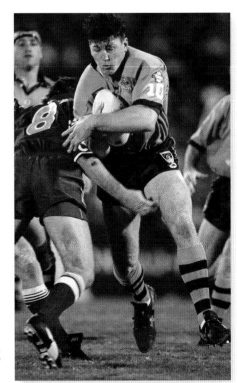

↓ NSW prop Mark Carroll made his test debut in 1990 but had to wait another five years before earning a state guernsey.

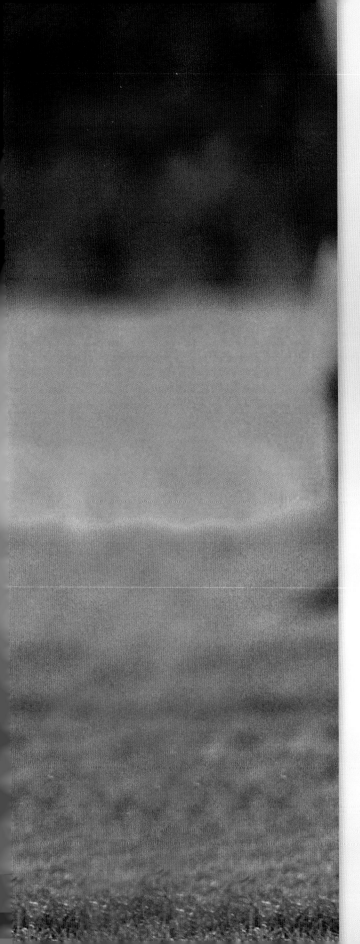

1996

Unchanged Southerners Bluewash Maroons Under a Queensland Referee

The ARL welcomed back Super League-aligned players for the 1996 series after the rebel competition was ruled illegal by the Federal Court. The rebels' return created a quandary for Queensland's selectors. Most of the Maroons from the historic 1995 series were available again, as were the Brisbane Bronco players whose team was in the top two on the ARL competition ladder. It was hard to say how many Super League-aligned players would be chosen because Queensland had lost the past three Origin series in which Brisbane players were involved. But, on the other hand, if the selectors stuck with players from the victorious 1995 team, would they measure up against a full-strength NSW side?

Queensland was without Hohn, who had retired, and Allen, now playing in England. Clyde and Stuart were unavailable for NSW.

Paul Vautin and Phil Gould continued as coaches. The 1996 series was to be the first to be played using unlimited interchange and there was no game scheduled for Melbourne this time.

← Geoff Toovey was NSW's first-choice halfback as Ricky Stuart was absent, and Andrew Johns moved to hooker. The Toovey-Johns combination was a winner for the Blues.

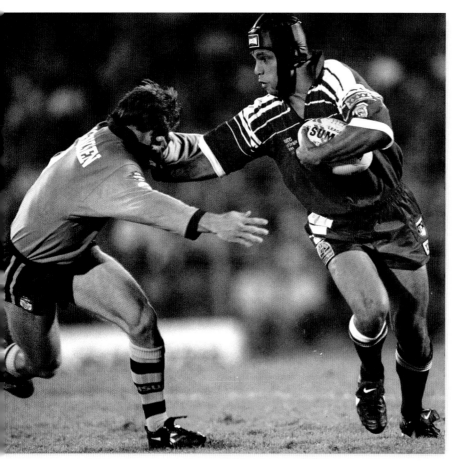

↑ Steve Renouf tries to brush off Andrew Ettingshausen. Renouf was unable to make an impact as the Maroons lacked cohesion throughout the game.

reached around him to plant the ball. Referee Manson ruled that one or two Blues were offside but replays disputed the decision. The Maroons received a follow-up penalty but didn't benefit. Fittler hooked a kick out on the full, then was questionably penalised for a high tackle. Hearn fumbled before Queensland was penalised from the scrum. A further penalty against Larson enabled Johns to open the scoring with a 25-metre goal. Queensland received the next penalty but it was followed by a Langer knock-on.

Continuing the trend, Brasher kicked out on the full, NSW was penalised and Queensland fumbled. Fittler put Brasher through a gap but Fittler's pass was dubiously ruled forward. After a knock-on from Renouf, Bartrim was punished for obstructing in the ruck. NSW ventured into Queensland's quarter, where Daley played the ball forward and was tackled by an off-side Moore, allowing Johns to kick his second penalty goal. NSW threatened again after another penalty, but Ettingshausen's pass to Wishart found the sideline as an overlap beckoned. Langer knocked-on again when he was about to kick.

Six minutes from the break, Smith fumbled a pass from Langer. Five tackles later, Fittler kicked to the right where an awkward bounce eluded Hancock, allowing Ettingshausen to swoop and

The Teams

Queensland's starting team included nine from the 1995 series: O'Davis, Dallas, Sing, Smith, Billy Moore, Gillmeister, Larson, Bartrim and Hearn. Lam was chosen as a reserve. Returning from Super League were Renouf, Langer and Hancock, and Super League-aligned Wendell Sailor, Brad Thorn, Alan Cann and Craig Greenhill were debutants.

NSW's selectors retained Brasher, Wishart, Fittler, Toovey, Muir, Pay, Harragon, Andrew Johns and Menzies. Returning from Super League were Ettingshausen, Mullins, Daley, Croker and Lazarus. Chosen to debut were David Furner, Jim Dymock and Jamie Ainscough. Fittler was named skipper ahead of Daley, and Johns was picked out of position at hooker with Toovey at halfback.

The Game

The twists and turns began within three minutes of play. Fittler put through a kick which bounced over O'Davis's head behind Queensland's tryline. As O'Davis hovered casually over the ball, Mullins

score. Johns's third goal gave NSW a 10–0 lead. Sailor saved Queensland twice in the shadows of half-time, wrapping up Menzies with a great tackle, then catching Fittler's towering bomb.

Three quick penalties after half-time allowed the Maroons to fight back. NSW survived the first two but the third proved costly. The Blues were caught offside and Langer took a quick tap just 5 metres out. He threw a dummy to the right and straightened before surging into Brasher and reaching out to ground the ball on the tryline. Bartrim converted, reducing the margin to four points.

But the Blues looked better and forced a repeat set, only for Muir to fumble in a scramble for a grubber-kick. A head clash with Moore forced Johns from the field. Within a minute, Daley veered towards the left corner but Sailor saved Queensland again, driving Daley sideways to prevent a sure try. The Maroons withstood another attacking raid following a knock-on by Larson.

A comedy of errors midway through the half saw Lazarus fumble, a misfired pass from Langer end in NSW hands, and Croker spill a pass. The tide seemed to be turning Queensland's way, but the game changed in an instant when Smith spilled Langer's shin-height pass from the scrum. On the ensuing tackle, Langer was questionably penalised in the ruck as Daley fumbled in the play-the-ball. Five tackles later, a running Hancock failed to reach Fittler's left-footed hooked kick on the full. It bounced wickedly for Hancock and Menzies was on the spot to pounce. Wishart's conversion attempt struck the left upright and NSW held an eight-point lead.

In the final 14 minutes, O'Davis copped another bad bounce near his tryline and was saved when Wishart collided with him and fumbled the ball; Mullins had another try disallowed following Johns's bomb, although this time replays supported referee Manson ruling the chasers offside; Queensland's dreadful ball security continued, including Smith fumbling another poor pass from Langer. The Blues forced two goal-line drop-outs in the last three minutes and kept their 14–6 lead.

The Verdict

NSW had won an Origin game on Brisbane turf under a Queensland referee for the first time. There were concerns from both teams about Manson's refereeing, with the chief focus the size of his 10 metres. The Blues deserved to win as their coordination was superior to that of the error-ridden Maroons. It seemed odd that NSW's two tries came from kicks that bounced fortuitously for them, although both tries came off the back of Queensland errors. Toovey was man of the match, although Lazarus must have come close after playing the full game, a rarity for a prop in Origin football.

← Geoff Toovey is wrapped up by debutant Queensland second-rower Brad Thorn.

↓ Steve Menzies (in headgear) receives a pat from Laurie Daley after scoring a decisive try.

➔ Brad Fittler's record as NSW captain had a lot more respectability about it after the 1996 series, compensating for his team's 3–0 loss in his first series as an Origin skipper.

↓ The two players who participated in the most consecutive Origin games for their respective states before the 2000s, ball-carrier Paul Harragon (20 games for NSW) and his tackler Gary Larson (24 for Queensland).

The Teams

The NSW selectors named an unchanged squad. By contrast, the Maroons dropped O'Davis, Bartrim, Gillmeister, Hancock and Cann. Gillmeister went from captain to the outer and it ended his Origin career. Langer took over the captaincy, and Coyne, Steve Walters, O'Neill and Gee were recalled. Several positional changes were made, including Sailor from wing to fullback, O'Neill was picked at five-eighth and Kevin Walters on the bench.

The Game

NSW was caught offside after just 30 seconds, and then Daley flattened Gee with a stunning shoulder-charge. Langer chip-kicked after only three tackles

and Brasher just beat Sailor to the ball in-goal. Queensland received another penalty straight after the goal-line drop-out but failed to make the most of an extended run of possession. A penalty to the Blues enabled them to apply pressure. After Thorn infringed in a play-the-ball, Johns's angled penalty kick from 30 metres struck the right upright. Gee conceded two penalties in a short space of time, and Brasher fumbled with Queensland's tryline under threat before Johns pulled a 36-metre penalty kick just wide. After a penalty against Hearn, NSW led 2–0 when Johns kicked from 38 metres.

Amid niggling in a scrum, Steve Walters was singled out and sent to the sin-bin for head-butting. The Blues turned over possession before a penalty to the Maroons enabled them to turn defence into attack. Five tackles later, Langer put up a bomb to the left which Sailor and Wishart contested. The ball went through Wishart's hands for Renouf to recover and dive over the line. O'Neill converted from wide out. A grubber from Langer forced a repeat set but a try-scoring chance went begging as the ball bounced off Sailor's shoulder when a swarm of players converged on a high punt.

Two minutes from the break, Kevin Walters riskily tried a chip-kick just inside NSW's half but it went straight to Daley, who sent Menzies charging away. Menzies fed Ettingshausen, who crossed the quarter-line and grubbered ahead before O'Neill brought him down. Kevin Walters grounded the ball in-goal but O'Neill's tackle was ruled to be late. Replays showed the penalty was harsh as O'Neill was committed to the tackle. A few tackles later, Toovey spread the ball right to Johns, Daley and Furner before an overlap appeared. Ettingshausen drew Sailor and fed

Wishart, who speared through and brought the ball towards the posts to benefit Johns's goal-kick. NSW led 8–6. The Maroons had survived when down a player for ten minutes, but Kevin Walters's blunder and questionable refereeing were crucial.

Soon after the break, Langer charged down Daley's kick but knocked it on. Brasher spilled a bomb from Daley in the next set but the Blues returned to the attack following an offside penalty. From dummy-half, Toovey caught out the defence on the blindside and linked with Ainscough, who sent Mullins over in the left corner. Johns hooked another goal-kick. NSW was under pressure when Lazarus dropped the ball from the restart, but Moore's unload went forward soon afterwards. After a penalty against Steve Walters, Johns sent Ettingshausen through a gap but Ettingshausen appeared to knock-on as Sailor tackled him just short of the line. From the play-the-ball, Johns kicked 30 metres to the left where Mullins got outside Dallas to catch the ball and touch down. Replays showed Ettingshausen had fumbled and, although Johns pulled another goal-kick, the Blues led 16–6 and were in sight of winning the series.

An offside penalty enabled Queensland to raid enemy territory, but Langer dropped a pass from Steve Walters. Langer finally had some success, jolting the ball out of Fittler's grasp, but O'Neill's bomb bounced off Sailor again as he leapt alongside Brasher. Queensland's sinking prospects plunged further when several players were caught in front of Langer when he hoisted a bomb, before Greenhill

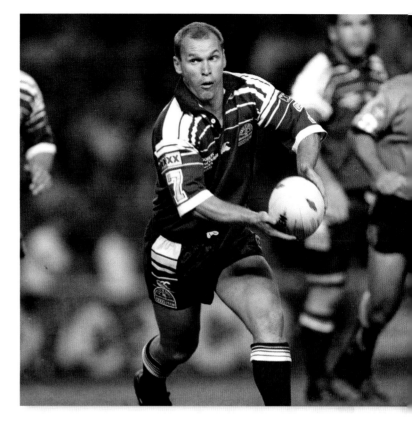

↑ After plenty of success early in his Origin career, Allan Langer was involved in four straight series losses in the 1990s.

earned the dubious honour of being the first player sent off in Origin football. He had mistimed a tackle and felled Harragon with a sickening right arm around the neck. The impact caused Harragon to fall backwards, and referee Manson instantly pointed Greenhill to the sheds.

Down to 12 players, Queensland battled in vain as the Blues defended resolutely. The Blues received a penalty six minutes from the end when a NSW player was ruled to have been tackled without the ball. Johns kicked his third goal, and the Blues kept their 18–6 lead until full-time. NSW's series win was its fourth in five years.

The Verdict

NSW again played better as a team but the result was controversial due to the lead-up to NSW's first and third tries. The undetected knock-on before the third try escaped scrutiny, but the Maroons were unhappy with the penalty against O'Neill that led to Wishart's try just before half-time. They cited this as the turning point in the game, as it gave NSW a two-point lead instead of trailing by four at the break. Johns's selection at hooker paid off and he was named man of the match.

Players & Statistics

NSW Tim Brasher, Rod Wishart, Andrew Ettingshausen, Laurie Daley, Brett Mullins, Brad Fittler (c), Geoff Toovey, Adam Muir, Dean Pay, David Furner, Paul Harragon, Andrew Johns, Glenn Lazarus. **RESERVES** Jim Dymock, Jamie Ainscough, Jason Croker, Steve Menzies. **COACH** Phil Gould

QLD Wendell Sailor, Brett Dallas, Steve Renouf, Mark Coyne, Matt Sing, Julian O'Neill, Allan Langer (c), Billy Moore, Brad Thorn, Gary Larson, Andrew Gee, Steve Walters, Tony Hearn. **RESERVES** Adrian Lam, Kevin Walters, Jason Smith, Craig Greenhill. **COACH** Paul Vautin

Result NSW 18 (Mullins 2, Wishart tries; Johns 3 goals) beat Queensland 6 (Renouf try; O'Neill goal)

Referee David Manson (Queensland)

Crowd 41 955

Man of the Match Andrew Johns (NSW)

↑ Tackled by Andrew
Gee, Glenn Lazarus shows
the strain.

The Game

Carne kicked the Maroons to a 2–0 lead after the Blues were caught offside in Queensland's first set of tackles. In the tenth minute, Brasher scurried left and drew Dallas to give Mullins an uninterrupted run to the tryline, but Brasher's long pass hit the ground before Mullins fumbled it with a try begging.

After a couple of errors from NSW, the Maroons put the Blues under enormous pressure, but Carne fumbled Langer's bomb near the tryline. After Queensland failed to profit from a penalty against Daley, Toovey threw a stray pass. Shearer raced through and kicked the loose ball but was unable to reach it before it went dead.

NSW somewhat unexpectedly broke through a few tackles later. From 15 metres in NSW's half, Harragon sent the ball to Ettingshausen, who instantly passed left to Johns. He stepped out of Coyne's tackle, shrugged off Langer and darted to the left. Held by Dallas near the 10-metre line, Johns flicked the ball right to the unmarked Ettingshausen, who scored behind the posts.

A knock-on by Harragon gave Queensland a chance to hit back. Veering right and drawing the defence, Langer fed an unmarked Moore but a certain try was butchered when Moore fumbled 5 metres out. Play was halted in the 30th minute as Smith left the field after copping a heavy knock. Shortly before half-time, Muir was penalised for impeding Langer after Langer grubber-kicked, and Carne's 32-metre goal-kick pushed to the right. NSW still led 6–2.

In the first minute after the break, NSW was fortunate to have a scrum feed rather than be penalised after Gee fumbled the ball against Muir, who was lying in the ruck. The Blues then forced two goal-line drop-outs, before Fittler's around-the-corner bomb soared between the posts. Mullins out-leapt Coyne and Menzies to score a try, which Wishart converted. The Maroons erred in the next five minutes and Wishart landed a goal to stretch NSW's lead to 12 points after Gee was penalised for a high tackle.

A couple of NSW errors led to Queensland attacking dangerously midway through the second half. Brasher was penalised and sent to the sin-bin for a professional foul after Langer took a penalty tap. But then Steve Walters surrendered possession on the first tackle when he tried to unload. The Maroons soon applied further pressure and won a scrum against the feed, only for Walters to fumble

The Teams

The Blues created history by fielding the same team for an entire Origin series. Furthermore, Manson became the first referee to control a full series. Queensland could not choose Greenhill (suspended) or Kevin Walters (injured). O'Neill was dropped. Carne and Shearer (at five-eighth) were recalled and reserve Owen Cunningham was named to debut.

Players & Statistics

NSW Tim Brasher, Rod Wishart, Andrew Ettingshausen, Laurie Daley, Brett Mullins, Brad Fittler (c), Geoff Toovey, Adam Muir, Dean Pay, David Furner, Paul Harragon, Andrew Johns, Glenn Lazarus. **RESERVES** Jim Dymock, Jamie Ainscough, Jason Croker, Steve Menzies. **COACH** Phil Gould

QLD Wendell Sailor, Brett Dallas, Steve Renouf, Mark Coyne, Willie Carne, Dale Shearer, Allan Langer (c), Billy Moore, Brad Thorn, Gary Larson, Andrew Gee, Steve Walters, Tony Hearn. **RESERVES** Adrian Lam, Matt Sing, Jason Smith, Owen Cunningham. **COACH** Paul Vautin

Result NSW 15 (Ettingshausen, Mullins tries; Wishart 2, Johns goals; Fittler field goal) beat Queensland 14 (Coyne, Dallas tries; Carne 3 goals).

Referee David Manson (Queensland)

Crowd 38 217

Man of the Match Steve Menzies (NSW)

again. Then the Maroons were caught offside, and Fittler kicked a decisive 33-metre field goal at the end of the ensuing tackle count, giving NSW a 13-point lead with 14 minutes left.

After Langer conceded a penalty for reefing the ball, NSW forced a repeat set before Wishart fumbled with the tryline beckoning. When Toovey was penalised for a dangerous tackle on Sing, Queensland returned to the attack and received six more tackles. Moments later, Coyne was tackled just short of the tryline. His play-the-ball was messy as he nearly tripped over, but the ball crossed the line where Coyne quickly pounced for a speculative try. Carne converted, and Queensland trailed 15–8 with seven minutes left.

The Maroons also had their next tackle count restarted as Croker fumbled a loose ball. From near halfway, Walters fired the ball right to Sailor and Sing, who drifted right and darted past Ainscough. Sing unloaded inside to Coyne, who drew Brasher and fed Dallas. He veered right and, as Mullins slipped over, dashed through to score near the posts. Following Carne's conversion, NSW suddenly led by just one point with barely four minutes left.

Queensland was controversially awarded a scrum feed after Coyne rather than Ainscough appeared to fumble Thorn's offload. Queensland attacked for five tackles before Brasher spilled Langer's bomb. An offside Fittler seemed to touch the loose ball 10 metres in from the left wing, but referee Manson restarted Queensland's tackle count rather than

penalise Fittler. The Maroons had 80 seconds to pull off a miracle and deny the Blues a series whitewash. NSW's defence held for five tackles before Langer hooked a grubber-kick towards the posts. Coyne beat Fittler to pounce behind the tryline with just 28 seconds left, but Coyne was 2 metres offside and was penalised. As in the third game of the Blues' previous clean-sweep (in 1986), Queensland had a match-winning try disallowed from a kick.

The Verdict

Menzies became the first reserve to win a man-of-the-match award in Origin football. The decision to field the same NSW team for all three games was well rewarded, since the Blues played better as a team throughout the series. Whether off-field issues had an impact is a matter of conjecture, but some post-series discussions made telling reading. While the Blues appeared to work in harmony, the ARL/Super League divide seemed to cause factions in the Queensland team.

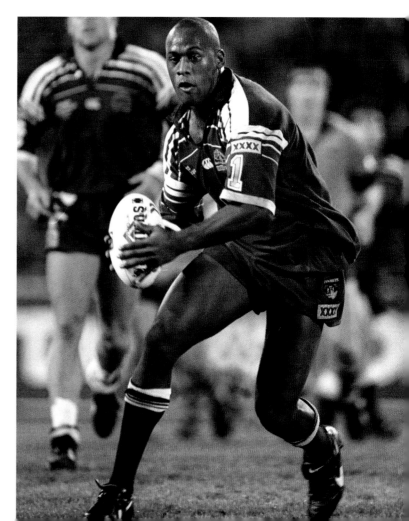

↓ Wendell Sailor was one of Queensland's shining lights in its disappointing Origin campaign. In the light of the ongoing ARL/Super League crisis, the usual mateship and bonding associated with Maroons teams seemed to be missing.

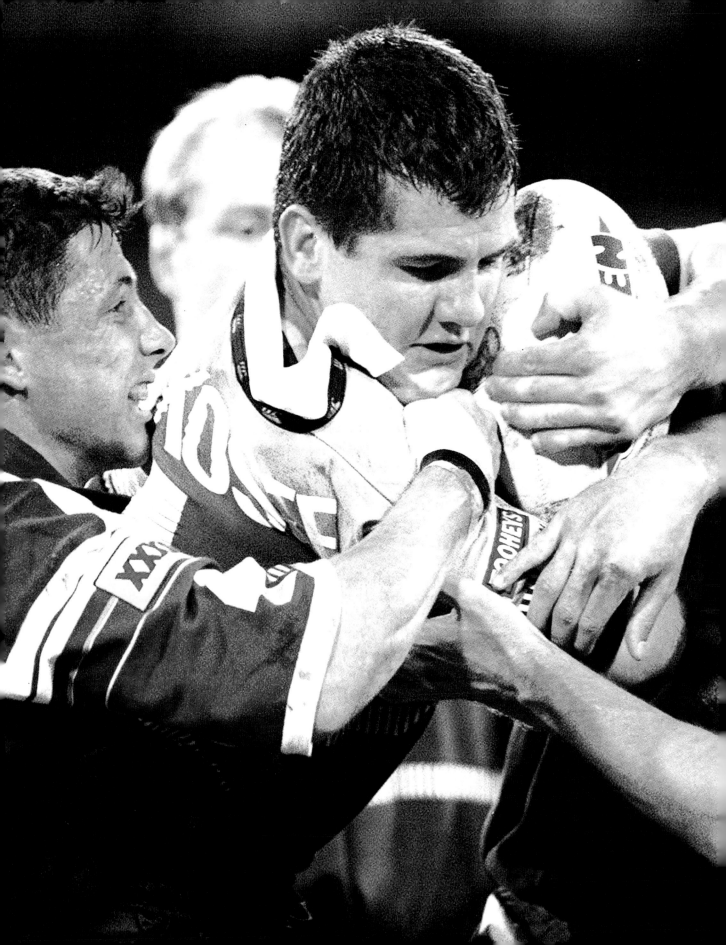

1997

The Blues Coach Lights Up

Rugby league took a dramatic twist in 1997 when the Super League concept came to fruition. The ARL and Super League competitions ran in direct competition and both offered a version of Origin football. The ARL continued with its proven series with only ARL-aligned players eligible, whereas Super League offered a tri-series involving NSW, Queensland and New Zealand.

The ARL-aligned Origin series had a lot to measure up against following a highly competitive Super League tri-series, which NSW won with wins over Queensland and New Zealand and then Queensland again in the final. The series decider was a thriller, with the scores locked at 22–all at full-time. Twenty minutes of extra-time failed to produce a winner before it became a case of 'next score wins'. NSW's Noel Goldthorpe kicked a field-goal to win the game after an amazing 103 minutes and 47 seconds.

Paul Vautin remained as Queensland's Origin coach, but Phil Gould stepped aside from Origin. Wests coach Tom Raudonikis took on the coaching job and became the first NSW coach with experience as an Origin player. He had become well known for his habit of chain-smoking while watching football.

Origin football returned to Melbourne, with game two played at the MCG.

← NSW forward Nik Kosef, in possession, is at the centre of attention. The Blues wore a new look jersey in 1997, the year that rugby league was divided into the Super League and ARL divisions.

→ Jamie Goddard was Queensland's debutant hooker in a year when Super League players were unavailable.

The Teams

The Blues fielded ten members from their successful 1996 squad, although an injured Fittler was absent for the series. Meanwhile, Hill, McGregor, Carroll, Fairleigh and Simon were recalled. The only Origin first-timers were Nik Kosef and Ken McGuinness. Toovey was named captain.

As in 1995, Queensland had plenty of players unavailable due to Super League. Recalled were O'Davis, Danny Moore, Ikin and Bartrim. Debutants were Jamie Goddard, Neil Tierney, Craig Smith, Jeremy Schloss and Stuart Kelly. Lam became the new captain.

Kelvin Jeffes was appointed to officiate his first Origin match.

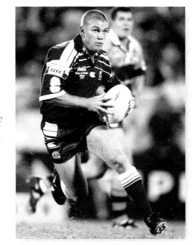

↓ Adam Muir is gang-tackled by Tony Hearn, Wayne Bartrim and Jason Smith while NSW captain Geoff Toovey looks on.

The Game

NSW suffered a setback in just the second minute when McGregor was forced off with a pinched nerve in his left shoulder. The opening ten minutes were marred by penalties and sloppy handling by both teams. On one occasion, Tierney dropped the ball from a goal-line drop-out. Referee Jeffes stamped his authority on the game and blew a number of penalties for slowing the play-the-ball. After one such penalty to NSW, Johns opened the scoring with a 38-metre goal.

A head knock forced Tierney off after 15 minutes. McGregor was able to return to the field a couple of minutes later. Jason Smith was penalised for high tackles in successive sets, and Johns attempted another long range goal but pushed it to the right. Within minutes, NSW suffered a big setback when Johns twisted his leg in a three-man tackle and exited the game. Scrappy play followed before Queensland had another casualty when Billy Moore was concussed.

The game took an unexpected and decisive turn in the 32nd minute. On the halfway line, Toovey passed right to Simon and Dymock, who unloaded inside to Simon. He drew O'Davis before firing the ball out to Wishart, who drew two defenders and linked up with McGregor on the inside. Wrong-footing O'Davis, McGregor veered right and crashed over. Wishart's wide-angled kick gave NSW an 8–0 lead.

The pendulum changed four tackles after the restart. Just inside NSW's half, Jason Smith charged down Simon's clearing kick and the ball rolled perilously close to NSW's tryline, where it was fielded by Brasher. Hill was held on the next tackle and Jeffes incorrectly awarded a handover after failing to restart the tackle count. This provided Queensland with an undeserved set of tackles in attacking territory, but it made no impact as Harragon took an intercept. A fumble by Brasher in the shadows of half-time forced a goal-line drop-out but the Blues held out until the siren.

Neither team looked like gaining the upper hand in the

Players & Statistics

NSW Tim Brasher, Rod Wishart, Terry Hill, Paul McGregor, Jamie Ainscough, Jim Dymock, Geoff Toovey (c), Nik Kosef, Adam Muir, Steve Menzies, Mark Carroll, Andrew Johns, Paul Harragon. **RESERVES** David Fairleigh, Dean Pay, John Simon, Ken McGuinness. **COACH** Tom Raudonikis

QLD Robbie O'Davis, Brett Dallas, Matt Sing, Mark Coyne, Danny Moore, Ben Ikin, Adrian Lam (c), Wayne Bartrim, Billy Moore, Gary Larson, Craig Smith, Jamie Goddard, Neil Tierney. **RESERVES** Jason Smith, Jeremy Schloss, Tony Hearn, Stuart Kelly. **COACH** Paul Vautin

Result NSW 8 (McGregor try; Johns, Wishart goals) beat Queensland 6 (Lam try; Bartrim goal)

Referee Kelvin Jeffes (NSW)

Crowd 28 222

Man of the Match Geoff Toovey (NSW)

second half until the Maroons received a penalty in the 51st minute. Grubber-kicks from Lam and Ikin forced consecutive goal-line drop-outs. Queensland created an opening as Sing turned a reverse pass inside to Danny Moore, but he spilled the ball with the tryline just 9 metres away. Play was stopped as Wishart exited the game with a shoulder injury.

Queensland had a string of possession after Lam broke through and linked up with Dallas in the 66th minute. Dallas was dragged over the sideline but Ainscough was penalised for an early tackle. Another penalty 10 metres from the posts saw the Maroons enticed to push for a try instead of taking the easy two points on offer. Bartrim was thwarted just short of the line before Goddard passed left to Lam, who threw a dummy, surged forward and barged over to score in a tackle. Bartrim converted to narrow NSW's lead to only two points with 11 minutes remaining.

In the 74th minute, Jason Smith put up a bomb, which bounced inside the NSW quarter as Brasher and Sing raced to it. Brasher appeared to touch the ball before it went loose and then O'Davis was tackled in NSW's 10-metre zone. Jeffes awarded a handover when a restart of the tackle count would have put the Maroons in ideal field position to press further for a potentially winning try. Smith conceded a relieving penalty, then Muir knocked on as the nail-biting tension remained. The Maroons threw everything at NSW before Lam put up a pressure bomb which Brasher fumbled backwards, but Ainscough was on the spot to save the situation.

The Blues relied on ball security and Simon's kicking game to keep Queensland at bay. In the final minute, the Maroons made good headway after a scrum win on their 30-metre line. But then they travelled mainly sideways as they threw the ball around, before Dallas put through an ineffective kick that Brasher defused as the siren sounded.

The Verdict

Following a tight game, each coach was displeased with a refereeing decision that went against his respective team. Raudonikis was unhappy that the tackle count did not restart for NSW after Jason Smith's charge-down of a Simon kick in the first half. Vautin was annoyed the Maroons did not receive an extra set of tackles after Brasher seemingly touched Jason Smith's kick in the 74th minute. Vautin nonetheless conceded that the Maroons made mistakes, and he was particularly unhappy with their kicking game.

↑ Terry Hill tries to evade Brett Dallas's tackle. Hill returned to Origin after being dropped in 1996.

↓ Dean Pay, named as reserve for the game, breaks out of a tackle.

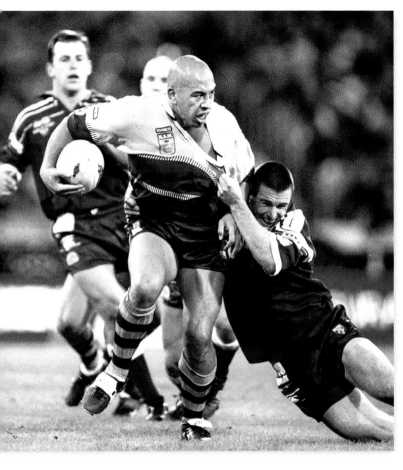

↑ Jim Dymock looks to unload as he is tackled by Ben Ikin. Dymock scored NSW's third try as the Blues jumped to a 14–0 lead before the Maroons came back.

The Teams

For NSW, the injured Wishart was replaced on the wing by McGuinness and Seers was recalled. In a later change, an injured Andrew Johns was replaced by the newcomer Aaron Raper, who is the son of the NSW selector and rugby league legend John Raper.

Queensland's selectors replaced the injured Hearn with newcomer Clinton O'Brien. Danny Moore was dropped, O'Neill was recalled, and several positional changes occurred. O'Neill had played for Australia in the first Super League test match and for Queensland in the first tri-series game, and then his club sacked him for disciplinary reasons. Signed by the ARL-aligned South Sydney, O'Neill achieved the distinction of selection for his state in both the Super League and ARL competitions in the same year.

→ Paul McGregor had a patchy game but did enough to win the man-of-the-match award. However, late in the contest he conceded a penalty that almost cost NSW the game.

The Game

The small crowd at the MCG was indicative of the fragmented nature of rugby league in 1997. After the sides exchanged handling errors, an offside penalty helped NSW downfield. Fifteen metres from the tryline, Dymock veered left but turned the ball to the blindside where Toovey fed McGregor. Kelly misread the play and McGregor flicked a back-handed pass inside to McGuinness, who crashed over to score. Simon missed the conversion.

NSW was caught inside the 10 metres, then Bartrim sliced a straightforward goal-kick. A darting run from Lam in the 12th minute set up a break by Moore, who looked left for support as two unmarked team-mates loomed on the right, allowing Brasher's tackle to ruin the opportunity.

NSW applied pressure but Sing, O'Davis and Dallas all fielded kicks safely. Dallas broke away towards his 20-metre line but lost the ball in a tackle, although replays showed Fairleigh should have been penalised for stripping. A few tackles later, Toovey passed left to Kosef, who broke out of Moore's tackle to dive over for a soft try. Simon's conversion gave NSW a handy ten-point lead after 21 minutes. Five minutes later, Queensland's defence held off on the last tackle but NSW took the initiative from 40 metres out. Toovey spread the ball right to Simon and Dymock, who confused the defence and fired a pass to McGregor. Drawing Sing, McGregor fed McGuinness. He drew O'Davis and passed inside to Dymock, who dived over the tryline. Despite Simon slicing another goal-kick, NSW led 14–0.

After errors by Muir and McGregor soon after the restart, the Maroons created an overlap but Moore's high pass to Dallas was fumbled into touch. Further NSW mistakes gave the Maroons another

opportunity in the 33rd minute. Near the right corner, Coyne spun the ball to Smith, Lam, Ikin and Moore. This time Moore threw a well-timed pass to Sing, who flashed past McGuinness and touched down as he stumbled. Sing could have brought the ball closer to the posts, and his momentary lack of aware-ness proved crucial when O'Neill pulled the wide-angled goal-kick.

Queensland coughed up posses-sion immediately but O'Davis intercepted a poor unload from Dymock to put the Maroons back on the offence. A few metres short of the tryline, Jason Smith passed right to Lam, who drew the defence and created a gap before slipping a pass for O'Davis to crash over the line. O'Neill converted, and NSW's lead was reduced to 14–10 at half-time.

Dymock left the field injured soon after the break. Simon sliced a clearing kick out on the full from inside his half to gift Queensland vital field possession. Long passes from Goddard to Jason Smith and on to Dallas allowed the winger to get outside his opponent and dive to score in the right corner. O'Neill's conversion attempt sliced badly and the score remained level.

After a period of scrappy play, Seers broke through and looked trybound before Kelly produced a superb tackle. The Blues sent the ball right, again looking like scoring, but a swarm of defenders held McGregor up in-goal. Back in possession, Queensland threatened to score through O'Neill but Kosef thwarted him just short of the line. McGuinness caught a high punt before Simon legally stole the ball from Dallas in the 61st minute. NSW forced a goal-line drop-out but then Menzies knocked-on. Both sides exchanged errors before Simon drilled an impressive field-goal from an awkward angle to put NSW ahead 11 minutes from full-time. McGregor fumbled late in the next set, and then Queensland forced a repeat set of tackles. Five tackles later, a long pass back to O'Davis gave him ample time to kick an equalising field-goal, but his 20-metre attempt barely rose off the ground.

Five minutes from full-time, McGregor conceded a penalty after being wrong-footed in defence and tackling Sing too high. O'Neill lined up a potentially winning penalty kick 34 metres out and 8 metres inside the left wing. He struck his kick well but it landed agonisingly just under the crossbar. Tierney and Ikin both spilled the ball in the last three minutes as the Maroons failed to overcome their single-point deficit.

The Verdict

The Blues had racked up a five-match winning streak, their longest in Origin history. Yet they had won the first two games of 1997 by only two points and one point respectively. The Maroons could easily have levelled the series or won both games: poor goal-kicking and other missed chances was the difference.

↓ Nik Kosef prepares for a heavy landing. Kosef was one of few NSW players to make his Origin debut in the year marred by the Super League/ARL split.

↑ Ben Ikin breaks through on his way to touch down near the posts for the first try of the game.

↓ Craig Smith, playing in his only Origin series, feels Jamie Ainscough's tackle.

The Teams

NSW omitted McGregor (suspended for his high tackle on Sing in Origin II), Dymock (injured) and Raper (dropped after spending all the previous game on the bench). Johns returned from injury, Michael Buettner and Trent Barrett were newcomers, and some positional changes occurred.

Keeping the faith, Queensland selectors named an identical squad but made some positional changes.

The Game

Following excellent field kicks by Ikin and Brasher, Muir was penalised for a swinging arm that just missed Moore's head. Two tackles later, Lam drifted left near the 40-metre line but turned the ball right to Ikin. Evading Muir, Ikin flashed through and scored near the posts. Five tackles later, O'Neill followed Lam's kick and pinned Seers in-goal. After a late hit by Johns on Goddard, Goddard retaliated with punches and was penalised. Some typical Origin brutality and mayhem followed.

O'Brien was knocked out when ball-carrier Carroll powered into him. Opposing props Carroll and Craig Smith clashed in a scrum and swung punches as a melee erupted. Johns and Goddard

renewed hostilities, and Goddard floored Johns with a right hook. Johns left the field for treatment to his bloodied face but referee Ward called him back and sent him and Goddard to the sin-bin.

As a result of the scuffle, the Maroons lost a concussed Craig Smith. However, they received the penalty, then forced a goal-line drop-out. The teams exchanged knock-ons before Jason Smith copped a late high tackle from Pay. On the last tackle, Moore spun the ball right to Ikin and O'Neill, who drifted then barged through to score. O'Neill's sideline conversion gave Queensland a 12–0 lead. How different could the series have been if Queensland's goal-kicking were that accurate in game two?

Following an offside penalty to the Blues, Bartrim escaped penalty for a swinging arm that missed Toovey. NSW, however, received a penalty within moments after a late hit on Ainscough. Simon opened NSW's account with a 10-metre goal. Queensland lost a badly concussed Ikin in the 27th minute after he copped an accidental knee while tackling Buettner.

Successive penalties against the Maroons gave NSW territorial advantage leading up to the break Near the tryline, the Blues swept the ball right where Johns's clever pass sent Menzies through. Menzies scurried over the tryline and veered towards the posts but a certain try was incredibly bombed as Sing and Jason Smith held him up. Soon after a knock-on by Tierney, Brasher beat two Maroons to Johns's grubber but Brasher fumbled as he tried to swoop on the ball. He celebrated but Ward checked with his fellow officials and correctly disallowed the try. Queensland led 12–2 at half-time but had lost Craig Smith, Ikin and Sing to injuries.

NSW's failure to close its deficit was compounded when Carroll fumbled as he ran onto Brasher's pass. Five tackles later, Lam chip-kicked left into open space where Coyne raced to pounce and score. Another goal by O'Neill opened up a 16-point lead for the visitors, with rain falling in the second half.

Errors by the Maroons invited the Blues to fight back, with a goal-line drop-out followed by a penalty to NSW. Barrett was hit high by Bartrim before a NSW error led Queensland back into the Blues' half. Jason Smith forced a goal-line drop-out, then butchered a scoring chance with a bad pass and conceded a penalty for a high tackle on Barrett. The Blues entered the red zone, and Johns changed the point of attack to the right, drew the defence and fed McGuinness. As Kelly moved in, McGuinness

Players & Statistics

QLD Robbie O'Davis, Brett Dallas, Mark Coyne, Julian O'Neill, Matt Sing, Ben Ikin, Adrian Lam (c), Billy Moore, Jason Smith, Gary Larson, Neil Tierney, Jamie Goddard, Clinton O'Brien. **RESERVES** Stuart Kelly, Jeremy Schloss, Craig Smith, Wayne Bartrim. **COACH** Paul Vautin

NSW Tim Brasher, Ken McGuinness, Jamie Ainscough, Terry Hill, Matt Seers, Trent Barrett, Geoff Toovey (c), Nik Kosef, Adam Muir, Steve Menzies, Paul Harragon, Andrew Johns, Mark Carroll. **RESERVES** John Simon, Michael Buettner, Dean Pay, David Fairleigh. **COACH** Tom Raudonikis

Result Queensland 18 (Ikin, O'Neill, Coyne tries; O'Neill 3 goals) beat NSW 12 (Ainscough, Johns tries; Johns, Simon goals)

Referee Eddie Ward (Queensland)

Crowd 33 241

Man of the Match Gary Larson (Queensland)

as they forced a couple of goal-line drop-outs, but the Maroons defended well before Buettner became a casualty when he twisted his leg while tackled. After NSW entered Queensland's quarter, Toovey darted left, catching the defence off guard, and managed to offload to Johns, who reached out to score under the posts. Johns's conversion closed the margin to one converted try with five minutes left.

The Maroons defended desperately in the closing minutes. McGuinness chased Simon's chip-kick towards the right corner but the ball rolled into touch. Brasher broke away on a kick return and reached halfway, but the Blues looked finished when Menzies was taken into touch. But with 30 seconds left, referee Ward mysteriously penalised the Maroons in possession to give NSW a final chance. O'Davis prevented any last-minute miracle when he caught Simon's bomb safely in Queensland's quarter.

↑ Even with Super League players missing, brawling was as likely as ever to break out. The most spiteful match of the 1997 series was game three, even though the series had been decided.

fed Ainscough, who dived over in the corner. Johns's sliced goal-kick left the score 18–6 to Queensland.

With 18 minutes remaining, O'Neill miscued a field-goal attempt, then Lam missed with his effort a few moments later. A penalty against Carroll followed by Menzies being marched 10 metres allowed O'Neill to kick for goal, but he hooked the 28-metre shot. The Blues remained in the contest

The Verdict

The Maroons deserved the win. They established a lead whereas NSW blew golden opportunities through Menzies and Brasher. Queensland's win was particularly impressive given that a concussed O'Brien was its only available reserve after half-time.

The tight nature of the series ensured Origin lost nothing in comparison with Super League's tri-series.

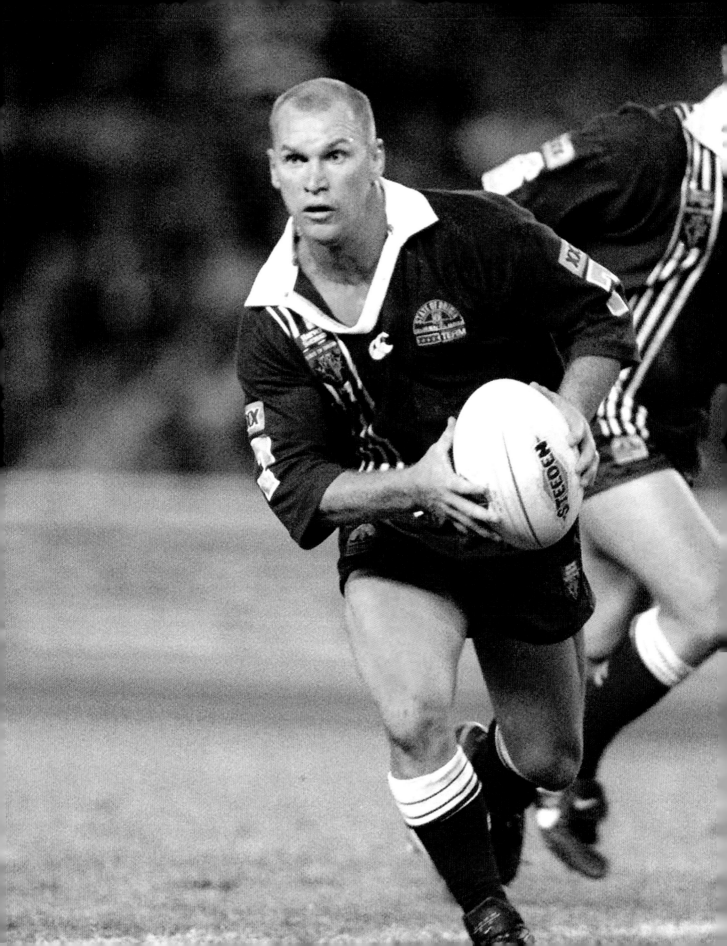

1998

Alfie's Return to Origin Glory

After the turmoil of the ARL/Super League 'war', 1998 was a significant year for rugby league as the two factions reunited to form the National Rugby League. With both states having a full quota of players eligible for selection, the 1998 Origin series attracted heightened appeal and interest. In a significant change, Origin games were scheduled on Friday nights. This caused great discomfort to NRL clubs because players would be needed to back up for their clubs later in the weekend. Also new was the video referee, a new technology that had been introduced in Super League.

Tom Raudonikis remained NSW's coach. Queensland appointed Wayne Bennett for his second coaching stint in Origin football. Bennett had coached the Maroons in the 1997 Super League tri-series, after his previous year as an Origin coach in 1988. The Brisbane Broncos were a new club that year, and ten years on Bennett was still coaching the team, having guided them to premierships in 1992 and 1993, as well as the 1997 Super League title. But Queensland had lost its past four Origin series that involved Broncos players (1992–94 and 1996), as well as the Super League tri-series games against NSW.

NSW was somewhat set back as injury or illness forced Stuart, Clyde, Mullins and Muir to miss the Origin series.

← Allan Langer was instrumental in Queensland's 1998 series win. It was the first time in seven years that he and and some of his Brisbane Broncos team-mates were part of an Origin series-winning team.

The Teams

Queensland named the former ARL-aligned players Sing, Ikin, Jason Smith, Larson and Bartrim. Origin newcomers Darren Lockyer, Shane Webcke, Peter Ryan and Tonie Carroll played in the Super League tri-series, but Jason Hetherington had not. Tallis (suspension) and Thorn (injured) were later replaced by debutants Steve Price and Martin Lang (the son of John Lang).

NSW's only debutants were Adam MacDougall and Rodney Howe. The Blues fielded many experienced Origin campaigners. Daley, Ettingshausen and Howe were NSW's only former Super League players. Wishart was recalled after an injured McGregor withdrew.

Bill Harrigan was appointed to referee the game.

The Game

Lockyer defused a high ball before Brasher fumbled one alongside Sailor as a NSW try beckoned. Queensland attacked after a penalty against Kosef. Langer's grubber hit Harragon's leg and Langer kicked the rebound where Walters pounced for a try, which the left-footed Lockyer converted. Three minutes later, Jason Smith broke through and sent Renouf scurrying to the posts. But a certain 12–0 lead went begging when Sing was penalised for colliding with Hill in backplay.

After Sailor dropped Fittler's high kick in the 17th minute, Andrew Johns fed the scrum and then speared a pass right to Daley, who drifted as Hill ran a decoy. Daley fed Brasher, who drew Sing and sent an unmarked Wishart flying for the corner. NSW trailed 6–4.

With NSW at halfway on tackle five, Wishart steered the ball left to Johns as Price rushed to pressure the likely kicker. However, Johns spun the ball to Daley as a gap opened in the defensive line. Daley turned a reverse ball to Brasher, who flashed through and scored. NSW led 8–6.

Seven minutes from half-time, Johns put up a bomb to the right, where Sing fumbled over his head as Wishart pressured him. Daley fielded the loose ball and juggled it low as he veered right before bouncing over the line. Johns hooked another wide-angled goal-kick, ensuring NSW led 12–6, despite scoring three tries to one. Johns stretched the margin to seven points with a 38-metre field goal just before the break.

After play resumed, MacDougall was lucky not to be penalised for dragging Sailor over the sideline after Sailor's momentum had stopped. Queensland regrouped, although NSW's defence held. But soon after a knock-on by Brasher, Langer grubbered to the right of the posts, where MacDougall astonishingly fumbled over his shoulder in a rolling motion. Price swooped for a converted try to close the margin to one point. Soon after the restart, Langer put in a deep kick where

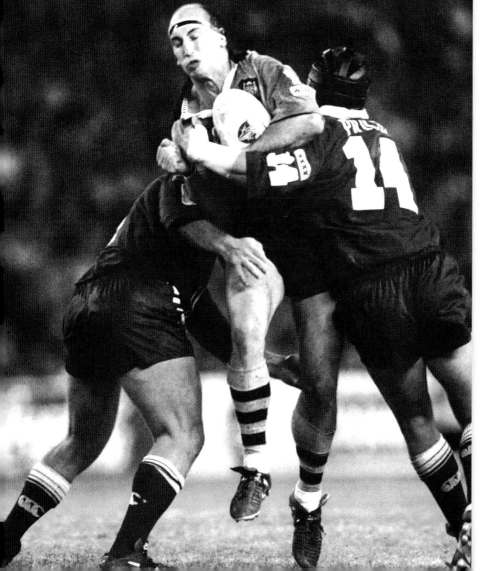

↓ David Barnhill feels the force of the Queensland defence.

Players & Statistics

QLD Darren Lockyer, Wendell Sailor, Steve Renouf, Darren Smith, Matt Sing, Kevin Walters, Allan Langer (c), Peter Ryan, Jason Smith, Wayne Bartrim, Gary Larson, Jason Hetherington, Shane Webcke. **RESERVES** Steve Price, Martin Lang, Ben Ikin, Tonie Carroll. **COACH** Wayne Bennett

NSW Tim Brasher, Rod Wishart, Andrew Ettingshausen, Terry Hill, Adam MacDougall, Laurie Daley (c), Andrew Johns, Brad Fittler, Nik Kosef, Dean Pay, Paul Harragon, Geoff Toovey, Rodney Howe. **RESERVES** David Barnhill, Steve Menzies, Matthew Johns, Ken McGuinness (not used). **COACH** Tom Raudonikis

Result Queensland 24 (Walters, Price, Langer, Carroll tries; Lockyer 4 goals) beat NSW 23 (Wishart, Brasher, Daley, Fittler, Menzies tries; A Johns goal; A Johns field goal)

Referee Bill Harrigan (NSW)

Crowd 36 070

Man of the Match Allan Langer (Queensland)

Brasher was forced in-goal. Five tackles later, Langer grubbered to the left of the posts, where Daley uncharacteristically dropped the ball near the tryline. Langer beat Lockyer to the loose ball. Queensland suddenly led 18–13 after Lockyer converted.

A few minutes later, Fittler's bomb to the left was spilled by a leaping Sailor and caught by MacDougall. On his back, MacDougall threw the ball inside, where Howe fired it to Fittler. He drifted, then straightened, stepped out of Darren Smith's tackle and scored in Sing's tackle. Johns finally landed a goal and NSW was back in front by one point.

From the restart, Lockyer's kick found the sideline but Queensland was unable to capitalise. Following Langer's next grubber, the ball ricocheted before Harragon slapped it towards the tryline, where Brasher just beat Sing to it. The Maroons pressed hard numerous times, and NSW was reprieved when Jason Smith fumbled Hetherington's pass.

The Maroons again failed to profit after Harragon restarted their tackle count in the 72nd minute. Walters's shallow kick was fielded by Wishart, who broke away. Replacement front-rower Lang astonishingly pursued Wishart closely before Sing stopped Wishart near halfway. Within the next few tackles, in the quarter, NSW moved the ball left with Fittler and Johns performing a run-around movement before Fittler fed Ettingshausen. He drew Ikin and Sailor to send the unmarked Menzies in to score. Johns pushed his crucial goal-kick to the right, and NSW led 23–18 with five minutes left.

Hanging on by a thread, the Maroons regained the ball in their 10-metre zone in the 79th minute. With Brasher in the defensive line on the next tackle, Walters kicked over the NSW defence. The ball bounced awkwardly but Ikin raced to it before being tackled 5 metres inside NSW's half. The Maroons threw the ball around as NSW's defence struggled to regroup. After four tackles, 11 metres from the tryline, Langer spun the ball right to Jason Smith. He delayed his pass to brother Darren, who drew Fittler and fed Walters as Carroll loomed behind Walters's right. With Ettingshausen and Brasher advancing towards him, Walters sent a short ball to Carroll, who flashed through the gap to score with 46 seconds left. Carroll brought the ball to within 10 metres of the posts and Lockyer calmly landed the do-or-die conversion, giving his side a sensational 24–23 victory.

The Verdict

State of Origin was back to its best with the fever-pitch intensity and tempo of the game and the lead changing four times. Yet the result pivoted largely on handling errors from kicks that cost Queensland three tries and NSW two. The Blues scored five tries to four, so goal-kicking was also decisive as Lockyer landed four from four to Andrew Johns's one from five.

↑ Allan Langer's short-kicking game led to three Queensland tries.

↓ A front-rower chasing a winger? Seeing is believing. Martin Lang pursues Rod Wishart.

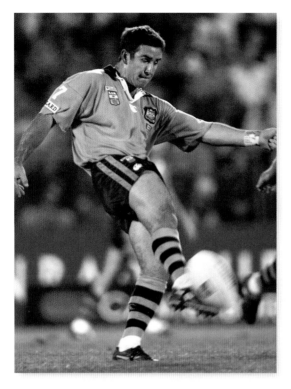

→ Andrew Johns cemented the halfback spot for the Blues after having spent much of the previous two series playing at hooker.

Players & Statistics

NSW Tim Brasher, Rod Wishart, Paul McGregor, Terry Hill, Adam MacDougall, Laurie Daley (c), Andrew Johns, Brad Fittler, David Barnhill, Dean Pay, Paul Harragon, Geoff Toovey, Rodney Howe. **RESERVES** Glenn Lazarus, Andrew Ettingshausen, Nik Kosef, Steve Menzies. **COACH** Tom Raudonikis

QLD Darren Lockyer, Wendell Sailor, Steve Renouf, Darren Smith, Matt Sing, Kevin Walters, Allan Langer (c), Wayne Bartrim, Brad Thorn, Gorden Tallis, Gary Larson, Jason Hetherington, Shane Webcke. **RESERVES** Steve Price, Martin Lang, Ben Ikin, Tonie Carroll. **COACH** Wayne Bennett

Result NSW 26 (McGregor 2, MacDougall, Fittler, Brasher tries; Johns 3 goals) beat Queensland 10 (Sailor, Sing tries; Lockyer goal)

Referee Bill Harrigan (NSW)

Crowd 40 447

Man of the Match Rodney Howe (NSW)

The Teams

Thorn and Tallis returned for the Maroons, who omitted Ryan and Price. However, Price was brought back when the suspended Jason Smith was ruled out.

For NSW, McGuinness and Matthew Johns were dropped as McGregor and Lazarus returned.

The Game

The Blues were quickly on the back foot when Toovey fumbled from dummy-half as Langer swamped him. Three tackles later, Langer chip-kicked to the right. With MacDougall in from his wing, the ball soared over his head and Sailor pounced for a try. Lockyer's sideline conversion gave the Maroons a dream start with a 6–0 lead. Five minutes later, Andrew Johns hoisted a bomb from just inside Queensland's half. The ball bounced near the posts after Smith misjudged its flight and Sailor was caught out of position. MacDougall collected the ball and passed right to Howe, who off-loaded to Daley. He drew Langer and Sailor before switching play to the left and lofting a pass to MacDougall, who scurried to the tryline. NSW trailed by two points.

From the restart, Webcke hammered Harragon in a tackle so brutal that both players had to leave the field for treatment before returning with head bandages. At the 15-minute mark, Langer sent Tallis

→ Terry Hill on the burst. Hill finally established himself as a first-choice centre for NSW when a full quota of players was available for selection.

a pass that referee Bill Harrigan questionably ruled forward. The Blues threw the ball around and got to within 2 metres of the uprights. Toovey rifled the ball right to Johns, who fired a cut-out pass to Kosef. He released the ball back to Daley, who threw a basketball pass to McGregor. Stepping inside and evading Sing, McGregor charged over the line in a tackle. As Johns sliced the conversion attempt, NSW led 8–6.

The first penalty came after 19 minutes when MacDougall impeded Sailor after Johns hoisted a high ball. However, the Blues were back on the attack

in their next set when Johns made a powerful, weaving run before he was tackled on the 20-metre line. Dummy-half Brasher ran to the right on the last tackle, drew the defence and fed Kosef, who unloaded to McGregor. He stepped outside Sing and spun, then planted the ball on the line. From wide out, Johns finally landed a goal to give NSW an eight-point lead.

McGregor exited the game soon afterwards with a shoulder injury. Vulnerable under the high ball, Sailor dropped a bomb from Johns, who soon sliced a surprising field-goal attempt. The Blues gained the initiative, sometimes appearing offside in defence as well as slowing down Queensland at the play-the-ball. The Maroons did not seem to adapt to the situation. But this had nothing to do with any of NSW's tries, nor the next key moment. Ikin spilled an inside pass from Walters when he ran into Barnhill's heavy tackle inside Queensland's half. From a play-the-ball a few tackles later, Fittler accepted the first pass and fooled Bartrim with a dummy before stepping through some shoddy defence for a soft try. Johns converted from in front of the posts and the Blues led 20–6 at the break.

NSW made good ground in the 45th minute before Fittler sent a spiralling bomb towards Sing, who dropped it. Brasher fielded the loose ball and whirled around before fending off Lockyer to score. Johns converted to give NSW a 20-point lead. Hill made a long break after a Queensland defensive lapse a couple of minutes later and, although the Blues did not score again, they looked comfortable.

In the 52nd minute, Lockyer ran the ball out of his quarter with Sing in support. But Sing tripped over one of Lockyer's tacklers and his boot hit Lockyer in the jaw. Lockyer left the field. Hetherington dropped the ball before the Maroons finally gained good yards in the 60th minute. Inside NSW's territory, Walters drifted right from dummy-half before veering left and feeding Langer, who threw a long pass to Ikin. Stepping right, Ikin drew Fittler to create a gap before turning an inside pass to Sing, who burst through. Sing attracted Brasher and shaped to feed an unmarked Renouf on the inside but instead kept going and plunged across the line in Wishart's tackle. Ikin hooked the conversion attempt wide.

The game continued at a lively pace. The Maroons mounted a few attacking raids but NSW's defence held firm. Lang was concussed and left the field after fiercely running from a goal-line drop-out and copping a heavy front-on tackle from Kosef. Howe made a couple of strong hit-ups late in the game, and

his strong all-round performance earned him man of the match. The score remained 26–10.

The Verdict

The 16-point margin equalled NSW's biggest Origin win. The Blues took their chances, especially in the first half, and controlled the pace at the play-the-ball. The Maroons rarely got into the game after opening the scoring and failed to adapt to referee Harrigan's leniency in the ruck.

↑ Paul McGregor was injured in game two, but not before he scored two tries as the match swung NSW's way.

→ Robbie O'Davis was recalled for game three, and was one of only a few Maroons to have been involved in Queensland's 1995 and 1998 series wins.

The Teams

Queensland omitted Hetherington, Bartrim and Lang, preferring Goddard, Jason Smith and Gee. In a late setback, Carroll and Thorn withdrew due to injury. Their places were taken by O'Davis and Ryan, and some positional changes occurred.

The Blues initially named an unchanged line-up but were set back when McGregor, Ettingshausen, Harragon and Howe were ruled out with injury. They were replaced in the squad by McGuinness, Dymock, Kearns and debutant Tony Butterfield. Kosef was suspended after a club match, and his place went to Furner. NSW suffered a further blow when Toovey pulled out with a virus on match day and was replaced by Matthew Johns.

Harrigan became the second referee to control an entire Origin series, after Manson two years earlier.

The Game

In a fierce opening few minutes, Lockyer was injured on a kick return but played on. Ikin received a cut above his eye and briefly left the field for treatment. In the eighth minute, Fittler targeted Sailor with a bomb but Sailor caught it somewhat awkwardly, jumped to his feet and scurried away before being tackled on halfway. Acting-half Renouf turned the ball right, where Lockyer, Walters, Langer, Jason Smith and Ikin handled before Ikin turned an inside pass to O'Davis. He fed Smith, who drew a defender and released a backhand flick pass to Walters. Sandwiched by MacDougall and Daley, Walters sold them a dummy and broke away to run in to score. For the third time in the series, Queensland jumped to a 6–0 lead.

After receiving consecutive penalties, the Blues worked their way into a scoring position before a leaping Brasher fumbled Andrew Johns's bomb. The teams exchanged penalties, then Fittler drew the defence and fed Hill. He charged towards the right corner but fumbled as Renouf tackled him into the corner post. Several minutes later, Tallis broke through ineffective tackles on a damaging charge from inside Queensland's half. Standing in the tackle, Tallis released a one-handed pass inside to Ikin, who steamed onto the ball and punched the air as he ran 35 metres untouched to score under the crossbar. With Lockyer's conversion, Queensland suddenly led 12–0.

Price dropped a straightforward pass soon after the restart to allow NSW to return to the offence. In the 10-metre zone, Andrew Johns moved right and floated a long pass to Hill, who veered towards the sideline and drew Renouf. Hill switched the ball inside to McGuinness as Renouf slipped over, allowing McGuinness to step through and reach out to score. Andrew Johns's conversion attempt sprayed wide to the right, leaving NSW eight points down.

NSW returned downfield soon after the kick-off following a penalty against Jason Smith. On tackle five, Andrew Johns's well-weighted grubber was knocked dead by Sailor as Wishart closed in. However, referee Harrigan unaccountably awarded Queensland

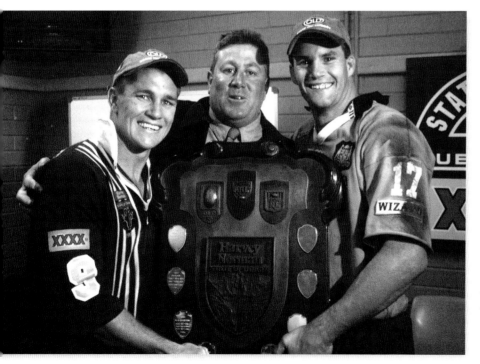

↓ Jamie Goddard, the Maroons manager Chris Close and Peter Ryan savour Queensland's decisive series win.

a 20-metre restart. The Maroons were quick to take advantage and it was too late for Harrigan to correct his error. The Blues were able to launch one more raid before the break, but they were thwarted when Jason Smith pulled off a vital tackle on Brasher.

The Maroons appeared in control after the resumption with good ball control and solid defence, while their defence did what NSW's defence had done in game two. The Blues suffered an injury blow in the 48th minute when MacDougall failed to clean up a kick and was hurt as Ikin tripped over him before Gee pounced on him. In the 54th minute, the referee erroneously awarded a handover to NSW after Langer's last-tackle chip-kick was touched by Matthew Johns before Sing recovered it. Andrew Johns launched a testing bomb a couple of minutes later but O'Davis caught it and broke away.

After the NSW halfback put in a poor clearing kick with 16 minutes remaining, the Maroons ventured into NSW's quarter. On the last tackle, dummy-half Gee looked left but turned the ball the other way to Langer, who stepped left then right, wrong-footing Fittler. Fooling the defence into thinking that he might kick, Langer stepped and weaved his way past Matthew Johns and

↑ Wendell Sailor accelerates away from NSW's Ken McGuinness.

Brasher before scoring near the posts. O'Davis converted to extend Queensland's lead to 18–4.

The Blues threw the ball around desperately but repeatedly went sideways rather than forwards. They continued to attack with gusto but Queensland's defence held. In the last few minutes, Ikin collared Butterfield within a metre of the tryline before Sailor defused another bomb. A knock-on by Brasher enabled the Maroons to work their way downfield, where Jason Smith landed a field goal with just one minute remaining.

The Verdict
Although the Maroons won convincingly, there was little between the sides in the first half. Unlike games one and two, Queensland struck after a high ball went towards Sailor. A chance for NSW to hit back went begging before the Maroons took their very next chance to ensure a 10- or 12-point turnaround. After NSW's first try, the Blues were not helped by Johns's missed conversion and a refereeing lapse. Unlike the first two games, Queensland went on with the job after scoring first. The match-winning converted try in game one was perhaps the most crucial part of Queensland's series win.

Players & Statistics

QLD Darren Lockyer, Robbie O'Davis, Steve Renouf, Ben Ikin, Wendell Sailor, Kevin Walters, Allan Langer (c), Darren Smith, Jason Smith, Gorden Tallis, Gary Larson, Jamie Goddard, Shane Webcke. **RESERVES** Steve Price, Matt Sing, Peter Ryan, Andrew Gee. **COACH** Wayne Bennett

NSW Tim Brasher, Rod Wishart, Laurie Daley (c), Terry Hill, Adam MacDougall, Brad Fittler, Andrew Johns, Jim Dymock, David Barnhill, David Furner, Tony Butterfield, Matthew Johns, Glenn Lazarus. **RESERVES** Robbie Kearns, Ken McGuinness, Dean Pay, Steve Menzies. **COACH** Tom Raudonikis

Result Queensland 19 (Walters, Ikin, Langer tries; Lockyer 2, O'Davis goals; J Smith field goal) beat NSW 4 (McGuinness try)

Referee Bill Harrigan (NSW)

Crowd 38 952

Man of the Match Shane Webcke (Queensland)

1999

Defence Controls Drawn Series

Both Wayne Bennett and Tom Raudonikis stood down as coaches of their respective states because of their club commitments. Queensland's new coach was the former Maroons halfback Mark Murray, who had coached Brisbane Norths to the QRL premiership in 1998. Another former State of Origin star, Wayne Pearce, was appointed as NSW coach.

In further changes, the states were forced to feature different-looking teams. NSW was without Harragon, Ettingshausen and Pay, all of whom had retired from representative football. McGregor was injured and Brasher and Wishart were struggling for form. For Queensland, Langer had retired from football, while Renouf and Larson had quit representative football. Lockyer was injured at the beginning of the series but there was a chance of him returning for the later games.

Another notable change was that NSW had a new home ground, Stadium Australia, based at Homebush. The venue was built for the 2000 Olympic Games and could host up to 100 000 people.

← Queensland captain Adrian Lam holds the Origin trophy aloft after the competition's first drawn series, which resulted in the Maroons retaining the shield since they had won the previous series.

The Teams

NSW's selectors named eight debutants: Robbie Ross, Darren Albert, Matt Geyer, Ryan Girdler, Bryan Fletcher, Jason Stevens, Craig Gower and Anthony Mundine. Meanwhile, Clyde was chosen for the first time in five years. But coach Pearce's innovative horse-riding bonding session backfired when Clyde and Kearns suffered injuries that cost them their places. Lazarus replaced Kearns and debutant Luke Ricketson came into the squad. Meanwhile, Fittler replaced Daley as captain.

With Langer unavailable, Lam regained the Queensland halfback and captaincy roles. Tonie Carroll, Lang, Greenhill and Hetherington were also recalled. The only new faces were Mat Rogers and Chris McKenna, both of whom played for Queensland in the 1997 Super League tri-series.

The Game

After an early knock-on by Stevens and an offside infringement by NSW, Rogers opened the scoring with a 35-metre penalty goal. The Maroons muscled up in defence with Hetherington particularly dominant before Lazarus conceded two penalties for holding down. From the second of these, Rogers kicked Queensland to a 4–0 lead. Rogers and Darren Smith pursued Geyer for the second time following a kick and they pounded him into the turf. Queensland enjoyed field position but Jason Smith twice squandered possession to let NSW off the hook.

In the 26th minute, Rogers made a weaving run but twisted his knee and was forced off the field. Jason Smith had another horror moment when he kicked out on the full from inside Queensland's territory. NSW forced a goal-line drop-out but Fittler dropped an inside pass from Andrew Johns in the repeat set.

Forty metres from Queensland's uprights, Ross passed right to Johns, who fired the ball to Hill. He stepped off his right foot, broke past Sing's one-on-one tackle, evaded O'Davis and sent Mundine in to score behind the posts. Girdler kicked the conversion to give NSW a 6–4 lead. The Maroons had held the

↑ Darren Albert tries to break through in his only Origin appearance for the Blues.

upper hand but just one lapse was all it took for them to lose their advantage.

Five minutes before half-time, O'Davis made a break from a kick return but lost the ball on halfway. Jason Smith was penalised for holding Stevens down in a tackle but Girdler sliced a penalty kick from the left of the posts. Queensland went on the attack just before half-time but an inside pass from Lam to Walters was dubiously ruled forward.

Rogers returned for the second half. After a forward pass from Girdler, Queensland forced a goal-line drop-out. After Kosef dropped a pass, Tallis got within 3 metres of the tryline. Queensland spread the ball right through Hetherington, Walters, Lam and the Smith brothers as the defence seemed disorganised. Darren Smith drew Girdler and sent Rogers across in the corner but replays showed the ball came loose millimetres before it hit the ground. Video referee Graeme West disallowed the try.

The teams exchanged handling errors before play was halted twice in quick succession as Gower and O'Davis were treated for injuries. Howe was penalised for holding Jason Smith down in a tackle, although the decision appeared questionable considering Smith briefly held Howe by the jersey. Rogers levelled the scores with the subsequent penalty goal.

Both teams faltered in possession before Johns made a costly error as his penalty kick failed to find touch. This gifted Queensland handy field position, and then Howe cost NSW again when he hit Tallis high within range of the uprights. Rogers landed his fourth goal to nose his side in front. Soon after, Ikin

Players & Statistics

QLD Robbie O'Davis, Mat Rogers, Darren Smith, Matt Sing, Wendell Sailor, Kevin Walters, Adrian Lam (c), Jason Smith, Chris McKenna, Gorden Tallis, Craig Greenhill, Jason Hetherington, Shane Webcke **RESERVES** Ben Ikin, Steve Price, Tonie Carroll, Martin Lang **COACH** Mark Murray

NSW Robbie Ross, Darren Albert, Laurie Daley, Terry Hill, Matt Geyer, Brad Fittler (c), Andrew Johns, Nik Kosef, David Barnhill, Bryan Fletcher, Rodney Howe, Craig Gower, Jason Stevens **RESERVES** Glenn Lazarus, Luke Ricketson, Ryan Girdler, Anthony Mundine **COACH** Wayne Pearce

Result Queensland 9 (Rogers 4 goals; Rogers field goal) beat NSW 8 (Mundine try; Girdler 2 goals)

Referee Bill Harrigan (NSW)

Crowd 38 093

Man of the Match Jason Hetherington (Queensland)

← Steve Price attempts to bust the tackles of Glenn Lazarus and David Barnhill.

↑ Mat Rogers scored all of Queensland's points in the first two games of the 1999 series.

dropped a straightforward pass near his 20-metre line before O'Davis was incorrectly penalised for supposedly stripping the ball in a three-man tackle. The scores were tied up again as Girdler landed a penalty goal.

After fielding a kick in his in-goal area, Rogers headed down the shortside and into the field of play but was forced into touch by Geyer. Fletcher was thwarted within a metre of the tryline, then Gower burrowed for the line from dummy-half but was turned on his back and held up. Ross, Tallis, Gower and Lang traded fumbles as the pressure was on. With 11 minutes left, Johns surprisingly pushed a close-range field-goal attempt to the right. Three minutes later, Lam's long-range effort fell short.

Darren Smith crucially jolted the ball from Mundine in a one-on-one tackle. Jason Smith fielded the loose ball and was deemed tackled when Mundine stripped him of the ball and was penalised. The Maroons attacked and, after three tackles, Hetherington threw a long pass back to Rogers, who stab-kicked a wobbly 15-metre field goal to give his side a one-point lead with six minutes remaining.

Webcke conceded a critical penalty three minutes later to help NSW enter Queensland's half. After three tackles, Barnhill gave the ball to Fittler, who attempted an equaliser but he sliced it well wide. The Maroons held on before a fumble from Geyer brought the game to a close in the final 30 seconds as a brawl threatened to erupt.

The Verdict

In a game of twists and turns, near misses at the tryline and failed field-goal attempts, NSW scored the only try but ended up on the wrong side of the scoreline. The most telling factor was NSW's lack of discipline. Queensland received only two more penalties than NSW (8–6) but four of these were within goal-kicking range and another allowed the Maroons to work their way into position for the winning field goal.

The Teams

For NSW, Albert, Gower and Lazarus were dropped, an injured Barnhill was missing and Stevens (suspension) was unavailable. Toovey, MacDougall and Mark Carroll were recalled. Michael Vella and Ben Kennedy were named to debut.

Queensland made one forced change with the injured Lam replaced by Origin debutant Paul Green, another player from the 1997 Super League tri-series. Walters was Queensland's new captain.

The referee was Steve Clark, appointed to control his first Origin match.

↑ A triumphant Laurie Daley farewells the Stadium Australia crowd after his final Origin game in Sydney.

The Game

Even though heavy rain kept some spectators away, an Origin record crowd of 88 336 was present. They had reason to cheer after just three tackles. From NSW's 20-metre line, Toovey passed left to Johns, who spun a torpedo pass to Daley. Veering farther left, Daley drew Darren Smith and delayed a pass to Girdler, who broke through before drawing O'Davis to send Ross sprinting 40 metres to score near the left post. The electrifying try came after just 42 seconds, easily the fastest try in an Origin game, and NSW quickly led 6–0.

With Greenhill already in the blood bin, referee Clark penalised McKenna for being slow to get off a tackled player. Mark Carroll dropped a pass a few moments later before copping a shoulder-charge from Webcke. Hill reacted to a tackle from Tallis in NSW's next set: the two held jerseys and clashed face-to-face before being dragged apart.

Neither side made headway despite penalties and goal-line drop-outs both ways. Green failed to find

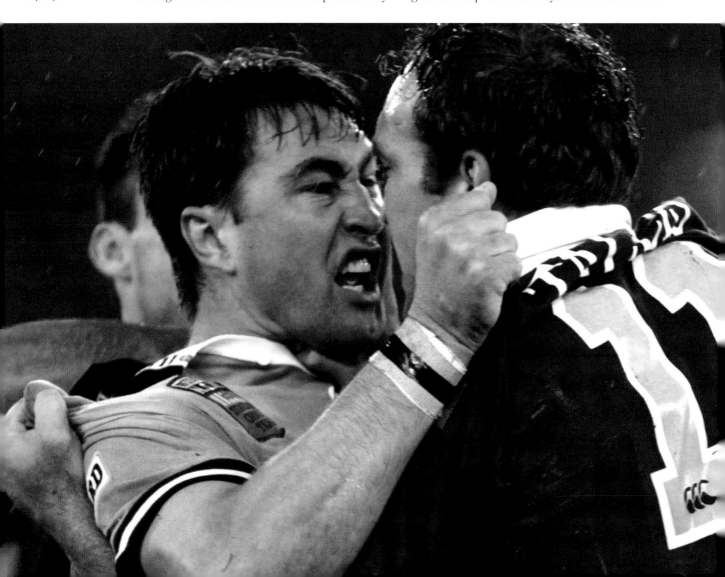

Players & Statistics

NSW Robbie Ross, Adam MacDougall, Ryan Girdler, Terry Hill, Matt Geyer, Laurie Daley, Andrew Johns, Brad Fittler (c), Bryan Fletcher, Nik Kosef, Rodney Howe, Geoff Toovey, Mark Carroll **RESERVES** Luke Ricketson, Michael Vella, Ben Kennedy, Anthony Mundine **COACH** Wayne Pearce

QLD Robbie O'Davis, Mat Rogers, Matt Sing, Darren Smith, Wendell Sailor, Kevin Walters (c), Paul Green, Jason Smith, Chris McKenna, Gorden Tallis, Craig Greenhill, Jason Hetherington, Shane Webcke **RESERVES** Ben Ikin, Steve Price, Tonie Carroll, Martin Lang **COACH** Mark Murray

Result NSW 12 (Ross, Daley tries; Girdler 2 goals) beat Queensland 8 (Rogers try; Rogers 2 goals)

Referee Steve Clark (NSW)

Crowd 88 336

Man of the Match Laurie Daley (NSW)

the sideline with a penalty kick when an acrobatic Ross kept the ball in play, only to see Geyer fumble seconds later. After Rogers made a long, weaving run, an offside penalty allowed Rogers to land a goal. In the 26th minute, Hetherington evaded two defenders as he made a darting run from dummy-half. Eight metres inside NSW's territory, Green passed right to Walters, who dummied inside before drifting right and drawing two defenders. Girdler's attempt to intercept Walters's pass to Jason Smith failed, allowing Smith to exploit the gap left by Girdler. Smith dummied inside and evaded Ross before drawing MacDougall and passing to the unmarked Rogers, who scored. Rogers kicked a superb sideline conversion to give Queensland an 8–6 lead.

Ross fumbled near his own line after Walters placed a kick to the corner. The Maroons attacked for five tackles before Green put up a bomb to the right. Rogers beat MacDougall in the jump for the ball but lost it as he came down, spoiling a golden opportunity to extend Queensland's lead. To make matters worse, Rogers was injured and forced from the field.

Five tackles later at the other end of the field, referee Clark ruled O'Davis knocked-on a Johns bomb even though O'Davis faced his own line and spilled the ball that way. NSW was suddenly on the attack before Sailor fumbled an intercept attempt. Five metres from the tryline, Johns drifted left before turning a reverse pass to Daley, who charged through Tonie Carroll's tackle and powered over the line. Girdler converted for a 12–8 lead to NSW. The Maroons had an immediate chance to hit back after

Johns's clearing kick sliced out on the full, but the Blues held on and stayed in front at half-time.

A penalty against Greenhill put NSW on the attack early in the second half. Ross and Johns went tantalisingly close to the tryline before NSW forced a goal-line drop-out. But Queensland held out, then had a chance after a penalty against Toovey. Tallis charged for the line from close range but crashed into the right upright to help Daley and Carroll thwart him. The Maroons forced a goal-line drop-out before Fittler retrieved a kick and broke away.

Queensland forced another goal-line drop-out before another scoring chance went begging when a bomb bounced off a leaping Sailor's shoulder over the tryline. The Maroons forced another drop-out but Walters was penalised for an obstruction. Mark Carroll was on the end of an 'Origin special' as Hetherington and Webcke flattened him with a fierce shoulder-charge. Play continued briefly before it was halted to allow trainers to help the groggy Carroll off the field.

The Maroons lost O'Davis a few minutes later after his leg twisted as he was tackled. With about ten minutes left, the teams took it in turns to fumble in good field position. After a Queensland mistake, Fittler veered right and lofted a cut-out pass to Hill. He drew Tonie Carroll but his pass to a trybound Geyer was forward. With five minutes left, referee Clark ruled that Green had illegally stripped the ball from Geyer. Replays confirmed that Geyer dropped the ball cold. The Blues went on to dominate field position without scoring before a knock-on from Green in the final minute ensured NSW victory.

↓ Jason Smith is well held by Brad Fittler and Luke Ricketson. Smith locked the scrum for Queensland throughout the series.

The Verdict

It was a tale of opportunities taken and lost as well as the odd questionable refereeing decision. Rogers, Tallis and Sailor were each all but over the line but none registered a score, and O'Davis got a poor call. NSW swooped twice and scored enough points to win. Daley was man of the match in his last Origin game on home soil and, interestingly, it was his first such award in Origin football.

← Confrontation—State of Origin style. Terry Hill and Gorden Tallis come face to face.

↑ Rodney Howe feels the pain of a tackle from Jason and Darren Smith.

The Teams

Daley was named NSW captain for his farewell Origin game when Fittler withdrew because of injury. Barnhill was recalled before being ruled out after being suspended in club football and Furner was called up.

For Queensland, Rogers and Sing were injured. Green was dropped, then recalled when Kevin Walters pulled out on the game eve with a hamstring strain. Lockyer, Lam and Thorn were recalled and some positional changes were made.

The Game

Rain made the Suncorp Stadium surface slippery. Johns's first kick went awry, and some chasers were offside. The attacking Maroons spread the ball right, where O'Davis headed for the corner but was knocked into the sideline by Johns. Queensland had better field position as both sides faltered, with McKenna and Kosef repeatedly erring. An offside penalty gave the Blues their first attacking chance. Near the posts, Toovey moved the ball right to Johns and Daley. He scooped up the low pass one-handed

and fed Hill, who drew Sailor and sent an unmarked Geyer over in the right corner. Girdler sliced the goal-kick and NSW led 4–0.

McKenna blundered again as he conceded a penalty on the last tackle. The game see-sawed amid errors from both sides. Ikin left the field dazed after a strong tackle by Daley. In the 23rd minute, Johns's well-placed bomb bounced away from Lockyer and rolled towards the tryline. Kennedy fielded the ball and unloaded to Ricketson, but he fumbled the wayward pass with support looming and no defence in sight. Almost immediately, Webcke fumbled in Howe's sturdy tackle. However, Daley knocked-on after NSW won the scrum, although replays suggested Jason Smith dislodged it and was fortunate not to be penalised.

In NSW's next tackle count, Vella fumbled as he was hammered. Webcke neared NSW's 10-metre line before Green darted right from dummy-half, straightened and dummied before burrowing under two tacklers and plunging over the line. Queensland hit the lead as Lockyer converted. But Tonie Carroll made a mistake, and then Jason Smith floored Mark Carroll with a swinging arm. Carroll pushed the offender in retaliation, and tempers threatened to flare as players from both sides converged. Clark warned Smith and penalised him although replays suggested Smith's first point of contact was with Carroll's shoulder. Girdler levelled the scores with the penalty goal on offer.

Officials missed a slight knock-on by Geyer as he escaped from his in-goal area after fielding a kick.

Lockyer's fumble on a kick return helped NSW with half-time looming. The scores remained deadlocked at the break after Daley narrowly missed a field-goal attempt.

Geyer fumbled in a tackle in his quarter within five minutes of the resumption. A couple of tackles later, Green passed left to Lam, who was swamped but released a one-handed pass to Ikin. He drew Ross and Geyer and fed an unmarked Lockyer, who stumbled over the line. The Maroons led 10–6 as Lockyer's conversion attempt hooked marginally. Queensland returned to the attack, helped by MacDougall conceding a penalty for ball-stripping, but Webcke lost the ball as he rucked it up. Queensland dominated field position for a while. Lam darted from dummy-half, only to be thwarted a metre from the tryline. He sniped again from dummy-half but was held up by three defenders.

The Blues finally crossed halfway but errors cruelled their chances. As the rain became heavier, O'Davis dropped a straightforward kick on his 10-metre line. With NSW attacking, MacDougall fielded Daley's stray pass, stepped right and unloaded to Ross. The ball went to Johns and Howe, who put through a grubber to the right. Sailor was out of position and Geyer easily beat him to ground the ball in-goal and level the scores. Girdler sliced the difficult conversion attempt and a drawn match and drawn series looked possible with eight minutes left. The players knew that a draw would enable Queensland to regain the Origin crown after its 1998 series win.

As time ticked away, NSW could not get into an attacking position. Daley's hopes of a successful farewell looked gone when he dropped a pass in his quarter with three minutes left. The Maroons played out their tackle count conservatively, not

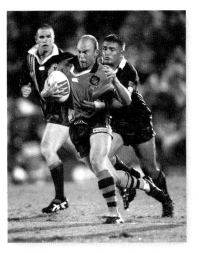

seeing any need for a field goal. The Blues regained the ball but they had to go the length of the field. They reached Queensland's half on the last tackle before Hill hoisted a bomb towards Queensland's 10-metre line. O'Davis scooped up the loose ball but fumbled when he met the defence. With 50 seconds left, the Blues worked towards a position for a series-winning field goal. Queensland's defence appeared offside before Howe played the ball near the posts. Daley drew several defenders as he veered right from dummy-half and turned an inside pass to Ross. However, Ross overran the ball and spilled it with a gaping hole in front of him. The game and Daley's winning prospects were as good as over, and the Maroons rejoiced when full-time arrived.

The Verdict

It would be unfair to pay too much attention to NSW's final chance going begging, as there were so many twists and turns throughout the series. The wafer-thin margin between success and failure could not have been better exemplified.

← Ben Kennedy surges forward as Shane Webcke seeks to halt his progress.

↓ Darren Lockyer tries to break away from Laurie Daley and Geoff Toovey.

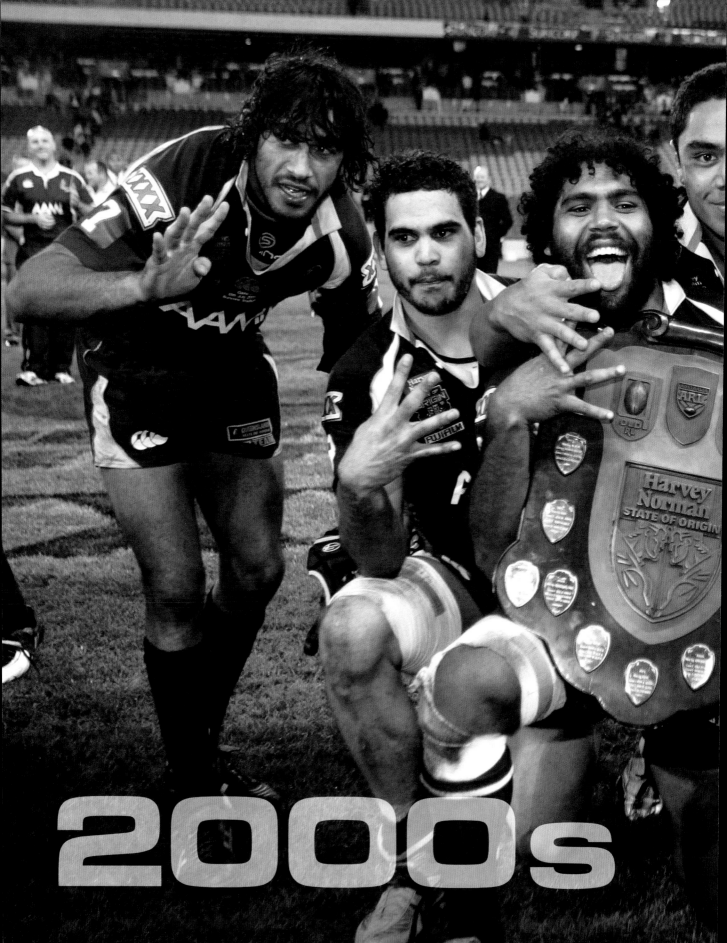

2000s

2000

Harrigan and Blues Take Centre Stage

Stadium Australia was scheduled to host the first and third games of the 2000 Origin series, before the venue was used for the Olympic Games later in the year. After the previous year's drawn series, both states looked to a more decisive outcome as they began the third decade of State of Origin football. Wayne Pearce and Mark Murray remained as coaches.

The Blues had to make some changes to their personnel after Mark Carroll joined Laurie Daley in retirement from representative football. Injuries kept Kosef and Mundine on the sidelines, and an injured Andrew Johns was unavailable for game one.

For the Maroons, Kevin Walters's State of Origin career ended due to injury problems. McKenna, Sing and O'Davis also had injuries and were sidelined.

← Ben Kennedy is wrapped up by the Queensland defence, which was fragile at times as NSW clean-swept the series. Talks of a NSW dynasty were common after the Blues won comprehensively in the second and third games.

The Teams

NSW chose a squad blending youth and experience. Geyer and Ricketson were dropped and Fittler and Kearns recalled. Debutants were Shaun Timmins, Brett Kimmorley, Scott Hill and Eric Grothe Jnr. But Grothe and Ross were forced out with injuries, with Ainscough recalled and David Peachey called up to debut.

Queensland's selectors named a similar side to the previous year. , Greenhill lost his place. Rogers was recalled and Paul Bowman and Russell Bawden were the only debutants.

The Game

The Maroons forced an early goal-line drop-out, before Tallis charged from dummy-half and was held up over the line on tackle five. A few minutes later, Lam left the field with a pinched nerve in his collarbone after a late, high shot from Fletcher, who escaped penalty. NSW received a relieving penalty and another penalty five tackles later when Hetherington infringed in a tackle. Girdler subsequently kicked NSW to an early 2–0 lead.

↑ Adrian Lam, who was always a danger when he ran with the ball, scored two tries after suffering an injury early in the game.

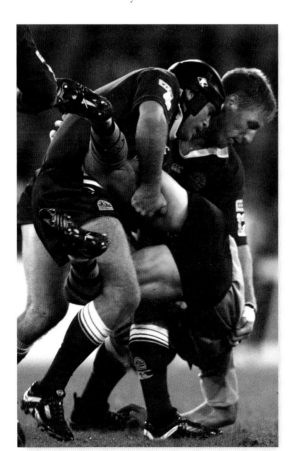

→ Darren Smith and Brad Thorn send an opponent crashing into the turf.

After the teams exchanged fumbles, NSW received six more tackles after Price smothered Kimmorley's kick. On the last play, Fittler drew the defence and sent Girdler across the tryline, but the pass was ruled forward. In NSW's next set, Scott Hill deflected a pass forward. From the scrum near halfway, Green fired the ball right to Ikin, who kicked downfield. MacDougall slipped over and the ball rolled in-goal, where Rogers pounced for a try. Rogers's conversion attempt hit the right post and Queensland led 4–2.

Lang fumbled as he tried to play the ball in his quarter. Scott Hill soon drifted left and fed Fittler, whose cut-out pass found Girdler. Girdler put through a grubber for MacDougall, who outpaced Rogers and scored. NSW's lead was two points after Girdler hooked the goal-kick.

In the 28th minute, Bowman wrong-footed Terry Hill and sent Ikin scurrying away, but Green fumbled in support with a try beckoning. Nine minutes from the break, Scott Hill fumbled in a heavy front-on tackle. Within the next few tackles, Lam veered left, evaded Furner and then ducked under Terry Hill's attempted tackle to score a soft try. Queensland led 8–6 as Rogers's kick missed again. As half-time arrived, Sailor dived to catch a chip-kick while Lockyer raced across and couldn't stop. His leg collided with Sailor, knocking the winger unconscious.

Soon after the resumption, Lam set up a break by Thorn before Hetherington was tackled on the 20-metre line on the last tackle. From dummy-half,

Lam veered right and threw dummies before sliding under Fittler's last-ditch tackle. Rogers's sideline conversion extended Queensland's lead to 14–6. On a kick-return a few minutes later, Lockyer crucially fumbled in Kearns's hammering tackle. Furner regained possession and passed left to Fittler and Girdler, who sprinted towards the corner. Ikin appeared to produce a try-saving tackle but Girdler released the ball inside for MacDougall to score. The Maroons held an insecure two-point lead after Girdler converted.

NSW pressed Queensland's line for three sets in quick succession but Queensland held out. Carroll made a threatening break before the Blues were caught offside. The Maroons accepted the two points, courtesy of Lockyer. MacDougall looked set to score again, but Sailor made a try-saving tackle. Ikin's jaw was fractured when Furner's shoulder charge went wrong. After Terry Hill knocked on, the Maroons sought a potentially winning try. Carroll stepped through and crossed the tryline but was turned on his back and held up. As Queensland applied further pressure, Scott Hill took an intercept and sent the ball right, where Furner spilled it sideways and seemingly forward. Terry Hill fumbled the loose ball in a forward motion but the referee awarded play-on, and Kimmorley made a break. Two tackles later, Scott Hill stepped left and fed Peachey, who sent Girdler scampering away before he beat Lockyer's and Jason Smith's tackles to score in the corner. NSW was lucky as replays confirmed Furner and Hill knocked on. Harrigan then sin-binned a dissenting Tallis before changing the decision to a send-off as Tallis continued a verbal barrage. The scores remained level when Girdler hooked the conversion marginally. But the controversy left Queensland a player down for the last nine minutes.

Lam hooked a long-range field-goal attempt in the 75th minute. Then Bowman inadvertently knocked down a pass but was ruled to have played at it, allowing the Blues to head downfield. With four minutes left, Fittler looped to the right and offloaded to Toovey. He turned the ball to Howe, who stepped right and lofted a risky pass to Ainscough. Sailor reached to intercept but the ball just passed his fingers, and Ainscough sent Peachey diving across

in the corner, giving NSW a 20–16 lead. Despite Girdler's missed conversion, the Blues maintained the pressure. Lam made a break in the last 20 seconds but was thwarted just short of halfway.

The Verdict

The refereeing dominated post-match discussion, especially in Queensland. The overlooked knock-ons before Girdler's try and Tallis's dismissal were deemed to have cost the state the game. Yet the Maroons could still have won—had Lam succeeded with his field-goal attempt or Sailor intercepted Howe's pass in the lead-up to the final try. Luck went NSW's way, particularly in the last ten minutes.

↑ David Furner is tackled by Darren and Jason Smith. Furner later come under scrutiny for fracturing Ben Ikin's jaw with a shoulder charge that went wrong.

The Teams

Queensland lost Sailor and Ikin to injuries sustained in Origin I. Sing and O'Neill were recalled. NSW omitted Vella and had to replace the injured Peachey and Terry Hill. Brasher, Johns (reserve) and Muir (reserve) were recalled. Despite his controversial influence in game one, Bill Harrigan was re-appointed to referee the game.

The Game

The field was slippery after rain before the game. After being booed by the parochial crowd, referee Harrigan detected an obvious knock-on by Fittler in the first minute. Kearns was caught offside on the next tackle, enabling Rogers to open the scoring with a 30-metre goal. Heavy but legal tackles were regular early on.

The Blues launched attacks but lacked the finishing touch. Two quick penalties to NSW were wasted when Kimmorley kicked in the red zone after only three tackles. From a set move, Fletcher spilled Brasher's pass with the tryline beckoning. MacDougall kneed O'Neill in the ribs in a tackle but escaped punishment. Moments later, Kimmorley sliced through and fed Muir, but he fumbled as Rogers produced a try-saving tackle. After rain began to fall, Howe escaped penalty when he hit Lang high with a swinging arm, much to the ire of the crowd.

Harrigan controversially penalised Rogers for stripping the ball from Girdler, who subsequently missed a goal-kick from the left of the posts. The Maroons soon received a contentious stripping penalty, and then they forced a goal-line drop-out before Tallis fumbled a pass from Lam. Timmins gave away a penalty for holding Bawden off the ball

after Jason Smith's bomb bounced. Rogers kicked Queensland to a 4–0 lead. NSW launched some further raids as half-time neared but the Maroons held out.

An injured Jason Smith was unable to resume. Toovey gifted Queensland a handy penalty immediately after the resumption. The Maroons reached the 10-metre zone but Bowman's kick went too deep. A couple of minutes later, Darren Smith was penalised for not allowing Brasher to play the ball. Three tackles later, Brasher fed Fittler on the left. Fittler stepped both ways and rushed past Thorn before reaching to score in Lockyer's tackle. The visitors led 6–4 after Girdler's conversion.

From the restart, Fletcher found an opening and gained nearly 50 metres but NSW turned over possession. A couple of minutes later, Bowman passed right to Lam. He took the ball up and switched back inside to Sing, who weaved past Howe. Held by Toovey, Sing unloaded to a rampaging Tallis, who stepped out of Timmins's tackle and charged over the tryline with MacDougall clinging to him. In typical Origin brutality, Tallis hit Mac-Dougall in the face. Rogers goaled and Queensland were back in front by four points.

The close scoreline gave no indication of what was to follow. With the game and the series on a knife's

↑ Scott Hill's progress is brought to a stop. Hill scored a crucial try in the second half as the Blues romped to victory.

→ Adam Muir handled the ball several times as the Blues scored three tries in the space of five minutes in the second half.

edge, Johns inspired a rout that reaped NSW three tries in just five minutes. A superb yet freakish try began the onslaught in the 60th minute, after NSW ran the ball on the last tackle 45 metres from the uprights. Johns darted right from dummy-half and fed Muir, who slipped and off-loaded to Furner. He drew Lam to create a gap on the inside, turning the ball to Timmins, who raced through and chip-kicked wide of Lockyer. The ball ricocheted off Lockyer's outstretched left hand and uncannily flew straight to Timmins, who had an uninterrupted run to the line.

Two tackles later, Fletcher produced a superb offload to Brasher, who broke away. On the next tackle, Muir looked left but turned the ball right, where Fittler fired it on to Johns, who drew Bowman before sending a well-timed pass to Scott Hill. He threw a dummy and flashed between Lam and Sing before diving for the line. During the next set of tackles, Johns began a passing movement featuring Kearns, Kimmorley, Muir, Furner, Johns again and Kennedy. Inside the quarter-line, Kennedy stepped off both feet, wrong-footed Lockyer, veered right and sent Furner crashing over in the right corner. Girdler converted all three tries and, seemingly in a flash, NSW's 10–6 deficit became a 24–10 lead. The Maroons had no possession during this five-minute period as their defence was at sixes and sevens and their opponents executed brilliantly. Andrew Johns's contribution was reminiscent of Wally Lewis at his best.

Kennedy came close to scoring in the 71st minute before Queensland finally showed some enthusiasm with the ball. In the last four minutes, Bowman was tackled just centimetres from the tryline. Within the final two minutes, Girdler intercepted Green's cut-out pass and sent

MacDougall down the left wing before Girdler backed up in support and scored. Johns took the conversion attempt but pulled it.

The Verdict

NSW's series-clinching 28–10 victory produced the state's highest score and winning margin in Origin football. But the score did not reflect how close and hard-fought the game was for the first 60 minutes. NSW's three quick tries midway through the contest were breathtaking in style and decisive in the context of the game. And for the second successive match, the Blues overcame a deficit at half-time, something that they had done only once in State of Origin football before this series.

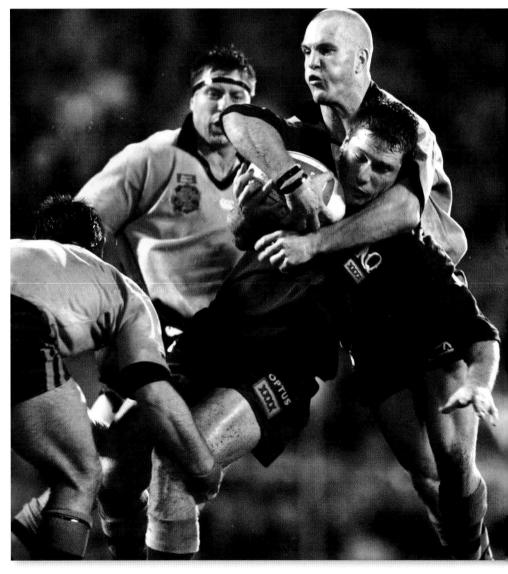

↓ Paul Bowman has nowhere to go as he is wrapped up. Bowman's Origin career began with three losses.

↑ The Maroons are dejected after suffering the heaviest defeat in State of Origin football. Amid talks of a gloomy future, it was easy to forget other facts: Queensland was unlucky to lose game one, the series was very close until three-quarters of the way through game two, and NSW's series win was its first for three years.

→ Matt Gidley receives congratulations after scoring one of his two tries on debut. He crossed the line two other times, but was denied because of forward passes.

The Teams

Queensland's selectors dropped Bawden, Price and Green, and Jason Smith was ruled out with injury. Sailor, Ikin and McKenna returned from injury and Greenhill was recalled. For NSW, the injured Timmins and suspended Howe were out of contention. Vella was recalled and Matt Gidley was named for his Origin debut.

The Game

The contest began at a frantic pace with strong attack, gang tackles, offloads and indiscretions. The penalty count was 3–1 to the Maroons within seven minutes. After eight minutes, Hetherington burrowed from dummy-half but was thwarted agonisingly short. NSW came close to scoring in the 13th minute but Kimmorley's offload went forward. Kennedy and Ikin were early casualties. After 16 minutes,

O'Neill fired the ball towards Sailor, but Girdler's superb anticipation enabled him to intercept and race 39 metres to score near the posts and grab a 6–0 lead for NSW. Three tackles after the restart, Johns, Kimmorley and Girdler combined to send MacDougall away. On the last play, Fittler stepped right and drew the defence before slipping a well-timed pass to Muir. He sliced between two Maroons before stepping inside Lockyer to score near the posts. The Blues shot to a 12–0 lead after a relatively even opening 15 minutes of play.

A knock-on by Stevens after the restart enabled Queensland to attack. Five tackles later, Lockyer hoisted a bomb to the left where Brasher fumbled in-goal. Rogers followed through and grounded it for a try before landing an impressive conversion to close the margin to six points. At the end of NSW's next set, Kimmorley put up a high ball, which MacDougall chased and kicked as soon as it hit the ground. Lockyer retrieved the ball and looked for a way out of his in-goal area but Kimmorley's driving tackle forced a knock-on. Lockyer attempted to knock the ball dead but it hit Kimmorley in the face before Girdler pounced. The video referee awarded a try as replays showed Kimmorley did not knock-on. Another easy conversion by Girdler extended the lead to 12 points.

The Maroons received six more tackles at the end of their next tackle count when Furner charged down O'Neill's kick. Lam employed the bomb five tackles later and Sing knocked the ball back as he out-jumped Sailor and MacDougall. Sing regained the ball and shovelled it to Darren Smith, who stepped right and skirted around Girdler and MacDougall to score in the corner. Rogers's side-line conversion attempt pushed just to the right.

After a 'six more tackles' call in the 35th minute, Brasher chased Kimmorley's chip-kick but was impeded by Smith, and Girdler kicked NSW to a 20–10 lead. A Girdler fumble soon after the restart saw the Maroons within 20 metres at the end of the ensuing tackle count. Smith passed to Lam, who sucked in two defenders and sent Bowman striding through. Bowman ran over two Blues and crossed the tryline but was held up by Johns from front-on. This decisive save allowed NSW to hold a comfortable ten-point lead at the break.

Within four minutes of play resuming, Johns, Kimmorley, Hill, Fletcher and Ainscough handled

before Ainscough unloaded to Kearns. The ball moved via Furner to Fittler, who sold Sing a dummy, drew Lockyer and sent Johns skidding over beside the left post. Girdler's goal made the score 26–10. Clearly on top, the Blues went on to produce a point-scoring blitz as the Maroons were deflated. Fragile Queensland defence coupled with brilliant execution and teamwork from NSW led to Girdler (52nd minute), Gidley (58th), Fletcher (65th) and MacDougall (71st) running in converted tries. It might have been worse for Queensland as forward passes denied Gidley further tries in the 61st and 63rd minutes, and Brasher was held up over the line just before MacDougall's try. After Fletcher scored, he pretended to throw a hand grenade as his team-mates ducked and fell. It was a pantomime but some observers claimed it was bad sportsmanship.

Tallis scored a try with three minutes left but NSW ensured it was no consolation. In the last 30 seconds, ten passes were thrown in a mesmeric movement, which ended with Gidley scoring in the right corner. Girdler iced the cake with a superb kick for a final 56–16 score.

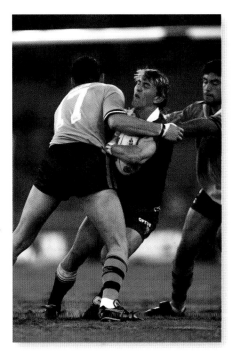

↑ Mat Rogers finds there is no way through the NSW defence. It was to be his last Origin series.

Players & Statistics

NSW Tim Brasher, Adam MacDougall, Ryan Girdler, Matt Gidley, Jamie Ainscough, Brad Fittler (c), Brett Kimmorley, Scott Hill, Ben Kennedy, Bryan Fletcher, Jason Stevens, Geoff Toovey, Robbie Kearns. **RESERVES** Andrew Johns, David Furner, Adam Muir, Michael Vella. **COACH** Wayne Pearce

QLD Darren Lockyer, Mat Rogers, Paul Bowman, Matt Sing, Wendell Sailor, Ben Ikin, Adrian Lam (c), Darren Smith, Chris McKenna, Gorden Tallis, Martin Lang, Jason Hetherington, Shane Webcke. **RESERVES** Julian O'Neill, Brad Thorn, Tonie Carroll, Craig Greenhill. **COACH** Mark Murray

Result NSW 56 (Girdler 3, Gidley 2, Muir, Johns, Fletcher, MacDougall tries; Girdler 10 goals) beat Queensland 16 (Rogers, Smith, Tallis tries; Rogers 2 goals)

Referee Bill Harrigan (NSW)

Crowd 58 767

Man of the Match Ryan Girdler (NSW)

The Verdict

The scoreline looked demoralising for Queensland as the fine line between winning and losing was not reflected in the result. Queensland gifted NSW two tries in the first half, Hetherington went very close early on and Bowman was held up just before half-time. It was a case of opportunities missed at one end and taken at the other. Then, once the Blues got on a roll, they kept their foot on the accelerator to go on and crush Queensland with an authoritative display. Consequently, the magnitude of the result was impossible to ignore. Chris Close described it as the most humiliating loss in Origin football and the blackest day in Queensland rugby league history. Girdler was named man of the match, after he and his team broke numerous Origin point-scoring records in a game and in a series.

2001

The Turnaround, Return to Square One and the Return of Alfie

After Queensland's heavy series loss in 2000, the QRL made major changes before the 2001 series. Wayne Bennett returned for his third stint as coach, rugby league was added to the Queensland Academy of Sport, a pre-season training camp for emerging Origin candidates was established and a new panel of selectors was appointed.

The scheduling of Origin games took another twist with games fixed for Sunday nights and club football scrapped on the same weekend. There was to be a five-week gap between the first and second matches, then a three-week gap between the second and third games. In another change, teams were restricted to making 12 interchanges per game. However, an interchange would not be counted if an injured player were replaced because of illegal play that had been penalised.

Queensland was certain to field a new-look team because injuries and player unavailability were an issue, in addition to the notion that mass changes were needed after the 2000 series. Lam, Carroll, Hetherington and Jason Smith (all to England) and Thorn (rugby union) moved overseas, while McKenna, Rogers and Ikin were injured. NSW had injury problems too, with Johns, Girdler, Brasher and Peachey on the sidelines.

The third game of the series was played at Brisbane's ANZ Stadium because the redevelopment of Suncorp Stadium had begun.

← Darren Lockyer offloads to a support player. Lockyer showed his true talent as the Maroons recovered from the disappointment of 2000 to reclaim the Origin crown.

The Teams

Queensland's squad contained ten debutants: Lote Tuqiri, Daniel Wagon, Kevin Campion, Petero Civoniceva, John Buttigieg, John Doyle, Chris Walker, Chris Beattie, Brad Meyers and Carl Webb. Green was named at halfback and Gorden Tallis was the Maroons' new captain.

NSW retained many players from the 2000 series, and recalled Croker and Barrett. The debutants were Mark Hughes, Michael De Vere, Luke Priddis and Nathan Hindmarsh. Scott Hill and St George Illawarra winger Nathan Blacklock were surprise omissions from the squad.

The Game

After Queensland somewhat changed its starting line-up, rookies Buttigieg, Civoniceva and Meyers made hit-ups in the first set of tackles. At the end of NSW's first set, Kimmorley kicked straight to Lockyer, who veered left from his quarter and drew the defence before sending Tuqiri away between two defenders. Tuqiri stumbled but stepped inside

↓ John Doyle played a key role as Queensland broke away from NSW in the second half. His footwork from dummy-half was particularly fine.

Players & Statistics

QLD Darren Lockyer, Lote Tuqiri, Paul Bowman, Darren Smith, Wendell Sailor, Daniel Wagon, Paul Green, Brad Meyers, Petero Civoniceva, Gorden Tallis (c), John Buttigieg, Kevin Campion, Shane Webcke. **RESERVES** Chris Walker, Chris Beattie, Carl Webb, John Doyle. **COACH** Wayne Bennett

NSW Mark Hughes, Jamie Ainscough, Matt Gidley, Michael De Vere, Adam MacDougall, Brad Fittler (c), Brett Kimmorley, Jason Croker, Bryan Fletcher, Nathan Hindmarsh, Robbie Kearns, Luke Priddis, Jason Stevens. **RESERVES** Trent Barrett, Michael Vella, Ben Kennedy, Rodney Howe. **COACH** Wayne Pearce

Result Queensland 34 (Lockyer, Smith, Webb, Doyle, Buttigieg, Walker tries; Lockyer 5 goals) beat NSW 16 (Gidley, Fittler, Barrett tries; De Vere 2 goals)

Referee Bill Harrigan (NSW)

Crowd 38 909

Man of the Match Gorden Tallis (Queensland)

Hughes before sending Lockyer in for a try near the posts. Lockyer converted and the Maroons led 6–0 after just three minutes.

A penalty against Buttigieg a few minutes later gave NSW a chance. Gidley ran onto Fittler's bullet-like pass and lunged for the line. However, Tuqiri turned Gidley on his back and stripped the ball from his grasp. Priddis and Hindmarsh conceded a crucial penalty for holding Sailor down too long, and Queensland forced a goal-line drop-out before Tallis was held 10 metres from the tryline. From acting-half, Smith darted and wrong-footed Kearns to create a gap on the right before diving through the gap to score. Lockyer converted and Queensland led 12–0 after as many minutes.

With the Maroons attacking again, Tallis busted two tackles but was stopped a metre from the try-line. Following a penalty against Meyers, Croker made a 40-metre break downfield. Entering the 10-metre zone, NSW spun the ball right through Priddis, Kimmorley and Gidley, who scored despite last-ditch tackles by Smith and Tuqiri. De Vere's kick struck the right post, leaving the Maroons with an eight-point lead.

An offside penalty against NSW enabled Queensland to raid enemy territory again before Webcke's charge for the tryline was thwarted by three defenders, who forced a knock-on. Lockyer sliced through NSW's defence on a kick return but his pass to Tuqiri was intercepted by Ainscough. Green produced a 40-20 kick to put the Maroons on the attack again. In the ensuing set, Webb shrugged off two tacklers but was foiled by four defenders just centimetres from the tryline.

Three minutes from half-time, Howe committed the deadly sin of conceding a penalty on the last tackle when he slowed a play-the-ball. In NSW's quarter just moments later, Webb charged to the left, spun out of Croker's and Gidley's shoulder-grabbing tackles, powered into Ainscough and surged across the line in Croker's tackle. Queensland led 16–4 at half-time but lost the injured Meyers and Smith for the rest of the game.

NSW had the first chance to strike shortly after the break. Fletcher stepped out of a tackle and scurried for the line. But as he reached to score in a tackle, the ball came loose as it hit Lockyer's knee. Three tackles later, Doyle veered right from dummy-half and stepped out of Fittler's tackle. Doyle fed Lockyer, who scurried past De Vere and committed Hughes and MacDougall before sending unmarked Doyle running to score near the posts. The Maroons held a commanding 22–4 lead as they again profited soon after NSW blew a scoring chance.

Webcke left the field injured. An offside infringement against Lockyer gave NSW an opportunity but Gidley threw a pass into open space. Tuqiri fielded the loose ball. Stepping from dummy-half, Doyle threw a dummy and darted between Howe and Priddis before standing in Hughes's tackle and unloading to Green. Green stepped left, drew Croker and fed Buttigieg, who charged for the line and crashed over.

Doyle was at it again in the 55th minute. He fed Tallis, who cut back inside and broke away from three Blues before sending Walker on a 32-metre run to the posts. Lockyer converted for a 34–4 lead. In the 60th minute, Tallis set up another line-break for Lockyer, only for Lockyer to send a forward pass to a try-bound Walker.

The Blues finally halted Queensland's momentum 15 minutes from full-time when Fittler intercepted a pass from Green and ran 60 metres to score under the crossbar. In the 71st minute, Hughes, Barrett, Fittler, De Vere and MacDougall

combined to draw the defence and send Barrett in to score behind the posts. De Vere's second goal brought up the final score of 34–16.

The Verdict

Many followers claimed that Queensland's victory was miraculous in the light of NSW's comprehensive wins in the two previous Origin games. But a closer look at the first 45 minutes reveals the fine line between success and failure. Twice the Blues crossed Queensland's tryline without grounding the ball before the Maroons quickly hit back. Furthermore, Webb's try just before half-time resulted from a costly mistake by Howe. Queensland's win, therefore, was really not an upset at all. Rather, it showed that each game could take on a course of its own—and that a team simply had to take its chances.

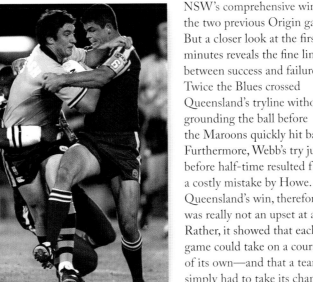

↑ Michael De Vere feels the force of a tackle from John Buttigieg and Petero Civoniceva. Buttigieg and Civoniceva were part of the Maroons' new-look forward pack.

← Nathan Hindmarsh tries to free himself from a tackle. But Queensland's defence was hard to crack.

→ Mark O'Meley had a strong debut for NSW, and set up a try for Brad Fittler.

The Teams

NSW sacked De Vere, Croker, Kimmorley, Hindmarsh and Kennedy. Stevens and Howe were injured. Girdler, Barrett, Ricketson, Muir and debutant Mark O'Meley came into the starting line-up. Debutants Matt Adamson and Andrew Ryan and the recalled Gower were named as reserves. When Kearns was ruled out with injury, Stevens returned after overcoming his neck injury.

Queensland received a serious setback when Tallis was ruled out for the season with a serious neck injury. Buttigieg (suspended) and Doyle (injured) were also out. Bawden was recalled, and Dane Carlaw and Nathan Fien were debutants. Lockyer took over the captaincy.

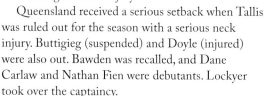

The Game

NSW earned good field position early on after Lockyer's clearing kick deflected off Ricketson. A penalty against Campion provided Girdler with a 35-metre penalty attempt, but he pulled it. Strong NSW defence pinned the Maroons on their 20-metre line but it went to waste when Priddis was penalised. After the teams traded handling errors, Girdler was punished in front of his posts for trying to play the ball prematurely. Lockyer's penalty goal gave Queensland a 2–0 lead after ten minutes.

The battle remained even until five minutes later when the NSW forwards muscled up in defence, giving Queensland little room to move. Green intercepted a pass as NSW threatened Queensland's tryline in the 20th minute. Sailor fielded a grubber-kick and threw a dangerous pass to Lockyer, who fielded it on the half-volley behind his line and broke through to the halfway line. Lockyer's grubber-kick a few tackles later forced a goal-line drop-out but the Maroons failed to profit. When Fittler sliced a clearing kick out on the full in the 26th minute, Queensland again failed to capitalise.

NSW sought to strike after Fien matched Fittler's mistake a few minutes later. Thirty-five metres from Queensland's uprights, the ball moved right to Barrett, who drew the defence and sent Ricketson striding between Wagon and Green for a try. Girdler's conversion gave NSW a 6–2 lead. After NSW forced a goal-line drop-out five minutes later, Barrett again cleverly confused the defence and fed Gidley and Ainscough, but the latter was tackled into the corner post by Tuqiri. NSW forced a goal-line drop-out just before half-time but Queensland held on.

With rain falling, conditions became slippery after the break. Four minutes in, Queensland threatened to create an overlap from its quarter as the ball moved left from Fien to Green, Lockyer and Smith. As Smith passed, Ainscough knocked the ball loose, toed it ahead, retrieved it and scored unopposed. Ainscough accidentally knocked the ball forward when tackling Smith, so the correct call was 'play on' following a recent rule change. It was lucky for NSW, which led 12–2 after Girdler's easy kick.

In the 48th minute, Sailor dropped an easy pass in his quarter. Gower swooped

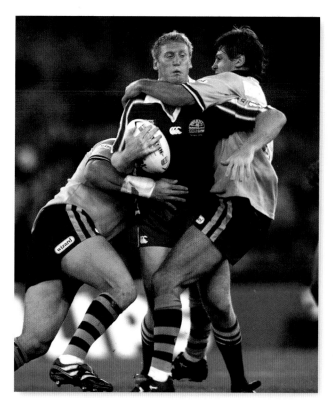

→ Brad Meyers is thwarted by NSW defence, which proved a lot harder to penetrate than in the previous game.

Players & Statistics

NSW Mark Hughes, Jamie Ainscough, Ryan Girdler, Matt Gidley, Adam MacDougall, Brad Fittler (c), Trent Barrett, Luke Ricketson, Adam Muir, Bryan Fletcher, Mark O'Meley, Luke Priddis, Jason Stevens. **RESERVES** Craig Gower, Michael Vella, Matt Adamson, Andrew Ryan. **COACH** Wayne Pearce

QLD Darren Lockyer (c), Lote Tuqiri, Darren Smith, Paul Bowman, Wendell Sailor, Daniel Wagon, Paul Green, Brad Meyers, Petero Civoniceva, Dane Carlaw, Russell Bawden, Kevin Campion, Shane Webcke. **RESERVES** Chris Walker, Chris Beattie, Carl Webb, Nathan Fien. **COACH** Wayne Bennett

Result NSW 26 (Fittler 2, Ricketson, Ainscough, Barrett tries; Girdler 3 goals) beat Queensland 8 (Walker try; Lockyer 2 goals)

Referee Bill Harrigan (NSW)

Crowd 70 249

Man of the Match Trent Barrett (NSW)

before fumbling as Sailor pounced. Referee Harrigan awarded Queensland a scrum feed even though NSW did not appear to benefit from Sailor's knock-on. What happened next proved more astonishing. Fittler argued with Harrigan that the Blues had had no advantage. Harrigan appeared to be swayed, overturning his decision to give NSW the scrum feed. It proved decisive. In the following set, Fittler, Barrett and Gidley combined, before Gidley found Barrett on the inside. He reached out and slammed the ball down as he was tackled. Harrigan awarded the try but replays detected a slight knock-on as the ball slipped from Barrett's fingertips just before hitting the ground. The score became 16–2.

Webcke was penalised for a high tackle on Gower soon after. Six metres in Queensland's half, Gower fed O'Meley, who burst through Webcke's tackle and charged ahead. Drawing Lockyer, O'Meley sent Fittler racing away to touch down beside the left post. Girdler converted, carrying NSW to a convincing 22–2 lead with 26 minutes left.

The game became scrappy. Carlaw fumbled 12 minutes from the end before Priddis stepped out

of a tackle and surged across the line as three Maroons tackled him. Referee Harrigan called on video referee Mick Stone, who disallowed the try when replays showed that the ball had come loose under Priddis's right arm. After MacDougall was penalised for lifting his knee as he ran with the ball at Civoniceva, the Maroons ventured to within 5 metres of NSW's line. Green passed left to Walker, who veered right and crashed over the line. Lockyer's conversion made the score 22–8.

After a knock-on from Walker, Adamson was tackled by Beattie, who went on with the tackle, resulting in a scuffle. Beattie was penalised, allowing NSW to attack. Three tackles later, Priddis flipped the ball left to Fittler, who put Wagon in two minds before stepping through his tackle and reaching for the line. NSW had an 18-point lead. Harrigan gave Queensland three inconsequential penalties in the last few minutes, but knock-ons by Beattie ended any chance of the Maroons finishing creditably.

The Verdict

Despite a few controversial decisions, the refereeing could not be blamed for Queensland's loss as the Blues took their chances to score five tries to one. Ainscough's try at a critical moment was fortuitous but perhaps reflected the overall trend of the game.

↓ Mark Hughes looks for a way through as Paul Bowman approaches. Picked at fullback despite being a regular centre in club football, Hughes was a consistent performer in what was to be his only Origin series.

→ A victorious Wayne Bennett with the player he recalled from England, Allan Langer. The duo tasted Origin success in each of the first three decades of Origin football.

The Teams

Queensland axed Fien, Beattie and Bawden, and Doyle and Buttigieg returned. At coach Bennett's request, the selectors sprang the biggest selection surprise in Origin history when they recalled Langer. Bennett deemed that Langer, who was nearing his 35th birthday, would be an ideal source of inspiration to the Maroons. Langer received permission from his English club Warrington to play.

For NSW, the injured Ricketson was replaced by Croker, who was then forced out after an injury in a club match. Menzies was added to the squad. In another setback, an injured Barrett withdrew and Kimmorley was recalled as his replacement. Fittler confirmed this would be his final Origin match.

↓ Carl Webb did an impressive job off the bench for the Maroons in the series.

The Game

Queensland began badly when Buttigieg knocked on in the first tackle. From the scrum, Kimmorley spread the ball left to Fittler and Girdler. Evading Bowman, Girdler sold Sailor a dummy and brushed off Smith to score in the corner. The try, the fastest in Origin football, came after just 38 seconds. Girdler's sideline conversion gave NSW an instant six-point lead.

In the tenth minute, Lockyer was tackled by Kimmorley but unloaded an inside pass to Meyers. He drifted left and busted Gidley's tackle before drawing Ainscough to send Tuqiri breaking away. Tuqiri drew Hughes and passed inside to Walker, who veered left and then scurried away from Priddis to score in the corner. Lockyer's conversion attempt missed and Queensland trailed 6–4.

Bowman and Smith were penalised for a lifting tackle on Hughes, before Stevens fumbled in Webcke's brutal front-on tackle. With the Maroons returning to the attack, Girdler fumbled Langer's chip-kick as Bowman pressured him. Buttigieg was tackled a metre from the right post before Langer fired the ball right to Smith, who turned it back to Bowman. He stepped off both feet and evaded Fittler before reaching out to score. Queensland led 8–6 after Lockyer sliced another goal-kick.

A forward pass by Green was followed by a stripping penalty to NSW, allowing Girdler to level the scores with a goal. Both teams surrendered possession after receiving a penalty. After a knock-on from Queensland, Kimmorley retrieved the loose ball and threw a marginally forward pass as he was driven towards his tryline. Although NSW did not appear to benefit from Queensland's knock-on, referee Harrigan strangely gave Queensland a penalty: he deemed Kimmorley's forward pass deliberate. Lockyer subsequently kicked Queensland to a two-point lead.

The even nature of the match gave no indication of the carnage that began shortly after the restart. The Maroons returned to enemy territory after NSW markers were caught offside. Five tackles after the penalty, Gower moved up too quickly on Langer, who stepped around him and offloaded right to Wagon. He unloaded in a tackle to Carlaw, who charged past MacDougall and Hughes and then crashed over near the right post. Lockyer kicked the conversion and Queensland led 16–8.

At the end of the next set, Doyle swung the ball left to Lockyer, who took it on his 30-metre line in centrefield. With the defence racing up, Lockyer stepped around Fletcher and threw a dummy before accelerating between Ryan and Gidley. Lockyer crossed NSW's 40-metre line and kicked ahead. Walker beat Tuqiri to the ball and dived past MacDougall to score in the corner. Queensland suddenly led 22–8 after Lockyer's conversion. NSW paid dearly for mistakes in defence on the last tackle in consecutive sets.

Kimmorley threw a forward pass in NSW's next set. Four tackles later, Smith veered left and fed Langer. He drew the defence and turned the ball inside to Lockyer, who scored. After a poor start, Queensland held a 28–8 lead at half-time.

In the 53rd minute, Doyle turned defence into attack when he inadvertently knocked the ball down and then recovered it. Near NSW's tryline four tackles later, Doyle passed right to Langer, who shaped to pass but then stepped left. He ducked under Vella's tackle and was flipped on his back by Muir, but managed to reach over his head to touch down. After Queensland received a penalty with 20 minutes remaining, Lockyer spiralled a cut-out pass right to Bowman, who stepped right, drew Fittler and Girdler, then stepped left through the gap and shrugged off O'Meley to score.

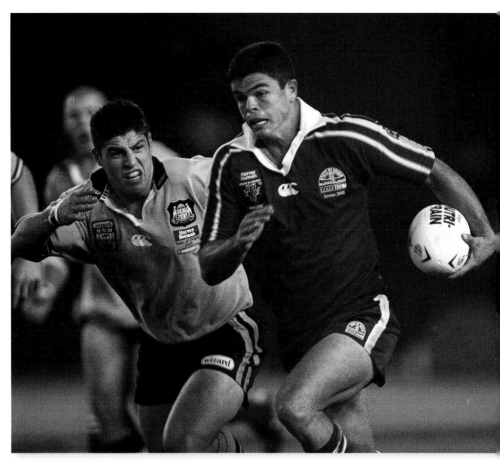

Queensland's momentum stalled when Green fumbled from dummy-half. Gower linked up on the left with Kimmorley, Fittler and Stevens, who drew Sailor and sent Girdler across in the corner. Girdler converted, but NSW's comeback was short-lived. Fletcher had the ball jolted loose as he charged for the line. In the next minute, Queensland forced a repeat set when Hughes had to take Lockyer's kick dead in-goal as Walker sprinted from well behind. Finally, Webb burst through Girdler before drawing Hughes and sending Lockyer in to score. Lockyer missed all three second-half conversion attempts, but the 40–14 score was the highest margin in a State of Origin decider.

The Verdict

As in game one, the Maroons won convincingly after regularly capitalising on mistakes from their slightly off-key opponents. Most of the post-match attention focused on Langer. His surprise recall could not have paid off more handsomely: he had produced a vintage performance.

↑ Daniel Wagon hares away from Luke Priddis. Wagon produced a crucial offload in the lead-up to Dane Carlaw's try, which began a Queensland onslaught.

2002

Triumph, Disappointment and Déjà Vu

The 2002 series saw the clash of the master coaches: Wayne Bennett of Queensland and Phil Gould of NSW. Boasting identical Origin records, both men had to juggle club and Origin commitments. In the lead-up to the series, Gould criticised Bennett, claiming that Bennett did not do enough to promote Origin football. In his memoir published several years later, Bennett responded that the players were the focus of the game because they were the ones the fans came to see.

The scheduling of Origin football changed again, as the games reverted to Wednesday nights while the NRL premiership rounds continued without interruption.

Following Fittler's retirement, Andrew Johns returned for NSW. Appointed as the new captain, he said that he wanted to dominate an Origin series. The Blues were unable to select injured players Peachey, MacDougall, Girdler and Stevens. Queensland had Bowman and Green on the injured list, and Sailor had transferred to rugby union. Langer remained eligible for Queensland after returning to the Broncos.

← Chris McKenna takes on the NSW defence. Recalled to Origin after missing the 2001 series, McKenna was named as the best on the ground in game two.

The Teams

NSW fielded a new-look side featuring eight debutants: Brett Hodgson, Timana Tahu, Jason Moodie, Jamie Lyon, Danny Buderus, Jason Ryles, Steve Simpson and Braith Anasta. Recalled were Hindmarsh, Timmins, Barrett, Johns, Kearns, Ricketson and Kennedy. Notable omissions were Gidley and Scott Hill. The suspended Ryles and injured Kearns were replaced by O'Meley and debutant Luke Bailey. When Timmins succumbed to a virus and withdrew on match day, he was replaced by Gidley.

Queensland retained 13 members from game three of 2001. Meyers had lost form, and Bowman, Green and Sailor were unavailable. The returning Tallis regained the captaincy. Origin debutants were Clinton Schifcofske and Shaun Berrigan. Having returned to the Broncos, Gee made a reappearance. An injured Wagon withdrew on match eve and was replaced by McKenna.

The Game

NSW earned good field position in the opening minutes through determined running with the ball and fast-moving defence. A line-break by Hodgson followed by a Johns grubber-kick forced a goal-line drop-out. Hodgson made another electrifying burst in the next set before he was tackled a metre from the tryline. Buderus looked left but turned the ball the other way where the defence was thin. Barrett drew McKenna and Tuqiri before sending a head-high pass to Gidley, who rolled over in the right corner in a tackle. Referee Harrigan awarded a try —replays showed it was a brave decision as the bottom point of the ball barely touched the ground. Johns's brilliant sideline conversion gave the Blues a 6–0 lead after five minutes.

Queensland had a chance soon after the restart but the Blues survived. Several minutes later, an offside penalty gave the Maroons attacking position well into NSW's half. Opting to run on the last tackle, the Maroons moved the ball left through Webcke, Langer and McKenna before Tuqiri touched down just inside the corner post. Schifcofske's conversion attempt pushed to the right to leave the Blues leading 6–4.

A missed opportunity took place at each end before the game swung decisively in NSW's favour. Receiving the ball from Buderus near halfway, Johns grubber-kicked through for Lyon to retrieve the ball and pass inside to Moodie. Although held, Moodie threw a speculative pass towards the left sideline. Johns recovered the ball and veered for the corner, where Lockyer almost drove him out. Johns managed to throw a wayward pass back infield, where Lyon scooped up the loose ball and dived over the line. Johns's touchline conversion brilliantly curled from outside the right post to soar over the crossbar.

Twelve minutes from half-time, Buderus sent Hodgson into open space again. The NSW fullback drew his opposite number to send Johns scampering beneath the posts for a converted try and an 18–4 scoreline. A 40–20 kick by Johns set up another attacking raid for the Blues, but a trybound Tahu was bundled into touch near the corner flag.

↓ Shaun Berrigan is tangled up in the NSW defence. Berrigan was unable to make an impact in his Origin debut as the Maroons were outclassed.

Hodgson made another break when he ran onto a short pass from Barrett inside Queensland's quarter, but Lockyer produced a try-saving tackle. The Maroons then conceded a second offside penalty in as many minutes, and Johns landed the penalty goal to make the score 20–4. When Langer was penalised for slowing a play-the-ball, referee Harrigan issued Tallis with a warning over Queensland's infringements. A few minutes later, Tallis was penalised for a ruck infringement and was controversially ordered to the sin-bin. Johns took the penalty kick and, from the restart, booted a 30-metre field goal to take the Blues to a very comfortable 17-point lead at half-time.

Queensland strengthened its defence early in the second half and prevented NSW from scoring while Tallis was off the field. However, the Maroons rarely threatened in attack and never looked capable of repairing the damage already caused. Midway through the second half, the Blues opted to run on the last tackle in Queensland's quarter. Buderus passed the ball right to Barrett and, as the defence held off, he passed to the unmarked Tahu, who punched the air before sliding over the tryline.

Barrett landed a field goal in the 70th minute, then Hodgson capped off a memorable debut with a spectacular try five minutes from the end. From an untidy scrum, Hodgson took the ball 10 metres from his own tryline, stepped through and sprinted the remaining length of the field before diving over beside the posts. Hodgson converted to take the final score to 32–4.

← A late inclusion in the NSW side, Luke Bailey tries to penetrate Darren Smith's and Dane Carlaw's tackle.

↓ Andrew Johns was named man of the match in NSW's 32–4 win. His sizzling form matched the burning desire he had revealed beforehand: that he wanted to dominate Origin football.

Players & Statistics

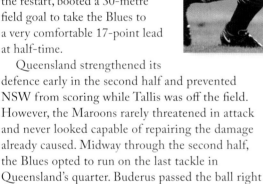

NSW Brett Hodgson, Timana Tahu, Jamie Lyon, Matt Gidley, Jason Moodie, Trent Barrett, Andrew Johns (c), Luke Ricketson, Ben Kennedy, Steve Simpson, Mark O'Meley, Danny Buderus, Luke Bailey. **RESERVES** Braith Anasta, Bryan Fletcher, Nathan Hindmarsh, Michael Vella. **COACH** Phil Gould

QLD Darren Lockyer, Lote Tuqiri, Chris McKenna, Darren Smith, Clinton Schifcofske, Shaun Berrigan, Allan Langer, Dane Carlaw, Petero Civoniceva, Gorden Tallis (c), John Buttigieg, Kevin Campion, Shane Webcke. **RESERVES** Chris Walker, John Doyle, Carl Webb, Andrew Gee. **COACH** Wayne Bennett

Result NSW 32 (Gidley, Lyon, Johns, Tahu, Hodgson tries; Johns 4, Hodgson goals; Johns, Barrett field goals) beat Queensland 4 (Tuqiri try)

Referee Bill Harrigan (NSW)

Crowd 55 421

Man of the Match Andrew Johns (NSW)

The Verdict

NSW's win was the state's second biggest in Origin football. The vast reshuffling of the side had paid dividends, while Queensland came crashing back to earth after winning two games with similar teams the previous year. Hodgson was very unlucky not to receive the man-of-the-match award, which went to Johns. Although NSW's win was convincing, Johns said the Blues needed to improve for the return clash because he anticipated that the Maroons would come back strongly in front of their home crowd.

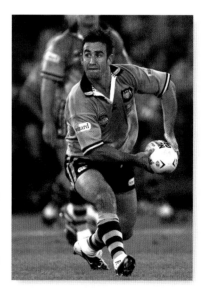

→ Lote Tuqiri touches down for the game's first try. He went on to score two more tries in the contest, and his match tally of 18 points was a record for a Queensland player in Origin football.

The Teams

Queensland axed Schifcofske, Campion, Buttigieg and Doyle. Injuries forced Civoniceva and Webb out of the team and Wagon was still injured. Into the starting line-up came debutants Justin Hodges, Travis Norton and PJ Marsh. Beattie and Price were recalled and Chris Flannery was the new reserve. Tuqiri received a one-match ban for a dangerous tackle in a club match, so the Queensland selectors named 'to be advised' in the number two jersey. This allowed Tuqiri to serve his suspension in club football before Origin II.

NSW made just one change: Timmins replaced Gidley. But injuries to Kennedy and Barrett forced late changes, with Scott Hill and Menzies recalled.

Despite criticism after game one, Bill Harrigan was appointed to control his 17th Origin match.

The Game

Both teams attacked vigorously early on. In the sixth minute, Timmins scored off a Johns bomb but he was denied when replays showed he was offside. Ten minutes later, Bailey beat two opponents to a Johns grubber but fumbled it, and video referee Eddie Ward denied NSW again. Queensland created a scoring opportunity on the left side in the next minute, but the pass from Tallis flew over McKenna's shoulder into touch.

After an error by Anasta, Queensland attacked in NSW's quarter, firing the ball left through Lockyer, Langer and Price, before McKenna drew two Blues and released an around-the-corner pass to Tuqiri. He stepped inside Hodgson and scored before badly hooking the sideline goal-kick.

The momentum soon changed when Walker was punished for interference when Johns hoisted a bomb. Just two tackles later, Johns grubbered behind the tryline, where Hodges fielded the ball and stumbled as Hindmarsh confronted him. Seeing Lockyer to his left, Hodges shovelled a wild pass and Anasta beat Vella to the loose ball near the posts. It was a gift six points, and NSW led 6–4.

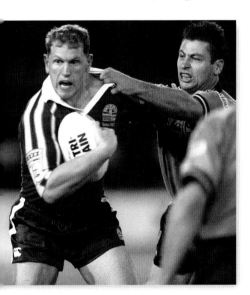

↑ Travis Norton tries to shrug off Luke Ricketson. Norton took a key intercept late in the game as the Maroons staved off a NSW comeback.

From the restart, Moodie caught the ball but his backwards momentum took him across the dead-ball line. The Maroons didn't strike but NSW was kept in its own half. After Hodgson retired with a punctured lung, Moodie paid dearly for gripping the ball one-handed when he met the defence. Queensland subsequently pressed the tryline. Lockyer's grubber-kick rebounded off Fletcher's leg and the ball ballooned to McKenna, who drew Tahu and sent the unmarked Tuqiri across in the corner. Tuqiri hooked another goal-kick. NSW had another scoring opportunity after a crossfield kick from Johns, but Ward gave another red light when replays showed Tahu knocked on in the lead-up. The Maroons led 8–6 at the break.

Queensland had the first chance of the second half after Hindmarsh fumbled in a tackle. Langer and Berrigan moved the ball left when a mistake by Fletcher created a hole for Tallis to burst through and score. Tuqiri converted and Queensland led 14–6 as a heavy shower arrived. After Lockyer fumbled in a gang tackle, Queensland's markers were offside to enable Johns to kick a penalty goal. Lockyer then sent the kick-off out on the full before Smith fumbled a Johns chip-kick near the posts. Menzies was on the spot to score, but Ward denied NSW again as replays showed Menzies fumbled the ball as he attempted to bring it over the line.

In the 57th minute, Langer drew Bailey and Johns before sending Carlaw through a gap with a short pass. Carlaw powered to the line and Tuqiri converted from the right wing, extending the

Maroons' lead to 12 points. But Queensland was still error-prone. Lockyer's clearing kick ricocheted off Simpson, giving NSW good field position. Hill grubbered through to where Hodges retrieved the ball and ran towards the uprights before changing direction as he tried to escape from his in-goal area. Caught by Moodie, Hodges bungled again as the greasy ball slipped from his grasp as he tried to pass. Tahu dived at the ball but inadvertently deflected it sideways past Lockyer where Ricketson pounced. Ward finally ruled in NSW's favour, and Johns's conversion closed the deficit to a converted try. Hodges was replaced immediately.

After Lockyer miscued another clearing kick, the Blues forced two consecutive goal-line drop-outs. Harrigan missed a knock-on by Bailey as the front-rower rose to play the ball. One tackle later, a movement featuring Buderus, Johns, Hill, Menzies and Timmins resulted in a try to Timmins near the left touchline. Johns's conversion attempt agonisingly struck the left post, leaving Queensland with a slender 20–18 lead. The rain had eased and a tense final ten minutes remained.

NSW fell apart as handling errors gifted Queensland territorial advantage. In the 77th minute, Lockyer appeared to score but he was penalised for running a shepherd behind Walker. NSW worked its way past halfway but Norton saved Queensland with an intercept. Then Moodie lost the ball on a kick return. Tuqiri surged over between the posts in the ensuing moments, and then added the extras to make the final scoreline 26–18.

The Verdict

Eight of the nine tries awarded followed mistakes by the opposition, but it was telling that the Blues had bombed four tries. Although the fine margin between success and failure was evident in numerous ways, Hodges's in-goal blunders were a focal point of post-match reviews. However, he was defended by Phil Gould, who said that Hodges was young and playing out of position, and that he would be back in Origin again.

↑ Mark O'Meley, one of very few NSW survivors from the 2001 series, is brought to a halt.

The Teams

Predictably, Hodges was dropped from the Queensland team and was replaced by O'Davis. Beattie gave way to the returning Civoniceva, and debutant Brent Tate replaced Flannery.

For NSW, Barrett returned in place of Anasta. The Blues were forced to leave out the injured Lyon and O'Meley, with Gidley returning and Ryles finally making his Origin debut.

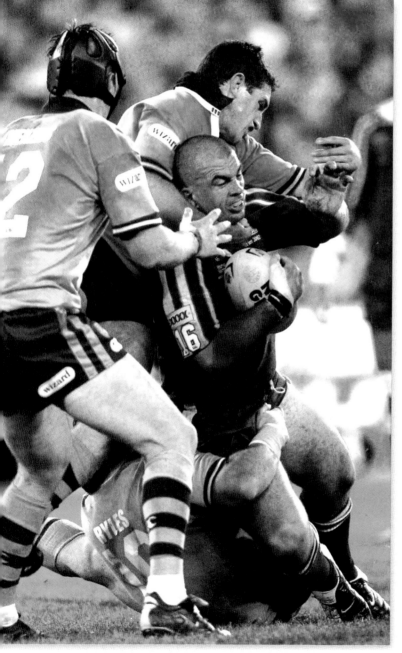

↓ Andrew Gee is safely held. A surprise selection, Gee came off the bench for Queensland in all three games of the series.

The Game

Marsh, Carlaw, Langer and Walker combined to send O'Davis away in the third minute, but O'Davis failed to pass to a trybound Lockyer. A few minutes later, Tahu lost the ball as he unwisely tried to unload in heavy traffic. Queensland spread the ball left through Langer, Berrigan and Lockyer, who grubbered to the left corner for Tuqiri to pounce. Tuqiri hooked the conversion attempt.

The Blues enjoyed field position after Tuqiri butchered an intercept. Buderus passed right to Johns, who threw a long ball to Barrett. He stopped almost to a standstill and, changing the point of play, slipped a short pass inside, where Menzies burst past Tallis, stepped out of Lockyer's last-ditch tackle and flopped over to score. Johns converted to nose his side in front.

Tallis atoned a few minutes later when he collared Hodgson and dragged him 17 metres across field and over the sideline in a sensational tackle. From the scrum, Langer, Berrigan and Lockyer combined to send Walker scurrying down the right flank, but his wayward inside pass was spilled by O'Davis with the tryline in sight.

A penalty against Barrett and a handling error from Tahu gave Queensland prolonged possession in an attacking position. Marsh passed left to Langer, whose long and well-timed bullet-like pass sent Berrigan through a gap to reach out and score in Simpson's tackle. Tuqiri hooked the conversion from a handy position.

In the 27th minute, Ricketson turned a short ball left to Barrett, who stepped, dummied and accelerated between Carlaw and Walker. Barrett drew Lockyer and sent the unmarked Moodie running to the posts for a converted try. NSW made a couple of attacking raids in the last seven minutes of the first half, but nothing materialised. The score remained 12–8 to NSW.

After the interval, both sides struggled to score the decisive try. NSW went close in the 55th minute following a Johns kick but Lockyer saved the Maroons. The Blues broke away in the next minute. Running on the last tackle, Buderus passed right to Johns and Hill. He sent a cut-out pass to Tahu, who dived for the corner as Tuqiri neared. Video referee Chris Ward disallowed the try as replays showed Tahu dropped the ball as he tried to force it left-handed.

Two minutes later, Johns dropped an easy pass. A few moments later, Langer veered left and turned the ball right to Webcke, who surged past Bailey's despairing tackle and bulldozed over the top of Hodgson to crash over for a try. Suddenly the Maroons were back in front by two points as Tuqiri converted.

The sides traded handling mistakes as the pressure built. After Hill kicked out on the full in the 68th minute, Langer's chip-kick bounced awkwardly beside the left upright. Tahu fumbled and Lockyer beat Hodgson in the jump for the ball, before grounding it between his feet just inside the dead-ball line. Video evidence showed that Lockyer momentarily lost his grip on the ball but still clung to it and applied downward pressure. Chris Ward astonishingly ruled that Lockyer had knocked on, leaving the Maroons with a narrow two-point lead.

With six minutes left, Buderus passed left to Ryles, who linked with Johns, Hill, Fletcher and Barrett. Drawing two tacklers, Barrett released an around-the-corner pass to Timmins. He drew Lockyer and reverse-passed to Moodie, who dived over the line. Johns's brilliant sideline conversion made it 18–14.

Lockyer's short kick-off rolled into touch to earn Queensland a scrum feed. Queensland's attack was sluggish but its defence was speedy, pinning the Blues in their half. When Queensland regained possession, NSW only needed to hang on for 90 seconds and the Maroons had to produce something special. Five metres inside NSW territory, Smith fed Langer, who passed right to Carlaw.

↑ Queensland's eventual and unlikely saviour Dane Carlaw prepares to take on Steve Menzies.

From a standing start, Carlaw brushed off Moodie and charged through open space down the right side with nobody near him. Stepping out of Hodgson's tackle, Carlaw crashed over for a try, levelling the scores with 52 seconds remaining. Like in 1999, a drawn series was enough for Queensland to regain the shield. Tuqiri had the opportunity to kick the Maroons to a series victory, but he sliced the wide-angled goal-kick.

The Verdict

Langer, man of the match, confirmed it was his last Origin game. Post-match discussion in Queensland centred on Lockyer's disallowed try, which left the Maroons seething. They may have won had the try been awarded—and if Tuqiri had not missed three goals from four attempts.

In NSW, the major talking point focused on the desire for extra time to determine an outright winner in the event of a drawn decider. It is hard to know whether the Blues would have pushed for extra time had they retained the Origin trophy through a drawn series.

↓ Jason Ryles looks for support under pressure. Ryles finally made his Origin debut after being ruled out of game one through suspension.

Players & Statistics

QLD Darren Lockyer, Lote Tuqiri, Chris Walker, Chris McKenna, Robbie O'Davis, Shaun Berrigan, Allan Langer, Darren Smith, Dane Carlaw, Gorden Tallis (c), Petero Civoniceva, PJ Marsh, Shane Webcke. **RESERVES** Travis Norton, Steve Price, Andrew Gee, Brent Tate. **COACH** Wayne Bennett

NSW Brett Hodgson, Timana Tahu, Matt Gidley, Shaun Timmins, Jason Moodie, Trent Barrett, Andrew Johns (c), Luke Ricketson, Steve Menzies, Steve Simpson, Jason Ryles, Danny Buderus, Luke Bailey. **RESERVES** Scott Hill, Bryan Fletcher, Nathan Hindmarsh, Michael Vella. **COACH** Phil Gould

Result Queensland 18 (Tuqiri, Berrigan, Webcke, Carlaw tries; Tuqiri goal) drew with NSW 18 (Moodie 2, Menzies tries, Johns 3 goals)

Referee Bill Harrigan (NSW)

Crowd 74 842

Man of the Match Allan Langer (Queensland)

2003

Joey Johns Fulfills Origin Dream

After the drawn series in 2002, the ARL adopted a 'golden-point' rule for Origin football. If scores were level at full-time, the teams would play extra-time until one team hit the lead. If scores remained unchanged after five minutes of extra-time, the sides would change ends and play on until the deadlock was broken. NSW officials had the numbers to launch the proposal, despite disapproval from north of the border.

Phil Gould and Wayne Bennett continued as coaches, although Gould considered stepping down after developing a confrontational relationship with several News Limited journalists. He again became involved in a pre-series controversy, this time involving Andrew Johns. Gould was critical of Johns's form, and the coach was photographed poking Johns in the chest.

NSW had to make some changes to its squad as Barrett, Stevens, Simpson and Hodgson were injured. Queensland lost Langer and Darren Smith to retirement, and Tuqiri (who had swapped to rugby union) and McKenna (playing in England) had moved on.

State of Origin returned to Suncorp Stadium after the redevelopment of 'The Cauldron' as a seats-only venue. In another amendment, sponsorship led to Stadium Australia having its named changed to Telstra Stadium.

← Luke Bailey makes a menacing charge. He played a major role in the Blues clinching the series in the first two games.

→ In his Origin debut, NSW second-rower Craig Fitzgibbon runs away from Shane Webcke.

↓ Michael De Vere spills blood for the Blues after suffering a head gash. De Vere's wound re-opened a couple of times, and staples were inserted once, making for graphic television footage.

The Teams

NSW's selectors introduced five newcomers: Anthony Minichiello, Craig Fitzgibbon, Phil Bailey, Josh Perry and Craig Wing. De Vere and Kearns returned to the side. Timmins was something of a surprise choice at five-eighth.

For Queensland, the selectors stuck largely with players from 2002, with Hodges earning a recall along with Ikin and Carroll. Schifcofske and the uncapped Rhys Wesser were surprisingly overlooked. O'Davis was forced out with injury and was replaced by Shannon Hegarty, the team's only debutant.

The Game

The forwards immediately engaged in hard-hitting attack and defence. As he was tested with a series of bombs, Minichiello grew in confidence. Lyon sent De Vere sprinting away in the seventh minute and a try looked possible until Lockyer came across to drive him over the sideline.

Queensland forced two goal-line drop-outs in quick succession, and De Vere was twice treated for a head cut that spilled blood. Two tackles after the latter goal-line drop-out, the Maroons moved the ball right. Marsh, Ikin and Lockyer handled before Lockyer sold a dummy, darted between two defenders and busted Minichiello's tackle to crash over the line. Lockyer converted from the sideline for a handy 6–0 lead.

Carlaw made a crucial knock-on in a tackle before NSW forced a goal-line drop-out. In the repeat set, Buderus spun a pass left to Johns, who drew the defence and fired the ball to Minichiello. He veered inside, rushed past Ikin's tackle and scored near the posts. Johns converted, tying the scores.

Ikin landed a 40-20 kick three minutes later to give Queensland a scrum feed in NSW's quarter. But Hodges drifted too far right, where Lyon and De Vere easily took him over the touchline. NSW fortuitously received a scrum feed in the 25th minute when a linesman ruled that Hegarty touched and played at the ball after Johns kicked for the sideline. Replays showed Hegarty attempted to evade the ball and did not appear to touch it. Two tackles later, Buderus passed right to Johns, who created a hole as Gidley ran a decoy. Johns delayed a pass to Minichiello, who crashed over to score. Referee Harrigan checked for an obstruction but video referee Eddie Ward awarded a try. Johns converted, making it 12–6 to NSW.

The old 'state against state, mate against mate' notion was displayed when De Vere copped a high tackle from his club captain Tallis. De Vere spilled more blood before Bowman exited the game with medial ligament damage just after he entered the fray. Johns hooked a field-goal attempt six minutes from the break before Gidley conceded a penalty for a high tackle on Lockyer as half-time neared. Clever lead-up work from Ikin sent Gee surging for the line, but he lost the ball agonisingly short in a tackle. NSW led 12–6 at the break.

Hegarty made a 40-metre break from dummy-half to put the Maroons on the attack soon after the resumption. On the last tackle of the set, Tallis veered left and surged for the line with four defenders swarming him. Video referee Ward referred the call back to Harrigan, who awarded a try. Lockyer's conversion levelled the scores.

In a bruising encounter of explosive hit-ups and tackles, Hodges suffered a season-ending knee injury and exited on a medicab. Tallis tried to bustle through for another try, and he juggled the ball before planting it. The crowd roared at first but Ward disallowed the try as replays showed the ball struck Gidley as Tallis juggled it forward, constituting a knock-on.

The evenly matched battle continued before NSW lifted the intensity. Timmins dropped the ball with the tryline under threat, and then Luke Bailey beat Lockyer to Johns's grubber in-goal but failed to ground it. Johns broke through but kicked ahead without result.

In the 62nd minute, a botched intercept by Price proved crucial as Timmins made a half-break before the tackle count restarted 25 metres from Queensland's line. Johns drifted left, drew two Maroons and sent a perfectly timed pass to Wing, who evaded Ikin and Lockyer before scampering under the crossbar. Johns's conversion gave NSW an 18–12 lead and momentum.

NSW dominated field position as the injury-plagued Maroons scrambled desperately in defence and were tiring. Carlaw made a rampaging break with ten minutes remaining, shrugging off Ricketson and trampling Minichiello, but he lost the ball at halfway as he was swamped by Tahu.

The Blues worked their way downfield and on the last tackle Johns booted a field goal, which gave NSW a seven-point lead with nine minutes remaining. In desperation, Lockyer tried a short kick from the restart but he hooked it out on the full. Tate fumbled as he tried to pounce on a loose ball soon after. Then Johns strolled through some slow defence for an easy try a few moments later, ending any hope for the Maroons.

The Verdict

The 25–12 score belied the closeness of the contest. Both sides had scoring opportunities but after NSW capitalised on Price's moment of misfortune, it was always going to be hard for the injury-ravaged Maroons to recover. Nonetheless, it was a high-quality game, one of the most brutal and thrilling Origin matches ever.

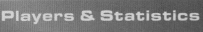

Players & Statistics

NSW Anthony Minichiello, Timana Tahu, Matt Gidley, Jamie Lyon, Michael De Vere, Shaun Timmins, Andrew Johns (c), Luke Ricketson, Ben Kennedy, Craig Fitzgibbon, Jason Ryles, Danny Buderus, Robbie Kearns. **RESERVES** Luke Bailey, Craig Wing, Josh Perry, Phil Bailey. **COACH** Phil Gould

QLD Darren Lockyer, Shannon Hegarty, Brent Tate, Justin Hodges, Matt Sing, Ben Ikin, Shaun Berrigan, Tonie Carroll, Dane Carlaw, Gorden Tallis (c), Petero Civoniceva, PJ Marsh, Shane Webcke. **RESERVES** Steve Price, Chris Flannery, Andrew Gee, Paul Bowman. **COACH** Wayne Bennett

Result NSW 25 (Minichiello 2, Wing, Johns tries; Johns 4 goals; Johns field goal) beat Queensland 12 (Lockyer, Tallis tries; Lockyer 2 goals)

Referee Bill Harrigan (NSW)

Crowd 52 420

Man of the Match Luke Bailey (NSW)

The Teams

NSW made just one forced change, with Fletcher replacing the suspended Perry.

Queensland selectors showed faith and retained the bulk of the side. Hodges, Flannery, Bowman and Marsh were unavailable due to injury. Norton was recalled, and Michael Crocker, Scott Sattler and Matt Bowen were named to debut.

The Game

Rain before the match ensured that the surface was damp and slippery in places. After the first tackle, Lockyer struggled to regain his composure after sustaining a head knock. In the opening exchanges, both sides again looked switched on and hit hard in defence. Johns was in form with his kicking game and repeatedly found open space, while Lockyer and Ikin kept finding Minichiello on the full.

In the 12th minute, Johns's banana kick struck the left upright and ricocheted to the left. De Vere lost the ball backwards and bumped into referee Harrigan before Kennedy beat Crocker in the dive for the ball. Johns converted and NSW led 6–0. Having conceded the first try in an unlucky fashion, Queensland forced a goal-line drop-out a few minutes later, but Ikin fumbled in a tackle to release the pressure before Tate was penalised for interfering in a play-the-ball. Suddenly the Blues were back on the attack. As Gidley veered left near the 20-metre line, he shaped to pass and, as the defence held off him, stepped through for a very soft try. NSW led 12–0. Even at this early stage of the game, the Maroons looked beaten.

Kennedy hit Price with a swinging arm in the 25th minute, unsighted by referee Harrigan. Play continued and Carroll lost the ball before video referee Phil Cooley intervened. Harrigan subsequently placed Kennedy on report but ordered a scrum to NSW because the tackle on Carroll had been completed after the Kennedy-Price incident. Price appeared to be groggy as he was assisted from the field, but he summoned up enough energy to berate a linesman for overlooking Kennedy's hit. Two tackles after NSW won the scrum, Fletcher unloaded in a tackle to Lyon, who crossed the Queensland quarter-line and then fed Minichiello. He powered over his opposite number and forced his way over in the left corner, for NSW to establish a commanding 16–0 lead.

Just before the break, Johns punted the ball from a 20-metre restart and found the sideline to earn NSW the scrum feed. Timmins hoisted a bomb infield as the siren sounded two tackles later, and the ball bounced before Johns veered right and snapped a field goal for NSW to lead 17–0.

↓ A shock selection for the Blues after being omitted from NSW preliminary squads, Phil Bailey attempts to break out of a tackle.

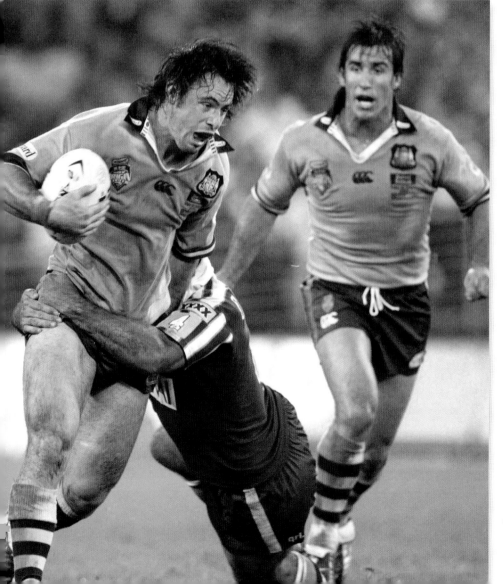

Players & Statistics

NSW Anthony Minichiello, Timana Tahu, Matt Gidley, Jamie Lyon, Michael De Vere, Shaun Timmins, Andrew Johns (c), Luke Ricketson, Craig Fitzgibbon, Ben Kennedy, Jason Ryles, Danny Buderus, Robbie Kearns. **RESERVES** Luke Bailey, Craig Wing, Bryan Fletcher, Phil Bailey. **COACH** Phil Gould

QLD Darren Lockyer, Shannon Hegarty, Brent Tate, Tonie Carroll, Matt Sing, Ben Ikin, Shaun Berrigan, Dane Carlaw, Petero Civoniceva, Gorden Tallis (c), Steve Price, Michael Crocker, Shane Webcke. **RESERVES** Travis Norton, Andrew Gee, Scott Sattler, Matt Bowen. **COACH** Wayne Bennett

Result NSW 27 (Tahu 2, Kennedy, Gidley, Minichiello tries; Johns 3 goals; Johns field goal) beat Queensland 4 (Crocker try)

Referee Bill Harrigan (NSW)

Crowd 79 132

Man of the Match Andrew Johns (NSW)

After the break, NSW continued to control the game as the Maroons continually looked out of their depth. Carroll drove Luke Bailey back in a tackle but Bailey shrugged off the tackler and stormed upfield, leaving multiple defenders in his wake. A fumble by Civoniceva was followed by a blatant infringement by Gee, allowing Johns to kick a goal to make the score 19–0.

A strip in a three-man tackle gifted the Blues another penalty a couple of minutes later, and the Maroons were marched 10 metres when Hegarty back-chatted the referee. At the end of the ensuing set, Timmins angled a grubber-kick to the right where Hegarty had an air swing at it and missed. Tahu beat Gidley in the dive for the ball, and the score blew out to 23–0.

Phil Bailey came on for NSW and became involved in the action almost immediately when he swung his arm at Webcke in a tackle. Webcke chased Bailey and threw several punches, causing a short-lived scuffle. Queensland was awarded a penalty but continued to disappoint when Berrigan coughed up possession inside the quarter.

Bowen was introduced and lost the ball with his first touch. With 11 minutes remaining, Lockyer hoisted a bomb, which bounced before Crocker regathered it. Crocker reached for the line as Lyon tackled him from behind and Harrigan gave the try. However, replays showed the ball slipped out of Crocker's grasp as he reached out before putting his hand over the top of the ball to force it down—a knock-on because he did not catch

the ball after losing it forward. Crocker hooked the conversion attempt and then knocked on as he attempted to play the ball soon after the restart.

Inside Queensland's quarter soon afterwards, NSW moved the ball right with Timmins, Johns and Gidley handling. As the defence approached, Gidley tripped over, but he produced a backhand flick to the unmarked Tahu, who scooped up the ball at bootlace level in a classy piece of handling before diving over the line. The score remained unchanged for the final seven minutes. The Blues won 27–4, and tied up the series.

The Verdict

With its first series win in three years, NSW had plenty to smile about. Meanwhile, the Maroons had much soul-searching to do—their performance was arguably one of the worst in Origin history. Both their general play and their handling were well below State of Origin standards. In his memoir, Bennett rated it as the most disappointing Origin game he had ever coached. He said he didn't know what had happened to the Maroons, but he was quite definite about that they were never in the contest

↑ Thwarted from behind here, Timana Tahu made some strong contributions to NSW's series win after some horror moments in game three of 2002.

↓ Jamie Lyons feeds try-bound Anthony Minichiello as NSW romp to a lead in the first half.

→ Like many of the Maroons, Shaun Berrigan was on song in game three after failing to impress earlier in the series.

The Teams

Queensland's heavy defeat gave its selectors the opportunity to blood new players and look ahead. But oddly, the only players to cop the axe were reserves Sattler and Gee. Cameron Smith and Josh Hannay were selected for the first time. The NSW selectors made only forced changes, with Kennedy (suspended) and Fitzgibbon (injured) unavailable. Anasta was recalled and Willie Mason was named to debut.

The Game

Johns was ill in the lead-up to the game but he looked fit when he produced a thumping tackle that left Tate clutching at his shoulder. Carroll was penalised for a swinging arm on De Vere in the next minute before Ryles was on the receiving end of a heavy, driving tackle by Civoniceva, Webcke and Carroll. The momentum swung Queensland's way when Tallis fielded a loose ball on the halfway line. At the end of that set, Ikin put up a bomb in the in-goal area. Sing out-jumped De Vere to knock the ball back, where Tate caught it and fell over to score. The left-footed Hannay converted for an early 6–0 lead to the Maroons.

A kick from Johns into Queensland's in-goal area provided an ideal chance for the Blues to force a goal-line drop-out. However, Sing weaved his way through four defenders to get into the field of play before Lockyer, Berrigan and Ikin combined with Smith to take play towards NSW's 30-metre line on tackle five. Berrigan sucked in the defence and lofted a pass, which cut out three players, creating an overlap for Sing to beat Minichiello to the right corner. Hannay's sideline conversion made the score 12–0 as Ryles was forced off the field with a recurring shoulder injury.

↑ Gorden Tallis leads the Maroons out for the last time in his Origin career. He finished on a happy note, although his team had lost the series.

The Blues were caught in front of the kicker from the restart and were subsequently penalised. The Maroons were in NSW's quarter just one tackle later, with Lockyer throwing a cut-out pass for Sing to score his second try in the corner. NSW was in disarray while Queensland was firing on all cylinders to lead 16–0 after just 17 minutes. The Maroons looked nothing like the team that had lost the series after meekly surrendering in game two only three weeks earlier. Queensland received a setback though when Carroll left the field with a hamstring injury.

Ikin missed a field-goal attempt in the 21st minute before Sing showed the fickle nature of the game when he spilled a high punt. Two tackles after the resultant scrum, Johns stepped from dummy-half but fumbled as he attempted to score. General play from both sides was scrappy for the remainder of the first period and there was no change in the score before the break.

Wing made his side's first line-break for the game in the 47th minute, gaining 36 metres. Anasta put in a long, rolling kick to the right corner, where Tahu raced to swoop on the ball ahead of Lockyer. Johns converted from the right touchline to narrow the scores to 16–6. NSW released the pressure shortly after the restart when Phil Bailey dropped the ball as he tried to play it. Fletcher threw a loose pass on Queensland's 30-metre line, and Price scooped up the ball and fended off Wing to make a surprisingly long break. Price brushed off Tahu but stumbled in the process and he fell to ground just 5 metres short of the tryline.

Seven minutes later, Hegarty charged into Gidley and scampered to the right, before linking up with Lockyer, Norton and Webcke. After busting a tackle, Webcke charged ahead and managed to pass to Lockyer as he was tackled. Lockyer stepped right and then lofted the ball to the unmarked Tate, who dashed for the right corner and planted the ball with only centimetres to spare. Hannay pocketed another conversion kick from the touchline to give Queensland a 22–6 lead.

With all the momentum, the energetic Maroons went on a scoring spree against a waning NSW team. With 11 minutes left, Bowen took a high pass from Lockyer inside his 10-metre zone before stepping through the defence and sprinting 75 metres. One tackle later, Berrigan fired a pass left to Lockyer. He drew Tahu and fed Smith, who rolled over the line to score on debut. Then five minutes from the end, as a gap appeared in the NSW defence, Tallis linked with Berrigan, who veered left and then right past Minichiello to send Sing scampering over for his third try. Hannay converted from wide out to increase the score to 32–6.

Three tackles later, the Maroons were in their own half when Ikin chip-kicked to the right, where Sing caught the ball 6 metres in NSW's half. Sing passed inside to Lockyer. He drifted left and drew two Blues before spinning an overhead pass right to the unmarked Crocker, who scurried away from Minichiello to score. Hannay sliced a relatively easy conversion, with the 36–6 scoreline equalling Queensland's biggest win in the competition.

The Verdict

Game three was a complete reversal from the previous encounter. On this occasion, Queensland took its early opportunities, established momentum and took the game away from a lacklustre NSW side. The result showed again that there are no favourites in State of Origin games.

↓ As Robbie Kearns and Luke Bailey drive him to ground, Shane Webcke prepares himself for a heavy landing.

2004

Gus Recalls Freddie and Says Farewell

Phil Gould opted to continue as NSW coach after being undecided at the end of the 2003 series. He cited the commitment of the players and the passion of the fans as factors that enticed him to carry on. By contrast, club commitments again induced Wayne Bennett to stand down from Origin duty. Queensland's new coach was Michael Hagan, who took Newcastle to the 2001 NRL premiership in his first year as coach.

Both states were forced into major team overhauls. For NSW, Kearns and Ricketson had retired from representative football, Lyon had quit the NRL, and Andrew Johns, Tahu, Ryles and Luke Bailey were injured. The Maroons also lost Tallis and Ikin to retirement from representative football, and injuries accounted for Sing, Berrigan, Hegarty and Marsh.

There were changes in the refereeing department too after long-time referee Bill Harrigan retired.

← After coming out of retirement from Origin football, Brad Fittler helped the Blues to their second straight series win.

The Teams

Forced to make many changes since the 2003 Origin series, NSW's selectors introduced Ben Hornby, Luke Lewis, Mark Gasnier, Ryan O'Hara, Brent Kite and Trent Waterhouse to State of Origin football. Gower, Fitzgibbon, Ryan and Hindmarsh were recalled, and Anasta, Fletcher and Phil Bailey were overlooked. Buderus was named the captain.

After mischievous conduct during NSW's lead-up camp, Gasnier and Minichiello were expelled and Mason, Waterhouse, O'Meley, Gower and Wing were fined. The disruptions incensed coach Gould, who decided that this would be his last series. De Vere was recalled and Luke Rooney received a call-up to Origin honours.

Queensland's four debutants were Rhys Wesser, Billy Slater, Scott Prince and Ben Ross. Hodges and Bowman were recalled. The Maroons suffered a major blow when Lockyer, now a five-eighth, pulled out with a rib injury. He was replaced by Flannery. Webcke took over the captaincy.

Sean Hampstead was appointed referee.

↑ Sean Hampstead refereed after the retirement of Bill Harrigan, who had officiated at the previous 12 Origin games.

↓ Scott Prince had a fine debut for the Maroons, scoring the first try and setting up the last one.

The Game

NSW gained early ascendancy after Queensland was pinned in its own territory and then caught offside following Prince's clearing kick. Buderus burrowed for the line but was held up by two defenders. Another opportunity was lost when a Gidley pass went astray. Price smothered Gower's kick but NSW regained the ball. At the end of the repeat set, Slater and Timmins dived at a Hornby grubber. The ball appeared to ricochet before De Vere grounded it. Replays were inconclusive but video referee Steve Clark ruled a knock-on against Timmins.

Queensland forced a handling error in the 20th minute and, five tackles later, Slater chased Tate's grubber but just failed to ground the ball before it rolled dead. The Maroons returned to the attack within minutes after Fitzgibbon was caught offside. Two metres from the line, acting-half Prince threw a dummy to the left and then plunged over the line. The left-footed Smith's goal-kick struck the left post.

Mason was jeered by his home crowd when he came on. NSW lost a certain scoring opportunity in the 30th minute when, following Gower's bomb, Ryan dropped the ball with the tryline in sight. Mason lost possession in the next minute and, soon afterwards, Queensland forced three consecutive goal-line drop-outs. But NSW's defence held firm and the score remained 4–0 in Queensland's favour at half-time.

From the restart, Wing and Hornby got in each other's way and spilled the ball. Gower rescued NSW with an intercept in the following set. At the other end, Hodges was slow to recover a kick in his in-goal area and conceded a repeat set to the Blues. Timmins surged into a three-man tackle from close range and freed his left arm to place the ball over the line. Fitzgibbon's conversion put NSW in front 6–4. A few minutes later, Fitzgibbon extended that lead to four points with a penalty goal after Webcke impeded Hornby as he chased Gower's chip-kick.

Neither side looked like taking a grip on the game, although NSW often had better field position. A rare line-break by Flannery saw him step off both feet and then spin the ball to Prince, who threw a dummy and evaded Fitzgibbon. Crossing the quarter-line, Prince drew Hornby and Lewis before firing a long pass to Tate, who sprinted to score in the left corner. Smith hooked his goal-kick, leaving the scores deadlocked.

Players & Statistics

NSW Ben Hornby, Luke Rooney, Michael De Vere, Matt Gidley, Luke Lewis, Shaun Timmins, Craig Gower, Craig Fitzgibbon, Andrew Ryan, Nathan Hindmarsh, Mark O'Meley, Danny Buderus (c), Ryan O'Hara. **RESERVES** Willie Mason, Brent Kite, Trent Waterhouse, Craig Wing. **COACH** Phil Gould

QLD Rhys Wesser, Justin Hodges, Paul Bowman, Brent Tate, Billy Slater, Chris Flannery, Scott Prince, Tonie Carroll, Dane Carlaw, Michael Crocker, Steve Price, Craig Smith, Shane Webcke. **RESERVES** Ben Ross, Petero Civoniceva, Travis Norton, Matt Bowen. **COACH** Michael Hagan

Result NSW 9 (Timmins try; Fitzgibbon 2 goals; Timmins field goal) beat Queensland 8 (Prince, Tate tries)

Referee Sean Hampstead (NSW)

Crowd 68 344

Man of the Match Shaun Timmins (NSW)

↑ Debutant Luke Lewis is surrounded by Maroons as he leaps for a high kick.

In the 71st minute, Webcke went to the shortside and found a runaway Slater in support but referee Hampstead correctly ruled the pass forward. A half-break by Ryan tipped the scales NSW's way. The Maroons were caught offside but Fitzgibbon was offline with his penalty attempt from the left of the posts. NSW chasers tackled Wesser in-goal before Gidley burrowed for the tryline but was thwarted by three Maroons, then lost the ball as he got up to play it. With four minutes left, Gower pulled a field-goal attempt as Smith and Price charged at him.

In the 78th minute, a thumping tackle by Mason on Webcke forced a crucial handling error near Queensland's quarter-line. NSW set up for another field goal. Gower had time and space for his kick, but he glanced at the uprights as the ball came to him and he knocked-on. Queensland had one final chance of snatching victory within a minute of full-time when Slater forced Lewis in-goal after Smith's downfield kick. Slater caught the goal-line drop-out with less than ten seconds left, steadied and attempted a field goal but Buderus charged it down. For the first time, an Origin match went into extra time.

NSW had the first chance but Gower's field-goal attempt was smothered by Carroll. The Maroons made little ground as NSW's defence moved up quickly, and Tate and Wesser lost their footing. On tackle five of NSW's ensuing set, Buderus threw a long pass back to Timmins, who steadied and booted a towering 37-metre field goal, deciding the game after 82 minutes and 20 seconds.

The Verdict

For the fourth time in Origin football, a side had lost after scoring more tries than the opposition. Smith's two failed conversions, including one near-miss, could have swung the game, and Fitzgibbon's two goals were decisive. There were other missed chances from both sides as the little things played out. The game was always tight, but the absence of playmakers such as Lockyer and Johns made a huge difference.

The Teams

For Queensland, Sing and Lockyer returned from injury, and Hodges and Norton were dropped. The Maroons were set back when Crocker (suspended) and Tate (injured) were ruled out. Corey Parker and Willie Tonga were named to debut.

For NSW, Hornby, O'Hara and De Vere were left out, and Timmins and Gower were injured. Stevens, Minichiello and Tahu were recalled. Fittler returned at five-eighth after Gould invited him to make a comeback. Finding a halfback proved complicated. Kimmorley was named, only to withdraw injured; Barrett declined; Matt Orford was called in then ruled out with injury. The Blues settled on Brett Finch, who played alongside Fittler in club football.

The Game

Fittler was greeted with a punishing three-man tackle. In the fourth minute, Buderus spread the ball right to Fittler, Finch and Gidley, who grubbered towards the corner. Wesser fumbled the ball overhead and Tahu caught it with an outstretched hand to spin over in the in-goal area. Fitzgibbon's goal-kick hit the left upright, leaving the score 4–0.

Minichiello produced a weaving run soon after, evading several tackles before crossing the tryline, but referee Hampstead penalised him for running an obstruction. A handling error by NSW a few minutes later gave the Maroons a chance. They sent the ball left with the NSW defence at sixes and sevens, but Price's wayward pass was fumbled by Slater.

Wesser made another mistake when he spilled a bomb, before Price was penalised for a ruck infringement. Fitzgibbon accepted the gift two points. Wesser soon made amends, dragging Rooney over the sideline in a try-saving tackle. NSW controlled play, and dummy-half Hindmarsh made a 60-metre break from inside his quarter.

A penalty against Finch eight minutes from the break put Queensland on the attack. Prince spun a long ball right to Lockyer, who fired it to Wesser. He drew Fittler and slipped an inside ball to Slater, who raced through and stepped inside Minichiello to score. Smith's conversion levelled the scores. NSW wasted a chance to reply almost immediately when Rooney kicked too deep after the second tackle.

With half-time barely a minute away, Wing veered right, drew the defence and fed Gidley. Gidley was held but he released his trademark backhand flick-pass to Tahu, who had an open run to the corner. Fitzgibbon converted brilliantly and NSW took a crucial 12–6 lead just before the break.

↓ Dane Carlaw touches down for the Maroons. It was his fourth Origin try, and all of them came at crucial times.

In the 44th minute, Tahu accidentally knocked down a pass but was ruled to have played at the ball. The tackle count restarted before Webcke surged into Wing and underarmed a pass left to Lockyer, who spun a long ball. It bounced before Tonga fielded it and stepped outside Tahu to touch down in the corner. Smith's hooked goal-kick left NSW leading 12–10.

Unlike the first half, Queensland now looked more threatening, with Tonga particularly dangerous. Flannery lost the ball in a tackle just short of the tryline after good lead-up work from Prince. After a stripping penalty against Fittler, Lockyer pushed a goal-kick to the left.

With 18 minutes remaining, Lockyer grubbered to the left from his 40-metre line. Slater scooped up the ball, raced away and attempted to wrong-foot Minichiello. As Minichiello and Lewis closed in, Slater chip-kicked to his left and swooped on the bouncing ball to score in a breathtaking play. Referee Hampstead called for replays since Slater looked offside. However, replays showed it was line-ball and video referee Tim Mander awarded the try. Prince's conversion gave Queensland a 16–12 lead.

After Fittler was stopped just short of the line, NSW spread the ball right where Slater shoulder-charged Tahu as he dived for the corner. Tahu was denied as replays showed his arm had touched the corner post and he'd dropped the ball. In the next set, Lockyer hoisted a bomb towards the left corner where Tahu dropped an overhead catch under

pressure from Slater. Carlaw gathered it to touch down for a try. Queensland had some breathing space with a 20–12 lead.

Mason made a good break in the 73rd minute to get the ball near halfway. Fittler linked with Finch and Hindmarsh, who bumped off Prince, changed direction twice and underarmed the ball left to Ryan. Drawing Sing, Ryan fed Rooney, who ran past Bowman and stepped inside Sing before diving for the line. Fitzgibbon kicked the conversion, reducing Queensland's lead to a mere two points.

Hindmarsh evaded a couple of tackles from the restart and powered ahead to maintain NSW's momentum, but Waterhouse dropped the ball two tackles later. The Blues threatened to attack from inside their half with three minutes left, but Fittler's pass to Rooney found the sideline. Then Lewis gave away a penalty near his tryline. As Smith used up time preparing a goal-kick, Gould conceded defeat as he headed for the dressing room. Smith landed the goal and then fielded Fittler's short kick-off.

The Verdict

Most post-match reviews focused on Slater's sizzling try, which immediately entered folklore as one of the all-time great Origin tries. The Maroons had just done enough to win, having scored four tries to three. As in game one, a goal-kick hitting the post was a good example of how close the games were.

↑ Billy Slater scores one of the most sensational tries in Origin football with a chip-and-chase as he scurries away.

Players & Statistics

QLD Rhys Wesser, Matt Sing, Paul Bowman, Willie Tonga, Billy Slater, Darren Lockyer (c), Scott Prince, Tonie Carroll, Dane Carlaw, Petero Civoniceva, Steve Price, Cameron Smith, Shane Webcke. **RESERVES** Ben Ross, Corey Parker, Chris Flannery, Matt Bowen. **COACH** Michael Hagan

NSW Anthony Minichiello, Timana Tahu, Matt Gidley, Luke Lewis, Luke Rooney, Brad Fittler, Brett Finch, Craig Fitzgibbon, Andrew Ryan, Nathan Hindmarsh, Mark O'Meley, Danny Buderus (c), Jason Stevens. **RESERVES** Willie Mason, Brent Kite, Trent Waterhouse, Craig Wing. **COACH** Phil Gould

Result Queensland 22 (Slater 2, Tonga, Carlaw tries; Smith 2, Prince goals) beat NSW 18 (Tahu 2, Rooney tries; Fitzgibbon 3 goals)

Referee Sean Hampstead (NSW)

Crowd 52 478

Man of the Match Billy Slater (Queensland)

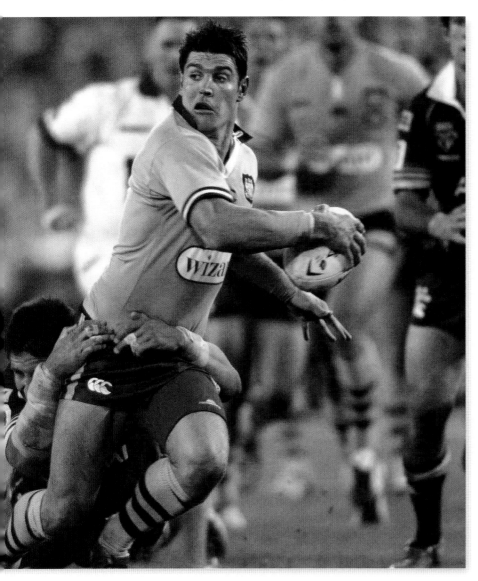

↑ Recalled after an injury layoff, Trent Barrett played a leading role for NSW at halfback as the Blues won the series decider.

The Teams

NSW dropped Gidley, Tahu, Finch, Waterhouse, Stevens and Ryan. Barrett, Ryles, Timmins and Kennedy returned, as did Gasnier. Matt Cooper was named to debut. Queensland's selectors omitted Carroll and Parker, recalled Tate and Crocker and made some positional changes. Parker earned a reprieve when an injured Bowman withdrew.

Paul Simpkins was named to referee his first State of Origin match.

The Game

In the second minute, Slater was slammed on his back by Hindmarsh and Fitzgibbon in a lifting tackle. Referee Simpkins ignored Lockyer's claim of a dangerous tackle, although replays showed that the defenders had lifted Slater's legs into a vertical position. Fortunate to have possession, NSW set up an overlap but Slater jolted the ball out of Lewis's grasp.

Smith kicked Queensland to a 2–0 lead from an offside penalty. A few minutes later, Slater's one-handed carry cost him as he fumbled in a tackle. As NSW attacked, Fittler threw a cut-out ball right to Gasnier, who drifted, straightened and busted Slater's tackle before barging over the tryline. Fitzgibbon converted. After Slater fumbled a kick return backwards, an all-in brawl developed after O'Meley flopped on a tackled player. The Maroons received a penalty but could not penetrate.

Midway through the first half, Tate grubbered into NSW's in-goal area. As Sing zeroed in, Minichiello coat-hangered him to illegally prevent a likely try. Referee Simpkins did not sin-bin Minichiello or award a penalty try or even seek replays, but he simply awarded a penalty. Two tackles later, Flannery turned the ball left to Lockyer, who spun it to Tonga. He drew Lewis and sent Slater over in the corner. Smith's conversion gave his side a two-point lead, but NSW appeared fortunate not to have been punished further for Minichiello's indiscretion.

Eleven minutes from the break, Fittler's kick rolled in-goal after Sing fumbled it backwards, and a pursuing Kennedy knocked Wesser over before Minichiello grounded the ball. Kennedy was penalised on video evidence. After Queensland was penalised for offside, Barrett veered right and accelerated between Webcke and Flannery, then skipped past Slater's diving tackle to score. Fitzgibbon converted again.

Webcke was penalised for flopping in a tackle immediately after the restart, allowing the Blues to return downfield. The Blues were 2 metres out on the last tackle, to the right of the posts. Wing rifled the ball to the blindside, where Fittler exploited a three-on-two overlap to send Gasnier over in the corner. Fitzgibbon's goal-kick bounced over the crossbar, and NSW had quickly struck two crucial blows to lead 18–8. Just before half-time, Kennedy botched an attempted intercept to help Queensland. But Rooney palmed Prince's grubber dead, before Lewis defused Lockyer's chip-kick.

Just after the resumption, Sing was taken off after a head clash with Fittler. Fittler charged for the tryline in the next minute but was held up. The Maroons regrouped as Prince and Lockyer combined to send Slater racing away. Slater's chip-kick rolled beyond the tryline but Wesser's missed tackle enabled Minichiello to escape from the in-goal area. Two minutes later, Tonga made a 30-metre break before Wesser stepped from dummy-half and reached for the left corner in Minichiello's tackle. But video referee Hampstead disallowed the try when replays showed that Wesser's left foot touched the sideline before he grounded the ball.

In the 55th minute, Queensland lost possession after a pass from Webcke went awry. Fittler's cut-out pass to the left created an overlap as Cooper ran a decoy, before Wing unloaded to Rooney, who crossed in the corner as Tate just failed to drag his legs into touch. The tiny margin between Wesser's loss and Rooney's gain decisively turned the match.

The Blues maintained their impetus when Barrett landed a 40-20 kick. Lockyer chip-kicked towards Slater's wing but the linesman incorrectly ruled Slater had stepped into touch as he scooped the ball back. Bowen chanced an intercept but knocked on, before Barrett ran from the scrum to within 5 metres

← A tower of strength in NSW's series win, Craig Fitzgibbon was replaced with 13 minutes left after having been on the field for every minute of the series until then.

of the tryline. Timmins drew the defence and sent Minichiello barging over for a converted try to make the score 28–8. Smith hooked the kick-off out on the full before the Blues forced a goal-line drop-out. Then Parker was penalised for stripping the ball as he prevented Cooper scoring a try. Fitzgibbon landed the goal on offer.

In the 72nd minute, Mason ran onto a short pass and made a long break, but fumbled short of the line, thwarted by a desperate Slater. Lockyer chip-kicked inside his 30-metre zone, only for Fittler to charge it down, collect the ball and score behind the posts.

Inside the last four minutes, Bowen scored a consolation try when he dummied, straightened and stepped through the NSW defence. The 36–14 score produced NSW's highest winning margin in an Origin decider and provided Fittler and Gould with a triumphant finish to Origin football.

↓ Brad Fittler says goodbye for the last time. Having played against Wally Lewis in his first Origin series and opposing Darren Lockyer in his last, Fittler said he couldn't have written the script any better way.

The Verdict

There were several telling aspects in the game. Whereas Queensland led only 8–6 after receiving the first five penalties, the Blues capitalised on their first two penalties with a converted try each time. In fact, NSW's first five tries followed Queensland mistakes.

The Maroons had a couple of chances to fight back in the first ten minutes after half-time, but they could not grasp the opportunities. In addition, Queensland missed 51 tackles to NSW's 21.

Players & Statistics

NSW Anthony Minichiello, Luke Lewis, Mark Gasnier, Matt Cooper, Luke Rooney, Brad Fittler, Trent Barrett, Shaun Timmins, Craig Fitzgibbon, Nathan Hindmarsh, Mark O'Meley, Danny Buderus (c), Jason Ryles. **RESERVES** Willie Mason, Brent Kite, Ben Kennedy, Craig Wing. **COACH** Phil Gould

QLD Rhys Wesser, Matt Sing, Brent Tate, Willie Tonga, Billy Slater, Darren Lockyer (c), Scott Prince, Dane Carlaw, Petero Civoniceva, Michael Crocker, Steve Price, Cameron Smith, Shane Webcke. **RESERVES** Chris Flannery, Ben Ross, Corey Parker, Matt Bowen. **COACH** Michael Hagan

Result NSW 36 (Gasnier 2, Barrett, Rooney, Minichiello, Fittler tries; Fitzgibbon 5, Gasnier goals) beat Queensland 14 (Slater, Bowen tries; Smith 3 goals)

Referee Paul Simpkins (NSW)

Crowd 82 487

Man of the Match Craig Fitzgibbon (NSW)

2005

The Intercept, the X-factor and the Close of an Era

Ricky Stuart had big shoes to fill when he took over as NSW coach. However, he brought with him a strong record of his own as a premiership-winning coach (2002) and runner-up twice (2003 and 2004). Furthermore, he worked at the same club as Phil Gould. For Queensland, Michael Hagan was under pressure after the 2004 series loss and, additionally, his club side was winless after ten games in the 2005 season.

Queensland faced life after Webcke (retired from representative football), while Tate and Tonga had season-ending injuries. The Blues had lost Fittler and Timmins to retirement, while Andrew Johns, Mason and O'Meley were injured. But there was a chance that Johns could return during the Origin series.

← Andrew Johns returned from injury to play a major role for the Blues after NSW lost game one. It was to be his last Origin series.

The Teams

Queensland recalled Berrigan, Webb and Thorn, but Wesser and Prince were overlooked. First caps were given to Ty Williams and Johnathan Thurston. Casey McGuire became another debutant when Tonie Carroll withdrew injured.

Simpson, Ryan and Kimmorley were recalled for NSW, and Matt King and Anthony Watmough were chosen to debut.

The Game

NSW was plugged in its own half early on after Price smothered Kimmorley's clearing kick. Minichiello was penalised for flopping and Smith opened the scoring from the resultant kick. Lockyer and Kimmorley tried the high ball without success before Rooney made a break, only for Thurston to pull off a try-saving tackle.

At the other end, Queensland forced a goal-line drop-out before a penalty against Buderus for interference led to another two points for Smith. Near NSW's quarter-line five tackles later, Lockyer passed to Slater, who tried to catch the ball as he was tackled from behind. It struck his knee and floated over Minichiello's arm before Williams scooped the ball up and dived over between the posts. Replays were unable to show if the ball touched Slater's hands, but video referee Graeme West awarded the try. Queensland led 10–0 after Smith converted.

After Bailey accidentally hit Flannery high, Webb reacted and was penalised for pushing Bailey and

↓ Mark Gasnier feels the force of a dominant tackle. Gasnier broke through a couple of times in the second half, and scored a try as the Blues fought back from a seemingly hopeless position.

Players & Statistics

QLD Billy Slater, Ty Williams, Shaun Berrigan, Paul Bowman, Matt Sing, Darren Lockyer (c), Johnathan Thurston, Chris Flannery, Brad Thorn, Michael Crocker, Petero Civoniceva, Cameron Smith, Steve Price. **RESERVES** Ben Ross, Carl Webb, Casey McGuire, Matt Bowen. **COACH** Michael Hagan

NSW Anthony Minichiello, Matt King, Mark Gasnier, Matt Cooper, Luke Rooney, Trent Barrett, Brett Kimmorley, Ben Kennedy, Craig Fitzgibbon, Nathan Hindmarsh, Jason Ryles, Danny Buderus (c), Luke Bailey. **RESERVES** Craig Wing, Steve Simpson, Andrew Ryan, Anthony Watmough. **COACH** Ricky Stuart

Result Queensland 24 (Williams, Crocker, Bowen tries; Smith 5 goals; Lockyer, Thurston field goals) beat NSW 20 (Rooney, Gasnier, Fitzgibbon, Buderus tries; Fitzgibbon 2 goals)

Referee Paul Simpkins (NSW)

Crowd 52 484

Man of the Match Steve Price (Queensland)

pinning him down. Webb immediately continued his campaign against Bailey, conceding another penalty for rough play before forcing a knock-on with a thumping tackle. Then Kimmorley was penalised for stealing the ball from Webb and tempers threatened to flare. Queensland regained the initiative and forced successive repeat sets of six. After Barrett hit Thurston high, Smith kicked his third penalty goal. Queensland foiled a couple of NSW attacking raids before Lockyer landed a field goal within a minute of half-time to make the score 13–0.

Early in the second half, Rooney retrieved Barrett's bomb within sight of the tryline and attempted to burrow through three tacklers. Due to inconclusive replays, West referred the call back to Simpkins, who ruled Rooney was held up. Next, Ryles dropped a regulation pass in his half to enable the Maroons to apply pressure. Lockyer fired a bullet-like pass left to Crocker, who veered inside and scored a try which Smith converted. Not long after NSW was arguably unlucky not to have bridged a 13-point deficit, Queensland led 19–0.

Webb knocked-on after the restart before Barrett drifted left and drew the defence. He linked up with Cooper, who drew Sing and sent Rooney diving for the left corner. Fitzgibbon's conversion attempt hooked wide to leave the score at 19–4 to Queensland. At the hour mark, Minichiello broke out of Lockyer's tackle before drawing Slater and sending Gasnier scampering 30 metres to score. Slater's chase ensured Gasnier scored wide out, and stop-gap kicker Kimmorley's conversion attempt pulled wide.

In the 68th minute, NSW spread the ball left through Buderus, Kimmorley and Cooper. Buderus's and Kimmorley's passes were clearly forward but were overlooked. Cooper grubbered infield towards the tryline where three Maroons converged but muddled up. Fitzgibbon was on the spot to score, then converted from close range. The margin was suddenly just five points.

Four tackles after the restart, Buderus linked up with Barrett and Gasnier, both of whom drew in defenders, before Gasnier sent King scurrying down the right touchline. He flung a long and patently forward pass inside to Buderus, who ran to score near the posts. Fitzgibbon converted and the Blues had unexpectedly but luckily turned a 19–0 deficit into a 20–19 lead in 20 minutes.

The Blues launched another raid when Gasnier made a break with the Queensland defence in tatters, before Kimmorley's grubber-kick rolled too deep. Half-breaks by Bowen and Berrigan gained vital field position for Queensland with just five minutes left. Fitzgibbon and Bailey were caught offside, and Lockyer pulled a crucial 33-metre penalty kick just wide.

The Maroons attacked again from the 20-metre drop-out and were 10 metres out on tackle five. Bowen spun the ball infield to Thurston whose field-goal attempt just wobbled over the crossbar after Ryan touched it in flight. The teams were tied 20–all with two minutes left. Lockyer attempted a long-range field goal in the last minute but was well short.

In NSW's first set in extra-time, the Blues only made it to their 30-metre line in five tackles. Queensland's defence rushed up to put pressure on Kimmorley and Barrett, who only managed to put through a grubber to the halfway line. The Maroons worked their way into field-goal position but Lockyer's 34-metre attempt missed. Three tackles later and 12 metres short of halfway, Buderus passed left to Kimmorley, who spun the ball wide, where Cooper had open space in front of him. However, Bowen rushed to intercept and ran away unopposed for the winning try. It was breathtaking stuff. After a fascinating 83 minutes and 20 seconds, Queensland won 24–20.

The Verdict

The Blues felt that the match officials had cost them dearly. Among their complaints were: that Slater had knocked on during the Maroons' first try, that Rooney's disallowed try should have been awarded and that Webb should have been sin-binned for scuffling with Bailey. On the other hand, the palpably forward passes in the lead-up to NSW's final two tries were virtually overlooked.

Other factors NSW supporters had to concede included the Blues' missed goal-kicks and the penalties they conceded within goal-kicking range.

← After returning to rugby league following a four-year stint in rugby union, Brad Thorn savours being on a winning Origin team for the first time.

↓ Luke Rooney catches a high ball safely. Rooney was disallowed a try before he scored NSW's first try.

The Teams

Kimmorley unfairly copped the brunt of criticism for NSW's loss in game one, and he was dropped along with Watmough. Anasta and Menzies were recalled. After moving to halfback, an injured Barrett withdrew, leading to the reinstatement of Johns. Queensland was set back as an injured Price was ruled out for the series. Webb moved into the second-row and Carlaw was recalled as a reserve.

Steve Clark was appointed as referee and Graeme West remained as video referee.

↑ Paul Bowman is well caught by the NSW defence.

↓ In full voice…the 'Blue Army' had plenty to smile about as Queensland remained winless at the Telstra Stadium.

The Game

The Maroons threatened twice early on but were let down by ineffective kicks. Williams put through a kick which Berrigan toed ahead but it bounced into touch near the tryline with Williams in close pursuit. After appearing to knock-on Johns's banana kick, Crocker broke through and fed Slater, who dashed past the halfway line and kicked, but King beat Berrigan to the ball. King steamed onto a Minichiello pass to put the Blues in a try-scoring position five minutes later, but Crocker intercepted King's inside pass.

On the 14-minute mark, Johns kicked downfield from 40 metres out. Slater and Sing ambled towards the ball but it ricocheted off the left upright for Minichiello to swoop and score. Replays suggested that Minichiello was marginally offside but the video referee ruled a try, which Fitzgibbon converted. NSW received successive penalties after the restart and, after the latter, Fitzgibbon landed a penalty goal to extend NSW's lead to 8–0.

Bailey dropped a pass in his half, and Queensland forced a goal-line drop-out before Ryles was penalised for a flop. Queensland opted to push for a try. Lockyer put up a last-tackle bomb, and Thorn jumped over Anasta to take an overhead mark before surging into Cooper and rolling over to score. Smith converted from in front to close NSW's lead to two points.

Webb exited the match with a groin injury in the 26th minute. Successive Johns bombs forced a goal-line drop-out and a Slater fumble near Queensland's tryline. However, Minichiello spilled Anasta's reserve pass from the scrum. Slater caught the ball and sprinted 88 metres to beat Minichiello to the other end. Rooney retired from the match with a thigh injury just before Smith landed the conversion attempt. Queensland showed some ill-discipline later in the half, but led 12–8 at the break.

Fitzgibbon erred from the restart, running to the blindside, where four Maroons tackled him into touch. On the last tackle, Queensland moved the ball left through Bowen, Crocker, Lockyer and Berrigan, who drew Menzies and rushed his pass. Williams collected the ball after it bounced and stepped inside Minichiello and Bailey to touch down, but Berrigan's pass was ruled forward by the linesman. Replays suggested the pass was line-ball.

Johns caught Queensland off guard just three tackles later with a 40-20 kick, putting the Blues back on the attack. The Maroons held out but Ross lost possession as he tried to offload in a tackle. In the next set, Johns fired the ball right to Anasta. He stepped inside and unloaded in a tackle to Minichiello, who crashed over the line in a tackle. Johns landed the conversion for NSW to lead 14–12. The sequence of a few successive incidents was crucial

Players & Statistics

NSW Anthony Minichiello, Matt King, Mark Gasnier, Matt Cooper, Luke Rooney, Braith Anasta, Andrew Johns, Ben Kennedy, Craig Fitzgibbon, Nathan Hindmarsh, Jason Ryles, Danny Buderus (c), Steve Simpson. **RESERVES** Luke Bailey, Craig Wing, Andrew Ryan, Steve Menzies. **COACH** Ricky Stuart

QLD Billy Slater, Ty Williams, Shaun Berrigan, Paul Bowman, Matt Sing, Darren Lockyer (c), Johnathan Thurston, Chris Flannery, Carl Webb, Michael Crocker, Petero Civoniceva, Cameron Smith, Brad Thorn. **RESERVES** Ben Ross, Dane Carlaw, Casey McGuire, Matt Bowen. **COACH** Michael Hagan

Result NSW 32 (Minichiello 2, Menzies, Cooper, Buderus tries; Fitzgibbon 3, Johns 3 goals) beat Queensland 22 (Thorn, Slater, Bowen, Civoniceva tries; Smith 3 goals)

Referee Steve Clark (NSW)

Crowd 82 389

Man of the Match Andrew Johns (NSW)

↑ The strain shows as Nathan Hindmarsh confronts a solid mass of the Queensland defence.

as Queensland could just as easily have led 16–8 or 18–8 and been well-placed to push for a series win.

Five tackles after Minichiello's try, Slater spilled yet another Johns bomb. A metre from the tryline, long passes to the right found Wing. Drawing the defence, Wing cleverly slipped a short ball that sent Menzies barging over to score. Johns converted, and NSW had an eight-point lead with 32 minutes left.

Johns showed again that he was back to his best when he sliced through the Queensland defence to set up another try, only for Buderus to throw a forward pass to Cooper. However, six minutes later, King began a passing movement that included Anasta, Johns and Cooper, who sent Gasnier running down the left wing. Slater thwarted Gasnier but he passed inside to Cooper, who raced to the line. NSW led comfortably at 26–12 after Johns made it three from three with the boot.

In the 64th minute, King produced an airborne driving tackle on Williams. Eleven minutes from the finish, Berrigan spun a long pass right to Thurston and Lockyer, who slipped the ball to Bowen. He sprinted through to score near the right corner, and the Maroons trailed 26–16 after Smith's stray goal-kick. But Queensland's comeback was short-lived. Bowen fumbled twice within six minutes, before Johns used some good footwork to commit multiple defenders before sending a well-timed pass to Buderus, who dived over the line unopposed. Fitzgibbon converted for NSW to lead 32–16. Queensland fought until the end and, with 20

seconds left, Civoniceva pushed forward and spun around with a swarm of defenders clinging to him to crash over for a try. Smith's conversion made the score look a little more respectable at 32–22.

The Verdict

Queensland was always going to find it tough to win if Johns hit his straps. But the refereeing came under fire, with the Maroons particularly rueing Williams's disallowed try. Queensland was also let down by poor ball handling in the second half.

The Teams

The Blues lost Rooney and Wing to injury. Tahu and Gower were recalled. For Queensland, the injured Webb was out and Slater, McGuire and Carlaw were omitted. Bowen moved to fullback, and Parker was recalled and Danny Nutley and Ashley Harrison were named to debut. One spot was left unnamed, with Carroll later called up.

The Game

An early fumble by Minichiello gave the Maroons possession, which they held for an unbelievable 29 consecutive tackles. But they never looked like scoring—their plays were predictable and NSW's defence never looked like cracking. At one stage, Johns appeared unsportsmanlike by feigning an injury to cause a stoppage and give his team a breather.

Queensland's attacking sequence ended when Minichiello fielded a shallow Lockyer grubber and broke away. Bowen chased from the opposite side to tackle his counterpart in Queensland's quarter before Sing came in late and flopped to concede a penalty. The Blues attacked and were near the posts when Nutley was penalised for slowing a play-the-ball. Fitzgibbon landed a penalty goal and NSW struck an important psychological blow after withstanding a flurry of Queensland attacks.

The Maroons failed to capitalise after forcing another goal-line drop-out. A few minutes later, Crocker made a catastrophic mistake on the last tackle by conceding a penalty for a play-the-ball infringement. The Blues attacked and received six more tackles after Thurston knocked-on attempting an intercept. Buderus spun the ball right to Johns whose delayed pass to Anasta allowed him to rush past Lockyer and cross the line. Johns converted for NSW to lead 8–0. The Blues returned downfield after Carroll dropped a regulation pass. On the last tackle, Johns hoisted a bomb to the right of the posts where Gasnier out-jumped Berrigan and crashed over to score. Johns raised the flags for a 14–0 scoreline.

Ten minutes from the break, a wrong-footed Crocker stuck out his right arm and cuffed ball-carrier Kennedy across the chin. Kennedy fell to ground and lay motionless as the Queenslanders angrily claimed he'd taken a dive to milk a penalty. Replays showed that his actions looked unsporting but, nevertheless, referee Simpkins penalised Crocker. Kennedy rose to his feet and resumed playing as though nothing had happened.

In the next set, Menzies passed right to Johns, who stepped off both feet, surged into Parker and shovelled the ball to Minichiello. He sucked in the defence and fed King, who stepped out of Williams's tackle and touched down. Johns's conversion attempt pushed just wide but NSW held a strong 18–0 lead at half-time.

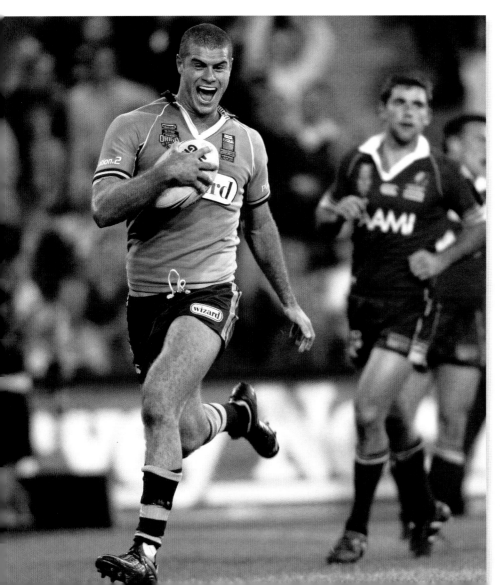

↓ A joyful Matt King runs in for one of his three tries in NSW's convincing win.

Players & Statistics

NSW Anthony Minichiello, Matt King, Mark Gasnier, Matt Cooper, Timana Tahu, Braith Anasta, Andrew Johns, Ben Kennedy, Craig Fitzgibbon, Nathan Hindmarsh, Jason Ryles, Danny Buderus (c), Steve Simpson. **RESERVES** Luke Bailey, Craig Gower, Andrew Ryan, Steve Menzies. **COACH** Ricky Stuart

QLD Matt Bowen, Ty Williams, Shaun Berrigan, Paul Bowman, Matt Sing, Darren Lockyer (c), Johnathan Thurston, Tonie Carroll, Brad Thorn, Michael Crocker, Petero Civoniceva, Cameron Smith, Danny Nutley. **RESERVES** Chris Flannery, Ben Ross, Ashley Harrison, Corey Parker. **COACH** Michael Hagan

Result NSW 32 (King 3, Anasta, Gasnier, Tahu tries; Johns 3, Fitzgibbon goals) beat Queensland 10 (Thurston, Bowen tries; Smith goal)

Referee Paul Simpkins (NSW)

Crowd 52 436

Man of the Match Anthony Minichiello (NSW)

Five minutes after the break, Sing passed to nobody. The ball rolled towards the left sideline, where Berrigan fielded it and was tackled into touch by King. On the last tackle, Kennedy spun the ball left to Johns, who stepped left and fooled the defence before turning the ball right. King veered left as he raced onto it and sped through the gap to score behind the posts. Johns kicked the conversion to make the score 24–0.

Cooper spilled a bomb from Lockyer and a knock-on from Thorn soon followed. Williams fielded Johns's downfield kick 35 metres from his line and passed to Bowen, who fumbled backwards. He dived at the ball but Johns picked it up and passed to Ryan and Hindmarsh. With Thorn approaching, Hindmarsh stepped left and fired the ball out to Cooper and then Tahu, who scored in the corner.

Queensland briefly lifted, forcing consecutive goal-line drop-outs, and a powerful hit-up by Nutley left Fitzgibbon dazed. But a knock-on by Bowen added to Queensland's night of woe. Sing fumbled a bomb before Queensland was penalised for a play-the-ball infringement. Buderus spiralled a pass right to Johns, who linked up with Menzies and Gasnier. With Williams in from the wing, Gasnier quickly fed King, who dived over in the corner. It was incredible to think that a team that had 29 consecutive tackles in possession early on could later trail 32-0.

With seven minutes left, Williams combined with Bowen and Sing from a kick return. Sing evaded Anasta and Kennedy before drawing Minichiello

and spinning a long pass to Smith. He drew the NSW fullback then sent Thurston running away to score near the posts. Ross initiated some pushing and shoving after he lashed out at Fitzgibbon and Buderus when they held onto him too long. Soon after the penalty, Queensland was 2 metres from the uprights. Smith spun a long pass left to Lockyer, who drew the defence before firing the ball to Bowen, who sprinted through and dived to score.

The Verdict

The 32–10 result produced NSW's highest score and winning margin in an Origin match in Brisbane. In a familiar scenario, the winning team scored all its points on the back of opposition errors. The Maroons had failed to capitalise on a feast of early scoring opportunities before paying the full price for a swag of unforced mistakes.

NSW had won three straight series, although the 2005 series could have been different were it not for Williams's crucial disallowed try in game two. But the extent to which NSW dominated and Queensland crumbled in the second half of the series meant the controversy over Williams's disallowed try was all but forgotten.

↓ A dejected Darren Lockyer wonders what might have been as the Maroons slip to a heavy defeat on home soil.

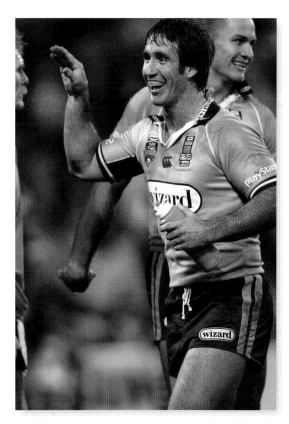

← Meanwhile, in the Blues corner, Andrew Johns is all smiles when NSW romps to a series victory.

2006

King Wally's Statue Turns Blue but Mal's Maroons Get Out of Jail

Melbourne was allotted a State of Origin match for the first time since 1997. The Melbourne Storm committed $23 million to the marketing and development of rugby league, and the funding was complemented with a package that included a tri-nations test and Origin game three. After Olympic Park and the MCG hosted previous Origin games in Melbourne, the 2006 match was to be played at Telstra Dome, featuring a closed roof.

There were coaching and management changes in both teams. Queensland implemented a coaching and support team structure in its quest to regain Origin supremacy. Mal Meninga stepped into the coaching position, with Neil Henry and Kevin Walters as assistants, and several former Origin players joined an extended management team. Ricky Stuart's elevation to Australian coach ruled him out of the NSW coaching job. The new Blues coach was Graham Murray, whose long coaching career had included stints in Australia and England. Royce Simmons was named his assistant coach and Laurie Daley an additional manager.

Eying an unprecedented fourth straight series win, NSW was without Johns and Kennedy, both of whom had retired from representative football. Minichiello, Ryles and Luke Bailey were injured, although Bailey had a chance of returning during the Origin series. The Maroons lost Sing and Bowman, who had both retired from representative football, and the suspended Slater and Crocker.

← Part of the new breed for the Maroons … Nate Myles takes the ball up. It was to be the start of a golden period for Queensland.

↑ The toast of NSW's victory: Brett Finch launches into the winning field goal. Drafted into the team less than 24 hours earlier, the fourth-choice halfback scored the opening try and had a hand in NSW's two other tries before his match-winning moment. His hero status was short-lived, and he was dropped after NSW lost the following game.

The Teams

Queensland's selectors recalled Hodges, Tate, Price and Webb, and named seven debutants: Greg Inglis, Steve Bell, Dallas Johnson, Matt Scott, David Stagg, Sam Thaiday and Nate Myles.

For NSW, Fitzgibbon was overlooked. Hodgson, Mason, Kite, Wing and O'Meley won recalls and Luke O'Donnell was named to debut. When an injured Cooper withdrew, Eric Grothe Jnr was recalled for his belated Origin debut after injury had denied him six years earlier. When halfback Gower was forced out, the Blues had trouble replacing him. Johns declined an offer, before Kimmorley and Matt Orford were considered but had injury problems. Like in game two of 2004, NSW settled with Finch.

The Game

Queensland was unable to capitalise on good field position after a knock-on from Gasnier and a penalty against Mason. O'Donnell pulled off several heavy tackles but a fractured thumb ended his Origin debut in the seventh minute. Bowen broke away after taking a bomb before Mason was penalised for a high tackle. Hodges got within a metre of scoring in the right corner before Bell, Bowen, Lockyer and Thurston handled, but Tate dropped Thurston's pass. Gasnier scooped the ball up and sent King away down the flank. With Tate chasing, King flung a pass inside to Finch, who

scurried 30 metres to score. Hodgson's kick missed but NSW led 4–0 against the run of play.

Inglis fumbled a bomb in a contest with King in the 15th minute. NSW soon sent the ball right via Finch, Hodgson and Gasnier, who drew Inglis and sent King across in the corner. Gasnier's pass looked forward but referee Hampstead awarded the try. Hodgson missed another kick and the score remained 8–0. Lockyer made a crucial error by sending the kick-off on the full. In Queensland's 30-metre zone a few minutes later, Finch's clever pass sent Mason through a gap. Mason shrugged off Bowen to score near the posts. Hodgson's conversion took NSW to a 14–0 lead.

A couple of NSW mistakes allowed the Maroons to hit back but they were incoherent. They twice lost possession on the first tackle, including when Tate spilled a hospital pass from Lockyer. NSW's forwards kept Queensland's forwards on the back foot. Just before the break, Thurston grubbered for Bell in the right corner, but Grothe bundled Bell into touch.

Fumbles by Inglis and Hodges kept the Maroons pinned in their quarter early in the second half. To their credit, they showed solid defence. After Hodges stole the ball from Grothe in a one-on-one tackle, a punch-up followed. Grothe was penalised for being the aggressor. Two rucks later, the Maroons spread the ball left in NSW's quarter as Smith combined with Price, Thurston and Lockyer. His cut-out pass put Inglis over in the left corner and Thurston's brilliant conversion cut NSW's lead to eight points.

Ten minutes later, Lockyer fumbled to slow Queensland's push. After Tate conceded a penalty with 16 minutes remaining, Hodgson landed a goal to make the score 16–6. In the next set, Gasnier retrieved an Anasta bomb and sent King diving across in the corner. But the try was disallowed after replays showed that Inglis knocked the ball loose as King reached to ground it.

In the 71st minute, Lockyer chip-kicked over the NSW defence and Hodgson fumbled the ball inside his quarter. Bowen almost tripped over the loose ball before Lockyer picked it up and fed Inglis, who scored in the left corner. Thurston's conversion hooked wide, leaving NSW with a six-point lead. Grothe knocked-on outside his quarter a couple of minutes later to present Queensland with another opportunity, but Lockyer fumbled on the last play. Buderus secured the ball and was tackled when Johnson gave him a little kick below the shoulder. Buderus played the ball, then punched Johnson in retaliation. Play continued but a linesman intervened. Johnson's indiscretion was missed by the officials and Buderus was penalised despite claiming he'd been kicked in the head. One tackle later, within 10 metres of the uprights, Thurston spun a pass right to Hodges, who drew Grothe and sent Bell plunging over in the corner. Facing a high-pressure sideline conversion attempt, Thurston's kick curled from right to left and raised the flags to level the scores with three minutes remaining.

Lockyer kicked from his 30-metre line after just three tackles in the next set. With Queensland's defenders standing deep late in the tackle count, a combination of Menzies's reverse

pass and Gasnier's half-break took NSW past halfway. On the final tackle, 18 metres inside Queensland territory, Buderus fired a long pass to the left, where Finch steadied and nailed a 35-metre field goal with 90 seconds remaining. A knock-on by Gasnier allowed Queensland a scrum feed with 20 seconds left. The Maroons threw the ball around but the defence was up quickly and snuffed out their last chance. Despite suffering a couple of frights, NSW finally prevailed 17–16.

The Verdict

Although the Maroons came close to stealing an unlikely win late in the game, the result flattered them in the light of their sub-par form for much of the contest. Their first half was arguably as bad as an Origin side had ever played. By contrast, the Blues played cohesively and took advantage of their opportunities.

↑ Eric Grothe and Justin Hodges come to blows as spite creeps into the game.

↓ Shaun Berrigan is swamped by Willie Mason and Nathan Hindmarsh.

The Teams

Queensland dropped Bowen, Stagg and Scott. Carroll and Flannery were recalled, and Karmichael Hunt was chosen to debut. Inglis and Carroll were forced out with injury, with their places going to surprise choices Adam Mogg and Jacob Lillyman.

NSW had the luxury of only one forced change. The injured O'Donnell was replaced in the squad by the recalled Luke Bailey.

The Game

On the morning of game two, the statue of Wally Lewis outside Suncorp Stadium was found covered in blue paint. A 'fan' defaced the statue with the sky blue of a NSW jersey, dark blue shorts, a sky blue wig and 'NSW' across the shield. The statue was cleaned before kick-off.

After being swarmed by four Maroons in the first tackle of the match, Mason looked at the defence on his next hit-up and spilled the ball. Queensland's ensuing raid was undone when Hodges's pass to Tate found the sideline. Thurston opened the scoring with a 30-metre penalty goal after Kite was punished in the fourth minute for lying on Webb in a tackle.

The Blues created an overlap several minutes later, but Hodgson's pass to an unmarked King went astray as Mogg hammered Hodgson. Both defences were solid, with three defenders often involved in tackles. After 19 minutes, Thurston put up a well-placed bomb towards the left corner, where Gasnier caught it safely, only to be nailed into touch by Mogg near the corner post. From the ensuing scrum, a rehearsed move saw Flannery pick up the ball from lock and pass inside to Webb as the scrum broke up. Webb raced through to score behind the posts. Thurston added the extras and Queensland led 8–0.

The Maroons maintained their intensity, with Civoniceva producing a thundering shoulder-charge on O'Meley. Thaiday took his aggression too far, dropping his elbow into Gasnier as the ball-carrier lay on the ground. Thurston sliced a kick out on the full to give the Blues good field position. On the left, Anasta fired the ball to Tahu, only to see Hodges intercept and race 90 metres to score. Thurston landed his third goal for the night. Just before half-time, Tate crossed the tryline but was held up by Hodgson and King. The Maroons led 14–0 at

the break—a reversal from the corresponding stage of game one. Despite the Queensland forwards' better form, the score could have been much closer were it not for Hodges's intercept try.

O'Meley took another battering in a Thaiday tackle just after the break. When NSW won a scrum near halfway, Finch passed right to Anasta, whose pass bounced in front of Gasnier, who lost the ball as he was tackled by Bell. Thurston toed the ball ahead, beat King to it, scooped it up and shovelled a pass to Mogg, who touched down. The try was awarded on video evidence, and Thurston converted to increase the score to 20–0.

The Blues continued to lack cohesion in attack. Mason and Finch messed up a decoy play and surrendered possession; a two-man overlap beckoned in the 58th minute but Menzies held onto the ball then lost it as Lockyer tackled. Berrigan stripped the ball from Finch in a one-on-one tackle in the 62nd minute. A few tackles later, the ball went left through

↑ Teenager Karmichael Hunt shows his footwork. Newcomer Hunt was overlooked for game one despite making his test debut earlier in the year.

→ An unexpected selection for the Maroons, Adam Mogg touches down for the second of his two tries in a memorable Origin debut.

Players & Statistics

QLD Karmichael Hunt, Brent Tate, Justin Hodges, Steve Bell, Adam Mogg, Darren Lockyer (c), Johnathan Thurston, Dallas Johnson, Carl Webb, Nate Myles, Petero Civoniceva, Cameron Smith, Steve Price. **RESERVES** Shaun Berrigan, Chris Flannery, Sam Thaiday, Jacob Lillyman. **COACH** Mal Meninga

NSW Brett Hodgson, Matt King, Mark Gasnier, Timana Tahu, Eric Grothe, Braith Anasta, Brett Finch, Andrew Ryan, Nathan Hindmarsh, Steve Simpson, Brent Kite, Danny Buderus (c), Willie Mason. **RESERVES** Luke Bailey, Mark O'Meley, Steve Menzies, Craig Wing. **COACH** Graham Murray

Result Queensland 30 (Mogg 2, Webb, Hodges, Berrigan tries; Thurston 5 goals) beat NSW 6 (Tahu try; Hodgson goal)

Referee Steve Clark (NSW)

Crowd 52 468

Man of the Match Darren Lockyer (Queensland)

Tate, Lockyer and Thurston, who spread it to Smith. Drawing King, Smith passed to the unmarked Mogg, who dived over in the corner in Gasnier's tackle.

A few minutes later, Price sucked in the defence as Myles ran a decoy and Price linked up with Thurston. He drew two defenders and sent Lockyer striding through a gap. Nearing the 10-metre line, Lockyer drew Hodgson and sent Berrigan in to score under the posts. After a knock-on from Johnson, five Blues combined to set Tahu up for a late consolation try. Hodgson converted for a final score of 30–6.

The Verdict

The Maroon forwards, bagged mercilessly after game one, dominated their better credentialled opponents. Two of Queensland's first three tries came against the run of play. But once they were on a roll, the Maroons were hard to stop. The Blues lacked cohesion, made too many mistakes and were rarely in the game. In another good sign for the Maroons, Lockyer shone at five-eighth. Their only misfortune was that Bell was forced out of the decider, after suffering a fractured cheekbone in the 67th minute.

↑ Timana Tahu and Brent Tate contest a high kick. Tahu scored NSW's only try late in the game.

when Thurston floated a kick to the in-goal area on the left. Mogg caught the ball and grounded it as he fell backwards over the sideline in Grothe's tackle. The linesman raised his flag but referee Clark asked for replays—one showed Mogg touched down just before he landed out. The try was awarded and Schifcofske's goal-kick just missed.

A number of errors followed. Gower threw a forward pass to Gasnier; O'Donnell drove Thaiday backwards in a bone-jarring tackle but slowed the play-the-ball and was penalised, as was O'Meley for taking an intercept in an offside position. With the Maroons attacking, Thurston passed left, where Hannay and Mogg outnumbered Grothe. But Grothe intercepted the pass to save a try, then sprinted 95 metres to score at the other end. Hodgson's kick missed. NSW gained momentum in the last ten minutes of the half, but the score remained 4–4.

Three tackles after the break, Grothe fumbled in a tackle on his 30-metre line. He kicked the loose ball back before Carroll kicked it ahead and pounced behind the posts. Replays showed that Price touched the ball as it came loose but seemingly did not intend to strip it as he and Civoniceva tackled Grothe. But video referee Graeme West called it a strip and awarded NSW a penalty.

Several minutes later, NSW entered Queensland's quarter. Thurston rolled over a loose ball with his stomach but was incorrectly ruled to have knocked-on. The Maroons held out for four tackles before O'Donnell surged into the defence and passed back to Buderus, who found support on the right. Hodgson drew Thurston and fed Gasnier and King, who dived through to score. Hodgson converted and NSW fortuitously led 10–4.

At the end of the next set, Gower put up a bomb on the right. As the

The Teams

NSW dropped Anasta, Finch, Ryan, Kite and Wing and recalled Gower, O'Donnell, Cooper and Hornby. Paul Gallen was the only newcomer and some positional changes were made, most notably that of Gasnier to five-eighth.

Queensland lost Bell and Hunt to injury and Lillyman was omitted. Hannay, Schifcofske and Carroll were recalled. An injured Hodges was forced to withdraw after team selection, with Tate moving to centre and Wesser recalled as a winger.

The Game

Gallen copped Tate's elbow in a tackle to draw a penalty in just the second minute. A few minutes later, the Maroons were on the last tackle

↑ Having been promoted to the starting line-up in his Origin debut, Paul Gallen's progress is stopped by Darren Lockyer and Rhys Wesser.

→ In his recall to Origin football, Clinton Schifcofske made a decisive dart from dummy-half and kicked two crucial goals as the Maroons scraped home.

ball came down, Hodgson spilled it to his right. Menzies beat Mogg to the loose ball and fed Grothe, who beat Schifcofske to the line. Replays showed the ball touched Hodgson's chest, then projected forward off his right arm. Unbelievably, West awarded the try, a decision that television commentator Peter Sterling labelled disgraceful. NSW led 14–4 after a run of good fortune, and an historic fourth straight series win beckoned.

Queensland threw everything at NSW in the next 20 minutes and achieved nothing more than goal-line drop-outs. The Blues had another chance with 21 minutes left, but Cooper fumbled in-goal after he out-jumped Wesser as they contested another Gower bomb. This time West denied the try. King hammered Thurston with a brutal tackle in the 65th minute and King swung his arm around Thurston's neck but escaped penalty. The Maroons finally launched a promising raid in the 69th minute but Wesser threw a forward pass to Smith.

The game changed complexion two minutes later. Deep in Queensland's territory, Schifcofske veered right from acting-half, drew three defenders and fed Thurston, who threw a dummy, wrong-footed O'Donnell and scurried through. Thurston fired the ball to Tate, who flashed 60 metres down the right wing before running to score at the posts. Schifcofske's conversion bridged the margin to four points.

Five tackles after the restart, Grothe fielded Lockyer's clearing kick and was held on NSW's 20-metre line. Acting-half Hodgson's pass infield went astray, and Lockyer raced through, collected

↑ Brent Tate runs in for a try as the Maroons start to fight back in a seemingly lost cause.

the ball and broke out of Bailey's tackle to plunge over behind the posts. Schifcofske nailed the conversion and Queensland suddenly led by two points with five minutes left.

Two minutes later, Wesser fielded Gower's kick and was carried behind his tryline by defenders. However, referee Clark had called 'held' while Wesser was still in the field of play and a penalty was given to Queensland rather than a goal-line drop-out. Mogg almost scored again as he chased Smith's downfield kick, forcing a goal-line drop-out when Hodgson kicked the ball dead. King regained possession from a short drop-out but, very close to the sideline, his wayward pass inside was fumbled by Hornby. The Blues got the ball back with 20 seconds remaining and 90 metres to travel, but they could not get out of their half and Grothe's desperate kick went out on the full.

The Verdict

After an incredible 80 minutes, Queensland won 16–14 despite being on the wrong end of some puzzling decisions from match officials. The game demonstrated that, in spite of having all the latest technology available to eliminate mistakes, human error could not be totally removed from the field. Having overcome a poor first half in game one and adversity in game three, the Maroons were rightly rewarded with their first series win in five years.

Players & Statistics

QLD Clinton Schifcofske, Rhys Wesser, Brent Tate, Josh Hannay, Adam Mogg, Darren Lockyer (c), Johnathan Thurston, Dallas Johnson, Carl Webb, Nate Myles, Petero Civoniceva, Cameron Smith, Steve Price. **RESERVES** Shaun Berrigan, Chris Flannery, Sam Thaiday, Tonie Carroll. **COACH** Mal Meninga

NSW Brett Hodgson, Timana Tahu, Matt King, Matt Cooper, Eric Grothe, Mark Gasnier, Craig Gower, Luke O'Donnell, Nathan Hindmarsh, Paul Gallen, Willie Mason, Danny Buderus (c), Luke Bailey. **RESERVES** Steve Simpson, Mark O'Meley, Steve Menzies, Ben Hornby. **COACH** Graham Murray

Result Queensland 16 (Mogg, Tate, Lockyer tries; Schifcofske 2 goals) beat NSW 14 (Grothe 2, King tries; Hodgson goal)

Referee Steve Clark (NSW)

Crowd 54 833

Man of the Match Brent Tate (Queensland)

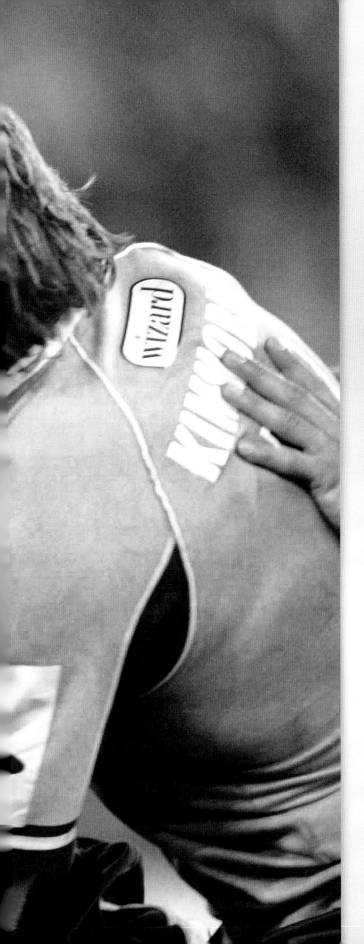

2007

Maroons Break Homebush Hoodoo

Queensland set about its State of Origin defence by maintaining its structures from the previous series. Mal Meninga stayed on as coach and again called on a number of former Origin players to join the Queensland squad during its pre-series build-up. Neil Henry remained as assistant coach, with Bob Lindner as media manager and Steve Walters the team manager. NSW retained Graham Murray as coach.

The Maroons could not call on Mogg (who was playing in France) or Schifcofske (moved to rugby union) and Thaiday was injured. NSW had Gasnier and O'Donnell on the injured list.

← Dallas Johnson feels the force of the NSW defence. Johnson was one of the key players for the Maroons, and made an Origin record 62 tackles in game two.

The Teams

Queensland's selectors remained loyal to players from the 2006 series. Reserve forward Neville Costigan was the only debutant, before Antonio Kaufusi became another newcomer after Webb pulled out on match eve with injury.

NSW recalled Minichiello, Lyon, Anasta, Ryan and Kite. Debutants were Jarryd Hayne, Jarrod Mullen, Brett White, Anthony Tupou and Kurt Gidley (the brother of Matt Gidley).

The Game

Johnson and Carroll welcomed White to Origin football with a pummelling tackle in the first minute. Hunt copped a heavy tackle from Ryan before Mason was penalised for a high shot on Price. Five tackles later, Thurston floated a kick to the left and,

as Bell ran a decoy to draw King, Inglis jumped for the ball uncontested and scored. Thurston's conversion curled from right to left between the posts. Thurston threw a bad pass to Inglis a few minutes later, and then NSW forced a goal-line drop-out before Myles was penalised for a lifting tackle on White. Two tackles later, Mullen spun the ball left to Anasta, who stepped through and, while held by Lockyer, threw a forward pass to Hindmarsh. He crashed over the line in tackles from Hodges and Hunt. The Queenslanders claimed Hindmarsh was held up but referee Simpkins awarded the try. Replays suggested Hindmarsh did not ground the ball, and the forward pass was overlooked. Lyon added the extras, levelling the scores.

White continued to be targeted by Queensland forwards and King was on the receiving end of a heavy tackle by Carroll. In defence, King again moved in too far and Bell juggled the ball, then fumbled as he headed for the corner unopposed. A try went begging. Then Carroll was penalised for a high tackle on Cooper. The Blues ventured into Queensland's 10-metre zone and spread the ball left through Buderus, Mullen and Ryan, who drew Hodges and Tate and sent an unmarked Cooper across. Lyon converted from wide out and NSW led 12–6.

The Maroons appeared to tire in attack they returned to the danger zone after successive mistakes by their opponents. Buderus's kick flew out on the full, then NSW was caught off-side. Inside NSW's 10-metre zone, Smith's well-timed pass sent Price through to score but the pass was ruled forward. The Maroons appeared unlucky as the replays showed that Smith's pass was flatter than Anasta's pass in the lead-up to Hindmarsh's try. Queensland received another penalty and forced a repeat set before Smith was held up over the line on the last tackle. Mason left the field injured in the 33rd minute. Lyon extended NSW's

Brett White copped a hammering from the Maroons several times in his Origin debut.

Players & Statistics

QLD Karmichael Hunt, Brent Tate, Steve Bell, Justin Hodges, Greg Inglis, Darren Lockyer (c), Johnathan Thurston, Dallas Johnson, Nate Myles, Tonie Carroll, Petero Civoniceva, Cameron Smith, Steve Price. **RESERVES** Shaun Berrigan, Jacob Lillyman, Antonio Kaufusi, Neville Costigan. **COACH** Mal Meninga

NSW Anthony Minichiello, Matt King, Jamie Lyon, Matt Cooper, Jarryd Hayne, Braith Anasta, Jarrod Mullen, Andrew Ryan, Nathan Hindmarsh, Willie Mason, Brent Kite, Danny Buderus (c), Brett White. **RESERVES** Luke Bailey, Steve Simpson, Anthony Tupou, Kurt Gidley. **COACH** Graham Murray

Result Queensland 25 (Inglis 2, Price, Lockyer tries; Thurston 4 goals; Thurston field goal) beat NSW 18 (Hindmarsh, Cooper, Hayne tries; Lyon 3 goals)

Referee Paul Simpkins (NSW)

Crowd 52 498

Man of the Match Johnathan Thurston (Queensland)

↑ Queensland's two try hero Greg Inglis attempts to break out of a tackle.

lead to eight points with a penalty goal after Thurston ran a shepherd behind Costigan.

As the siren sounded, Queensland spread the ball right through Smith, Thurston, Lockyer and Tate, whose kick went straight into Hayne's shins. Hayne picked up the ball, fended off Hodges and scurried down the touchline. He kicked ahead as Lillyman approached, before beating Hodges to the ball for a try out wide. It was a vital blow after the siren sounded. Lyon's wide-angled kick missed, but NSW held a handy and somewhat fortuitous 18–6 lead at half-time.

Eight minutes after the break, Kaufusi was injured after falling awkwardly in a tackle. Soon after, Ryan conceded a penalty in possession for impeding Lockyer as Buderus darted from dummy-half. The Maroons soon moved the ball left, with Smith and Price handling before Lockyer drew Mullen and speared a pass to Hunt. Drawing King as Bell ran a decoy, Hunt sent an unmarked Inglis in for his second try. Thurston landed another sideline conversion and the margin was just one converted try.

The Maroons attacked after another NSW handling error. Quick hands saw Tate cross in the right corner but Hodges's pass to Tate was well forward. White was penalised for holding Inglis down and, when NSW touched the ball, they had to defend for another set of tackles. A metre from the tryline, Berrigan fired a well-timed pass right to Price, who dived between two defenders for a legitimate try near the posts this time. The scores

were locked up at 18-all after Thurston added the extras.

As Smith's downfield kick rolled towards NSW's 10-metre line in the ensuing tackle count, Hayne dived to retrieve it near the sideline, thinking it was a 40-20 kick. He scooped a wayward pass to Minichiello, only for Lockyer to gather the ball after one bounce and run in to score behind the posts. Thurston made it four from four and Queensland suddenly led 24–18.

NSW received a penalty after Hayne was hit across the jaw by a wrong-footed Lillyman. The Blues tried to break through but were foiled when Mason was penalised for passing off the ground in a tackle. It was a dubious call but it allowed Queensland to work its way downfield, where Thurston kicked a field goal to give Queensland breathing space. NSW threw everything at the Maroons in the final stages but the home side remained composed to win 25–18.

The Verdict

For the second successive game, the Maroons overcame some tough luck and a double-digit deficit to win. Their strong defence, second-half control, increasing errors by NSW and Thurston's goal-kicking were all factors that turned the game Queensland's way.

Thurston was named the man of the match.

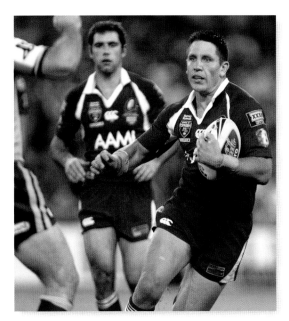

← Thirty-three-year-old Steve Price was a tower of strength for the Maroons, and was unlucky not to be named man of the match.

front-on tackle, Simpson raced onto a reverse pass from Anasta a few tackles later and was stopped just 2 metres short. From dummy-half, Stewart looked left but stepped right to dive over the line. The Blues led 6–0 after Lyon converted.

Stewart saved NSW in the 19th minute when he beat Tate to a Hodges kick into NSW's in-goal area. NSW defended well until the fifth tackle when Smith stepped to the blindside and drew three defenders. Smith looked to have erred as it was the last tackle, but he flicked a left-handed pass that hit the ground before an unmarked Inglis fielded it and ran in to score. Thurston's conversion levelled the scores.

In the 25th minute, Lyon threw a bad pass to Cooper, who dropped it in Tate's tackle. The Blues endured some anxious moments but survived a sequence of attacks on their line. Queensland forced a goal-line drop-out before Carroll was held up over the line. Possession finally changed when a Thurston chip-kick rolled dead, and the scores remained level at the break. Incredibly, no penalties were awarded in the first half. Shayne Hayne appeared lenient with the size of his 10 metres and the time he allowed defenders to get off their opponents. Thus, defenders from both sides took advantage to smother their opponents as the game turned into a slugfest.

Inglis just failed to score in the 48th minute when Thurston's grubber-kick rolled into touch in-goal. The first penalty of the match came a couple of minutes later when Civoniceva was caught for slowing a play-the-ball. With NSW on the attack, Kimmorley chip-kicked to the left but Tate leapt

↑ Brett Stewart was safe at the back for NSW in his Origin debut. He scored the first try of the game.

The Teams

Queensland made just one change to its squad, with Webb returning to replace the injured Kaufusi. NSW omitted Tupou and the injured duo Mullen and Gidley. Kimmorley was recalled and first caps given to reserves Greg Bird and Ryan Hoffman. NSW's hopes were dealt a blow when Minichiello was ruled out with injury. Brett Stewart was the new fullback. Shayne Hayne was appointed to officiate.

The Game

Lockyer and Kimmorley peppered their opposing backlines with bombs early on but they were safely defused. Stewart showed particularly good composure. Hindmarsh hit Lockyer around the chin but escaped punishment. After NSW forced a handling error, the Blues threatened but King was barrelled into touch. After Price fumbled in Buderus's solid

Players & Statistics

QLD Karmichael Hunt, Brent Tate, Steve Bell, Justin Hodges, Greg Inglis, Darren Lockyer (c), Johnathan Thurston, Dallas Johnson, Carl Webb, Tonie Carroll, Petero Civoniceva, Cameron Smith, Steve Price. **RESERVES** Shaun Berrigan, Jacob Lillyman, Nate Myles, Neville Costigan. **COACH** Mal Meninga

NSW Brett Stewart, Matt King, Jamie Lyon, Matt Cooper, Jarryd Hayne, Braith Anasta, Brett Kimmorley, Andrew Ryan, Nathan Hindmarsh, Willie Mason, Brett White, Danny Buderus (c), Brent Kite. **RESERVES** Luke Bailey, Steve Simpson, Ryan Hoffman, Greg Bird. **COACH** Graham Murray

Result Queensland 10 (Inglis, Bell tries; Thurston goal) beat NSW 6 (Stewart try; Lyon goal)

Referee Shayne Hayne (NSW)

Crowd 76 924

Man of the Match Cameron Smith (Queensland)

high and saved Queensland with an acrobatic overhead catch. After a grubber by Kimmorley forced a goal-line drop-out, NSW failed to strike after Lockyer's subsequent drop-kick went 70 metres. Buderus escaped punishment for a blatant offside infringement before NSW received another penalty for a play-the-ball indiscretion. The Blues earned a repeat set after Tate slapped Kimmorley's bomb dead. Tate exited the game a few minutes later with suspected medial ligament damage. Neither team looked like producing a game-breaking play in the defence-dominated contest.

In the 62nd minute, Bailey prepared to play the ball in the Maroons' half when he grabbed marker Price's leg, causing the Queenslander to fall backwards. Referee Hayne penalised Bailey, and the Maroons turned defence into attack. In the following set, Webb took the ball up and passed right to Price, who unloaded to Thurston in a tackle. Thurston drifted right and kicked through, where Bell scooped up the ball low down and dived over in the corner. The Maroons were lucky to be awarded the try because replays showed that Webb's pass was forward. Thurston's goal-kick sailed to the left, and Queensland led 10–6.

Price was penalised when he stripped the ball in a two-man tackle. The Blues went on the attack and Price was punished again for lingering in the ruck. NSW tried to break through but Queensland's defence held before Mason's pass found Hodges. With three minutes remaining, Kite lost the ball backwards in a driving tackle. Berrigan knocked on attempting an intercept before scurrying away to score under the posts. Video referee Bill Harrigan rightly awarded a scrum to NSW near the halfway line.

The Blues failed to pierce Queensland's defence, but NSW retained possession after Hayne's chip-kick for the left corner forced Hodges to take the ball dead. NSW had a scrum feed 10 metres out with one minute left. The Maroons held on as NSW threw the ball around in an effort to keep the series alive, but Lyon dropped it with 30 seconds left.

← Brent Tate takes an impressive catch to defuse a cross-field kick under pressure in the second half.

Queensland looked home and hosed, but Myles fumbled in a gang-tackle to present the Blues with one final chance. NSW again threw the ball around desperately and, as the siren sounded, Cooper kicked over the top where Inglis caught the ball unopposed behind the tryline. The Maroons had clinched the series. Queensland had posted back-to-back series wins for the first time since 1989.

The Verdict
Queensland had finally won at Telstra Stadium. Both sides criticised referee Hayne and pointed to several decisions unfavourable to them. The penalty count was 4–1 to NSW, although the Maroons' only penalty—an unusual one which displeased the Blues—proved game-breaking.

It was telling that a decisive try to Queensland in each of the two games had resulted from the Blues being penalised in possession—always a deadly sin in rugby league.

↓ Steve Bell scored the winning try for the Maroons as they finally broke their drought at the Homebush-based stadium.

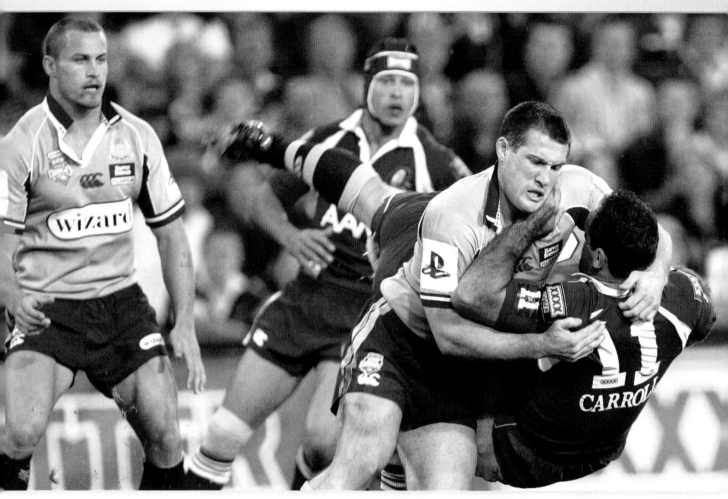

↑ Paul Gallen sends Tonie Carroll crashing to earth with a fierce tackle.

→ Hazem El Masri scored a try and kicked three goals in his only Origin appearance.

The Teams

The NSW selectors dropped White and were unable to consider Anasta because of injury. Gallen and Kurt Gidley were recalled. Lyon pulled out later and debutant Hazem El Masri was named on the wing as King moved to centre. NSW made some positional changes, including that of Bird at five-eighth.

For the first time in Origin history, the Maroons named an unchanged side for all three games in one series. But they were forced into later changes when Lillyman and Costigan were injured and replaced by Bowen and Carlaw.

The Game

Queensland suffered an immediate setback when Johnson was concussed in the first tackle. Then two minutes later Kimmorley suffered a leg injury but was able to continue. Referee Simpkins blew three penalties each way by the 14th minute as infringements were regular. Handling errors were frequent too as players struggled to reach any great heights.

After 21 minutes, King ran the ball back from a kick and took advantage of slow Queensland chasers. Nearing the Maroons' 30-metre line, Kimmorley spun a cut-out pass left to Cooper and Hayne, who stepped infield before fending off Hunt to score in the left corner. El Masri landed a brilliant conversion. The Maroons were further set back when they lost Inglis for the rest of the match with a knee injury.

Queensland had the chance to strike back when Gallen unloaded a forward pass to Hindmarsh shortly after the restart. Four tackles later on the 10-metre line, Smith passed right to Thurston, who spun the ball to Hunt. As the defence bunched to cover the

Players & Statistics

NSW Brett Stewart, Hazem El Masri, Matt King, Matt Cooper, Jarryd Hayne, Greg Bird, Brett Kimmorley, Paul Gallen, Andrew Ryan, Nathan Hindmarsh, Willie Mason, Danny Buderus (c), Brent Kite. **RESERVES** Luke Bailey, Steve Simpson, Ryan Hoffman, Kurt Gidley. **COACH** Graham Murray

QLD Karmichael Hunt, Brent Tate, Steve Bell, Justin Hodges, Greg Inglis, Darren Lockyer (c), Johnathan Thurston, Dallas Johnson, Carl Webb, Tonie Carroll, Petero Civoniceva, Cameron Smith, Steve Price. **RESERVES** Shaun Berrigan, Nate Myles, Matt Bowen, Dane Carlaw. **COACH** Mal Meninga

Result NSW 18 (Hayne, King, El Masri tries; El Masri 3 goals) beat Queensland 4 (Hodges try)

Referee Paul Simpkins (NSW)

Crowd 52 469

Man of the Match Greg Bird (NSW)

decoy runners, a tackled Hunt sent the ball to an unmarked Hodges who touched down. Ten metres in from the right wing, Thurston hooked the goal-kick. Tate sustained a match- and season-ending knee injury when he fell awkwardly after he kicked ahead and was tackled by Hayne and Cooper. NSW led 6–4 after a substandard 40 minutes of football.

The Queensland dressing room looked like a casualty ward whereas the Blues returned with vigour soon after the break. From inside NSW's quarter, Hoffman ran onto a well-timed pass from Mason and showed impressive speed as he accelerated ahead. Hoffman drew Hunt inside Queensland's 30-metre zone and passed to Stewart, who linked up with Cooper. However, he was tackled just short of the tryline by Thurston and Hunt. In the 50th minute, Stewart off-loaded to Cooper in a tackle inside Queensland's territory. Cooper scampered away, but Bell produced a sensational try-saving tackle with Cooper just a breath away from scoring.

In spite of Cooper's two near-misses, the standard of football remained lacklustre. Johnson courageously returned in the 45th minute and put in a typical effort. Myles suffered a shoulder injury in the 47th minute but carried on until the 69th minute because of the limited replacements available. The mediocre standard of the game persisted as both sides failed to capitalise on their opponents' errors. NSW enjoyed better field position while the injury-ridden Maroons defended admirably but did not look penetrating in attack.

Hunt and Hodges suffered ankle injuries but a depleted bench forced them to continue playing.

Eight minutes from full-time, Lockyer ran the ball on the last tackle from inside his half but threw a poor pass, which Carroll fumbled. A few tackles later, Stewart passed right to Bird who cleverly delayed his pass to King, who crashed through tackles from Bowen and Smith to score. NSW had a handy eight-point lead when El Masri kicked the conversion superbly from wide out.

Three minutes from the end, Hayne fielded a kick and made a long break through tired defence to put NSW in good field position. At the end of that set, a metre from the tryline, Gallen surged into Bowen and Thurston. As Gallen fell in the tackle, he threw a miraculous pass right to El Masri, who banged the ball down. El Masri again converted from near the right sideline. The series-losing Blues had salvaged a face-saving 18–4 win and had scored more points in the three games than the series winners.

The Verdict

Queensland's injury-ridden team did well to contain the Blues to just one try in the first 72 minutes. However, the numbers were always going to take their toll. In a match of surprisingly poor quality, NSW did enough to grind out a morale-boosting victory. The selection of Bird at five-eighth was rewarded as he was named man of the match.

← Despite being a forward in club football, Greg Bird was promoted to five-eighth for NSW, and was named best player on the ground.

2008

Maroon Melburnians Reap Rewards

Although State of Origin has always been a contest between NSW and Queensland, there was little doubt Melbourne was the most influential club leading into the 2008 series. The Storm had convincingly beaten every team on their way to the 2007 premiership and all its Australian-born players were from NSW or Queensland.

Melbourne coach Craig Bellamy was appointed to guide the Blues. Bellamy had been Wayne Bennett's assistant at the Broncos for several years before becoming Melbourne's head coach. Bellamy's team lost to the Bennett-coached Broncos in the 2006 grand final but came back stronger, trouncing Manly in the 2007 decider. Bellamy had assumed the mantle of rugby league's best coach, an honour that had been bestowed on Bennett.

Bellamy had formerly played for Canberra, where one of his teammates was Mal Meninga, who remained Queensland's coach. This created a scenario somewhat similar to 1989, when Jack Gibson opposed Arthur Beetson. On both occasions, the incoming NSW coach was widely regarded as the best in rugby league and came up against a successful Origin coach who used to be a club colleague. Also, Queensland was again shooting for its third successive series win.

A number of players from recent series were no longer in the picture. The Maroons lost Carroll to retirement and Berrigan and Carlaw to England. Costigan, Lockyer and Price were injured, but Lockyer and Price had the chance of returning. For NSW, King had moved to England, and Kurt Gidley was absent for at least game one of the series.

Telstra Stadium had had its name changed to ANZ Stadium—not to be confused with the Queensland venue that hosted an Origin match in 2001 and 2002.

← Greg Inglis proved hard to tackle when he found open space. He was one of several Melbourne players to play a major role for the Maroons.

The Teams

Slater, Thaiday, Crocker, Webb, Marsh, and Lillyman were recalled for Queensland. Teenager Israel Folau and reserve forward Ben Hannant were newcomers. The in-form Prince was the most glaring omission and surprisingly Hunt was picked at five-eighth. Smith, one of six Melbourne players in the team, was named captain after leading his club and country.

NSW's selectors picked four debutants: Anthony Quinn, Peter Wallace, Anthony Laffranchi and Ben Cross. Gasnier, Fitzgibbon, Tupou and White were recalled. Buderus retained the captaincy.

Tony Archer was appointed to control his first Origin match.

The Game

NSW's defence dominated to keep Queensland back-pedalling in the opening stages. The Maroons were pinned in their quarter as a succession of them ineffectively ran from dummy-half. In an early raid, Buderus spun the ball left to Wallace and Bird, who threw a cut-out pass to Hoffman. Surging into a tackle, Hoffman

↑ NSW half Peter Wallace, like Greg Bird (see below), was too good for his Maroons counterpart.

→ Greg Bird again did well in his unusual position of five-eighth, but the Maroons move to play Karmichael Hunt at five-eighth did not pay off.

released a one-handed around-the-corner pass, which Stewart caught with an outstretched right hand before drawing Slater to provide Quinn with a clear path to the corner. Fitzgibbon converted for a 6–0 lead.

Queensland briefly looked dangerous in attack but the Blues made much greater impact in defence. The Maroons failed to capitalise on a penalty against Mason and a knock-on by Cooper. After a stray pass from Slater, NSW returned to the attack. Folau defused a Wallace bomb but was driven in-goal. Five tackles later, Wallace kicked to the left. With Tate caught off guard, Quinn leapt for the ball and scored to continue a dream start to Origin football. Fitzgibbon hooked his kick and the lead was 10–0.

Hunt pummelled Hoffman with a couple of heavy hits, one of which left Hoffman with a bleeding nose. After the Maroons threatened briefly, a succession of errors left them defending grimly again. Thirty metres from the tryline, Stewart turned the ball left to Laffranchi, who stood in a tackle and passed to Stewart on the blindside. Stewart fed Gasnier, who threw a dummy and darted through before drawing several defenders and sending a one-handed pass inside to Stewart. He ran in to score before stand-in kicker Wallace missed the conversion.

The Blues were keen to keep their 14–0 lead until half-time, but Wallace hooked a kick out on the full to improve Queensland's field position. The Maroons subsequently forced a goal-line drop-out with one minute left on the clock. On the last tackle, Johnson passed right to Thurston, who grubbered towards the right corner where Tate ran outside Quinn and beat him in the dive for the ball. The grounding looked questionable but replays showed Tate had forced the ball down with one or two fingers. Video referee Bill Harrigan awarded the try and NSW's lead was ten points after Thurston's conversion attempt curved too far across.

Both teams made handling errors but also created scoring opportunities early in the second half. Inglis and Stewart defused attacks at their respective ends. After making some earlier mistakes, Slater initiated a spectacular raid after keeping Wallace's kick in close to the sideline. Breaking away from NSW, he fed Inglis, who continued the thrust. A speculative pass inside was touched by a defender and an overlap developed on the right before Hodges was tackled just short of the try-line. The good work came undone two tackles later when Myles threw a terrible pass. Ill-discipline by the Maroons (backchatting) and Gallen (obstructing Hunt without the ball) plagued both sides. The latter gave Queensland possession in NSW's quarter, but a fumble botched the scoring chance.

Fumbles by Lillyman and Thurston proved decisive when play returned to the Maroons' half. After the latter, Hornby spread the ball right to Fitzgibbon, Wallace and Bird, who sent a cut-out pass to Gasnier. With Inglis moving up too soon, Gasnier stepped ahead and threw a familiar one-handed pass inside, this time to Laffranchi to score. NSW held a 14-point lead with 11 minutes left in spite of Fitzgibbon missing the conversion.

Folau caught the ball from a short kick-off and linked with Inglis, who was thwarted frustratingly short of the tryline. The Maroons enjoyed an extended run of possession via restarted tackle counts and a penalty against Mason. From the tap, Queensland made use of an overlap on the right, where Tate dived over in the corner. But the try was disallowed when replays showed Tate's leg touched the sideline before he grounded the ball. In the last two minutes, Smith moved the ball left to Thurston and Hodges. Hunt fielded Hodges's wayward pass and sent a cut-out ball to Folau, who squeezed over in the corner. Thurston converted for a NSW 18–10 win.

The Verdict

The final scoreline suggested that the match was relatively close but in fact Queensland struggled to stay within striking distance. The Blues' vastly superior defence ensured that they controlled the flow of the game. Three of their four tries followed mistakes by the Maroons, who regularly displayed poor coordination when they could have threatened NSW's tryline.

Bird was named man of the match, his second successive award in only his third State of Origin game. Although he played as a forward in club football, he was shining at five-eighth for his state and for his country.

↑ Ben Hannant came off the bench for the Maroons in all three games in his first Origin series.

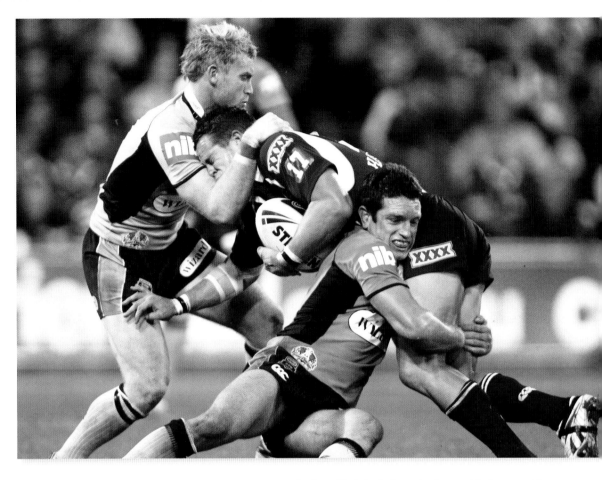

→ In his recall to Origin, Ashley Harrison is brought down by Peter Wallace and Danny Buderus.

The Teams

Queensland's prospects were boosted when Lockyer and Price returned from injury, but Hodges was suspended and ruled out of games two and three. Webb, Marsh and Lillyman were dumped and Hunt relegated to the bench. Winger Darius Boyd was the only debutant. Tate moved to centre, Harrison was recalled and Prince left out again. But when an injured Lockyer withdrew, Prince was named at halfback and Thurston moved to five-eighth. The line-up changed further, with Hunt and Harrison starting instead of Slater and Thaiday.

Cross was injured and unavailable for NSW and Hornby was omitted. Simpson and Gidley were recalled. In a late change, the suspended Jarryd Hayne was replaced by debutant Steve Turner.

↓ After initially being controversially left out of the Queensland side, Scott Prince fitted in well.

The Game

Both teams began inauspiciously, as NSW was penalised after just 32 seconds before Inglis spilled the ball on the first tackle. Just outside Queensland's quarter-line in the seventh minute, Smith began a passing movement to the left involving Thurston, Prince and Inglis. Fending off Gasnier, Inglis pushed Turner away and raced ahead, drawing Stewart and sending Boyd towards the posts to score.

Ten minutes later, the Blues forced a repeat set but Gallen subsequently fumbled in a tackle. Almost straight away, the Maroons produced another sweeping ball movement to the left from inside their half. Two second-man plays confused the defence and created room for Inglis, who again broke through and drew the NSW fullback to send Boyd in to score near the posts. Inglis's pass was clearly forward but referee Archer let it go. Thurston converted for the second time to set up a lucky 12–0 lead for Queensland. By scoring the game's first two tries in his Origin debut, Boyd replicated Quinn's achievement in the previous game, a feat previously achieved by Ziggy Niszczot and Michael O'Connor.

A scrappy period of play followed, with both sides guilty of errors. After a penalty against Quinn, the

Players & Statistics

QLD Karmichael Hunt, Darius Boyd, Greg Inglis, Brent Tate, Israel Folau, Johnathan Thurston, Scott Prince, Dallas Johnson, Ashley Harrison, Michael Crocker, Petero Civoniceva, Cameron Smith (c), Steve Price. **RESERVES** Billy Slater, Ben Hannant, Sam Thaiday, Nate Myles. **COACH** Mal Meninga

NSW Brett Stewart, Steve Turner, Mark Gasnier, Matt Cooper, Anthony Quinn, Greg Bird, Peter Wallace, Paul Gallen, Ryan Hoffman, Willie Mason, Brett White, Danny Buderus (c), Craig Fitzgibbon. **RESERVES** Kurt Gidley, Anthony Tupou, Steve Simpson, Anthony Laffranchi. **COACH** Craig Bellamy

Result Queensland 30 (Boyd 2, Hannant, Folau tries; Thurston 7 goals) beat NSW 0

Referee Tony Archer (NSW)

Crowd 52 416

Man of the Match Greg Inglis (Queensland)

Maroons attacked and then received a penalty closer to the posts when Gallen performed a high tackle on Thaiday. Thurston landed the two points on offer. After NSW failed to capitalise on a penalty, Thurston set up another electrifying break by Inglis, but this time he had no support and was brought down by Stewart. Hoffman was penalised for holding Smith down in a tackle, and Thurston's fourth goal brought up the half-time score of 16–0. The Blues looked out of form, particularly in attack, although Queensland was lucky to be awarded its second try.

Both teams were unable to capitalise on a penalty soon after play resumed, before a penalty against Cooper was followed by a penalty against Mason for ball stripping in a two-man tackle. Thurston then landed another goal to extend Queensland's lead to three converted tries. After another error from Mason, Queensland attacked the blindside, where Smith, Thurston and Slater linked to send Boyd over in the left corner. Having awarded Boyd an earlier try from an obviously forward pass, Archer ruled Slater's pass forward, although replays suggested it was fair. Thanks to a break by Folau, it wasn't long before the Maroons were on the attack again. Five metres out, Smith passed left to Hannant, who surged over the tryline in Gasnier's tackle. Archer called for the video referee but replays were unable to determine the verdict. On 'ref's call', Archer ruled in Queensland's favour and Thurston's sixth goal took the home team to a 24–0 lead.

The Blues turned over possession in their next set and Queensland was soon camped on NSW's

10-metre line. Smith spun the ball right to Thurston and Prince, who saw the Blues were short in defence on the right. Prince chip-kicked that way where Folau pounced for a try after the ball bounced away from Quinn. Thurston landed a great goal from wide out to take the score to 30–0. The Maroons had also levelled the state's record-winning margin in Origin football. Hunt hooked a field-goal attempt in the 76th minute, and Crocker knocked on with a try beckoning as Queensland's record-winning margin remained the same. NSW was scoreless for just the second time in Origin football.

The Verdict

The Blues were uncoordinated and paid for their errors. According to Meninga, the Maroons had responded really well to the criticism they copped after game one, but the 30–0 score was something he had not anticipated. Bellamy described his players as going into panic mode, although he was perplexed by referee Archer, who awarded 16 penalties compared with only six in game one.

Nine minutes before Origin II finished, the Channel Nine commentators were already talking about possible changes to the NSW team for game three. Ironically, Phil Gould targeted Greg Bird, the man of the match in the two previous games, who finally had a below-par game at five-eighth in representative football. Gould emphasised that Bird was a forward and that what NSW needed was a specialist five-eighth.

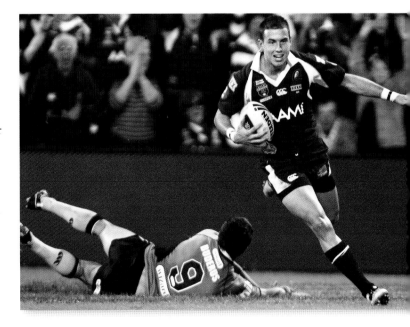

↓ Darius Boyd runs in for one of his two tries, which made him part of a select group of players to score two tries on debut.

↑ Nate Myles, Steve Price and Petero Civoniceva are all smiles after Queensland secured its third straight series win.

The Teams

Queensland named an unchanged team. For NSW, Gasnier, Bird and Wallace were unavailable through injury. Turner and Simpson were dropped; Cross, Hayne and Anasta were recalled, and Joel Monaghan and Mitchell Pearce were debutants. The Blues were keen to send Buderus out a winner in his Origin farewell. Both teams made some positional changes.

Archer retained the whistle, becoming the third referee to control an entire Origin series.

The Game

A knock-on by Hunt enabled the Blues to attack soon after kicking off. White dropped the ball after he copped a high shot from Civoniceva and a brawl broke out. Civoniceva was penalised and Fitzgibbon kicked NSW to a 2–0 lead. In the fifth minute, Prince's last tackle bomb towards the right corner struck Quinn's shoulder and was caught by Folau, who scored. Queensland led 4–2.

Boyd defused an Anasta bomb before a handling mistake by Myles put NSW in an attacking position. Prince was hurt in the ensuing set, and then Buderus passed left to Gidley, who opted to run the ball on the last tackle. Receiving a superbly timed pass, Cooper stepped between Tate and Folau to reach out and score near the left corner. Fitzgibbon's

→ Michael Crocker needs assistance after a clearing kick struck him in the head during a tense second half.

wide-angled conversion gave NSW an 8–4 lead. Prince exited with a broken forearm, and Hunt returned to five-eighth.

Inglis made a break soon after but he looked outside for support when Boyd was unmarked on the inside with the tryline only 20 metres away. Hoffman was penalised moments later for striking Smith after he kicked, and the Maroons soon forced a goal-line drop-out. When Thurston sent a crossfield bomb to the right, Folau and Quinn contested it in the in-goal area. Folau soared over Quinn, AFL-style, and grounded the ball spectacularly over his head as he fell to the ground. The scores remained level after Thurston pushed the goal-kick to the right. After an offside infringement by Crocker in NSW's next set, Fitzgibbon kicked a goal to put NSW in front 10–8.

Hayne suffered a head knock while attempting to tackle Slater. The Maroons struggled in attack and the Blues made some errors. Queensland missed a chance just before the break after Boyd put in a kick. Hunt knocked on with the tryline beckoning. NSW led 10–8 at half-time.

After Inglis was penalised soon after half-time, the Blues went on the attack. Pearce's chip-kick landed near the posts, where Johnson missed the ball as Gidley tackled him. The bouncing ball was knocked down by Buderus before Anasta grounded it. Replays showed that Gidley tackled Johnson without the ball and that Anasta was several metres in front of the kicker. NSW was penalised for Gidley's infringement rather than Anasta's. Five tackles later, Gallen coat-hangered Thurston as he chased his own grubber-kick. It provided a gift penalty goal for Thurston to level the scores at 10–all.

The game erupted in NSW's next set of six after Cross ran onto a forward pass and was upended in Myles's tackle. Cross landed on his head and, after restoring order, referee Archer penalised Myles and placed him on report. Within five minutes, Crocker became a casualty, after Pearce's clearing kick cannoned into the back of his head.

In a very even battle, the Maroons consistently struggled for rhythm in attack. In the 67th minute, commentators began talking about the prospects of a field goal to resolve the game, a discussion that ceased when Smith fed Thurston. He threw a dummy, darted between White and Pearce, drew Stewart and sent Slater away to score at the posts. Thurston's conversion gave the Maroons a 16–10 lead.

The Blues dominated field position in the ensuing minutes but Queensland defended well. Inglis defused an Anasta bomb, Gallen and Hunt made successive knock-ons and Pearce put in a couple of ineffective kicks, the latter charged down and regained by Price. Gallen's horrors continued when he gave Queensland a relieving penalty for a high tackle on Crocker. The Maroons entered field-goal territory, but Smith grubbered on the last tackle, only to see Slater just fail to get to the ball before it rolled dead in-goal.

The Blues thus remained alive, and they gained a vital repeat set in Queensland's quarter with two minutes remaining when Anasta's bomb touched a Maroon. On tackle three, Archer pulled up a marginally forward pass from Anasta, who then stole the ball from Smith with 13 seconds left. However, NSW was unable to break through and Pearce's last-ditch kick was run dead by Slater. Even with Lockyer sidelined, Queensland had won three consecutive series.

↑ Israel Folau leaps above his Melbourne team-mate Anthony Quinn on his way to score his second try of the game. 'Flying through the air like Superman' was commentator Ray Warren's description.

The Verdict

The decider could have gone either way as it went down to the wire. But the bigger picture showed that the Maroons were worthy series winners, having scored nine tries to five in the series. To put it in perspective, three of NSW's tries came before half-time in game one and only one in the final 170 minutes. The series was memorable for the Melbourne-based Queenslanders, but unsuccessful for their club coach and for Buderus.

2009

Mal's Awesome Foursome

Queensland sacrificed a home game for the 2009 series as part of the deal involving funding for the Melbourne Storm. Consequently, the first game was played at Etihad Stadium—formerly the Telstra Dome—in Melbourne under a closed roof. A significant focus of the series was the possibility of Queensland becoming the first state to win four consecutive Origin series.

Queensland had virtually the same playing stocks as in 2008, apart from the injured Tate. Crocker was still in the NRL after initially planning to play in England. In addition to Buderus, NSW lost Bird and Gasnier to overseas football, although Barrett was back in the NRL and eligible for State of Origin. An injured Brett Stewart was also unavailable.

Craig Bellamy and Mal Meninga continued their coaching roles.

← Johnathan Thurston was one of Queensland's best as the Maroons secured an historic fourth straight series win. He was man of the match in game one.

↑ Jarryd Hayne was always a danger when he had the ball. He came achingly close to scoring the first try of the series, with his foot just touching the edge of the sideline on his way to the tryline.

↓ Billy Slater touches down just inside the dead-ball line for the first try.

The Teams

Queensland's selectors stayed loyal to their success-ful squad. But there was no room for Prince, and Hodges and Lockyer returned.

NSW's selectors chose eight debutants: Michael Jennings, James McManus, Terry Campese, Ben Creagh, Robbie Farah, Justin Poore, Glenn Stewart and Michael Weyman. Recalled were Wallace, Luke Bailey, Kite, O'Donnell and Wing. Fullback Kurt Gidley was named captain. NSW recalled Luke Lewis and Laffranchi when Stewart (suspended) and Gallen (injured) were forced out.

In line with the recently introduced club foot-ball practice, two on-field referees were appointed: Tony Archer and Shayne Hayne.

The Game

Price knocked-on in Queensland's first set of tackles, before a penalty against Smith for ball-stripping enabled Gidley to kick NSW to an early 2–0 lead.

A few minutes later, Farah darted near halfway and sent Jarryd Hayne breaking away past Folau. Hayne tiptoed along the left sideline before throwing Slater a dummy and crossing in the corner. Replays showed Hayne's heel barely clipped the sideline: video referees Harrigan and Mander took more than two minutes to reach a no-try verdict.

The disappointed Blues conceded a penalty before Jennings knocked the ball down to restart Queensland's tackle count. Three tackles later, Smith stepped left and grubbered through for Slater to touch down millimetres inside the dead-ball line with a spectacular dive. Thurston's goal took Queensland to a fortuitous 6–2 lead.

A few minutes later, Hayne was penalised for impeding Folau as he chased Lockyer's high punt. Replays suggested Hayne was harshly treated as he watched the ball and not Folau. One tackle later, Thurston, Lockyer, Harrison, Slater and Inglis combined before Inglis surged for the line amid three defenders to score. Thurston's conversion from the left wing made the score 12–2.

Four tackles after the restart, Smith shaped to kick but was harassed and unloaded to Thurston, who combined with Harrison to reach NSW's 20-metre line. The ball was passed right through Thurston, Lockyer, Thaiday, Lockyer again, Hodges and Folau before Folau grubbered infield past three defenders where Thurston swooped to score. Thurston converted, taking the Maroons to a 16-point lead. Medial ligament damage forced Hodges to exit the game.

Hayne made a 60-metre break from a kick return before Slater was controversially penalised for stripping the ball from him. Three tackles later, O'Donnell surged into Slater on the tryline but the impact of the hit forced a knock-on.

The Blues were unable to capitalise on good field position before an offside penalty against Inglis enabled them to return downfield. After tackle four, Campese chip-kicked towards the left corner, where Hayne collected the ball and flung it infield and Creagh pounced to score. Hayne's pass was clearly forward but the video referees, not empowered to rule on forward passes, had to award the try. Gidley sliced his conversion before Thurston botched a field-goal attempt just before the break. The score remained 18–6 to Queensland at half-time.

In Queensland's quarter just two minutes after the resumption, Myles unloaded brilliantly in a lifting tackle to Thurston, whose pass found Inglis positioned outside McManus. Inglis sprinted down the left side and scored a 73-metre try, which Thurston converted. Queensland led 24–6.

Wing was introduced with about 25 minutes remaining. Thirty metres from Queensland's tryline, Wallace's chip-kick touched Thurston's hand and the ball bounced favourably for Lewis. He attracted Slater and slipped an inside pass to Wing, who scored a try that Gidley converted. NSW gained momentum as Queensland's defence tired. Inglis defended well, once soaring high to catch a bomb near his tryline and later barrelling Lewis to force a knock-on.

In the 63rd minute, Creagh dislodged the ball from Folau but fumbled it. Nevertheless, NSW was awarded a scrum feed. A few minutes later, Farah stepped left and kicked straight into Price's arm as the advancing Price turned. Farah caught the

rebound before drawing Slater and sending Hayne in behind the posts. Farah's pass appeared a little forward but Gidley's conversion closed Queensland's lead to one converted try with 11 minutes left.

Almost immediately, an O'Donnell offload set up a half-break by Lyon, who kicked ahead but Slater saved Queensland. Soon after, Thurston's downfield kick lingered in-goal. As he picked up the ball, Gidley inadvertently placed one foot out to concede a goal-line drop-out. At the end of the ensuing tackle count, Lockyer had time for a field-goal attempt but pushed it to the left.

NSW's hopes died in the last minute when Gidley reached to field Thurston's clearing kick and spilled it in his quarter. Thurston fed the scrum and switched play to the left, where Inglis fended off Wing before drawing McManus and throwing an around-the-corner pass to send Boyd scampering over in the corner. Queensland had won 28–18.

The Verdict

The difference between success and failure was as tiny as ever, particularly in the first half. NSW post-match analysis highlighted two decisions that upset the Blues: Hayne's disallowed try and the penalty against him for impeding Folau. The Maroons could have argued the Blues received some favourable decisions too. Phil Gould pointed to Queensland doing the little things right: getting to the loose ball first, a superior kicking game and not dropping their heads in adversity.

↑ Robbie Farah, playing in his Origin debut shapes to pass from dummy-half.

Players & Statistics

QLD Billy Slater, Darius Boyd, Greg Inglis, Justin Hodges, Israel Folau, Darren Lockyer (c), Johnathan Thurston, Dallas Johnson, Sam Thaiday, Ashley Harrison, Petero Civoniceva, Cameron Smith, Steve Price. **RESERVES** Ben Hannant, Nate Myles, Karmichael Hunt, Michael Crocker. **COACH** Mal Meninga

NSW Kurt Gidley (c), Jarryd Hayne, Michael Jennings, Jamie Lyon, James McManus, Terry Campese, Peter Wallace, Anthony Laffranchi, Ben Creagh, Luke O'Donnell, Luke Bailey, Robbie Farah, Brent Kite. **RESERVES** Justin Poore, Luke Lewis, Michael Weyman, Craig Wing. **COACH** Craig Bellamy

Result Queensland 28 (Inglis 2, Slater, Thurston, Boyd tries; Thurston 4 goals) beat NSW 18 (Creagh, Wing, Hayne tries; Gidley 3 goals)

Referees Tony Archer (NSW) and Shayne Hayne (NSW)

Crowd 50 967

Man of the Match Johnathan Thurston (Queensland)

↑ Luke O'Donnell tries to escape the clutches of Ben Hannant. O'Donnell made a crucial error late in the game as Queensland wrapped up the series.

The Game

Errors by Civoniceva and Thurston gifted the Blues the early initiative. But then Gallen flicked a one-handed pass to nobody and Folau pounced and broke away. Queensland received an offside penalty within easy goal-kicking range but took a tap instead. One tackle later, Smith passed left to Thurston, who turned the ball inside for Inglis to exploit soft goal-line defence and power through Gidley to score. Thurston kicked the Maroons to a 6–0 lead.

Williams fumbled in Tonga's front-on tackle on a kick return. Tonga dropped the ball a few tackles later with the tryline under threat, before Inglis made another bust from Queensland's quarter. At the start of NSW's next set, Williams stepped from his 20-metre line and again knocked on as Tonga tackled him. Folau fielded the ball, shrugged off Gidley, and burst through fragile defence from Farah and Poore to score under the crossbar.

Williams made a half-break but threw a stray inside pass, which Inglis fielded before copping a head-high tackle from Barrett. Concussed, Inglis exited the game. In the next minute, Farah's pass to the left went to ground inside NSW's 10-metre zone and Creagh spilled it before Lockyer pounced for another easy try. Unforced mistakes had gifted Queensland three tries for an 18-0 lead.

Poore fumbled to give the Maroons field position again. Smith moved the ball right to Lockyer and Slater, who lofted a pass to the unmarked Folau. Hayne intercepted and ran 93 metres to score. Gidley's conversion saw NSW trailing 18–6.

O'Donnell conceded a penalty when he reacted to an accidental kick from Hannant in a play-the-ball. Thurston opted to run the ball at the end of the set, and Tonga tried to unload in a tackle by Williams and Lyon. The ball went to ground, then Harrison fielded it and dived over the line. Replays showed that as Tonga pushed the ball backwards it struck Williams's head; however, the video referees ruled a knock-on against Tonga. Two tackles later, a brawl erupted between Poore and Crocker, who was penalised for throwing the first punch.

The Teams

NSW lost Bailey, McManus and Lewis to injury, and Campese and Laffranchi were axed. Glenn Stewart, Gallen, Watmough and Barrett were recalled, and David Williams was chosen to debut. Later injuries to Jennings and Wing led to the recall of Monaghan and the debut of Josh Morris.

The Maroons replaced the injured Hodges with Tonga. A virus affected several Queenslanders in the lead-up, but they remained fit to play.

The Blues attacked two minutes before half-time. O'Donnell played the ball to Hayne near the left corner on tackle five. Hayne stepped left and swivelled over the line in tackles by Hunt and Thurston. Replays showed that O'Donnell's arm obstructed Folau after the play-the-ball. But the video referees awarded the try via the 'benefit of the doubt' rule. Gidley sliced the conversion attempt. Queensland led 18–10 at the break.

Crocker made a few handling mistakes soon after the break, and Williams erred again when he threw a forward pass after making a threatening break. Queensland was in further trouble when Harrison and Hannant left the field injured (Hannant returned later). NSW gained a repeat set of tackles after Slater spilled Barrett's high punt. Gidley spread the ball left to Stewart and Barrett, who changed the point of attack and scooped a one-handed pass to Williams. He burrowed into three defenders but managed to plant the ball in the corner. Gidley missed his kick and the margin was down to four points with 16 minutes remaining.

Gidley forced another knock-on from Crocker, before Monaghan went for the line but was safely held up. Price charged down a Wallace kick but Creagh fumbled the loose ball. Stewart knocked-on but then Civoniceva fumbled in a hit-up. NSW enjoyed better field position for several minutes. Wallace's bomb beyond the tryline was propelled forwards by Monaghan as he contested with Folau, but referee Archer ruled a goal-line drop-out. The Maroons were on the back foot while the Blues

searched for the breakthrough. O'Donnell produced a vital offload on tackle one but then Williams put in a wasteful kick. Next, Lyon chanced the sliding defence and was tackled over the sideline.

In the ensuing tackle count, Lockyer's pin-point bomb forced a goal-line drop-out with three minutes left. The ball deflected NSW's way from a chip-kick but O'Donnell fumbled. On the last tackle, Thurston floated a kick to the right of the posts. Slater out-leapt Barrett but knocked the ball to O'Donnell, who was driven back between his uprights and lost the ball. Smith gathered the loose ball and dived over the line, and the video referees' green light sealed Queensland's historic fourth straight series triumph. Thurston converted for a 24–14 score.

↑ Ashley Harrison, who was controversially disallowed a crucial try in the first half, uses his fend.

↓ Sam Thaiday was voted man of the match in game two, which the Maroons won to seal the state's record fourth consecutive series triumph.

The Verdict

The Blues had only themselves to blame, with Bellamy deeming the first three tries the softest ones he had ever seen in Origin football. Gould commented in the *Sydney Morning Herald* that the Blues were awful, and that only the football gods and the video referees kept them in the game. Queensland meanwhile had good reason to be happy, and coach Meninga earned a unique place in Origin history.

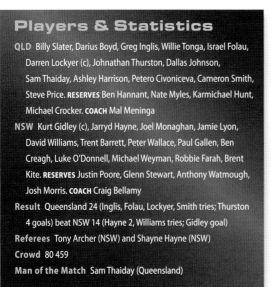

Players & Statistics

QLD Billy Slater, Darius Boyd, Greg Inglis, Willie Tonga, Israel Folau, Darren Lockyer (c), Johnathan Thurston, Dallas Johnson, Sam Thaiday, Ashley Harrison, Petero Civoniceva, Cameron Smith, Steve Price. **RESERVES** Ben Hannant, Nate Myles, Karmichael Hunt, Michael Crocker. **COACH** Mal Meninga

NSW Kurt Gidley (c), Jarryd Hayne, Joel Monaghan, Jamie Lyon, David Williams, Trent Barrett, Peter Wallace, Paul Gallen, Ben Creagh, Luke O'Donnell, Michael Weyman, Robbie Farah, Brent Kite. **RESERVES** Justin Poore, Glenn Stewart, Anthony Watmough, Josh Morris. **COACH** Craig Bellamy

Result Queensland 24 (Inglis, Folau, Lockyer, Smith tries; Thurston 4 goals) beat NSW 14 (Hayne 2, Williams tries; Gidley goal)

Referees Tony Archer (NSW) and Shayne Hayne (NSW)

Crowd 80 459

Man of the Match Sam Thaiday (Queensland)

The Teams

Queensland lost Folau, Hannant and Civoniceva to injury and Myles to suspension. Hodges, Matt Scott and Costigan were recalled and David Shillington was named to debut.

NSW's selectors dropped Monaghan, Wallace, Kite, Farah and Morris. Gallen, O'Donnell and Weyman were out through injury. Recalled were Kimmorley, Waterhouse, Perry, White, Wing and Jennings. Michael Ennis and Tom Learoyd-Lahrs were debutants. Morris returned when Lyon was ruled out with injury.

The Game

Brutal tackling and poor handling were prominent early on, and the Blues' defence showed renewed vigour. NSW was caught offside in the tenth minute, before Thurston grubbered inside NSW's 30-metre zone. Williams fumbled the ball over his head as he slid to gather it, and it rolled in-goal where Johnson pounced. Thurston's goal gave Queensland a 6–0 lead.

Hayne and Watmough made breaks before Inglis uncharacteristically fumbled an overhead mark from Barrett's bomb. On the next tackle, Ennis passed left to Watmough, whose superbly timed pass sent Creagh through to score. Ennis converted to tie the scores.

When Tonga had the ball stripped, it went onto his foot and rolled in-goal, where Smith pounced. Referee Hayne awarded NSW a scrum feed, but seeking a replay may have resulted in a try. When Queensland attacked again, Hunt kicked to the right corner, where Boyd collided with Jarryd Hayne. The ball was in the air and going out but Hodges leapt spectacularly high and reached to plant the ball as he was airborne. But the video

Players & Statistics

NSW Kurt Gidley (c), Jarryd Hayne, Michael Jennings, Josh Morris, David Williams, Trent Barrett, Brett Kimmorley, Anthony Watmough, Ben Creagh, Trent Waterhouse, Justin Poore, Michael Ennis, Josh Perry. **RESERVES** Craig Wing, Tom Learoyd-Lahrs, Glenn Stewart, Brett White. **COACH** Craig Bellamy

QLD Billy Slater, Darius Boyd, Greg Inglis, Justin Hodges, Willie Tonga, Darren Lockyer (c), Johnathan Thurston, Dallas Johnson, Michael Crocker, Ashley Harrison, Steve Price, Cameron Smith, David Shillington. **RESERVES** Karmichael Hunt, Neville Costigan, Matt Scott, Sam Thaiday. **COACH** Mal Meninga

Result NSW 28 (Creagh 2, Williams, Morris tries; Gidley 3, Ennis 3 goals) beat Queensland 16 (Johnson, Hodges, Slater tries; Thurston 2 goals)

Referees Tony Archer (NSW) and Shayne Hayne (NSW)

Crowd 52 439

Man of the Match Anthony Watmough (NSW)

referees disallowed the try since Hodges just failed to force the ball.

Within moments, Hayne made another break before his kick hit an upright and bounced favourably for NSW. Barrett grubbered on the last tackle and Slater fumbled the ball into Williams. He went to ground before his face copped a boot from Thurston, who belatedly attempted to save a try. Replays showed Williams had fumbled the ball against his leg, but video referees Simpkins and Hampstead ruled for NSW and controversially awarded an eight-point try for Thurston's indiscretion. Gidley landed both goal-kicks on offer, and NSW led 14–6 at half-time.

Just after the resumption, the Blues fumbled near halfway. Several tackles later, Smith passed right to Lockyer and Hodges, who busted Morris's tackle and spun over to score in a tackle. Down 14–10, Queensland soon faltered when Tonga fumbled in Kimmorley's tackle. Eleven metres from the uprights, Gidley passed left to Kimmorley and Barrett. He stepped through and unloaded inside to Morris, who touched down in Johnson's tackle. Barrett's pass was forward but it was missed

↓ Kurt Gidley pulls off a brilliant tackle on a runaway Darius Boyd to help foil Queensland's comeback.

by the referee, and Gidley's conversion gave NSW a ten-point lead.

After Kimmorley kicked out on the full, the Maroons spread the ball left where Inglis fended off Williams and broke away before kicking ahead, where Slater beat Williams to the ball in-goal. The video referees awarded the try, although replays showed Slater lost his grip when forcing the ball. Thurston's conversion reduced NSW's lead to four points with 27 minutes left.

The Blues made a few errors to give Queensland attacking chances. After a penalty against Waterhouse, Tonga lunged for the line but Gidley arrived and knocked the ball loose with his knee. In the 65th minute, a knock-on from Smith was soon followed by a break from Watmough. In Queensland's quarter, Creagh stepped right from dummy-half and exploited some slow defence to reach out and score. NSW took a ten-point lead with Ennis's conversion.

Inglis broke away from inside his half, but Kimmorley's brilliant covering tackle took him over the sideline. An infringement by Crocker saw Ennis kick a penalty goal, giving NSW a 12-point lead. The Maroons regained the ball from a short kick-off, then received a penalty. Queensland created an overlap on the left, but Williams moved in to force a fumble from Costigan. In Queensland's next set, Lockyer's cut-out pass sent Boyd away down the wing. Boyd twice fended off Hayne but Gidley's cover tackle forced him into touch. Queensland's best efforts were not quite enough this time.

In the final two minutes, White reacted after Price niggled him in a tackle. Play continued and Hayne crossed in the corner while White and Price scuffled. As Price fell from a punch, Waterhouse came from behind and forced him down. Poore lifted the unconscious Price, then let him go, infuriating the Maroons. Play was halted for several minutes and the teams were separated, but ill-feeling was apparent. Hayne's try was disallowed and the concussed Price was placed on a medicab. Waterhouse was sent off for being the third man in during the fight, and was the first NSW player sent off in Origin football.

Queensland received a penalty and kicked for touch, before Smith

immediately hoisted a bomb as the Maroons sought vengeance. Thaiday knocked Watmough down before Gidley caught the ball and was set upon by several Maroons. Brawling continued before Creagh and Thaiday were sent to the sin-bin, and more scuffling occurred until, mercifully, the siren sounded.

The Verdict

Controversial tries, great cover defence, passion, questionable video refereeing decisions, some old-fashioned antagonism—the game had them all. The Blues were angry over Thurston's kicking action and Queensland's revenge-driven behaviour at the end. The Maroons seethed over Waterhouse's attack on Price and Poore's treatment of the prostrate player. In the end, though, the Blues earned their win.

↑ Justin Hodges leaps high but just fails to control the ball for what would have been one of the most spectacular tries ever.

← Anthony Watmough was named man of the match in game three. Their win allowed the Blues to regain some lost pride.

Statistics

Throughout these statistics, the winning team is listed first.

Coaches

1980
ONE-OFF ORIGIN GAME
QLD John McDonald
NSW Ted Glossop

1981
ONE-OFF ORIGIN GAME
QLD Arthur Beetson
NSW Ted Glossop

1982
QLD Arthur Beetson
NSW Frank Stanton

1983
QLD Arthur Beetson
NSW Ted Glossop

1984
QLD Arthur Beetson
NSW Frank Stanton

1985
NSW Terry Fearnley
QLD Des Morris

1986
NSW Ron Willey
QLD Wayne Bennett

1987
QLD Wayne Bennett
NSW Ron Willey

EXHIBITION GAME
NSW Ron Willey
QLD Wayne Bennett

1988
QLD Wayne Bennett
NSW John Peard

1989
QLD Arthur Beetson
NSW Jack Gibson

1990
NSW Jack Gibson
QLD Arthur Beetson

1991
QLD Graham Lowe
NSW Tim Sheens

1992
NSW Phil Gould
QLD Graham Lowe

1993
NSW Phil Gould
QLD Wally Lewis

1994
NSW Phil Gould
QLD Wally Lewis

1995
QLD Paul Vautin
NSW Phil Gould

1996
NSW Phil Gould
QLD Paul Vautin

1997
NSW Tom Raudonikis
QLD Paul Vautin

1998
QLD Wayne Bennett
NSW Tom Raudonikis

1999
QLD Mark Murray
NSW Wayne Pearce

2000
NSW Wayne Pearce
QLD Mark Murray

2001
QLD Wayne Bennett
NSW Wayne Pearce

2002
QLD Wayne Bennett
NSW Phil Gould

2003
NSW Phil Gould
QLD Wayne Bennett

2004
NSW Phil Gould
QLD Michael Hagan

2005
NSW Ricky Stuart
QLD Michael Hagan

2006
QLD Mal Meninga
NSW Graham Murray

2007
QLD Mal Meninga
NSW Graham Murray

2008
QLD Mal Meninga
NSW Craig Bellamy

2009
QLD Mal Meninga
NSW Craig Bellamy

Captains

1980
ONE-OFF ORIGIN GAME
QLD Arthur Beetson
NSW Tom Raudonikis

1981
ONE-OFF ORIGIN GAME
QLD Wally Lewis
NSW Steve Rogers

1982
QLD Wally Lewis
NSW Max Krilich

1983
QLD Wally Lewis
NSW Max Krilich (I & III),
Ray Price (II)

1984
QLD Wally Lewis
NSW Ray Price (I & II),
Steve Mortimer (III)

1985
NSW Steve Mortimer (I & II),
Wayne Pearce (III)
QLD Wally Lewis

1986
NSW Wayne Pearce
QLD Wally Lewis

1987
QLD Wally Lewis
NSW Wayne Pearce

EXHIBITION GAME
NSW Peter Sterling
QLD Wally Lewis

1988
QLD Paul Vautin (I),
Wally Lewis (II & III)
NSW Wayne Pearce

1989
QLD Wally Lewis
NSW Gavin Miller

1990
NSW Ben Elias
QLD Paul Vautin (I),
Wally Lewis (II & III)

1991
QLD Wally Lewis
NSW Ben Elias

1992
NSW Laurie Daley
QLD Mal Meninga

1993
NSW Laurie Daley
QLD Mal Meninga

1994
NSW Laurie Daley
QLD Mal Meninga

1995
QLD Trevor Gillmeister
NSW Brad Fittler

1996
NSW Brad Fittler
QLD Trevor Gillmeister (I),
Allan Langer (II & III)

1997
NSW Geoff Toovey
QLD Adrian Lam

1998
QLD Allan Langer
NSW Laurie Daley

1999
QLD Adrian Lam (I & III),
Kevin Walters (II)
NSW Brad Fittler (I & II),
Laurie Daley (III)

2000
NSW Brad Fittler
QLD Adrian Lam

2001
QLD Gorden Tallis (I),
Darren Lockyer (II & III)
NSW Brad Fittler

2002
QLD Gorden Tallis
NSW Andrew Johns

2003
NSW Andrew Johns
QLD Gorden Tallis

2004
NSW Danny Buderus
QLD Shane Webcke (I),
Darren Lockyer (II & III)

2005
NSW Danny Buderus
QLD Darren Lockyer

2006
QLD Darren Lockyer
NSW Danny Buderus

2007
QLD Darren Lockyer
NSW Danny Buderus

2008
QLD Cameron Smith
NSW Danny Buderus

2009
QLD Darren Lockyer
NSW Kurt Gidley

Time, place and crowd

1980

ONE-OFF ORIGIN GAME
Lang Park, Brisbane, 8 July
CROWD: 33 210

1981

ONE-OFF ORIGIN GAME
Lang Park, Brisbane, 28 July
CROWD: 25 613

1982

GAME ONE
Lang Park, Brisbane, 1 June
CROWD: 27 326

GAME TWO
Lang Park, Brisbane, 8 June
CROWD: 19 435

GAME THREE
Sydney Cricket Ground, Sydney, 22 June
CROWD: 20 242

1983

GAME ONE
Lang Park, Brisbane, 7 June
CROWD: 29 412

GAME TWO
Sydney Cricket Ground, Sydney, 21 June
CROWD: 21 620

GAME THREE
Lang Park, Brisbane, 28 June
CROWD: 26 084

1984

GAME ONE
Lang Park, Brisbane, 29 May
CROWD: 33 662

GAME TWO
Sydney Cricket Ground, Sydney, 19 June
CROWD: 29 088

GAME THREE
Lang Park, Brisbane, 17 July
CROWD: 16 559

1985

GAME ONE
Lang Park, Brisbane, 28 May
CROWD: 33 011

GAME TWO
Sydney Cricket Ground, Sydney, 11 June
CROWD: 39 068

GAME THREE
Lang Park, Brisbane, 23 July
CROWD: 18 825

1986

GAME ONE
Lang Park, Brisbane, 27 May
CROWD: 33 066

GAME TWO
Sydney Cricket Ground, Sydney, 10 June
CROWD: 40 707

GAME THREE
Lang Park, Brisbane, 1 July
CROWD: 21 097

1987

GAME ONE
Lang Park, Brisbane, 2 June
CROWD: 33 411

GAME TWO
Sydney Cricket Ground, Sydney, 16 June
CROWD: 42 048

GAME THREE
Lang Park, Brisbane, 15 July
CROWD: 32 602

EXHIBITION GAME
Veterans Stadium, Long Beach, California, 6 August
CROWD: 12 349

1988

GAME ONE
Sydney Football Stadium, Sydney, 17 May
CROWD: 26 441

GAME TWO
Lang Park, Brisbane, 31 May
CROWD: 31 817

GAME THREE
Sydney Football Stadium, Sydney, 21 June
CROWD: 16 910

1989

GAME ONE
Lang Park, Brisbane, 23 May
CROWD: 33 088

GAME TWO
Sydney Football Stadium, Sydney, 14 June
CROWD: 40 000

GAME THREE
Lang Park, Brisbane, 28 June
CROWD: 33 268

1990

GAME ONE
Sydney Football Stadium, Sydney, 9 May
CROWD: 41 235

GAME TWO
Olympic Park, Melbourne, 30 May
CROWD: 25 800

GAME THREE
Lang Park, Brisbane, 13 June
CROWD: 31 416

1991

GAME ONE
Lang Park, Brisbane, 8 May
CROWD: 32 400

GAME TWO
Sydney Football Stadium, Sydney, 29 May
CROWD: 41 520

GAME THREE
Lang Park, Brisbane, 12 June
CROWD: 33 226

1992

GAME ONE
Sydney Football Stadium, Sydney, 6 May
CROWD: 40 039

GAME TWO
Lang Park, Brisbane, 20 May
CROWD: 31 500

GAME THREE
Sydney Football Stadium, Sydney, 3 June
CROWD: 41 878

1993

GAME ONE
Lang Park, Brisbane, 3 May
CROWD: 33 000

GAME TWO
Sydney Football Stadium, Sydney, 17 May
CROWD: 41 895

GAME THREE
Lang Park, Brisbane, 31 May
CROWD: 31 500

1994

GAME ONE
Sydney Football Stadium, Sydney, 23 May
CROWD: 41 859

GAME TWO
Melbourne Cricket Ground, Melbourne, 8 June
CROWD: 87 161

GAME THREE
Suncorp Stadium, Brisbane, 20 June
CROWD: 40 665

1995

GAME ONE
Sydney Football Stadium, Sydney, 15 May
CROWD: 39 841

GAME TWO
Melbourne Cricket Ground, Melbourne, 31 May
CROWD: 52 994

GAME THREE
Suncorp Stadium, Brisbane, 12 June
CROWD: 40 189

1996

GAME ONE
Suncorp Stadium, Brisbane, 20 May
CROWD: 39 348

GAME TWO
Sydney Football Stadium, Sydney, 3 June
CROWD: 41 955

GAME THREE
Suncorp Stadium, Brisbane, 17 June
CROWD: 38 217

1997

GAME ONE
Suncorp Stadium, Brisbane, 28 May
CROWD: 28 222

GAME TWO
Melbourne Cricket Ground, Melbourne,
11 June
CROWD: 25 105

GAME THREE
Sydney Football Stadium, Sydney,
25 June
CROWD: 33 241

1998

GAME ONE
Sydney Football Stadium, Sydney, 22 May
CROWD: 36 070

GAME TWO
Suncorp Stadium, Brisbane, 5 June
CROWD: 40 447

GAME THREE
Sydney Football Stadium, Sydney,
19 June
CROWD: 38 952

1999

GAME ONE
Suncorp Stadium, Brisbane, 26 May
CROWD: 38 093

GAME TWO
Stadium Australia, Sydney, 9 June
CROWD: 88 336

GAME THREE
Suncorp Stadium, Brisbane, 23 June
CROWD: 39 371

2000

GAME ONE
Stadium Australia, Sydney, 10 May
CROWD: 61 511

GAME TWO
Suncorp Stadium, Brisbane, 24 May
CROWD: 38 796

GAME THREE
Stadium Australia, Sydney, 7 June
CROWD: 58 767

2001

GAME ONE
Suncorp Stadium, Brisbane, 6 May
CROWD: 38 909

GAME TWO
Stadium Australia, Sydney, 10 June
CROWD: 70 249

GAME THREE
ANZ Stadium, Brisbane, 1 July
CROWD: 49 441

2002

GAME ONE
Stadium Australia, Sydney, 22 May
CROWD: 55 421

GAME TWO
ANZ Stadium, Brisbane, 5 June
CROWD: 47 989

GAME THREE
Stadium Australia, Sydney, 26 June
CROWD: 74 842

2003

GAME ONE
Suncorp Stadium, Brisbane, 11 June
CROWD: 52 420

GAME TWO
Telstra Stadium, Sydney, 25 June
CROWD: 79 132

GAME THREE
Suncorp Stadium, Brisbane, 16 July
CROWD: 52 130

2004

GAME ONE
Telstra Stadium, Sydney, 26 May
CROWD: 68 344

GAME TWO
Suncorp Stadium, Brisbane, 16 June
CROWD: 52 478

GAME THREE
Telstra Stadium, Sydney, 7 July
CROWD: 82 487

2005

GAME ONE
Suncorp Stadium, Brisbane, 25 May
CROWD: 52 484

GAME TWO
Telstra Stadium, Sydney, 15 June
CROWD: 82 389

GAME THREE
Suncorp Stadium, Brisbane, 6 July
CROWD: 52 436

2006

GAME ONE
Telstra Stadium, Sydney, 24 May
CROWD: 72 773

GAME TWO
Suncorp Stadium, Brisbane, 14 June
CROWD: 52 468

GAME THREE
Telstra Dome, Melbourne, 5 July
CROWD: 54 833

2007

GAME ONE
Suncorp Stadium, Brisbane, 23 May
CROWD: 52 498

GAME TWO
Telstra Stadium, Sydney, 13 June
CROWD: 76 924

GAME THREE
Suncorp Stadium, Brisbane, 4 July
CROWD: 52 469

2008

GAME ONE
ANZ Stadium, Sydney, 21 May
CROWD: 67 620

GAME TWO
Suncorp Stadium, Brisbane, 11 June
CROWD: 52 416

GAME THREE
ANZ Stadium, Sydney, 2 July
CROWD: 78 751

2009

GAME ONE
Etihad Stadium, Melbourne, 3 June
CROWD: 50 967

GAME TWO
ANZ Stadium, Sydney, 24 June
CROWD: 80 459

GAME THREE
Suncorp Stadium, Brisbane, 15 July
CROWD: 52 439

Teams

1980

ONE-OFF ORIGIN GAME

QLD Colin Scott, Kerry Boustead, Mal Meninga, Chris Close, Brad Backer, Alan Smith, Greg Oliphant, Wally Lewis, Rod Reddy, Rohan Hancock, Arthur Beetson (c), John Lang, Rod Morris
RESERVES: Norm Carr (not used), Bruce Astill (not used)

NSW Graham Eadie, Chris Anderson, Steve Rogers, Michael Cronin, Greg Brentnall, Alan Thompson, Tom Raudonikis (c), Jim Leis, Graeme Wynn, Bob Cooper, Craig Young, Steve Edge, Gary Hambly
RESERVES: Steve Martin, Robert Stone

1981

ONE-OFF ORIGIN GAME

QLD Colin Scott, Brad Backer, Mal Meninga, Chris Close, Mitch Brennan, Wally Lewis (c), Ross Henrick, Chris Phelan, Rohan Hancock, Paul McCabe, Paul Khan, Greg Conescu, Rod Morris
RESERVES: Norm Carr, Mark Murray

NSW Phil Sigsworth, Terry Fahey, Michael Cronin, Steve Rogers (c), Eric Grothe, Terry Lamb, Peter Sterling, Ray Price, Les Boyd, Peter Tunks, Ron Hilditch, Barry Jensen, Steve Bowden
RESERVES: Garry Dowling, Graham O'Grady (not used)

1982

GAME ONE

NSW Greg Brentnall, Chris Anderson, Michael Cronin, Steve Rogers, Ziggy Niszczot, Alan Thompson, Steve Mortimer, Ray Price, John Muggleton, Tony Rampling, Craig Young, Max Krilich (c), John Coveney
RESERVES: Brad Izzard, Royce Ayliffe

QLD Colin Scott, John Ribot, Mitch Brennan, Mal Meninga, Kerry Boustead, Wally Lewis, Mark Murray, Paul Vautin, Paul McCabe, Bruce Walker, Paul Khan, John Dowling, Rohan Hancock
RESERVES: Bob Kellaway, Gene Miles

GAME TWO

QLD Colin Scott, John Ribot, Graham Quinn, Gene Miles, Brad Backer, Wally Lewis (c), Mark Murray, Norm Carr, Paul McCabe, Rod Morris, Paul Khan, John Dowling, Rohan Hancock

RESERVES: Paul Vautin, Greg Holben

NSW Greg Brentnall, Tony Melrose, Brad Izzard, Steve Rogers, Ziggy Niszczot, Alan Thompson, Steve Mortimer, Ray Price, John Muggleton, Tony Rampling, Craig Young, Max Krilich (c), John Coveney
RESERVES: Brett Kenny, Royce Ayliffe

GAME THREE

QLD Mitch Brennan, John Ribot, Gene Miles, Mal Meninga, Kerry Boustead, Wally Lewis (c), Mark Murray, Norm Carr, Paul McCabe, Rohan Hancock, Paul Khan, John Dowling, Rod Morris
RESERVES: Paul Vautin, Tony Currie

NSW Phil Sigsworth, Terry Fahey, Michael Cronin, Brad Izzard, Phil Duke, Brett Kenny, Steve Mortimer, Ray Price, Les Boyd, Paul Merlo, Don McKinnon, Max Krilich (c), Royce Ayliffe
RESERVES: Alan Thompson, Craig Young

1983

GAME ONE

QLD Colin Scott, John Ribot, Mal Meninga, Gene Miles, Steve Stacey, Wally Lewis (c), Mark Murray, Wally Fullerton Smith, Paul Vautin, Bryan Niebling, Darryl Brohman, Greg Conescu, Brad Tessmann
RESERVES: Brett French (not used), Dave Brown

NSW Greg Brentnall, Chris Anderson, Brett Kenny, Phil Sigsworth, Eric Grothe, Alan Thompson, Peter Sterling, Ray Price, Wayne Pearce, Les Boyd, Geoff Bugden, Max Krilich (c), Geoff Gerard
RESERVES: Steve Ella, Ray Brown

GAME TWO

NSW Marty Gurr, Neil Hunt, Michael Cronin, Steve Ella, Eric Grothe, Brett Kenny, Peter Sterling, Ray Price (c), Paul Field, Gavin Miller, Lindsay Johnston, Ray Brown, Geoff Gerard
RESERVES: Steve Mortimer, Stan Jurd

QLD Colin Scott, Terry Butler, Mal Meninga, Gene Miles, Chris Close, Wally Lewis (c), Mark Murray, Paul Vautin, Wally Fullerton Smith, Bryan Niebling, Dave Brown, Greg Conescu, Brad Tessmann
RESERVES: Brett French (not used), Ross Henrick

GAME THREE

QLD Colin Scott, Steve Stacey, Mal Meninga, Gene Miles, Mitch Brennan, Wally Lewis (c), Mark Murray, Paul

Vautin, Wally Fullerton Smith, Bryan Niebling, Dave Brown, Greg Conescu, Brad Tessmann
RESERVES: Bruce Astill, Gavin Jones

NSW Marty Gurr, Neil Hunt, Michael Cronin, Steve Ella, Chris Anderson, Brett Kenny, Steve Mortimer, Gavin Miller, Paul Field, Stan Jurd, Lindsay Johnston, Max Krilich (c), Geoff Bugden
RESERVES: Kevin Hastings, Ray Brown

1984

GAME ONE

QLD Colin Scott, Kerry Boustead, Mal Meninga, Gene Miles, Chris Close, Wally Lewis (c), Mark Murray, Paul Vautin, Wally Fullerton Smith, Bryan Niebling, Dave Brown, Greg Conescu, Greg Dowling
RESERVES: Brett French, Bob Lindner.

NSW Garry Jack, Eric Grothe, Brett Kenny, Steve Ella, Ross Conlon, Alan Thompson, Peter Sterling, Ray Price (c), Wayne Pearce, Noel Cleal, Craig Young, Rex Wright, Steve Roach
RESERVES: Pat Jarvis, Brian Hetherington

GAME TWO

QLD Colin Scott, Kerry Boustead, Chris Close, Gene Miles, Mal Meninga, Wally Lewis (c), Mark Murray, Paul Vautin, Wally Fullerton Smith, Bryan Niebling, Dave Brown, Greg Conescu, Greg Dowling
RESERVES: Tony Currie (not used), Bob Lindner

NSW Garry Jack, Eric Grothe, Andrew Farrar, Brett Kenny, Ross Conlon, Terry Lamb, Steve Mortimer, Ray Price (c), Wayne Pearce, Noel Cleal, Peter Tunks, Royce Simmons, Steve Roach
RESERVES: Steve Ella, Pat Jarvis

GAME THREE

NSW Garry Jack, Steve Morris, Chris Mortimer, Brian Johnston, Ross Conlon, Brett Kenny, Steve Mortimer (c), Peter Wynn, Noel Cleal, Chris Walsh, Pat Jarvis, Royce Simmons, Steve Roach
RESERVES: Michael Potter, Peter Tunks

QLD Colin Scott, John Ribot, Mal Meninga, Brett French, Kerry Boustead, Wally Lewis (c), Ross Henrick, Bob Lindner, Wally Fullerton Smith, Chris Phelan, Dave Brown, Greg Conescu, Greg Dowling
RESERVES: Tony Currie, Bob Kellaway

1985

GAME ONE

NSW Garry Jack, Eric Grothe, Michael O'Connor, Chris Mortimer, John Ferguson, Brett Kenny, Steve Mortimer (c), Wayne Pearce, Peter Wynn, Noel Cleal, Steve Roach, Ben Elias, Pat Jarvis
RESERVES: Steve Ella (not used), Peter Tunks

QLD Colin Scott, John Ribot, Mal Meninga, Chris Close, Dale Shearer, Wally Lewis (c), Mark Murray, Bob Lindner, Paul McCabe, Paul Vautin, Dave Brown, Greg Conescu, Greg Dowling
RESERVES: Brett French (not used), Ian French (not used)

GAME TWO

NSW Garry Jack, Eric Grothe, Michael O'Connor, Chris Mortimer, John Ferguson, Brett Kenny, Steve Mortimer (c), Wayne Pearce, Peter Wynn, Noel Cleal, Steve Roach, Ben Elias, Pat Jarvis
RESERVES: Steve Ella, Peter Tunks (not used)

QLD Colin Scott, John Ribot, Mal Meninga, Chris Close, Dale Shearer, Wally Lewis (c), Mark Murray, Bob Lindner, Wally Fullerton Smith, Paul Vautin, Dave Brown, Greg Conescu, Greg Dowling
RESERVES: Tony Currie, Ian French

GAME THREE

QLD Colin Scott, John Ribot, Mal Meninga, Chris Close, Dale Shearer, Wally Lewis (c), Mark Murray, Paul Vautin, Wally Fullerton Smith, Ian French, Dave Brown, Greg Conescu, Greg Dowling
RESERVES: Tony Currie, Cavill Heugh

NSW Garry Jack, John Ferguson, Chris Mortimer, Michael O'Connor, Eric Grothe, Brett Kenny, Des Hasler, Wayne Pearce (c), David Brooks, Peter Wynn, Steve Roach, Ben Elias, Pat Jarvis
RESERVES: Steve Ella, Tony Rampling

1986

GAME ONE

NSW Garry Jack, Steve Morris, Michael O'Connor, Chris Mortimer, Andrew Farrar, Brett Kenny, Peter Sterling, Wayne Pearce (c), Noel Cleal, Steve Folkes, Peter Tunks, Royce Simmons, Steve Roach
RESERVES: Terry Lamb, David Gillespie

QLD Colin Scott, Dale Shearer, Mal Meninga, Gene Miles, Chris Close, Wally Lewis (c), Mark Murray, Bob Lindner, Gavin Jones, Bryan Niebling, Dave Brown, Greg Conescu, Greg Dowling
RESERVES: Peter Jackson, Ian French

GAME TWO

NSW Garry Jack, Brian Hetherington, Michael O'Connor, Chris Mortimer, Andrew Farrar, Brett Kenny, Peter Sterling, Wayne Pearce (c), Noel Cleal, Steve Folkes, Peter Tunks, Royce Simmons, Steve Roach
RESERVES: Terry Lamb (not used), David Gillespie

QLD Gary Belcher, Dale Shearer, Mal Meninga, Gene Miles, Les Kiss, Wally Lewis (c), Mark Murray, Ian French, Gavin Jones, Bob Lindner, Darryl Brohman, Greg Conescu, Cavill Heugh
RESERVES: Peter Jackson (not used), Brad Tessmann

GAME THREE

NSW Garry Jack, Brian Johnston, Michael O'Connor, Chris Mortimer, Eric Grothe, Brett Kenny, Peter Sterling, Wayne Pearce (c), Noel Cleal, Steve Folkes, Peter Tunks, Royce Simmons, Steve Roach
RESERVES: Terry Lamb, David Gillespie

QLD Gary Belcher, Dale Shearer, Mal Meninga, Gene Miles, Les Kiss, Wally Lewis (c), Mark Murray, Bob Lindner, Gavin Jones, Bryan Niebling, Cavill Heugh, Greg Conescu, Brad Tessmann
RESERVES: Grant Rix (not used), Ian French

1987

GAME ONE

NSW Garry Jack, Andrew Ettingshausen, Mark McGaw, Brian Johnston, Michael O'Connor, Brett Kenny, Peter Sterling, Wayne Pearce (c), Noel Cleal, Steve Folkes, Les Davidson, Royce Simmons, Pat Jarvis
RESERVES: David Boyle, Des Hasler (not used)

QLD Gary Belcher, Tony Currie, Peter Jackson, Gene Miles, Dale Shearer, Wally Lewis (c), Allan Langer, Ian French, Paul Vautin, Trevor Gillmeister, Martin Bella, Greg Conescu, Greg Dowling
RESERVES: Colin Scott (not used), Gary Smith

GAME TWO

QLD Gary Belcher, Colin Scott, Peter Jackson, Gene Miles, Dale Shearer, Wally Lewis (c), Allan Langer, Bob Lindner, Paul Vautin, Trevor Gillmeister, Martin Bella, Greg Conescu, Greg Dowling
RESERVES: Tony Currie (not used), Ian French

NSW Garry Jack, Michael O'Connor, Mark McGaw, Brian Johnston, Andrew Farrar, Brett Kenny, Peter Sterling, Wayne Pearce (c), Les Davidson, Steve Folkes, Pat Jarvis, Royce Simmons, David Boyle
RESERVES: Des Hasler, Paul Langmack

GAME THREE

QLD Gary Belcher, Colin Scott, Peter Jackson, Gene Miles, Dale Shearer, Wally Lewis (c), Allan Langer, Bob Lindner, Paul Vautin, Trevor Gillmeister, Bryan Niebling, Greg Conescu, Greg Dowling
RESERVES: Tony Currie, Ian French

NSW Garry Jack, Brian Johnston, Brett Kenny, Michael O'Connor, Andrew Ettingshausen, Cliff Lyons, Peter Sterling, Wayne Pearce (c), Les Davidson, David Boyle, Phil Daley, Royce Simmons, Peter Tunks
RESERVES: Mark McGaw, Steve Folkes

EXHIBITION GAME

NSW Jonathan Docking, Brian Johnston, Mark McGaw, Michael O'Connor, Andrew Ettingshausen, Cliff Lyons, Peter Sterling (c), Paul Langmack, Noel Cleal, Les Davidson, Peter Tunks, Royce Simmons, Phil Daley
RESERVES: Des Hasler, David Boyle

QLD Gary Belcher, Dale Shearer, Peter Jackson, Gene Miles, Tony Currie, Wally Lewis (c), Allan Langer, Bob Lindner, Paul Vautin, Trevor Gillmeister, Bryan Niebling, Greg Conescu, Greg Dowling
RESERVES: Colin Scott, Ian French

1988

GAME ONE

QLD Gary Belcher, Alan McIndoe, Tony Currie, Gene Miles, Joe Kilroy, Peter Jackson, Allan Langer, Paul Vautin (c), Bob Lindner, Wally Fullerton Smith, Sam Backo, Greg Conescu, Martin Bella
RESERVES: Brett French, Scott Tronc

NSW Jonathan Docking, Brian Johnston, Mark McGaw, Michael O'Connor, Andrew Ettingshausen, Cliff Lyons, Peter Sterling, Wayne Pearce (c), Noel Cleal, Steve Folkes, Steve Roach, Royce Simmons, Les Davidson
RESERVES: Terry Lamb, David Trewhella

GAME TWO

QLD Gary Belcher, Alan McIndoe, Peter Jackson, Gene Miles, Tony Currie, Wally Lewis (c), Allan Langer, Paul Vautin, Bob Lindner, Wally Fullerton Smith, Sam

Backo, Greg Conescu, Martin Bella

RESERVES: Brett French, Trevor Gillmeister

NSW Garry Jack, John Ferguson, Mark McGaw, Michael O'Connor, Andrew Ettingshausen, Terry Lamb, Peter Sterling, Paul Langmack, Steve Folkes, Wayne Pearce (c), Steve Roach, Ben Elias, Phil Daley

RESERVES: Paul Dunn, Des Hasler

GAME THREE

QLD Gary Belcher, Alan McIndoe, Peter Jackson, Tony Currie, Joe Kilroy, Wally Lewis (c), Allan Langer, Paul Vautin, Bob Lindner, Wally Fullerton Smith, Sam Backo, Greg Conescu, Martin Bella

RESERVES: Brett French, Trevor Gillmeister

NSW Garry Jack, John Ferguson, Mark McGaw, Michael O'Connor, Andrew Ettingshausen, Cliff Lyons, Des Hasler, Paul Langmack, Steve Folkes, Wayne Pearce (c), Steve Roach, Ben Elias, Steve Hanson

RESERVES: Noel Cleal, Greg Florimo

1989

GAME ONE

QLD Gary Belcher, Michael Hancock, Tony Currie, Mal Meninga, Alan McIndoe, Wally Lewis (c), Allan Langer, Bob Lindner, Gene Miles, Paul Vautin, Dan Stains, Kerrod Walters, Martin Bella

RESERVES: Trevor Gillmeister, Dale Shearer, Gary Coyne, Michael Hagan

NSW Garry Jack, Chris Johns, Andrew Farrar, Laurie Daley, John Ferguson, Terry Lamb, Des Hasler, Bradley Clyde, Gavin Miller (c), Paul Sironen, Paul Dunn, Mario Fenech, John Cartwright

RESERVES: Glenn Lazarus, Greg Alexander, Andrew Ettingshausen, Chris Mortimer

GAME TWO

QLD Gary Belcher, Alan McIndoe, Tony Currie, Mal Meninga, Michael Hancock, Wally Lewis (c), Allan Langer, Bob Lindner, Gene Miles, Paul Vautin, Sam Backo, Kerrod Walters, Martin Bella

RESERVES: Michael Hagan, Dale Shearer, Trevor Gillmeister, Gary Coyne

NSW Garry Jack, Chris Johns, Andrew Ettingshausen, Laurie Daley, John Ferguson, Chris Mortimer, Greg Alexander, Bradley Clyde, Gavin Miller (c), Bruce McGuire, Paul Dunn, Mario Fenech, Peter Kelly

RESERVES: Des Hasler, John Cartwright, Brad Mackay, Alan Wilson

GAME THREE

QLD Gary Belcher, Alan McIndoe, Tony Currie, Dale Shearer, Michael Hancock, Wally Lewis (c), Michael Hagan, Paul Vautin, Gene Miles, Dan Stains, Sam Backo, Kerrod Walters, Martin Bella

RESERVES: Peter Jackson, Gary Coyne, Trevor Gillmeister, Kevin Walters

NSW Garry Jack, Michael O'Connor, Brian Johnston, Chris Johns, John Ferguson, Des Hasler, Greg Alexander, Brad Mackay, Mark Geyer, Gavin Miller (c), Peter Kelly, David Trewhella, Bruce McGuire

RESERVES: Terry Matterson, John Cartwright, Phil Blake, Alan Wilson

1990

GAME ONE

NSW Andrew Ettingshausen, Rod Wishart, Michael O'Connor, Mark McGaw, Ricky Walford, Laurie Daley, Ricky Stuart, Bradley Clyde, David Gillespie, Bruce McGuire, Steve Roach, Ben Elias (c), Ian Roberts

RESERVES: Paul Sironen, Glenn Lazarus, Graham Lyons, Geoff Toovey

QLD Gary Belcher, Alan McIndoe, Dale Shearer, Mal Meninga, Les Kiss, Michael Hagan, Allan Langer, Bob Lindner, Paul Vautin (c), Wally Fullerton Smith, Martin Bella, Steve Walters, Dan Stains

RESERVES: Trevor Gillmeister, Gary Coyne, Kevin Walters, Mark Coyne

GAME TWO

NSW Andrew Ettingshausen, Rod Wishart, Brad Mackay, Mark McGaw, Graham Lyons, Des Hasler, Ricky Stuart, Bradley Clyde, David Gillespie, Bruce McGuire, Steve Roach, Ben Elias (c), Ian Roberts

RESERVES: Andrew Farrar, Glenn Lazarus, Paul Sironen, Brad Fittler

QLD Gary Belcher, Alan McIndoe, Dale Shearer, Mal Meninga, Les Kiss, Wally Lewis (c), Allan Langer, Bob Lindner, Dan Stains, Gary Coyne, Martin Bella, Kerrod Walters, Sam Backo

RESERVES: Trevor Gillmeister, Andrew Gee, Mark Coyne, Kevin Walters (not used)

GAME THREE

QLD Gary Belcher, Alan McIndoe, Dale Shearer, Peter Jackson, Willie Carne, Wally Lewis (c), Allan Langer, Bob Lindner, Trevor Gillmeister, Gary Coyne, Martin Bella, Steve Walters, Sam Backo

RESERVES: Andrew Gee, Kevin Walters, Steve Jackson, Michael Hagan

NSW Andrew Ettingshausen, Graham Lyons, Michael O'Connor, Mark McGaw, Rod Wishart, Brad Mackay,

Ricky Stuart, Bradley Clyde, David Gillespie, Bruce McGuire, Glenn Lazarus, Ben Elias (c), Ian Roberts

RESERVES: Mark Sargent, Paul Sironen, Greg Alexander, Andrew Farrar

1991

GAME ONE

QLD Paul Hauff, Michael Hancock, Peter Jackson, Mal Meninga, Willie Carne, Wally Lewis (c), Allan Langer, Gary Larson, Mike McLean, Andrew Gee, Steve Jackson, Steve Walters, Martin Bella

RESERVES: Kevin Walters, Steve Renouf, Gary Coyne, Gavin Allen

NSW Greg Alexander, Chris Johns, Andrew Ettingshausen, Laurie Daley, Michael O'Connor, Cliff Lyons, Ricky Stuart, Des Hasler, Paul Sironen, Mark Geyer, Ian Roberts, Ben Elias (c), Steve Roach

RESERVES: Glenn Lazarus, David Gillespie, Mark McGaw, Brad Fittler

GAME TWO

NSW Andrew Ettingshausen, Chris Johns, Laurie Daley, Michael O'Connor, Rod Wishart, Cliff Lyons, Ricky Stuart, Bradley Clyde, Mark Geyer, Ian Roberts, David Gillespie, Ben Elias (c), Steve Roach

RESERVES: Des Hasler, Mark McGaw, Brad Mackay, John Cartwright

QLD Paul Hauff, Michael Hancock, Peter Jackson, Mal Meninga, Willie Carne, Wally Lewis (c), Allan Langer, Gary Larson, Mike McLean, Andrew Gee, Steve Jackson, Steve Walters, Martin Bella

RESERVES: Kevin Walters, Dale Shearer, Gary Coyne, Gavin Allen

GAME THREE

QLD Paul Hauff, Michael Hancock, Peter Jackson, Mal Meninga, Willie Carne, Wally Lewis (c), Allan Langer, Gary Larson, Mike McLean, Andrew Gee, Steve Jackson, Steve Walters, Martin Bella

RESERVES: Dale Shearer, Gary Coyne, Bob Lindner, Kevin Walters (not used)

NSW Greg Alexander, Chris Johns, Mark McGaw, Michael O'Connor, Rod Wishart, Brad Fittler, Ricky Stuart, Brad Mackay, Bradley Clyde, John Cartwright, David Gillespie, Ben Elias (c), Steve Roach

RESERVES: Des Hasler, Brad Izzard, Craig Salvatori, David Fairleigh

1992

GAME ONE

NSW Andrew Ettingshausen, Rod Wishart, Paul McGregor, Brad Fittler, Graham Mackay, Laurie Daley (c), John Simon, Bradley Clyde, John Cartwright, Paul Sironen, Paul Harragon, Ben Elias, Glenn Lazarus

RESERVES: Robbie McCormack, Craig Salvatori, Brad Mackay, David Gillespie

QLD Dale Shearer, Michael Hancock, Peter Jackson, Mal Meninga (c), Willie Carne, Kevin Walters, Allan Langer, Gary Larson, Bob Lindner, Trevor Gillmeister, Steve Jackson, Steve Walters, Martin Bella

RESERVES: Mark Coyne, Gary Coyne, Steve Renouf, Gavin Allen

GAME TWO

QLD Dale Shearer, Michael Hancock, Mark Coyne, Mal Meninga (c), Adrian Brunker, Peter Jackson, Allan Langer, Billy Moore, Bob Lindner, Gary Larson, Gavin Allen, Steve Walters, Martin Bella

RESERVES: Kevin Walters, Trevor Gillmeister, Darren Smith, Mike McLean

NSW Andrew Ettingshausen, Rod Wishart, Paul McGregor, Brad Fittler, Graham Mackay, Laurie Daley (c), Ricky Stuart, Bradley Clyde, John Cartwright, Paul Sironen, Paul Harragon, Ben Elias, Glenn Lazarus

RESERVES: Craig Salvatori, Brad Mackay, David Gillespie, Steve Carter

GAME THREE

NSW Andrew Ettingshausen, Rod Wishart, Paul McGregor, Brad Fittler, Chris Johns, Laurie Daley (c), Ricky Stuart, Bradley Clyde, John Cartwright, Paul Sironen, Paul Harragon, Ben Elias, Glenn Lazarus

RESERVES: Craig Salvatori, David Gillespie, Tim Brasher, Brad Mackay

QLD Dale Shearer, Michael Hancock, Mark Coyne, Mal Meninga (c), Adrian Brunker, Peter Jackson, Allan Langer, Billy Moore, Mike McLean, Gary Larson, Gavin Allen, Steve Walters, Martin Bella

RESERVES: Kevin Walters, Darren Smith, Steve Jackson, Gary Coyne

1993

GAME ONE

NSW Tim Brasher, Rod Wishart, Brad Fittler, Paul McGregor, Andrew Ettingshausen, Laurie Daley (c), Ricky Stuart, Brad Mackay, Paul Harragon, Paul Sironen, Ian Roberts, Ben Elias, Glenn Lazarus

RESERVES: David Fairleigh, Craig Salvatori, Brett Mullins (not used), Jason Taylor (not used)

QLD Gary Belcher, Michael Hancock, Mal Meninga (c), Steve Renouf, Willie Carne, Kevin Walters, Allan Langer, Billy Moore, Gary Larson, Bob Lindner, Martin Bella, Steve Walters, Steve Jackson

RESERVES: Mark Coyne, Dale Shearer, Mark Hohn, Andrew Gee

GAME TWO

NSW Tim Brasher, Rod Wishart, Brad Fittler, Paul McGregor, Andrew Ettingshausen, Laurie Daley (c), Ricky Stuart, Brad Mackay, Paul Harragon, Paul Sironen, Ian Roberts, Robbie McCormack, Glenn Lazarus

RESERVES: David Fairleigh, David Gillespie, Jason Taylor, Jason Croker

QLD Dale Shearer, Willie Carne, Mal Meninga (c), Mark Coyne, Adrian Brunker, Kevin Walters, Allan Langer, Bob Lindner, Trevor Gillmeister, Gary Larson, Mark Hohn, Steve Walters, Martin Bella

RESERVES: Julian O'Neill, Steve Jackson, Darren Smith, Billy Moore

GAME THREE

QLD Dale Shearer, Brett Dallas, Mal Meninga (c), Mark Coyne, Willie Carne, Julian O'Neill, Allan Langer, Bob Lindner, Trevor Gillmeister, Gary Larson, Mark Hohn, Steve Walters, Martin Bella

RESERVES: Kevin Walters, Darren Smith, Steve Jackson, Billy Moore

NSW Tim Brasher, Rod Wishart, Brad Fittler, Andrew Ettingshausen, Graham Mackay, Laurie Daley (c), Ricky Stuart, Brad Mackay, Paul Harragon, Paul Sironen, David Fairleigh, Ben Elias, Glenn Lazarus

RESERVES: David Gillespie, Terry Hill, Scott Gourley, Jason Taylor

1994

GAME ONE

QLD Julian O'Neill, Michael Hancock, Mal Meninga (c), Steve Renouf, Willie Carne, Kevin Walters, Allan Langer, Billy Moore, Gary Larson, Trevor Gillmeister, Martin Bella, Steve Walters, Andrew Gee

RESERVES: Mark Coyne, Darren Smith, Mark Hohn, Darren Fritz

NSW Tim Brasher, Graham Mackay, Brad Fittler, Paul McGregor, Rod Wishart, Laurie Daley (c), Ricky Stuart, Brad Mackay, Paul Harragon, Paul Sironen,

Ian Roberts, Ben Elias, Glenn Lazarus

RESERVES: Andrew Ettingshausen, Chris Johns, David Gillespie, David Barnhill

GAME TWO

NSW Tim Brasher, Andrew Ettingshausen, Brad Fittler, Paul McGregor, Brett Mullins, Laurie Daley (c), Ricky Stuart, Bradley Clyde, Dean Pay, Paul Sironen, Paul Harragon, Ben Elias, Glenn Lazarus

RESERVES: Brad Mackay, David Barnhill, Ken Nagas, Chris Johns (not used)

QLD Julian O'Neill, Michael Hancock, Mal Meninga (c), Mark Coyne, Willie Carne, Kevin Walters, Allan Langer, Billy Moore, Gary Larson, Trevor Gillmeister, Darren Fritz, Kerrod Walters, Andrew Gee

RESERVES: Darren Smith, Mark Hohn, Gorden Tallis, Adrian Vowles

GAME THREE

NSW Tim Brasher, Andrew Ettingshausen, Brad Fittler, Paul McGregor, Brett Mullins, Laurie Daley (c), Ricky Stuart, Bradley Clyde, Dean Pay, Paul Sironen, Paul Harragon, Ben Elias, Ian Roberts

RESERVES: Ken Nagas, Chris Johns, Brad Mackay, David Barnhill

QLD Julian O'Neill, Michael Hancock, Mal Meninga (c), Steve Renouf, Willie Carne, Kevin Walters, Allan Langer, Jason Smith, Gary Larson, Billy Moore, Darren Fritz, Steve Walters, Mark Hohn

RESERVES: Mark Coyne, Darren Smith, Andrew Gee, Gorden Tallis

1995

GAME ONE

QLD Robbie O'Davis, Brett Dallas, Mark Coyne, Danny Moore, Matt Sing, Dale Shearer, Adrian Lam, Billy Moore, Gary Larson, Trevor Gillmeister (c), Tony Hearn, Wayne Bartrim, Gavin Allen

RESERVES: Terry Cook, Ben Ikin, Mark Hohn, Craig Teevan

NSW Tim Brasher, Rod Wishart, Terry Hill, Paul McGregor, Craig Hancock, Matthew Johns, Andrew Johns, Brad Fittler (c), Brad Mackay, Steve Menzies, Mark Carroll, Jim Serdaris, Paul Harragon

RESERVES: Greg Florimo, David Fairleigh, Matt Seers, Adam Muir

GAME TWO

QLD Robbie O'Davis, Brett Dallas, Mark Coyne, Danny Moore, Matt Sing, Jason Smith, Adrian Lam, Billy Moore, Gary Larson, Trevor Gillmeister (c), Tony Hearn, Wayne Bartrim, Gavin Allen

RESERVES: Ben Ikin, Terry Cook, Mark Hohn, Craig Teevan

NSW Tim Brasher, Rod Wishart, Terry Hill, Paul McGregor, John Hopoate, Brad Fittler (c), Andrew Johns, Brad Mackay, David Barnhill, Greg Florimo, Paul Harragon, Jim Serdaris, Dean Pay

RESERVES: Brett Rodwell, Adam Muir, Steve Menzies, David Fairleigh

GAME THREE

QLD Robbie O'Davis, Brett Dallas, Mark Coyne, Danny Moore, Matt Sing, Jason Smith, Adrian Lam, Billy Moore, Gary Larson, Trevor Gillmeister (c), Tony Hearn, Wayne Bartrim, Gavin Allen

RESERVES: Ben Ikin, Terry Cook, Mark Hohn, Craig Teevan

NSW Tim Brasher, Rod Wishart, Terry Hill, Paul McGregor, David Hall, Matthew Johns, Geoff Toovey, Brad Fittler (c), Adam Muir, Steve Menzies, Mark Carroll, Jim Serdaris, Paul Harragon

RESERVES: Matt Seers, Greg Florimo, David Fairleigh, David Barnhill

1996

GAME ONE

NSW Tim Brasher, Rod Wishart, Andrew Ettingshausen, Laurie Daley, Brett Mullins, Brad Fittler (c), Geoff Toovey, Adam Muir, Dean Pay, David Furner, Paul Harragon, Andrew Johns, Glenn Lazarus

RESERVES: Jim Dymock, Jamie Ainscough, Jason Croker, Steve Menzies

QLD Robbie O'Davis, Brett Dallas, Steve Renouf, Matt Sing, Wendell Sailor, Jason Smith, Allan Langer, Billy Moore, Brad Thorn, Trevor Gillmeister (c), Gary Larson, Wayne Bartrim, Tony Hearn

RESERVES: Adrian Lam, Michael Hancock, Alan Cann, Craig Greenhill

GAME TWO

NSW Tim Brasher, Rod Wishart, Andrew Ettingshausen, Laurie Daley, Brett Mullins, Brad Fittler (c), Geoff Toovey, Adam Muir, Dean Pay, David Furner, Paul Harragon, Andrew Johns, Glenn Lazarus

RESERVES: Jim Dymock, Jamie Ainscough, Jason Croker, Steve Menzies

QLD Wendell Sailor, Brett Dallas, Steve Renouf, Mark Coyne, Matt Sing, Julian O'Neill, Allan Langer (c), Billy Moore, Brad Thorn, Gary Larson, Andrew Gee, Steve Walters, Tony Hearn

RESERVES: Adrian Lam, Kevin Walters, Jason Smith, Craig Greenhill

GAME THREE

NSW Tim Brasher, Rod Wishart, Andrew Ettingshausen, Laurie Daley, Brett Mullins, Brad Fittler (c), Geoff Toovey, Adam Muir, Dean Pay, David Furner, Paul Harragon, Andrew Johns, Glenn Lazarus

RESERVES: Jim Dymock, Jamie Ainscough, Jason Croker, Steve Menzies

QLD Wendell Sailor, Brett Dallas, Steve Renouf, Mark Coyne, Willie Carne, Dale Shearer, Allan Langer (c), Billy Moore, Brad Thorn, Gary Larson, Andrew Gee, Steve Walters, Tony Hearn

RESERVES: Adrian Lam, Matt Sing, Jason Smith, Owen Cunningham

1997

GAME ONE

NSW Tim Brasher, Rod Wishart, Terry Hill, Paul McGregor, Jamie Ainscough, Jim Dymock, Geoff Toovey (c), Nik Kosef, Adam Muir, Steve Menzies, Mark Carroll, Andrew Johns, Paul Harragon

RESERVES: David Fairleigh, Dean Pay, John Simon, Ken McGuinness

QLD Robbie O'Davis, Brett Dallas, Matt Sing, Mark Coyne, Danny Moore, Ben Ikin, Adrian Lam (c), Wayne Bartrim, Billy Moore, Gary Larson, Craig Smith, Jamie Goddard, Neil Tierney

RESERVES: Jason Smith, Jeremy Schloss, Tony Hearn, Stuart Kelly

GAME TWO

NSW Tim Brasher, Ken McGuinness, Paul McGregor, Terry Hill, Jamie Ainscough, Jim Dymock, John Simon, Nik Kosef, Adam Muir, Steve Menzies, Mark Carroll, Geoff Toovey (c), Paul Harragon

RESERVES: David Fairleigh, Dean Pay, Matt Seers, Aaron Raper (not used)

QLD Robbie O'Davis, Brett Dallas, Stuart Kelly, Mark Coyne, Matt Sing, Ben Ikin, Adrian Lam (c), Billy Moore, Jason Smith, Gary Larson, Craig Smith, Wayne Bartrim, Neil Tierney

RESERVES: Jamie Goddard, Jeremy Schloss, Clinton O'Brien, Julian O'Neill

GAME THREE

QLD Robbie O'Davis, Brett Dallas, Mark Coyne, Julian O'Neill, Matt Sing, Ben Ikin, Adrian Lam (c), Billy Moore, Jason Smith, Gary Larson, Neil Tierney, Jamie Goddard, Clinton O'Brien

RESERVES: Stuart Kelly, Jeremy Schloss, Craig Smith, Wayne Bartrim

NSW: Tim Brasher, Ken McGuinness, Jamie Ainscough, Terry Hill, Matt Seers, Trent Barrett, Geoff Toovey (c), Nik Kosef, Steve Menzies, Adam Muir, Paul Harragon, Andrew Johns, Mark Carroll

RESERVES: John Simon, Michael Buettner, Dean Pay, David Fairleigh

1998

GAME ONE

QLD Darren Lockyer, Wendell Sailor, Steve Renouf, Darren Smith, Matt Sing, Kevin Walters, Allan Langer (c), Peter Ryan, Jason Smith, Wayne Bartrim, Gary Larson, Jason Hetherington, Shane Webcke

RESERVES: Steve Price, Martin Lang, Ben Ikin, Tonie Carroll

NSW Tim Brasher, Rod Wishart, Andrew Ettingshausen, Terry Hill, Adam MacDougall, Laurie Daley (c), Andrew Johns, Brad Fittler, Nik Kosef, Dean Pay, Paul Harragon, Geoff Toovey, Rodney Howe

RESERVES: David Barnhill, Steve Menzies, Matthew Johns, Ken McGuinness (not used)

GAME TWO

NSW Tim Brasher, Rod Wishart, Paul McGregor, Terry Hill, Adam MacDougall, Laurie Daley (c), Andrew Johns, Brad Fittler, David Barnhill, Dean Pay, Paul Harragon, Geoff Toovey, Rodney Howe

RESERVES: Glenn Lazarus, Andrew Ettingshausen, Nik Kosef, Steve Menzies

QLD Darren Lockyer, Wendell Sailor, Steve Renouf, Darren Smith, Matt Sing, Kevin Walters, Allan Langer (c), Wayne Bartrim, Brad Thorn, Gorden Tallis, Gary Larson, Jason Hetherington, Shane Webcke

RESERVES: Steve Price, Martin Lang, Ben Ikin, Tonie Carroll

GAME THREE

QLD Darren Lockyer, Robbie O'Davis, Steve Renouf, Ben Ikin, Wendell Sailor, Kevin Walters, Allan Langer (c), Darren Smith, Jason Smith, Gorden Tallis, Gary Larson, Jamie Goddard, Shane Webcke

RESERVES: Steve Price, Matt Sing, Peter Ryan, Andrew Gee

NSW Tim Brasher, Rod Wishart, Laurie Daley (c), Terry Hill, Adam MacDougall, Brad Fittler, Andrew Johns, Jim Dymock, David Barnhill, David Furner, Tony Butterfield, Matthew Johns, Glenn Lazarus

RESERVES: Robbie Kearns, Ken McGuinness, Dean Pay, Steve Menzies

1999

GAME ONE

QLD Robbie O'Davis, Mat Rogers, Darren Smith, Matt Sing, Wendell Sailor, Kevin Walters, Adrian Lam (c), Jason Smith, Chris McKenna, Gorden Tallis, Craig Greenhill, Jason Hetherington, Shane Webcke
RESERVES: Ben Ikin, Steve Price, Tonie Carroll, Martin Lang

NSW Robbie Ross, Darren Albert, Laurie Daley, Terry Hill, Matt Geyer, Brad Fittler (c), Andrew Johns, Nik Kosef, David Barnhill, Bryan Fletcher, Rodney Howe, Craig Gower, Jason Stevens
RESERVES: Glenn Lazarus, Luke Ricketson, Ryan Girdler, Anthony Mundine

GAME TWO

NSW Robbie Ross, Adam MacDougall, Ryan Girdler, Terry Hill, Matt Geyer, Laurie Daley, Andrew Johns, Brad Fittler (c), Bryan Fletcher, Nik Kosef, Rodney Howe, Geoff Toovey, Mark Carroll
RESERVES: Luke Ricketson, Michael Vella, Ben Kennedy, Anthony Mundine

QLD Robbie O'Davis, Mat Rogers, Matt Sing, Darren Smith, Wendell Sailor, Kevin Walters (c), Paul Green, Jason Smith, Chris McKenna, Gorden Tallis, Craig Greenhill, Jason Hetherington, Shane Webcke
RESERVES: Ben Ikin, Steve Price, Tonie Carroll, Martin Lang

GAME THREE

QLD Darren Lockyer, Robbie O'Davis, Tonie Carroll, Darren Smith, Wendell Sailor, Ben Ikin, Adrian Lam (c), Jason Smith, Chris McKenna, Gorden Tallis, Craig Greenhill, Jason Hetherington, Shane Webcke
RESERVES: Paul Green, Steve Price, Brad Thorn, Martin Lang

NSW Robbie Ross, Adam MacDougall, Ryan Girdler, Terry Hill, Matt Geyer, Laurie Daley (c), Andrew Johns, Nik Kosef, David Furner, Bryan Fletcher, Rodney Howe, Geoff Toovey, Mark Carroll
RESERVES: Luke Ricketson, Michael Vella, Ben Kennedy, Anthony Mundine

2000

GAME ONE

NSW David Peachey, Adam MacDougall, Ryan Girdler, Shaun Timmins, Jamie Ainscough, Brad Fittler (c), Brett Kimmorley, Ben Kennedy, David Furner, Bryan Fletcher, Rodney Howe, Geoff Toovey, Robbie Kearns
RESERVES: Scott Hill, Terry Hill, Michael Vella, Jason Stevens

QLD Darren Lockyer, Mat Rogers, Paul Bowman, Darren Smith, Wendell Sailor, Ben Ikin, Adrian Lam (c), Jason Smith, Brad Thorn, Gorden Tallis, Martin Lang, Jason Hetherington, Shane Webcke
RESERVES: Paul Green, Tonie Carroll, Russell Bawden, Steve Price

GAME TWO

NSW Tim Brasher, Adam MacDougall, Ryan Girdler, Shaun Timmins, Jamie Ainscough, Brad Fittler (c), Brett Kimmorley, Scott Hill, Ben Kennedy, Bryan Fletcher, Rodney Howe, Geoff Toovey, Robbie Kearns
RESERVES: Andrew Johns, David Furner, Adam Muir, Jason Stevens

QLD Darren Lockyer, Mat Rogers, Paul Bowman, Darren Smith, Matt Sing, Julian O'Neill, Adrian Lam (c), Jason Smith, Gorden Tallis, Brad Thorn, Martin Lang, Jason Hetherington, Shane Webcke
RESERVES: Paul Green, Tonie Carroll, Russell Bawden, Steve Price

GAME THREE

NSW Tim Brasher, Adam MacDougall, Ryan Girdler, Matt Gidley, Jamie Ainscough, Brad Fittler (c), Brett Kimmorley, Scott Hill, Ben Kennedy, Bryan Fletcher, Jason Stevens, Geoff Toovey, Robbie Kearns
RESERVES: Andrew Johns, David Furner, Adam Muir, Michael Vella

QLD Darren Lockyer, Mat Rogers, Paul Bowman, Matt Sing, Wendell Sailor, Ben Ikin, Adrian Lam (c), Darren Smith, Chris McKenna, Gorden Tallis, Martin Lang, Jason Hetherington, Shane Webcke
RESERVES: Julian O'Neill, Brad Thorn, Tonie Carroll, Craig Greenhill

2001

GAME ONE

QLD Darren Lockyer, Lote Tuqiri, Paul Bowman, Darren Smith, Wendell Sailor, Daniel Wagon, Paul Green, Brad Meyers, Petero Civoniceva, Gorden Tallis (c), John Buttigieg, Kevin Campion, Shane Webcke
RESERVES: Chris Walker, Chris Beattie, Carl Webb, John Doyle

NSW Mark Hughes, Jamie Ainscough, Matt Gidley, Michael De Vere, Adam MacDougall, Brad Fittler (c), Brett Kimmorley, Jason Croker, Bryan Fletcher, Nathan Hindmarsh, Robbie Kearns, Luke Priddis, Jason Stevens
RESERVES: Trent Barrett, Michael Vella, Ben Kennedy, Rodney Howe

GAME TWO

NSW Mark Hughes, Jamie Ainscough, Ryan Girdler, Matt Gidley, Adam MacDougall, Brad Fittler (c), Trent Barrett, Luke Ricketson, Adam Muir, Bryan Fletcher, Mark O'Meley, Luke Priddis, Jason Stevens
RESERVES: Craig Gower, Michael Vella, Matt Adamson, Andrew Ryan

QLD Darren Lockyer (c), Lote Tuqiri, Darren Smith, Paul Bowman, Wendell Sailor, Daniel Wagon, Paul Green, Brad Meyers, Petero Civoniceva, Dane Carlaw, Russell Bawden, Kevin Campion, Shane Webcke
RESERVES: Chris Walker, Chris Beattie, Carl Webb, Nathan Fien

GAME THREE

QLD Darren Lockyer (c), Lote Tuqiri, Chris Walker, Paul Bowman, Wendell Sailor, Daniel Wagon, Allan Langer, Darren Smith, Brad Meyers, Petero Civoniceva, John Buttigieg, Paul Green, Shane Webcke
RESERVES: Kevin Campion, Carl Webb, Dane Carlaw, John Doyle

NSW Mark Hughes, Jamie Ainscough, Ryan Girdler, Matt Gidley, Adam MacDougall, Brad Fittler (c), Brett Kimmorley, Andrew Ryan, Adam Muir, Bryan Fletcher, Mark O'Meley, Luke Priddis, Jason Stevens
RESERVES: Craig Gower, Michael Vella, Matt Adamson, Steve Menzies

2002

GAME ONE

NSW Brett Hodgson, Timana Tahu, Jamie Lyon, Matt Gidley, Jason Moodie, Trent Barrett, Andrew Johns (c), Luke Ricketson, Ben Kennedy, Steve Simpson, Mark O'Meley, Danny Buderus, Luke Bailey
RESERVES: Braith Anasta, Bryan Fletcher, Nathan Hindmarsh, Michael Vella

QLD Darren Lockyer, Lote Tuqiri, Chris McKenna, Darren Smith, Clinton Schifcofske, Shaun Berrigan, Allan Langer, Dane Carlaw, Petero Civoniceva, Gorden Tallis (c), John Buttigieg, Kevin Campion, Shane Webcke.
RESERVES: Chris Walker, John Doyle, Carl Webb, Andrew Gee

GAME TWO

QLD Darren Lockyer, Lote Tuqiri, Chris Walker, Chris McKenna, Justin Hodges, Shaun Berrigan, Allan Langer, Darren Smith, Dane Carlaw, Gorden Tallis (c), Chris Beattie, PJ Marsh, Shane Webcke
RESERVES: Travis Norton, Steve Price, Andrew Gee, Chris Flannery

NSW Brett Hodgson, Timana Tahu, Jamie Lyon, Shaun Timmins, Jason Moodie, Braith Anasta, Andrew Johns (c), Luke Ricketson, Nathan Hindmarsh, Steve Simpson, Mark O'Meley, Danny Buderus, Luke Bailey
RESERVES: Bryan Fletcher, Steve Menzies, Michael Vella, Scott Hill

GAME THREE

QLD Darren Lockyer, Lote Tuqiri, Chris Walker, Chris McKenna, Robbie O'Davis, Shaun Berrigan, Allan Langer, Darren Smith, Dane Carlaw, Gorden Tallis (c), Petero Civoniceva, PJ Marsh, Shane Webcke
RESERVES: Travis Norton, Steve Price, Andrew Gee, Brent Tate

NSW Brett Hodgson, Timana Tahu, Matt Gidley, Shaun Timmins, Jason Moodie, Trent Barrett, Andrew Johns (c), Luke Ricketson, Steve Menzies, Steve Simpson, Jason Ryles, Danny Buderus, Luke Bailey.
RESERVES: Scott Hill, Bryan Fletcher, Nathan Hindmarsh, Michael Vella

2003

GAME ONE

NSW Anthony Minichiello, Timana Tahu, Matt Gidley, Jamie Lyon, Michael De Vere, Shaun Timmins, Andrew Johns (c), Luke Ricketson, Ben Kennedy, Craig Fitzgibbon, Jason Ryles, Danny Buderus, Robbie Kearns
RESERVES: Luke Bailey, Craig Wing, Josh Perry, Phil Bailey

QLD Darren Lockyer, Shannon Hegarty, Brent Tate, Justin Hodges, Matt Sing, Ben Ikin, Shaun Berrigan, Tonie Carroll, Dane Carlaw, Gorden Tallis (c), Petero Civoniceva, PJ Marsh, Shane Webcke
RESERVES: Steve Price, Chris Flannery, Andrew Gee, Paul Bowman

GAME TWO

NSW Anthony Minichiello, Timana Tahu, Matt Gidley, Jamie Lyon, Michael De Vere, Shaun Timmins, Andrew Johns (c), Luke Ricketson, Ben Kennedy, Craig Fitzgibbon, Jason Ryles, Danny Buderus, Robbie Kearns
RESERVES: Luke Bailey, Craig Wing, Bryan Fletcher, Phil Bailey

QLD Darren Lockyer, Shannon Hegarty, Brent Tate, Tonie Carroll, Matt Sing, Ben Ikin, Shaun Berrigan, Dane Carlaw, Petero Civoniceva, Gorden Tallis (c), Steve Price, Michael Crocker, Shane Webcke
RESERVES: Travis Norton, Andrew Gee, Scott Sattler, Matt Bowen

GAME THREE

QLD Darren Lockyer, Shannon Hegarty, Brent Tate, Josh Hannay, Matt Sing, Ben Ikin, Shaun Berrigan, Tonie Carroll, Dane Carlaw, Gorden Tallis (c), Petero Civoniceva, Cameron Smith, Shane Webcke
RESERVES: Steve Price, Michael Crocker, Travis Norton, Matt Bowen

NSW Anthony Minichiello, Timana Tahu, Matt Gidley, Jamie Lyon, Michael De Vere, Shaun Timmins, Andrew Johns (c), Braith Anasta, Luke Ricketson, Bryan Fletcher, Jason Ryles, Danny Buderus, Robbie Kearns
RESERVES: Luke Bailey, Craig Wing, Willie Mason, Phil Bailey

2004

GAME ONE

NSW Ben Hornby, Luke Rooney, Michael De Vere, Matt Gidley, Luke Lewis, Shaun Timmins, Craig Gower, Craig Fitzgibbon, Andrew Ryan, Nathan Hindmarsh, Mark O'Meley, Danny Buderus (c), Ryan O'Hara
RESERVES: Willie Mason, Brent Kite, Trent Waterhouse, Craig Wing

QLD Rhys Wesser, Justin Hodges, Paul Bowman, Brent Tate, Billy Slater, Chris Flannery, Scott Prince, Tonie Carroll, Dane Carlaw, Michael Crocker, Steve Price, Craig Smith, Shane Webcke
RESERVES: Ben Ross, Petero Civoniceva, Travis Norton, Matt Bowen

GAME TWO

QLD Rhys Wesser, Matt Sing, Paul Bowman, Willie Tonga, Billy Slater, Darren Lockyer (c), Scott Prince, Tonie Carroll, Dane Carlaw, Petero Civoniceva, Steve Price, Cameron Smith, Shane Webcke
RESERVES: Ben Ross, Corey Parker, Chris Flannery, Matt Bowen

NSW Anthony Minichiello, Timana Tahu, Matt Gidley, Luke Lewis, Luke Rooney, Brad Fittler, Brett Finch, Craig Fitzgibbon, Andrew Ryan, Nathan Hindmarsh, Mark O'Meley, Danny Buderus (c), Jason Stevens
RESERVES: Willie Mason, Brent Kite, Trent Waterhouse, Craig Wing

GAME THREE

NSW Anthony Minichiello, Luke Lewis, Mark Gasnier, Matt Cooper, Luke Rooney, Brad Fittler, Trent Barrett, Shaun Timmins, Craig Fitzgibbon, Nathan Hindmarsh, Mark O'Meley, Danny Buderus (c), Jason Ryles
RESERVES: Willie Mason, Brent Kite, Ben Kennedy, Craig Wing

QLD Rhys Wesser, Matt Sing, Brent Tate, Willie Tonga, Billy Slater, Darren Lockyer (c), Scott Prince, Dane Carlaw, Petero Civoniceva, Michael Crocker, Steve Price, Cameron Smith, Shane Webcke
RESERVES: Chris Flannery, Ben Ross, Corey Parker, Matt Bowen

2005

GAME ONE

QLD Billy Slater, Ty Williams, Shaun Berrigan, Paul Bowman, Matt Sing, Darren Lockyer (c), Johnathan Thurston, Chris Flannery, Brad Thorn, Michael Crocker, Petero Civoniceva, Cameron Smith, Steve Price
RESERVES: Ben Ross, Carl Webb, Casey McGuire, Matt Bowen

NSW Anthony Minichiello, Matt King, Mark Gasnier, Matt Cooper, Luke Rooney, Trent Barrett, Brett Kimmorley, Ben Kennedy, Craig Fitzgibbon, Nathan Hindmarsh, Jason Ryles, Danny Buderus (c), Luke Bailey
RESERVES: Craig Wing, Steve Simpson, Andrew Ryan, Anthony Watmough

GAME TWO

NSW Anthony Minichiello, Matt King, Mark Gasnier, Matt Cooper, Luke Rooney, Braith Anasta, Andrew Johns, Ben Kennedy, Craig Fitzgibbon, Nathan Hindmarsh, Jason Ryles, Danny Buderus (c), Steve Simpson
RESERVES: Luke Bailey, Craig Wing, Andrew Ryan, Steve Menzies

QLD Billy Slater, Ty Williams, Shaun Berrigan, Paul Bowman, Matt Sing, Darren Lockyer (c), Johnathan Thurston, Chris Flannery, Carl Webb, Michael Crocker, Petero Civoniceva, Cameron Smith, Brad Thorn
RESERVES: Ben Ross, Dane Carlaw, Casey McGuire, Matt Bowen

GAME THREE

NSW Anthony Minichiello, Matt King, Matt Cooper, Matt Cooper, Timana Tahu, Braith Anasta, Andrew Johns, Ben Kennedy, Craig Fitzgibbon, Nathan Hindmarsh, Jason Ryles, Danny Buderus (c), Steve Simpson

RESERVES: Luke Bailey, Craig Gower, Andrew Ryan, Steve Menzies

QLD Matt Bowen, Ty Williams, Shaun Berrigan, Paul Bowman, Matt Sing, Darren Lockyer (c), Johnathan Thurston, Tonie Carroll, Brad Thorn, Michael Crocker, Petero Civoniceva, Cameron Smith, Danny Nutley
RESERVES: Chris Flannery, Ben Ross, Ashley Harrison, Corey Parker

2006

GAME ONE

NSW Brett Hodgson, Matt King, Mark Gasnier, Timana Tahu, Eric Grothe, Braith Anasta, Brett Finch, Luke O'Donnell, Nathan Hindmarsh, Andrew Ryan, Brent Kite, Danny Buderus (c), Willie Mason
RESERVES: Craig Wing, Steve Menzies, Mark O'Meley, Steve Simpson

QLD Matt Bowen, Greg Inglis, Justin Hodges, Brent Tate, Steve Bell, Darren Lockyer (c), Johnathan Thurston, Dallas Johnson, Matt Scott, David Stagg, Petero Civoniceva, Cameron Smith, Steve Price
RESERVES: Shaun Berrigan, Carl Webb, Sam Thaiday, Nate Myles

GAME TWO

QLD Karmichael Hunt, Brent Tate, Justin Hodges, Steve Bell, Adam Mogg, Darren Lockyer (c), Johnathan Thurston, Dallas Johnson, Carl Webb, Nate Myles, Petero Civoniceva, Cameron Smith, Steve Price
RESERVES: Shaun Berrigan, Chris Flannery, Sam Thaiday, Jacob Lillyman

NSW Brett Hodgson, Matt King, Mark Gasnier, Timana Tahu, Eric Grothe, Braith Anasta, Brett Finch, Andrew Ryan, Nathan Hindmarsh, Steve Simpson, Brent Kite, Danny Buderus (c), Willie Mason
RESERVES: Luke Bailey, Mark O'Meley, Steve Menzies, Craig Wing

GAME THREE

QLD Clinton Schifcofske, Rhys Wesser, Brent Tate, Josh Hannay, Adam Mogg, Darren Lockyer (c), Johnathan Thurston, Dallas Johnson, Carl Webb, Nate Myles, Petero Civoniceva, Cameron Smith, Steve Price
RESERVES: Shaun Berrigan, Chris Flannery, Sam Thaiday, Tonie Carroll

NSW Brett Hodgson, Timana Tahu, Matt King, Matt Cooper, Eric Grothe, Mark Gasnier, Craig Gower, Luke O'Donnell, Nathan Hindmarsh, Paul Gallen, Willie Mason, Danny Buderus (c), Luke Bailey
RESERVES: Steve Simpson, Mark O'Meley, Steve Menzies, Ben Hornby

2007

GAME ONE

QLD Karmichael Hunt, Brent Tate, Steve Bell, Justin Hodges, Greg Inglis, Darren Lockyer (c), Johnathan Thurston, Dallas Johnson, Nate Myles, Tonie Carroll, Petero Civoniceva, Cameron Smith, Steve Price
RESERVES: Shaun Berrigan, Jacob Lillyman, Antonio Kaufusi, Neville Costigan

NSW Anthony Minichiello, Matt King, Jamie Lyon, Matt Cooper, Jarryd Hayne, Braith Anasta, Jarrod Mullen, Andrew Ryan, Nathan Hindmarsh, Willie Mason, Brent Kite, Danny Buderus (c), Brett White
RESERVES: Luke Bailey, Steve Simpson, Anthony Tupou, Kurt Gidley

GAME TWO

QLD Karmichael Hunt, Brent Tate, Steve Bell, Justin Hodges, Greg Inglis, Darren Lockyer (c), Johnathan Thurston, Dallas Johnson, Carl Webb, Tonie Carroll, Petero Civoniceva, Cameron Smith, Steve Price
RESERVES: Shaun Berrigan, Jacob Lillyman, Nate Myles, Neville Costigan

NSW Brett Stewart, Matt King, Jamie Lyon, Matt Cooper, Jarryd Hayne, Braith Anasta, Brett Kimmorley, Andrew Ryan, Nathan Hindmarsh, Willie Mason, Brett White, Danny Buderus (c), Brent Kite
RESERVES: Luke Bailey, Steve Simpson, Ryan Hoffman, Greg Bird

GAME THREE

NSW Brett Stewart, Hazem El Masri, Matt King, Matt Cooper, Jarryd Hayne, Greg Bird, Brett Kimmorley, Paul Gallen, Andrew Ryan, Nathan Hindmarsh, Willie Mason, Danny Buderus (c), Brent Kite
RESERVES: Luke Bailey, Steve Simpson, Ryan Hoffman, Kurt Gidley

QLD Karmichael Hunt, Brent Tate, Steve Bell, Justin Hodges, Greg Inglis, Darren Lockyer (c), Johnathan Thurston, Dallas Johnson, Carl Webb, Tonie Carroll, Petero Civoniceva, Cameron Smith, Steve Price
RESERVES: Shaun Berrigan, Nate Myles, Matt Bowen, Dane Carlaw

2008

GAME ONE

NSW Brett Stewart, Jarryd Hayne, Mark Gasnier, Matt Cooper, Anthony Quinn, Greg Bird, Peter Wallace, Paul Gallen, Willie Mason, Ryan Hoffman, Craig Fitzgibbon, Danny Buderus (c), Brett White

RESERVES: Anthony Laffranchi, Anthony Tupou, Ben Cross, Ben Hornby

QLD Billy Slater, Brent Tate, Greg Inglis, Justin Hodges, Israel Folau, Karmichael Hunt, Johnathan Thurston, Dallas Johnson, Sam Thaiday, Michael Crocker, Petero Civoniceva, Cameron Smith (c), Carl Webb
RESERVES: PJ Marsh, Ben Hannant, Nate Myles, Jacob Lillyman

GAME TWO

QLD Karmichael Hunt, Darius Boyd, Greg Inglis, Brent Tate, Israel Folau, Johnathan Thurston, Scott Prince, Dallas Johnson, Ashley Harrison, Michael Crocker, Petero Civoniceva, Cameron Smith (c), Steve Price
RESERVES: Billy Slater, Ben Hannant, Sam Thaiday, Nate Myles

NSW Brett Stewart, Steve Turner, Mark Gasnier, Matt Cooper, Anthony Quinn, Greg Bird, Peter Wallace, Paul Gallen, Ryan Hoffman, Willie Mason, Brett White, Danny Buderus (c), Craig Fitzgibbon
RESERVES: Kurt Gidley, Anthony Tupou, Steve Simpson, Anthony Laffranchi

GAME THREE

QLD Karmichael Hunt, Darius Boyd, Greg Inglis, Brent Tate, Israel Folau, Johnathan Thurston, Scott Prince, Dallas Johnson, Ashley Harrison, Nate Myles, Petero Civoniceva, Cameron Smith (c), Steve Price
RESERVES: Billy Slater, Ben Hannant, Michael Crocker, Sam Thaiday

NSW Kurt Gidley, Jarryd Hayne, Joel Monaghan, Matt Cooper, Anthony Quinn, Braith Anasta, Mitchell Pearce, Paul Gallen, Ryan Hoffman, Craig Fitzgibbon, Brett White, Danny Buderus (c), Ben Cross
RESERVES: Brett Stewart, Willie Mason, Anthony Laffranchi, Anthony Tupou

2009

GAME ONE

QLD Billy Slater, Darius Boyd, Greg Inglis, Justin Hodges, Israel Folau, Darren Lockyer (c), Johnathan Thurston, Dallas Johnson, Sam Thaiday, Ashley Harrison, Petero Civoniceva, Cameron Smith, Steve Price
RESERVES: Ben Hannant, Nate Myles, Karmichael Hunt, Michael Crocker

NSW Kurt Gidley (c), Jarryd Hayne, Michael Jennings, Jamie Lyon, James McManus, Terry Campese, Peter Wallace, Anthony Laffranchi, Ben

Creagh, Luke O'Donnell, Luke Bailey,
Robbie Farah, Brent Kite
RESERVES: Justin Poore, Luke Lewis,
Michael Weyman, Craig Wing

GAME TWO

QLD Billy Slater, Darius Boyd, Greg Inglis,
Willie Tonga, Israel Folau, Darren
Lockyer (c), Johnathan Thurston, Dallas
Johnson, Sam Thaiday, Ashley Harrison,
Petero Civoniceva, Cameron Smith,
Steve Price
RESERVES: Ben Hannant, Nate Myles,
Karmichael Hunt, Michael Crocker

NSW Kurt Gidley (c), Jarryd Hayne, Joel
Monaghan, Jamie Lyon, David Williams,
Trent Barrett, Peter Wallace, Paul Gallen,
Ben Creagh, Luke O'Donnell, Michael
Weyman, Robbie Farah, Brent Kite
RESERVES: Justin Poore, Glenn Stewart,
Anthony Watmough, Josh Morris

GAME THREE

NSW Kurt Gidley (c), Jarryd Hayne,
Michael Jennings, Josh Morris, David
Williams, Trent Barrett, Brett
Kimmorley, Anthony Watmough, Ben
Creagh, Trent Waterhouse, Justin Poore,
Michael Ennis, Josh Perry
RESERVES: Craig Wing, Tom Learoyd-
Lahrs, Glenn Stewart, Brett White

QLD Billy Slater, Darius Boyd, Greg Inglis,
Justin Hodges, Willie Tonga, Darren
Lockyer (c), Johnathan Thurston, Dallas
Johnson, Michael Crocker, Ashley
Harrison, Steve Price, Cameron Smith,
David Shillington
RESERVES: Karmichael Hunt, Neville
Costigan, Matt Scott, Sam Thaiday

Results

1980

ONE-OFF ORIGIN GAME
QLD 20 (K Boustead, C Close tries;
M Meninga 7 goals) beat NSW 10
(G Brentnall, Raudonikis tries;
M Cronin 2 goals)

1981

ONE-OFF ORIGIN GAME
QLD 22 (B Backer, W Lewis, C Close,
M Meninga [penalty] tries; Meninga
5 goals) beat NSW 15 (E Grothe 2,
M Cronin tries; Cronin 3 goals)

1982

GAME ONE
NSW 20 (ZNiszczot 2, S Mortimer,
B Izzard tries; M Cronin 4 goals) beat
QLD 16 (J Ribot, M Brennan tries;
M Meninga 5 goals)

GAME TWO
QLD 11 (G Miles, J Ribot, P Vautin
tries; C Scott goal) beat NSW 7
(B Izzard try; T Melrose 2 goals)

GAME THREE
QLD 10 (R Hancock, W Lewis tries;
M Meninga 2 goals) beat NSW 5 (P Duke
try; M Cronin goal)

1983

GAME ONE
QLD 24 (W Lewis 2,M Murray tries;
M Meninga 6 goals) beat NSW 12
(E Grothe, S Ella tries; P Sigsworth
2 goals)

GAME TWO
NSW 10 (N Hunt, S Ella tries;
M Cronin goal) beat QLD 6
(M Meninga try; Meninga goal)

GAME THREE
QLD 43 (M Brennan 2, G Conescu,
S Stacey, B Niebling, D Brown, G Miles
tries; M Meninga 6, C Scott goals;
W Lewis field goal) beat NSW 22
(C Anderson 3, S Mortimer tries;
M Cronin 3 goals)

1984

GAME ONE
QLD 29 (K Boustead 3, P Vautin,
W Lewis, G Miles tries; M Meninga 2
goals; Lewis field goal) beat NSW 12
(N Cleal try; R Conlon 4 goals)

GAME TWO
QLD 14 (G Dowling, G Miles tries;
M Meninga 3 goals) beat NSW 2
(R Conlon goal)

GAME THREE
NSW 22 (B Johnston 2, N Cleal tries;
R Conlon 5 goals) beat QLD 12
(B Lindner, K Boustead tries;
M Meninga 2 goals)

1985

GAME ONE
NSW 18 (M O'Connor 2 tries;
O'Connor 5 goals) beat QLD 2
(M Meninga goal)

GAME TWO
NSW 21 (C Mortimer, B Elias, B Kenny
tries; M O'Connor 4 goals; O'Connor
field goal) beat QLD 14 (B Lindner,
I French tries; M Meninga 3 goals)

GAME THREE
QLD 20 (D Shearer 2, I French, J Ribot
tries; M Meninga 2 goals) beat NSW 6
(S Ella try; M O'Connor goal)

1986

GAME ONE
NSW 22 (Jack, Mortimer, Simmons,
Farrar tries; O'Connor 3 goals) beat
QLD 16 (Miles, Dowling tries; Meninga
4 goals)

GAME TWO
NSW 24 (Farrar, O'Connor, Pearce,
Kenny, Cleal tries; O'Connor 2 goals)
beat QLD 20 (French, Lindner, Kiss,
Shearer tries; Meninga 2 goals)

GAME THREE
NSW 18 (O'Connor, Pearce, Tunks tries;
O'Connor 3 goals) beat QLD 16
(Shearer, Belcher, Conescu, Kiss tries)

1987

GAME ONE
NSW 20 (M O'Connor 2, L Davidson,
M McGaw tries; O'Connor 2 goals) beat
QLD 16 (G Dowling, D Shearer,
T Currie tries; P Jackson, G Belcher
goals)

GAME TWO
QLD 12 (D Shearer, G Dowling, C Scott
tries) beat NSW 6 (A Farrar try;
M O'Connor goal)

GAME THREE
QLD 10 (B Lindner, D Shearer tries;
Shearer goal) beat NSW 8 (D Boyle try;
M O'Connor 2 goals)

EXHIBITION GAME
NSW 30 (A Ettingshausen, M McGaw,
J Docking, M O'Connor, C Lyons tries;
O'Connor 5 goals) beat QLD 18
(T Currie, G Miles, D Shearer tries;
Shearer 3 goals)

1988

GAME ONE
QLD 26 (A Langer 2, P Jackson,
A McIndoe, G Belcher tries; Belcher
3 goals) beat NSW 18 (M O'Connor,
Ettingshausen, McGaw tries; O'Connor
3 goals)

GAME TWO

QLD 16 (S Backo, A Langer tries;
G Belcher 4 goals) beat NSW 6
(M O'Connor try; O'Connor goal)

GAME THREE

QLD 38 (S Backo 2, W Lewis, A Langer,
P Jackson, J Kilroy, B French tries;
G Belcher 5 goals) beat NSW 22
(W Pearce, J Ferguson, S Hanson,
M O'Connor tries; O'Connor 3 goals)

1989

GAME ONE

QLD 36 (M Hancock 2, M Meninga 2,
A McIndoe, A Langer, B Lindner tries;
Meninga 4 goals) beat NSW 6
(A Ettingshausen try; L Daley goal)

GAME TWO

QLD 16 (M Hancock, Kerrod Walters,
W Lewis tries; M Meninga, G Belcher
goals) beat NSW 12 (L Daley, Johns
tries; G Alexander 2 goals)

GAME THREE

QLD 36 (D Shearer 2, A McIndoe,
M Hancock, Kerrod Walters, G Belcher,
T Currie tries; Shearer 4 goals) beat
NSW 16 (D Hasler, D Trewhella,
B McGuire tries; M O'Connor 2 goals)

1990

GAME ONE

NSW 8 (M McGaw try; M O'Connor
2 goals) beat QLD 0

GAME TWO

NSW 12 (R Stuart, B Mackay tries;
R Wishart 2 goals) beat QLD 6
(L Kiss try; M Meninga goal)

GAME THREE

QLD 14 (G Belcher, S Jackson tries;
Belcher 2, W Lewis goals) beat NSW 10
(G Lazarus, M McGaw tries;
R Wishart goal)

1991

GAME ONE

QLD 6 (M Meninga try; Meninga goal)
beat NSW 4 (L Daley try)

GAME TWO

NSW 14 (C Johns, M McGaw tries;
M O'Connor 3 goals) beat QLD 12
(W Carne, D Shearer tries; M Meninga
2 goals)

GAME THREE

QLD 14 (P Hauff, M Hancock,
D Shearer tries; M Meninga goal) beat
NSW 12 (C Johns, M O'Connor,
D Hasler tries)

1992

GAME ONE

NSW 14 (B Clyde, C Salvatori tries;
R Wishart 3 goals) beat QLD 6
(A Langer try; M Meninga goal)

GAME TWO

QLD 5 (B Moore try; A Langer field
goal) beat NSW 4 (R Wishart 2 goals)

GAME THREE

NSW 16 (R Stuart, A Ettingshausen,
J Cartwright tries; T Brasher 2 goals)
beat QLD 4 (M Meninga 2 goals)

1993

GAME ONE

NSW 14 (R Wishart, R Stuart tries;
Wishart 3 goals) beat QLD 10
(B Lindner, W Carne tries; M Meninga
goal)

GAME TWO

NSW 16 (L Daley, B Mackay, R Wishart
tries; Wishart 2 goals) beat QLD 12
(M Meninga, Kevin Walters tries;
A Brunker, D Shearer goals)

GAME THREE

QLD 24 (W Carne 2, S Walters, B
Lindner tries; M Meninga 2, J O'Neill
2 goals) beat NSW 12 (A Ettingshausen,
P Harragon tries; R Wishart 2 goals)

1994

GAME ONE

QLD 16 (J O'Neill, W Carne, M Coyne
tries; M Meninga 2 goals) beat NSW 12
(P Harragon, B Mackay tries; R Wishart,
G Mackay goals)

GAME TWO

NSW 14 (G Lazarus, P McGregor tries;
T Brasher 3 goals) beat QLD 0

GAME THREE

NSW 27 (B Clyde, L Daley, B Mullins,
B Fittler tries; T Brasher 4 goals; B Elias
2, Fittler field goals) beat QLD 12
(A Gee, S Renouf tries; J O'Neill 2 goals)

1995

GAME ONE

QLD 2 (W Bartrim goal) beat NSW 0

GAME TWO

QLD 20 (M Coyne, A Lam, B Dallas
tries; W Bartrim 4 goals) beat NSW 12
(B Rodwell, J Serdaris tries; R Wishart
2 goals)

GAME THREE

QLD 24 (J Smith, D Moore, B Dallas,
B Ikin tries; W Bartrim 4 goals) beat
NSW 16 (T Brasher, R Wishart, A Muir
tries; Wishart 2 goals)

1996

GAME ONE

NSW 14 (A Ettingshausen, S Menzies
tries; A Johns 3 goals) beat QLD 6
(A Langer try; W Bartrim goal)

GAME TWO

NSW 18 (B Mullins 2, R Wishart tries;
A Johns 3 goals) beat QLD 6 (S Renouf
try; J O'Neill goal)

GAME THREE

NSW 15 (A Ettingshausen, B Mullins
tries; R Wishart 2, A Johns goals;
B Fittler field goal) beat QLD 14
(M Coyne, B Dallas tries; W Carne
3 goals)

1997

GAME ONE

NSW 8 (P McGregor try; A Johns,
R Wishart goals) beat QLD 6 (A Lam
try; W Bartrim goal)

GAME TWO

NSW 15 (K McGuinness, N Kosef,
J Dymock tries; J Simon goal; Simon
field goal) beat QLD 14 ((M Sing,
R O'Davis, B Dallas tries; J O'Neill goal)

GAME THREE

QLD 18 (B Ikin, J O'Neill, M Coyne
tries; O'Neill 3 goals) beat NSW 12
(J Ainscough, A Johns tries; Johns,
J Simon goals)

1998

GAME ONE

QLD 24 (Kevin Walters, S Price, A
Langer, T Carroll tries; Lockyer 4 goals)
beat NSW 23 (R Wishart, T Brasher,
L Daley, B Fittler, S Menzies tries;
A Johns goal; Johns field goal)

GAME TWO

NSW 26 (P McGregor 2, A MacDougall, B Fittler, T Brasher tries; A Johns 3 goals) beat QLD 10 (W Sailor, M Sing tries; D Lockyer goal)

GAME THREE

QLD 19 (Kevin Walters, B Ikin, A Langer tries; D Lockyer 2, R O'Davis goals; J Smith field goal) beat NSW 4 (K McGuinness try)

1999

GAME ONE

QLD 9 (M Rogers 4 goals; Rogers field goal) beat NSW 8 (A Mundine try; R Girdler 2 goals)

GAME TWO

NSW 12 (R Ross, L Daley tries; R Girdler 2 goals) beat QLD 8 (M Rogers try; Rogers 2 goals)

GAME THREE

QLD 10 (P Green, D Lockyer tries; Lockyer goal) drew with NSW 10 (M Geyer 2 tries; R Girdler goal)

2000

GAME ONE

NSW 20 (A MacDougall 2, R Girdler, D Peachey tries; Girdler 2 goals) beat QLD 16 (A Lam 2, M Rogers tries; Rogers, D Lockyer goals)

GAME TWO

NSW 28 (B Fittler, S Timmins, S Hill, D Furner, R Girdler tries; Girdler 4 goals) beat QLD 10 (G Tallis try; M Rogers 3 goals)

GAME THREE

NSW 56 (R Girdler 3, M Gidley 2, A Muir, A Johns, B Fletcher, A MacDougall tries; Girdler 10 goals) beat QLD 16 (M Rogers, D Smith, G Tallis tries; Rogers 2 goals)

2001

GAME ONE

QLD 34 (D Lockyer, D Smith, C Webb, J Doyle, J Buttigieg, C Walker tries; Lockyer 5 goals) beat NSW 16 (M Gidley, B Fittler, T Barrett tries; M De Vere 2 goals)

GAME TWO

NSW 26 (B Fittler 2, L Ricketson, J Ainscough, T Barrett tries; Girdler 3 goals) beat QLD 8 (C Walker try; D Lockyer 2 goals)

GAME THREE

QLD 40 (D Lockyer 2, C Walker 2, P Bowman 2, D Carlaw, A Langer tries; Lockyer 4 goals) beat NSW 14 (R Girdler 2 tries; Girdler 3 goals)

2002

GAME ONE

NSW 32 (M Gidley, J Lyon, A Johns, T Tahu, B Hodgson tries; Johns 4, Hodgson goals; Johns, T Barrett field goals) beat QLD 4 (L Tuqiri try)

GAME TWO

QLD 26 (L Tuqiri 3, G Tallis, D Carlaw tries; Tuqiri 3 goals) beat NSW 18 (B Anasta, L Ricketson, S Timmins tries; A Johns 3 goals)

GAME THREE

QLD 18 (L Tuqiri, S Berrigan, S Webcke, D Carlaw tries; Tuqiri goal) drew with NSW 18 (J Moodie 2, S Menzies tries, A Johns 3 goals)

2003

GAME ONE

NSW 25 (A Minichiello 2, C Wing, A Johns tries; Johns 4 goals; Johns field goal) beat QLD 12 (D Lockyer, G Tallis tries; Lockyer 2 goals)

GAME TWO

NSW 27 (T Tahu 2, B Kennedy, M Gidley, A Minichiello tries; A Johns 3 goals; Johns field goal) beat QLD 4 (M Crocker try)

GAME THREE

QLD 36 (M Sing 3, B Tate 2, C Smith, M Crocker tries; J Hannay 4 goals) beat NSW 6 (T Tahu try; A Johns goal)

2004

GAME ONE

NSW 9 (S Timmins try; C Fitzgibbon 2 goals; Timmins field goal) beat QLD 8 (S Prince, B Tate tries)

GAME TWO

QLD 22 (B Slater 2, W Tonga, D Carlaw tries; C Smith 2, S Prince goals) beat NSW 18 (T Tahu 2, L Rooney tries; C Fitzgibbon 3 goals)

GAME THREE

NSW 36 (M Gasnier 2, T Barrett, L Rooney, A Minichiello, B Fittler tries; C Fitzgibbon 5, Gasnier goals) beat QLD 14 (B Slater, M Bowen tries; C Smith 3 goals)

2005

GAME ONE

QLD 24 (T Williams, M Crocker, M Bowen tries; C Smith 5 goals; D Lockyer, J Thurston field goals) beat NSW 20 (L Rooney, M Gasnier, C Fitzgibbon, D Buderus tries; Fitzgibbon 2 goals)

GAME TWO

NSW 32 (A Minichiello 2, S Menzies, M Cooper, D Buderus tries; C Fitzgibbon 3, A Johns 3 goals) beat QLD 22 (B Thorn, B Slater, M Bowen, P Civoniceva tries; C Smith 3 goals)

GAME THREE

NSW 32 (M King 3, B Anasta, M Gasnier, T Tahu tries; A Johns 3, C Fitzgibbon goals) beat QLD 10 (J Thurston, M Bowen tries; C Smith goal)

2006

GAME ONE

NSW 17 (B Finch, M King, W Mason tries; B Hodgson 2 goals; Finch field goal) beat QLD 16 (G Inglis 2, S Bell tries; J Thurston 2 goals)

GAME TWO

QLD 30 (A Mogg 2, C Webb, J Hodges, S Berrigan tries; J Thurston 5 goals) beat NSW 6 (T Tahu try; B Hodgson goal)

GAME THREE

QLD 16 (A Mogg, B Tate, D Lockyer tries; C Schifcofske 2 goals) beat NSW 14 (E Grothe 2, M King tries; B Hodgson goal)

2007

GAME ONE

QLD 25 (G Inglis 2, S Price, D Lockyer tries; J Thurston 4 goals; Thurston field goal) beat NSW 18 (N Hindmarsh, M Cooper, J Hayne tries; J Lyon 3 goals)

GAME TWO

QLD 10 (G Inglis, S Bell tries; J Thurston goal) beat NSW 6 (B Stewart try; J Lyon goal)

GAME THREE

NSW 18 (J Hayne, M King, H El Masri tries; El Masri 3 goals) beat QLD 4 (J Hodges try)

2008

GAME ONE
NSW 18 (A Quinn 2, B Stewart, A Laffranchi tries; C Fitzgibbon goal) beat QLD 10 (B Tate, I Folau tries; J Thurston goal)

GAME TWO
QLD 30 (D Boyd 2, B Hannant, I Folau tries; J Thurston 7 goals) beat NSW 0

GAME THREE
QLD 16 (I Folau 2, B Slater tries; J Thurston 2 goals) beat NSW 10 (M Cooper try; C Fitzgibbon 3 goals)

2009

GAME ONE
QLD 28 (G Inglis 2, B Slater, J Thurston, D Boyd tries; J Thurston 4 goals) beat NSW 18 (B Creagh, C Wing, J Hayne tries; K Gidley 3 goals)

GAME TWO
QLD 24 (G Inglis, I Folau, D Lockyer, C Smith tries; J Thurston 4 goals) beat NSW 14 (J Hayne 2, D Williams tries; K Gidley goal)

GAME THREE
NSW 28 (B Creagh 2, D Williams, J Morris tries; K Gidley 3, M Ennis 3 goals) beat QLD 16 (D Johnson, J Hodges, B Slater tries; J Thurston 2 goals)

Man-of-the-match awards

1980

ONE-OFF ORIGIN GAME
Chris Close (Queensland)

1981

ONE-OFF ORIGIN GAME
Chris Close (Queensland)

1982

GAME ONE
Mal Meninga (Queensland)

GAME TWO
Rod Morris (Queensland)

GAME THREE
Wally Lewis (Queensland)

1983

GAME ONE
Wally Lewis (Queensland)

GAME TWO
Peter Sterling (NSW)

GAME THREE
Wally Lewis (Queensland)

1984

GAME ONE
Wally Lewis (Queensland)

GAME TWO
Wally Lewis (Queensland)

GAME THREE
Steve Mortimer (NSW)

1985

GAME ONE
Peter Wynn (NSW)

GAME TWO
Wally Lewis (Queensland)

GAME THREE
Wally Fullerton Smith (Queensland)

1986

GAME ONE
Royce Simmons (NSW)

GAME TWO
Peter Sterling (NSW)

GAME THREE
Brett Kenny (NSW)

1987

GAME ONE
Les Davidson (NSW)

GAME TWO
Peter Sterling (NSW)

GAME THREE
Allan Langer (Queensland)

EXHIBITION GAME
Peter Sterling (NSW)

1988

GAME ONE
Allan Langer (Queensland)

GAME TWO
Sam Backo (Queensland)

GAME THREE
Sam Backo (Queensland)

1989

GAME ONE
Martin Bella (Queensland)

GAME TWO
Wally Lewis (Queensland)

GAME THREE
Kerrod Walters (Queensland)

1990

GAME ONE
Ben Elias (NSW)

GAME TWO
Ricky Stuart (NSW)

GAME THREE
Bob Lindner (Queensland)

1991

GAME ONE
Wally Lewis (Queensland)

GAME TWO
Steve Walters (Queensland)

GAME THREE
Martin Bella (Queensland)

1992

GAME ONE
Ben Elias (NSW)

GAME TWO
Bob Lindner (Queensland)

GAME THREE
Ricky Stuart (NSW)

1993

GAME ONE
Ricky Stuart (NSW)

GAME TWO
Tim Brasher (NSW)

GAME THREE
Dale Shearer (Queensland)

1994

GAME ONE
Willie Carne (Queensland)

GAME TWO
Paul Harragon (NSW)

GAME THREE
Ben Elias (NSW)

1995

GAME ONE
Gary Larson (Queensland)

GAME TWO
Jason Smith (Queensland)

GAME THREE
Adrian Lam (Queensland)

1996

GAME ONE
Geoff Toovey (NSW)

GAME TWO
Andrew Johns (NSW)

GAME THREE
Steve Menzies (NSW)

1997

GAME ONE
Geoff Toovey (NSW)

GAME TWO
Paul McGregor (NSW)

GAME THREE
Gary Larson (Queensland)

1998

GAME ONE
Allan Langer (Queensland)

GAME TWO
Rodney Howe (NSW)

GAME THREE
Shane Webcke (Queensland)

1999

GAME ONE
Jason Hetherington (Queensland)

GAME TWO
Laurie Daley (NSW)

GAME THREE
Wendell Sailor (Queensland)

2000

GAME ONE
Adam MacDougall (NSW)

GAME TWO
Tim Brasher (NSW)

GAME THREE
Ryan Girdler (NSW)

2001

GAME ONE
Gorden Tallis (Queensland)

GAME TWO
Trent Barrett (NSW)

GAME THREE
Darren Lockyer (Queensland)

2002

GAME ONE
Andrew Johns (NSW)

GAME, TWO
Chris McKenna (Queensland)

GAME THREE
Allan Langer (Queensland)

2003

GAME ONE
Luke Bailey (NSW)

GAME TWO
Andrew Johns (NSW)

GAME THREE
Matt Sing (Queensland)

2004

GAME ONE
Shaun Timmins (NSW)

GAME TWO
Billy Slater (Queensland)

GAME THREE
Craig Fitzgibbon (NSW)

2005

GAME ONE
Steve Price (Queensland)

GAME TWO
Andrew Johns (NSW)

GAME THREE
Anthony Minichiello (NSW)

2006

GAME ONE
Willie Mason (NSW)

GAME TWO
Darren Lockyer (Queensland)

GAME THREE
Brent Tate (Queensland)

2007

GAME ONE
Johnathan Thurston (Queensland)

GAME TWO
Cameron Smith (Queensland)

GAME THREE
Greg Bird (NSW)

2008

GAME ONE
Greg Bird (NSW)

GAME TWO
Greg Inglis (Queensland)

GAME THREE
Israel Folau (Queensland)

2009

GAME ONE
Johnathan Thurston (Queensland)

GAME TWO
Sam Thaiday (Queensland)

GAME THREE
Anthony Watmough (NSW)

Referees

1980

ONE-OFF ORIGIN GAME
Billy Thompson (Great Britain)

1981

ONE-OFF ORIGIN GAME
Kevin Steele (New Zealand)

1982

GAME ONE
Kevin Roberts (NSW)

GAME TWO
Barry Gomersall (Queensland)

GAME THREE
Don Wilson (New Zealand)

1983

GAME ONE
Barry Gomersall (Queensland)

GAME TWO
John Gocher (NSW)

GAME THREE
Robin Whitfield (England)

1984

GAME ONE
Kevin Roberts (NSW)

GAME TWO
Barry Gomersall (Queensland)

GAME THREE
Kevin Roberts (NSW)

1985

GAME ONE
Kevin Roberts (NSW)

GAME TWO
Barry Gomersall (Queensland)

GAME THREE
Barry Gomersall (Queensland)

1986

GAME ONE
Kevin Roberts (NSW)

GAME TWO
Barry Gomersall (Queensland)

GAME THREE
Kevin Roberts (NSW)

1987

GAME ONE
Mick Stone (NSW)

GAME TWO
Barry Gomersall (Queensland)

GAME THREE
Barry Gomersall (Queensland)

EXHIBITION GAME
Mick Stone (NSW)

1988

GAME ONE
Barry Gomersall (Queensland)

GAME TWO
Mick Stone (NSW)

GAME THREE
Greg McCallum (NSW)

1989

GAME ONE
Mick Stone (NSW)

GAME TWO
David Manson (Queensland)

GAME THREE
Greg McCallum (NSW)

1990

GAME ONE
David Manson (Queensland)

GAME TWO
Greg McCallum (NSW)

GAME THREE
David Manson (Queensland)

1991

GAME ONE
Bill Harrigan (NSW)

GAME TWO
David Manson (Queensland)

GAME THREE
Bill Harrigan (NSW)

1992

GAME ONE
David Manson (Queensland)

GAME TWO
Bill Harrigan (NSW)

GAME THREE
Eddie Ward (Queensland)

1993

GAME ONE
Greg McCallum (NSW)

GAME TWO
Eddie Ward (Queensland)

GAME THREE
Greg McCallum (NSW)

1994

GAME ONE
Bill Harrigan (NSW)

GAME TWO
Graham Annesley (NSW)

GAME THREE
Bill Harrigan (NSW)

1995

GAME ONE
Eddie Ward (Queensland)

GAME TWO
Eddie Ward (Queensland)

GAME THREE
David Manson (Queensland)

1996

GAME ONE
David Manson (Queensland)

GAME TWO
David Manson (Queensland)

GAME THREE
David Manson (Queensland)

1997

GAME ONE
Kelvin Jeffes (NSW)

GAME TWO
David Manson (Queensland)

GAME THREE
Eddie Ward (Queensland)

1998

GAME ONE
Bill Harrigan (NSW)

GAME TWO
Bill Harrigan (NSW)

GAME THREE
Bill Harrigan (NSW)

1999

GAME ONE
Bill Harrigan (NSW)

GAME TWO
Steve Clark (NSW)

GAME THREE
Steve Clark (NSW)

2000

GAME ONE
Bill Harrigan (NSW)

GAME TWO
Bill Harrigan (NSW)

GAME THREE
Bill Harrigan (NSW)

2001

GAME ONE
Bill Harrigan (NSW)

GAME TWO
Bill Harrigan (NSW)

GAME THREE
Bill Harrigan (NSW)

2002

GAME ONE
Bill Harrigan (NSW)

GAME TWO
Bill Harrigan (NSW)

GAME THREE
Bill Harrigan (NSW)

2003

GAME ONE
Bill Harrigan (NSW)

GAME TWO
Bill Harrigan (NSW)

GAME THREE
Bill Harrigan (NSW)

2004

GAME ONE
Sean Hampstead (NSW)

GAME TWO
Sean Hampstead (NSW)

GAME THREE
Paul Simpkins (NSW)

2005

GAME ONE
Paul Simpkins (NSW)

GAME TWO
Steve Clark (NSW)

GAME THREE
Paul Simpkins (NSW)

2006

GAME ONE
Sean Hampstead (NSW)

GAME TWO
Steve Clark (NSW)

GAME THREE
Steve Clark (NSW)

→ Steve Menzies looks for support as the Queensland
defence tries to halt his progress in 2005.

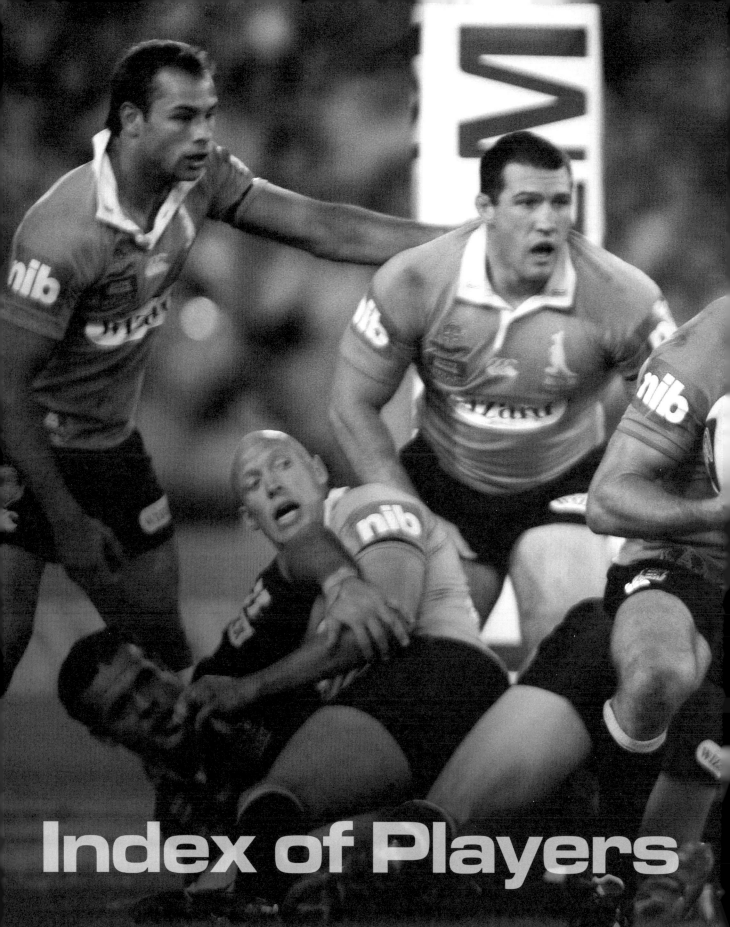

Index of Players

Acknowledgements

Special thanks go to my father Ian for his countless hours of proofreading and offering suggestions. Thanks are also extended to the following for their contributions: John Harms, Adrian McGregor, Michael Livingston, NRL Film Archives, Jim Pisanos, Andrew Slack, Alan Whiticker, my mother Bev and my sister Cindy.

I would also like to thank Lisa Hanrahan and Mary Trewby from Rockpool Publishing for taking on my project, for their assistance in helping me through the process and for bringing it to reality.

Photographic Acknowledgements

All photographs in this book have been supplied by Action Photographics, except for the following from Newspix/News Limited: pp 16–17, p 18 both, p 19, pp 20–21, p 23 both, pp 24–25, p 27, p 31, p 51, p 55.

Bibliography

Books

Malcolm Andrews, *Stampede 92: The Year of The Broncos*, Queensland Newspapers, Brisbane, 1992.

Arthur Beetson with Ian Heads, *Big Artie: The Autobiography*, ABC Books, Sydney, 2004.

Wayne Bennett and Steve Crawley, *Wayne Bennett: The Man in the Mirror*, ABC Books, Sydney, 2008.

Mario Fenech and Stephen Fenech, *Personal Best*, Pan Macmillan, Sydney, 1993.

Bret Harris, *Michael O'Connor: The Best of Both Worlds*, Pan Macmillan, Sydney, 1991.

Bret Harris, *Winfield State of Origin: 1980–1991*, Pan Macmillan, Sydney, 1992.

Gorden Tallis and Mike Colman, *Raging Bull*, Pan Macmillan, Sydney, 2003.

Max and Reet Howell, Peter Hastie, *State of Origin: The First Twelve Years*, Herron Publications, Brisbane, 1992.

Andrew Johns and Neil Cadigan, *The Two of Me*, HarperCollins, Sydney, 2007.

Brett Kenny and Neil Cadigan, *The Natural: Brett Kenny's Life in League*, Ironbark Press, Sydney, 1993.

John MacDonald, *Meninga*. Pan Macmillan, Sydney, 1995.

Paul Malone, *Alf: The Allan Langer Story*, Random House, Sydney, 1997.

Roy Masters, *Inside League*, Pan Books, Sydney, 1990.

Adrian McGregor, *Wally and the Broncos*, University of Queensland Press, Brisbane, 1989.

Mal Meninga and Alan Clarkson, *Meninga: My Life in Football*, HarperCollins, Sydney, 1995.

David Middleton, *Rugby League 1994*, Pan Macmillan, Sydney, 1994.

David Middleton, *Rugby League 1995*, HarperCollins, Sydney, 1995.

Ray Price with Neil Cadigan, *Perpetual Motion*, Angus & Robertson, Sydney, 1987.

Steve Price with Ben Blaschke, *Steve Price: Be Your Best*, Hachette, Sydney, 2008.

Kevin Walters, *Brave Hearts*, Pan Macmillan Australia Pty Limited, Sydney, 1999.

Newspapers

The Advertiser
The Age
The Australian
The Brisbane Telegraph
The Courier-Mail
The Daily Telegraph
The Herald Sun
The Newcastle Herald
The Sunday Mail
The Sunday Telegraph
The Sun-Herald
The Sydney Morning Herald
The Townsville Bulletin

Magazines

Big League
Rugby League Week

Internet sites

AAP
www.bronconet.com
www.ninemsn.com.au
http://nrl.rleague.com
www.qrl.com.au
rleague.com

CAPTIONS FOR COVER IMAGES

Front cover
Queensland's Greg Inglis steps out of a tackle in game one of the 2009 series.

Back Cover
BACKGROUND: 'The King', Wally Lewis, takes the ball up for Queensland in 1991, his last State of Origin season.

INSET IMAGES FROM TOP TO BOTTOM:
Steve Mortimer is carried from the field after NSW's breakthrough series win in 1985.
Mike McLean, Wally Lewis and Andrew Gee savour Queensland's 1991 series victory.
Allan Langer and Wendell Sailor after Queensland won the 2001 series.
Anthony Minichiello and Andrew Johns after NSW's series win in 2005.

www.rockpoolpublishing.com.au